T0350798

*Patrick J. Lucey*

# Patrick J. Lucey

*A Lasting Legacy*

## Dennis L. Dresang

WISCONSIN HISTORICAL SOCIETY PRESS

Published by the Wisconsin Historical Society Press
*Publishers since 1855*

The Wisconsin Historical Society helps people connect to the past by collecting, preserving, and sharing stories. Founded in 1846, the Society is one of the nation's finest historical institutions.
*Join the Wisconsin Historical Society:* wisconsinhistory.org/membership

Front cover: Lucey consults with his executive secretary Joe Sensenbrenner in 1977. Edwin Stein, *Wisconsin State Journal.* Back cover: Supporters of Lucey for governor distribute buttons and flyers in 1966. WHI Image ID 25349.

Printed in Canada
Cover design and typesetting by Tom Heffron

24 23 22 21 20    1 2 3 4 5

Library of Congress Cataloging-in-Publication Data

Names: Dresang, Dennis L., author.
Title: Patrick J. Lucey : a lasting legacy / Dennis L. Dresang.
Description: Madison : Wisconsin Historical Society Press, 2020. | Includes
   bibliographical references and index. | Summary: "As Wisconsin governor from 1971 to
   1977, Patrick J. Lucey pursued an unusually wide-ranging and ambitious progressive
   agenda, tempered by the concerns of a fiscal conservative and a pragmatic realist. He was
   known for bridging partisan divides, building coalitions, and keeping politics civil, even
   when dealing with his opponents. His legacy, which included merging Wisconsin's
   universities into one system and equalizing the funding formula for public schools,
   continues to impact Wisconsin residents and communities"—Provided by publisher.
Identifiers: LCCN 2019039552 (print) | LCCN 2019039553 (ebook) | ISBN 9780870209369
   (hardcover) | ISBN 9780870209376 (ebook)
Subjects: LCSH: Lucey, Patrick J., 1918–2014. | Governors—Wisconsin—Biography. |
   Wisconsin—Politics and government—1951–
Classification: LCC F586.42.L83 D74 2020  (print) | LCC F586.42.L83
   (ebook) | DDC 977.5/043092 [B]—dc23
LC record available at https://lccn.loc.gov/2019039552
LC ebook record available at https://lccn.loc.gov/2019039553

♾ The paper used in this publication meets the minimum requirements of the American National Standard for Information Sciences—Permanence of Paper for Printed Library Materials, ANSI Z39.48-1992.

*To the memory of David Adamany,*
*scholar, educator, and public servant.*

Publication of this book was made possible, in part, by generous gifts from

the Adamany family
Herb Kohl Philanthropies
Joe and Mary Ellyn Sensenbrenner

with additional support from
Robert Bartlett and Nancy Wenzel
Linda and Keith Clifford
Robert Dunn
David and Katie Lucey
Laurel Lucey
Linda Reivitz
Carol Skornicka
James B. Wood
JoAnn and Michael Youngman
and
Ruth Zubrensky, in memory of Leonard Zubrensky.

# CONTENTS

# PLANT GATES

O scar Mayer workers parked their cars and headed past the small building of Local 538 of the United Food and Commercial Workers on their way to make lunch meat and hot dogs. They passed the shiny Weinermobile, a motorized hot dog that drew cheers in parades and at local fairs. Many of the employees wore heavy Green Bay Packers jackets to protect against the cold. It was November 3, 1970, and the temperature was just above freezing. The chatter was mostly complaints about the weather and the loss to the San Francisco 49ers the previous Sunday.

The workers arriving for the six-o'clock morning shift were greeted by a man in a coat and tie accompanied by reporters and standing next to the plant gates. Many, but not all, of the workers recognized him as Patrick J. Lucey, Democratic candidate for governor of Wisconsin. He shook each person's hand, reminded each one that it was Election Day, and said he would appreciate their support.

Lucey had risen at four thirty that morning. As he got dressed and had breakfast, he reminisced about the time he encouraged John F. Kennedy to do a plant gate greeting at Oscar Mayer during the 1960 Wisconsin presidential primary campaign.[1] Kennedy initially rejected Lucey's suggestion, but Lucey insisted and the future president reluctantly agreed. Lucey pointed out the symbolic and substantive importance of making personal contact with individual voters. He noted that it was common for politicians in the state to court support by greeting people as they arrived for work. William Proxmire, who served as Wisconsin's US senator from 1957 to 1988, was the most prominent example of this approach to campaigning.[2] Afterward, Kennedy complained frequently—in jest—about doing plant gates in Wisconsin.

Patrick J. Lucey greets first-shift workers arriving at the Oscar Mayer plant on Election Day in 1970. BRUCE M. FRITZ, *CAPITAL TIMES*

After greeting the last of the shift workers, Lucey and his aides headed to the offices of Lucey Realty on University Avenue, in Madison. He and his wife, Jean, had started the business in 1954 and had grown it into the largest real estate business in the Madison area. It paid the bills during the years that Lucey was building the Democratic Party of Wisconsin and earned him a reputation as a successful businessperson. On Election Day, the office building was one of several locations where volunteers used union-funded telephones to remind supporters to get to the polls.

Next on the schedule was for Lucey himself to vote. He and his wife used the occasion as another opportunity to remind others it was Election Day. When they cast their ballots, a reporter and photographer from the *Capital Times* recorded the smiling couple at the polling booth and featured the story in the afternoon newspaper, which was delivered with plenty of time left for people to get to their own polling places before they closed. The *Capital Times* is a Madison progressive newspaper whose editorial board supported Lucey's candidacy for governor despite not having endorsed him in previous races.

Voter turnout would be key to ensuring victory. From the beginning, public opinion polls indicated a very close race between Lucey and Republican Jack Olson. Polls conducted just before the election favored Lucey, but the *Milwaukee Journal*, *Milwaukee Sentinel*, and *Wisconsin State Journal* forecast a tight conclusion to the campaign. The *Milwaukee Journal* predicted "Olson-Lucey Contest May Be a Photo Finish,"[3] and the *Wisconsin State Journal* asked, "Election: A Zero-to-Zero Deadlock?"[4] In any case, the polls that mattered were the ones where actual ballots were cast. A veteran of campaigns at the local, state, and national levels, Lucey was well aware of the need to get supporters to actually vote.

Once he had checked on the get-out-the-vote activities in Madison, Lucey stopped to buy detergent for the family dishwasher and then headed east to Milwaukee, where a high concentration of potential Democratic voters resided. Lucey and a couple of staffers rode with Pat Bauer at the wheel. Bauer was an undergraduate at Wesleyan University and a student of David Adamany, a longtime close adviser to Lucey. After assisting on the campaign of a Democratic candidate for secretary of state, Bauer served as Lucey's driver and liked to identify himself as "chair of the steering committee."[5]

As Bauer drove, everyone else in the car nodded off, and Bauer himself started to doze. Just as the car was speeding toward the back of a truck, he jolted awake, narrowly avoiding a collision. The adrenaline of the near-miss gave everyone a sudden shot of energy.[6]

They stopped to visit phone bank operations at a large building in State Fair Park, just outside of Milwaukee. Volunteers worked from computerized lists and used a new advance in communications technology: push-button telephones. Punching buttons was about 60 percent more efficient than using rotary dials and allowed for more phone calls in less time. In a two-day period, more than sixty thousand union members received calls reminding them to vote.[7] As a longtime political organizer and campaign manager, Lucey fully appreciated this feat.

To help ensure a large turnout in Milwaukee, Democratic Party activists, joined by union members, went door to door to urge people to vote.

After seeing Republicans dominate state government for twenty-three of the past thirty-one years, they were eager for change.

Those who were with Lucey on Election Day reported that he seemed relaxed. The polls gave him some reason for optimism, but he also felt confident about the campaign he had run and believed he was the stronger of the two candidates. He had beaten Jack Olson, a business owner from Wisconsin Dells, by forty thousand votes when the two ran for lieutenant governor in 1964. Although Olson was elected lieutenant governor in 1966 and reelected in 1968, Lucey considered Olson to be a vulnerable candidate and a poor campaigner, in spite of his respect for his opponent as a person. He thought the commercials in Olson's gubernatorial bid were poorly designed and, at times, silly, even joking toward the end of the campaign that he considered spending some of his own money to help Olson run more of his television ads rather than fund more Lucey ads.[8] While Lucey waited in the early evening of Election Day for returns to be reported, his daughter, Laurie, and some of her friends spoofed a Republican ad against her dad by doing a parody of "The Lucey Dance," chanting "one step forward, two steps back."[9] Television was only beginning to be a major instrument in the toolboxes of campaign strategists. Likewise, the major role of money was just starting to emerge.

Another reason for Lucey's cautious optimism was the unexpected level of support he appeared to be getting in Dane County. Although Madison and its neighbors were reliably Democratic, Lucey had not been able to deliver Dane County to John F. Kennedy in the 1960 primary. He suspected a major obstacle was Kennedy's Catholicism, which could have worked against Lucey, a devout Catholic himself, as well. Lucey also viewed the University of Wisconsin community as ideological purists, unwilling to be pragmatic.

But the opposition on campus to the war in Vietnam seemed to work in Lucey's favor. He had been an organizer and strategist for Robert F. Kennedy in his anti-war presidential bid. After Bobby Kennedy was assassinated, Lucey continued to work for US withdrawal from Vietnam and helped Eugene McCarthy in his anti-war efforts at the 1968 Democratic National Convention. On August 24, 1970, anti-war activists bombed Sterling Hall on the University of Wisconsin–Madison campus. Republicans in the state legislature criticized Lucey for not stridently condemning University of

Wisconsin students who were protesting the war. He was clear in speaking out against violence but was just as clear in identifying with the anti-war sentiment. Many on campus appreciated this distinction.[10]

In the car on the way back to Madison, Lucey jotted down a prediction: Olson would win the Third, Sixth, and Ninth Congressional Districts by a margin of fifty thousand votes and Lucey would win the First, Fourth, Seventh, and Tenth by seventy-five thousand. The remaining Second, Fifth, and Eighth Districts would break even, and Lucey would win by twenty-five thousand.[11] Later, he grew more optimistic and predicted he would win by one hundred thousand. Nonetheless, as the time for reporting results drew near, Lucey grew increasingly nervous.

The Luceys lived in Maple Bluff, one of Madison's most exclusive neighborhoods, a mile from the Wisconsin governor's official residence. Jean Lucey planned a roast beef dinner for Election Day and invited federal judge John Reynolds and his family.[12] Reynolds, a former governor, and Lucey had long been political allies, and their families had developed close personal friendships. As the Reynolds family arrived, Lucey was glued to television screens monitoring election news, including results of contests in states in the eastern time zone as well as in Wisconsin. He bounced nervously from chair to chair, watching the television set in one room and then in another, switching channels during commercials. Jean suggested he put all three of the family's sets in the recreation room, but he kept pacing.

Lucey also had two telephones installed in the recreation room in anticipation of calls from staffers and reporters.[13] Shortly after eight o'clock, when the polls closed, Lucey got a call from Adamany. The report was encouraging. A Republican-leaning ward in Madison recorded Lucey with 48 percent of the vote, a big improvement over his 1966 run for governor, when he got only 32 percent. Lucey smiled at the news but remained tense. The phones rang constantly with continued good news. Three key Milwaukee precincts had favored Lucey in 1966 with 58 percent of the vote. At 8:40, they reported Lucey won with 70 percent of the vote.

At 8:45 p.m., Walter Cronkite announced on CBS news that the projected winner of the contest for governor of Wisconsin was Patrick J. Lucey. Such a projection only forty-five minutes after the polls closed was an indicator of a very decisive victory. NBC confirmed the result minutes later.

For the first time all night, the governor-elect was still. The Lucey family piled into cars and made their way to greet relieved and almost giddy supporters who had gathered at Madison's Lorraine Hotel, a block from the ornate Wisconsin State Capitol where Lucey would soon spend his days. As Lucey entered the hotel lobby, a desk clerk told him he had a call from George McGovern. Senator Ted Kennedy sent his congratulations via a Wisconsin reporter who was in Massachusetts covering Kennedy's own race. Adamany stole a few private moments with Lucey and predicted a victory margin of 85,000 to 95,000.[14] In fact, the final tally was Lucey 728,408 and Olson 602,617[15]—a decisive difference of nearly 125,000 votes, more than anyone had anticipated.

The get-out-the-vote efforts of 1970 produced a record number of people voting in a Wisconsin election that did not include a presidential contest.[16] Turnout and Democratic Party success in 1970 was in large part the fruit of Lucey's organizational work as chair of the party from 1957 to 1963. Lucey was only the eighth Democrat elected governor since Wisconsin was admitted to the Union in 1848. Not only did he win, but Democrats also won sixty-seven of the then one hundred seats in the Wisconsin State Assembly.[17] That was a stunning increase from the forty-eight seats the party had won in 1968. Since 1893, Democrats had been in a distinct minority, except briefly in 1933 and 1965 when the party benefited from national landslides.[18] Lucey would take office with all the advantages of a two-thirds majority in one of the two houses of the legislature. The Republicans maintained a majority in the state senate—which had only one-half of its seats on the ballot—but the Democrats increased their numbers there, too. Adding to their woes, Republicans had failed to raise enough money to cover their campaign expenses. Their treasury was empty except for an IOU note of six hundred thousand dollars.

After thanking campaign workers and supporters in Madison, Lucey and company drove back to Milwaukee to attend a celebration at the Pfister Hotel. Olson and the GOP had also made arrangements to celebrate at the Pfister. A couple of Olson supporters were at the entrance to the hotel and booed when they spotted Lucey arriving. Although Olson did not make an appearance, he issued a press release congratulating his opponent. Reed Coleman, the chairperson of the Wisconsin Republican Party; John Erickson, the Republican candidate for US Senator who was defeated by

Bill Proxmire; and Bill Kraus, Erickson's campaign manager, graciously made an appearance at the Democratic victory party and conveyed their best wishes. John MacIver, Olson's campaign manager, ran into Lucey at the elevators, and the two heartily shook hands.[19]

In his victory speech, Lucey expressed his gratitude for all the work done by his supporters and noted the very impressive showing Democrats made that day. He was not a stirring orator with Kennedy-like charisma, but he had a dry wit and exuded competence and a confidence that many found reassuring. He spoke more like a professor than a politician, and he was gracious and civil, epitomizing Midwest "nice." But his victory speech at the Pfister Hotel clearly communicated his enthusiasm for the opportunity now before him.

In 1967, Wisconsin voters had approved an amendment to the state constitution that extended the term for governors from two to four years. The Wisconsin amendment took effect in 1970. This change was part of a national trend to increase the power of state executives in the wake of two US Supreme Court cases, *Baker v. Carr* (1962) and *Reynolds v. Sims* (1964), mandating application of the one-person-one-vote rule when drawing boundaries for state legislative districts. After the Supreme Court insisted on reapportionment, states made their governments more capable of problem-solving. These changes included longer terms for governors, allowing governors to serve consecutive terms, and providing governors with the authority to hire and fire the heads of major agencies. A study outlining these changes was published with the apt title *Goodbye to Good-Time Charlie: The American Governor Transformed.*[20]After Wisconsin adopted the longer gubernatorial term, only New Hampshire and Vermont continued with two-year terms.[21]

The four-year term made a big difference for Lucey. He knew he needed at least four years to accomplish significant reforms, and he had a very ambitious, progressive agenda. In fact, he said that he doubted that he would have run for the office if the term was still only two years.[22] He recognized that he—or anyone else elected to the office—would have to raise taxes, and that by itself, raising taxes would not have been politically feasible if he had to seek reelection in two years. During the campaign and again in his victory speech, he was candid about the need for more revenue and his plan to follow progressive principles of placing the heaviest

Lucey (center) celebrates his election as governor of Wisconsin with his running mate, Martin Schreiber (left), and Senator William Proxmire. WHI IMAGE ID 96394

burden on those with the greatest ability to pay.[23] He also pointed to the need to fund public schools on a fair and stable basis by enacting changes in how property was taxed and how state government provided aid to local school districts.

Lucey's speech was primarily an expression of gratitude to his supporters. But he took advantage of the occasion to summarize positions he had taken on the campaign trail. On the stump and in debates, Lucey spoke in informed and sometimes very detailed ways of his concerns and proposals, developed with input from advisers such as Adamany. He pledged to make state government more efficient and accountable. Lucey argued that the state had a responsibility to play an active role, along with local officials, in meeting Milwaukee's developmental and service needs. He envisioned an urban area that was an attractive place to live—not a place to flee. Lucey, who grew up in the tiny Mississippi River town of Ferryville, identified the importance of ensuring quality education and transportation in rural communities and preserving the state's environmental heritage.[24] He pleaded with his supporters to avoid rural–urban clashes.[25]

Finally, after a long but exhilarating Election Day, Pat and Jean headed to their room at the Pfister, accompanied by family, close friends, and campaign staffers, all feeling that mixture of exhaustion and exultation that comes with an exciting, tense event. Chatter and yawns filled the room. There were more congratulatory phone calls. At about three o'clock in the morning, the supporters left the Luceys to get some sleep. A long, memorable day came to an end.

At five o'clock the next morning, the governor-elect was out of bed and headed to South Milwaukee to the plant gates of Bucyrus-Erie, which manufactured steam shovels and mining equipment. As workers arrived, Lucey greeted them with, "Hi, I'm Pat Lucey, and I wanted to say thanks."[26]

With this example of plainspoken humility, Lucey kicked off a chapter in Wisconsin's history when politics and policy disagreements were civil even as historic progressive reforms were enacted. Remarkable for his willingness to listen, his unwillingness to bear a grudge, his intellect, his work ethic, and his ability to persuade, Lucey led the state from the relatively static 1960s to an era of reform in the 1970s. He developed an ambitious agenda of progressive and good government initiatives. He surrounded himself with talent, and he worked civilly and effectively with politicians and legislators of both parties. Without rhetorical flair or the initiation of a national movement, Lucey had an impact on Wisconsin and beyond that equaled, and in some ways exceeded, that of his predecessors, including his progressive heroes Robert M. La Follette Sr. and Francis McGovern. This is a book about an extraordinary person who believed government could accomplish good things if directed by the will of the people and well run.

Lucey demonstrated that politics and politicians could and should be synonymous with public service, not self-service. He was a man of integrity. His roots were in a small rural community, and he brought the values of his early upbringing with him as he traversed the halls of capitols and the rooms where policies are developed.

Lucey entered the political fray because he was concerned about the effects of the demagoguery of Joseph McCarthy. He organized progressives and socialists and mobilized farmers and labor to reinvent a Democratic Party—a party in Wisconsin that had opposed Franklin Delano Roosevelt and the New Deal. He was, of course, not alone, but as the chief convener and strategist, Lucey played a major role in transforming Wisconsin from a state dominated by the Republican Party to a competitive two-party state.

Lucey's list of progressive policy accomplishments is long and profound. Contrary to expectations that he might grow government and be a big spender, Lucey insisted on frugality. He restructured the public university systems to increase effectiveness and efficiency. He made state agencies more accountable by establishing cabinet government. He professionalized public management. He simplified the structure of state courts so cases would be decided more expeditiously and with more consistency.

One of the most fundamental legacies that he left was the reframing of state and local financial relationships. He replaced a policy of sending state money to local communities on the basis of how much each community raised in taxes with a policy of providing state money to localities on the basis of their need. An equalization formula pushed aside an approach whereby the wealthy got wealthier. He exchanged a policy that taxed manufacturers according to their property with one that taxed according to their income. Under Lucey, state government assumed financial responsibility for health and social services and for a major share of school funding, relieving local governments and providing programs to individuals without regard for their zip code. Under his leadership, Wisconsin pioneered policies addressing energy, transportation, civil rights, voting, and environmental issues.

Although Lucey was a partisan, he did not consider politics a blood sport. His main concern was not scoring points but winning victories for good government and progressive policies.

## CHAPTER 1

# THE LUCEYS AND FERRYVILLE

"Every time I come, they put up a sign," quipped Governor Patrick J. Lucey.[1] The occasion, on October 2, 2013, was a ceremony designating the twenty-four miles on Highway 35 from Ferryville to Prairie du Chien, Wisconsin, as the Governor Patrick Lucey Highway. Four years earlier, a historical marker was erected at the same roadside park noting that Wisconsin's thirty-eighth governor grew up in Ferryville. Those who made the journey in 2013 to the small town on the Mississippi River included former governors, state legislators, some who served on his staff, family, friends, and local officials.

The setting was improbable: a small village isolated from the mainstream of the nation's commerce and politics, whose initial reason for being was to provide a place to drink a beer. Ferryville was established as a drinking town. Until 1912, Ferryville was a section of the town of Freeman, which was dry. To quench the thirst of locals, a parcel of 1.9 square miles was carved out of Freeman and incorporated as the village of Ferryville, and three taverns were permitted. This hamlet is perched on a narrow shelf between the Mississippi River and the bluffs that run alongside it. Highway 35 is the main street, leading locals to quip that Ferryville is the only town in the world with a single, mile-long street. Another common jest is to suggest that someone acting offensively should take a walk around the block—there are no blocks in Ferryville.[2]

Long before it became Ferryville, the area was home to the Ho-Chunk. They had the area pretty much to themselves until, in the 1850s, Simeon Babcock came from Pennsylvania and George Hutson from Illinois to homestead, calling the area they settled Humble Bush. Early economic activities by white settlers in the area included farming, horse racing, and some support services, including the operation of ferries in the summer and horse-drawn sleds over the ice in the winter. Ferries were needed because the water was too shallow for steamboats. The town's first ferry, the *Julia Hadley*, traveled between Ferryville and Lansing, Iowa. The captain, T. C. Ankeney, named the vessel after his wife. She, in turn, renamed Humble Bush as Ferryville, a name that would become official when the village incorporated in 1912.[3]

The Burlington Railroad was built along the Mississippi and went through town in 1885. When the railroad was built, people no longer had to rely on transportation over water and ice. This new mode of carrying goods promoted economic activity and growth in the towns along the rails. Local businessman Henry Henderson took advantage of the opportunities provided by the railway by improving the general store he had been operating. He opened a hotel on the second story of his store. Soon more businesses and a warehouse opened in town. Projections were too optimistic, however. Actual commerce was insufficient to support all these vendors, and many went bankrupt. An increase in farming helped stabilize business fortunes, but at a modest level. Ferryville also saw a temporary influx in the 1930s of workers from the Army Corps of Engineers, who were put to work to make the Mississippi River navigable and minimize flooding as part of President Franklin D. Roosevelt's efforts to lead the country out of the Great Depression.

The hope for future growth has been to encourage tourists to enjoy the beauty of the area. This corner of Wisconsin was not leveled by the massive Laurentide Ice Sheet, also known as the Wisconsin Glacier, ten thousand years ago. The steep, wooded hills and ridges that border Old Man River are treasures for those who want pleasant but challenging outdoor recreation, as well as for those who want to capture nature with their cameras. But despite such picturesque scenery, Ferryville has seen little growth over the past century. The population was slightly more than three hundred in the 1940s and just below two hundred in the early twenty-first century. The village has continued through the years to be served by a handful of stores and, of course, three taverns.

The small rural village might seem an unlikely birthplace for a man who would go on to revitalize Wisconsin Democrats into a viable political party, who would accomplish an ambitious progressive agenda as governor, and who would be a confidant of and organizer for the Kennedys, a family that embodied an elite culture quite distant from the more rustic Midwest. But not all prominent public servants had the advantages of the Kennedys, the Rockefellers, or the Roosevelts. Indeed, part of the American lore is the ability of someone to rise from humble roots to the pinnacle of our institutions. Abraham Lincoln is the most visible example, and Lucey followed in this model.

The story of Patrick J. Lucey includes lessons of appreciating values acquired early in life and of perceiving as well as making opportunities. Importantly, the story also illustrates how governance can work both to achieve objectives and to foster civility.

## The Luceys

Two decades before the ceremony naming the highway for Governor Lucey, there was another celebration. On August 15, 1993, three hundred members of the Lucey family gathered at St. James Church in Rising Sun, eleven miles northeast of Ferryville, for a reunion. For the occasion, Lucey's youngest brother, Father Gregory Lucey, SJ, edited a seventy-page booklet that included family histories, photographs, and documents.[4] Governor Lucey contributed a biography of his great-grandfather, Patrick "Paddy" Lucey, who emigrated ahead of his wife, Hanora Sullivan, from County Cork, Ireland, to Crawford County in western Wisconsin.[5] Like more than a million others, they left their homeland because of the death and suffering caused by the infamous Irish potato famine.[6]

Paddy arrived in New York in 1862 and worked his way to Prairie du Chien to join some cousins. According to a story that Pat Lucey liked to tell, Paddy wanted to go from Prairie du Chien to Eastman, about thirteen miles away. He was on his way to stay with his cousin, Peter Lucey. He didn't know the way and roads were not marked well, so he decided to rely on the stagecoach. But he feared he might be robbed of the savings he had been able to accumulate and so wrapped his money around his leg and jogged behind the stagecoach all the way to Eastman.[7]

In two years, Paddy was able to pay for Hanora to join him. They were not to enjoy each other's company for long, however. When the US Civil

War began, Paddy was drafted into the Union Army. He knew that his wife was pregnant when he was mustered. He was not literate, and when the due date approached, he asked a buddy to write a letter for him, but his buddy had his own literary shortcomings. The letter inquired, "Is it a boy or a child?"[8]

It was a boy: John, Governor Lucey's grandfather.

After the war, Paddy and Hanora took advantage of the Homestead Act of 1862 to get a farm in Freeman, which surrounds Ferryville. The act provided up to 160 acres to those who cleared the land. Paddy was a successful farmer, and occasionally neighbors came to him to borrow money. If Paddy considered them a good risk, he would lend them the money and require the borrowers to leave the abstract of their farm as collateral. There were no written records, but Paddy always knew precisely the amounts and due dates of debts.

As the only child of Paddy and Hanora, John grew up on the family farm and ran it after his parents died. He married Margaret Connelly, who was the daughter of farmers near Rising Sun. Like Paddy and Hanora, Margaret's parents, Jeremiah Connelly and Bridget Collins, were born in County Cork and immigrated to Wisconsin via New York during the potato famine. John and Margaret married on April 7, 1890, in St. James Church, where the Lucey family reunited 103 years later. Unfortunately, Hanora died six months before being able to witness her son's wedding.[9]

## GC AND ELLA

John and Margaret had nine children, eight of whom lived to adulthood. Patrick Lucey's father, Gregory Charles "GC" Lucey, was born on February 28, 1896. He was their fourth child, following two older sisters and an older brother, Francis, who died before maturity. GC was an unusually hard worker and able entrepreneur. He made the most of the opportunities available in Ferryville. His childhood was one in which work demands on the family farm took priority, although education was highly prized. Summers were for planting, weeding, and harvesting. During the winter months when GC did not have to help with farm chores, he went to a one-room public school about two miles away in a valley called Buck Creek. The family lived at the time on South Buck

An old family photo shows four generations of Luceys. Pat Lucey as an infant is being held by his great grandfather Paddy, flanked by his father, Gregory Charles (GC), and grandfather John. COURTESY OF GREGORY LUCEY, SJ

Creek Ridge. When GC's oldest sister, Mary (nicknamed Maymie), was hired as the school's teacher, GC's behavior became a challenge, and his father pulled him out of school and increased his chores on the farm. He did not finish eighth grade.[10]

About a mile away, there was a public school where instruction was all in Norwegian. GC picked up some Norwegian from the students there. He took pride in his limited ability to speak Norwegian and used it more to impress than to communicate with the many Norwegian Lutherans in the area.

According to Lucey, his father and great-grandfather had a close relationship. GC was able at times to help Paddy, who lacked some of the skills acquired in a formal education. One example was when Paddy went to Gays Mills to purchase two carloads of distressed cows that were for sale because farmers in the Dakotas could not feed and water them due to a bad drought. GC, who was fifteen at the time, accompanied Paddy and had to count out the correct number of his grandfather's gold coins to complete the sale.

GC went to Wisconsin Business College for several months one winter. The college was fifty miles upriver in La Crosse, and GC learned basic accounting. While taking courses, he worked part-time at the Churness and Runice General Store in Ferryville. When GC was nineteen, Paddy staked him five hundred dollars—an enormous sum at the time—to purchase half ownership in the store in Ferryville. About a year later, GC bought the other half. That store had living quarters on the upper floor, which the Luceys used until they moved to Bagley when Pat began fourth grade. The store stayed in the Lucey family until it was sold in the mid-1970s.[11]

While going to school and getting started in the retail business, GC was also courting Ella McNamara. They met at the wedding of GC's sister Nora Lucey to James D. McNamara, Ella's brother, on February 3, 1915. GC, who was then nineteen, was asked to use a horse and buggy to fetch Ella, the groom's twenty-five-year-old sister. GC was immediately attracted to Ella and set his sights on making her his lifetime partner. He told his passenger that he intended to marry when he was twenty-one years old. Her response was, "Well, you will if you can find someone who will marry you!"[12]

Ella and her family lived on a farm located on a ridge about three and a half miles southeast of Lynxville, which is a little more than eight miles down the Mississippi River from Ferryville. Ella taught at a one-room school near the family farm. One early evening, GC took Ella home with his horse and buggy. Given the hour and the distance to Ferryville, she insisted he put the horse in the barn and stay the night. GC slept upstairs in her brothers' room. Meanwhile, her older sisters teased Ella for dating a teenager. Their father overheard the banter and intervened, confidently predicting that GC would be an excellent husband.[13]

GC turned twenty-one on February 28, 1917, and GC and Ella married on June 11. They honeymooned in La Crosse. As happened with Paddy and Hanora, the military draft cut short that first year together. And another repeated pattern: Ella was pregnant when the draft notice arrived, and GC's military obligation meant he would have to miss most of his son's first year of life. Ella gave birth at St. Francis Hospital in La Crosse on March 21, 1918, and GC left for France three weeks later.

While Ella was resting in bed at the hospital, a nun walked into her room and said, "St. Patrick's Day is the seventeenth; St. Joseph's Day is the

Gregory Charles (GC) and Ella Lucey, pictured in 1959.
*CAPITAL TIMES*

nineteenth. Your son was born on the twenty-first. I assume you'll want to call him Patrick Joseph."

Ella obediently replied, "Yes, Sister."[14]

GC spent ten months in the army. He served in France, but the war ended before he was sent to the front. While he was gone, Ella ran the store in addition to caring for young Patrick, whom they called Pat. The store did well and provided the family with above-average wealth in the community. In 1926, GC sold the store to his brother Joe and bought another store in Bagley, thirty-nine miles downstream from Ferryville. Bagley is a picturesque community located on the Mississippi. The family moved to Bagley and experienced life in a slightly larger village, then later took up residence in nearby Prairie du Chien.

The Bagley store started out selling general hardware and then expanded into farm implements. GC hired two employees to help with the business and became a John Deere dealer. Joe Lucey was having problems running the general store in Ferryville, and in 1931, GC bought it back from him. Tired of running back and forth between the communities, GC moved the family from Prairie du Chien back to Ferryville, confident the two employees in the Bagley store needed only minimal supervision. In Ferryville, GC not only resumed running the general store but also established another John Deere dealership.

Opened in 1926, the Lucey general store in Bagley sold general hardware and farm implements, later becoming a John Deere dealership. COURTESY OF GREGORY LUCEY, SJ

The Great Depression hit western Wisconsin hard, as it did the country as a whole. Lucey remembered the times as requiring frugality, but ones in which his family's basic needs were met. Menus were often dictated by the foods in the store that needed consumption before they spoiled.[15] While the Lucey family fared comparatively well during the Depression, they found themselves in position to help others who were less fortunate, and Pat grew up seeing this generosity pay off in noticeable ways. The most dramatic case was when Fred Baker, a hobo riding in a Burlington Railroad boxcar, got off in Ferryville and went to the Lucey grocery store to ask for something to eat. GC asked Fred if he were willing to do some work. When he replied that he was, GC asked if he knew anything about machinery, which the man did. GC then had Fred set up a cultivator, assuming that the task would take all afternoon. After less than an hour, Fred approached GC and asked if he had anything else that needed doing. Instead of returning to riding the rails, Fred became a long-term employee and was welcomed to many family events.[16]

GC's entrepreneurial success and ability to keep the stores afloat even during the Depression marked him as a leader in the community. During the time the family lived in Bagley, he served as village president, which automatically meant he also served on the Grant County Board. When the family returned to Ferryville, he was elected president of that village and a member of the Crawford County Board.

In Ferryville, he created an innovative way to maintain law and order. He thought that if misbehavior was going to occur, it was most likely to be in the village bars. GC therefore appointed the most senior barkeep as the village marshal and deputized the other two, authorizing them to deal directly with disorderly behavior. Not only were they authorized, they also were informed that keeping their liquor license was dependent on their effectiveness as marshals in maintaining order. GC also imposed a five-hundred-dollar annual license fee on each tavern.[17]

Lucey also recalled that his father was determined that Ferryville would have no local property tax. GC could not control taxation by the county, school district, or state, but he could affect the village. When the state improved a section of Highway 35 that went through the community, GC paid the village's share of the cost with the fees collected from the bars and kept his pledge to avoid levying a tax on homeowners.[18]

But GC was more interested in business than in politics—he left that to his son. Through watching GC's pragmatic approach to local government, his son learned lessons that he would apply when he became governor. Pat admired his father's creative approach to law enforcement, addressing the source of crime and devising a policy that put the heaviest tax burden on those who benefited most, the tavern owners. Pat appreciated at an early age that leaders can use the tools of governance—budgets and regulatory authority—to craft ways of serving the common good and minimizing costs to common people.

The Luceys were a devout Catholic family, and Pat took pride in his Irish Catholic identity.[19] One of his sisters, Genevieve, entered the Dominican Sisters and took the name Sister Mary Eleanor, OP. Two of his brothers, John Roger and Gregory Francis, were ordained as Jesuit priests. Pat himself seriously considered becoming a Jesuit. He attended Mass every week throughout his life and personally followed the practices of the Catholic Church.

As Irish Catholics, the Lucey family differed from their neighbors, who overwhelmingly were Norwegian Lutherans. The Democratic loyalties of the Luceys also set them apart. In a small town, ethnic, religious, and political identity is important and can be a source of social conflict. Lucey's siblings did not recall hostile treatment from their neighbors in Ferryville, but they did remember feeling distinct. Lucey later cited his Irish heritage as a primary reason he supported progressive causes and candidates. The stories passed along by family members and other Irish immigrants of centuries of persecution and harassment by the English prompted him to root for the lower and middle classes. He knew of the struggles and hopes of immigrants and the experiences of being part of an ethnic and religious minority in a small town.[20]

GC also felt distinct, although not in a hostile or threatened way. It was more a matter of taking pride in family heritage. He made it clear to his children that he wanted them, when the time came, to date and marry Irish Catholic Democrats. Pat's sister Kathleen once brought home a date who did not fit that description and recalled that GC was cold and unwelcoming to him.[21] But parental love prevailed over identity concerns. The children, including Pat, did not always heed the Irish-Catholic-Democrat preference and continued to be loved nonetheless.

## EDUCATION

Pat began his education at the public school in Ferryville. The school had no kindergarten, so he began first grade when he was five, in 1923. After his family relocated to Bagley following third grade, he attended public schools there.

Pat's formative years were filled with the family and educational issues common to most school-age children. But those years also contained some clues of his later interest in politics and his approach to public policy. His mother discouraged shyness and encouraged him to give public speeches as early as grade school. She arranged for him to give a speech to the local parent–teacher association once every year. As a fifth grader, he campaigned door to door for Democrat Al Smith, a Catholic, in the 1928 presidential contest. Pat was eager to see a Catholic become president. His disappointment when Smith lost led him, decades later, to briefly oppose the candidacy of John F. Kennedy because he did not want to see another failed attempt.

Pat's parents took to heart a sermon delivered at Sunday Mass that warned "parents who could afford to send their kids to a Catholic school and didn't do so might pay for it in eternity."[22] Pat and his sisters Eleanor and Verona transferred to St. Mary's Catholic School in Glen Haven, ten miles south of Bagley. GC had one of his employees drive the siblings to school every morning. When classes were finished, they walked to the railroad station near the river and took the northbound Burlington Northern and Quincy Railroad's *Black Hawk* back to Bagley.

Lucey confessed that he and Eleanor had a habit of losing their train tickets. The youngest of the three, Verona, was soon put in charge. She held on to the tickets and distributed them to her siblings as they boarded.[23]

When winter turned bitterly cold, the children stayed in Glen Haven with the Adrian family Monday through Friday, returning to Bagley on weekends. Fred Adrian and Pat were the same age and were both good friends and competitors in school. GC, of course, paid Fred's parents for caring for Pat and his sisters. This arrangement lasted through Pat's final three grades in elementary school.

When the family moved to Prairie du Chien in 1931, Pat enrolled at Campion Jesuit High School, and Eleanor and Verona went to St. Gabriel's, which was across the street from the house GC rented. Already at this age, Pat was showing a keen interest in national politics. He was elated when Franklin D. Roosevelt won the White House in 1932 and accompanied his father to the celebrations held in Prairie du Chien after Election Day. Lucey recalled racing to his grandmother's house to join her in listening to the broadcast of FDR's inaugural address. He was able to recite the names of every member of Roosevelt's cabinet—a feat he was not able to repeat for any subsequent administration.[24]

When GC moved the family back to Ferryville a year later, Pat stayed in Prairie du Chien so he could continue his high school education at Campion.[25] He lived with his grandmother Margaret Lucey, and GC paid her four dollars per week for his son's room and board.[26] Pat's grandfather John had died when Lucey was in the eighth grade, and Margaret welcomed the company of her grandson. Campion was a boarding school, but Pat was a day student. He biked the two miles from his grandmother's to campus, returning to have lunch with her and then going back to school. When he had an evening activity, he biked three trips in a day. He recalled that lunch was often "rather skimpy."[27] Sometimes it was just some soup and a five-cent candy bar. The Depression didn't allow for much more.

Campion Jesuit High School was founded in 1880 and initially named College of the Sacred Heart. In 1913, the school was renamed to honor St. Edmund Campion, SJ, who was tortured and hanged in 1581 when he refused to renounce Catholicism and acknowledge Queen Elizabeth I as the head of the Christian church. The state of Wisconsin chartered the school for both high school and college, but the latter was phased out in 1923. Campion enjoyed the reputation of being an intellectually rigorous school in the Jesuit tradition. It provided an opportunity in the Midwest akin to private boarding schools in the Northeast and attracted boys from throughout the United States, although most were from Illinois.[28]

The Lucey family had strong ties to Campion. GC was a major donor, and in 1959, when enrollment peaked at six hundred students, GC gave $100,000 ($880,000 in 2019) for the construction of a dormitory for sophomores and juniors. Campion named Lucey Residential Hall in GC's honor. Pat's brothers, Gregory and Roger, followed Pat to the school and became Jesuit priests. Their mother, Ella, later observed that she sent three sons to Campion and Campion kept two of them.[29] Gregory was president and acting rector when the school closed in 1975 after suffering the effects of a fire on campus and years of declining enrollment, staff shortages, and financial difficulties.[30]

Campion had a junior Reserve Officers' Training Corps (ROTC) program when Pat attended. His mother had a hard time picturing her then thirteen-year-old, eighty-three-pound boy drilling with guns. She had him take cornet lessons so he could be in the marching band instead of ROTC. Pat was not destined to be a virtuoso, however. The music teacher allowed Pat to join but told him to fake playing when the music got complicated.[31]

The athletic program at Campion was very competitive. Pat liked sports, but he was not an athlete. He would have liked to have played football but, realizing he would probably not be able to make the team, instead went out for boxing. He entered a tournament and lost the first fight, which he thought eliminated him. To his chagrin, the rules were that you were not out until you lost two fights. He won the second and then was soundly defeated in the third round. He switched to debate.

Pat also dabbled in journalism, convincing the school newspaper, *The Campionette*, to include a feature on the experiences and perspectives of day students. Pat and, for a time, one of his good friends, Bill Antwine, edited and contributed to the column, dubbing it the "Day Hops Deb." The stories and comments were primarily humorous, and the enterprise provided an opportunity for networking with other students that helped substitute for the relationships that more naturally developed among the boarders.[32]

Lucey credits his sophomore English teacher with sparking and nurturing his appreciation for literature, especially poetry. Father Robert Madigan, SJ, had worked for the *Chicago Tribune* before taking a teaching job at Campion as part of his training to become a Jesuit. In Pat's eyes, Madigan was especially enthusiastic and challenging. A particularly effective technique Madigan used was to recite a poem, then discuss the author and the circumstances in which the poem was written, and then read the verse once again.[33] This pedagogy made the students not only understand the poem better but also more genuinely appreciate it. Throughout his life, Pat turned to poetry for relaxation and inspiration. Pat's brother Gregory credits Madigan with introducing Pat to social justice issues as well as to English literature.[34]

While at Campion, Pat developed an interest in becoming a Jesuit priest. He did not, however, go to a Jesuit college. Instead, he followed the advice of his uncle, John McNamara, a priest in Ellsworth, Wisconsin. Father McNamara argued to Pat and his father that he should go to a Catholic college but one with a tradition different than that of the Jesuits. He encouraged application to the College of St. Thomas. Pat and GC visited the campus in St. Paul, Minnesota, and decided to follow McNamara's advice.[35]

Although Pat continued to harbor thoughts of becoming a Jesuit priest at the time he began college, he abandoned those thoughts during his freshman year. At the time, competence in the Greek language was a requirement for admission to the Jesuit ranks, but Pat struggled in his first Greek course, receiving a D for a grade. The instructor told Pat that he would not receive any credits for the course unless he was more successful in the second semester or he took and passed a related course, such as Greek mythology (in English!). Lucey took the advice and moved on to other aspirations.[36] Ironically, he would later marry a Greek American— who was fluent in modern Greek.

Debate was one of the strongest programs at St. Thomas. The team was nationally competitive and won several championships while Pat was at the college. Pat was a member of the team as a freshman and sophomore, earning him twelve credits in speech. His debate partner was Bob Short, who later distinguished himself as an owner of two professional sports teams—the NBA Lakers and the MLB Rangers—and became the treasurer of the National Democratic Party. Others on the team included Bob Sheran, who would become chief justice of the Minnesota Supreme Court, and Abe Kaplan, who became a distinguished professor at the University of California–Berkeley and the University of Michigan.

Pat also continued his interest in journalism. When he walked into the school newspaper office on his first day at St. Thomas and expressed an interest in being a reporter, the editor told him to interview the coach of the freshman football team about prospects for the coming season. Pat was a fan of football and was excited about the idea of covering sports, but he did the interview without any preparation and made a lousy impression on everyone. He did not know what league St. Thomas was in or even which teams were on the schedule. The coach was also taken aback when Pat showed up without pencil or pen and had to borrow one from the football office. The newspaper changed Pat's assignment from reporter to headline writer. Pat's self-assessment was that he was okay at his new task but not very clever or creative.[37]

Like most other students at St. Thomas, Pat lived on campus. He stayed at Ireland Hall and waited tables part-time at the rate of thirty cents per hour. His roommate was Joe Gabler, who was exceptionally bright. When the priest in charge of the dorm distributed report cards at the end of the semester, he observed that Pat and Joe's room contained both the student with the best academic record and the one with the biggest mess. Pat knew he did not have the best grades, so he concluded that the remark about the mess was directed at him.[38]

Pat did well both in and outside the classroom during his freshman and sophomore years at St. Thomas and started thinking about becoming a lawyer. But academic and occupational plans were put on hold. In 1937, GC bought another store and needed Pat's help. The store was in nearby Bloomington, in Grant County. GC asked Pat to take a semester off from his studies at St. Thomas to manage the newly acquired store. That semester stretched into three years, after which Uncle Sam took his share of Pat's time.

Lucey's early years could have laid the foundation for a path that he did not take. The entrepreneurial successes of his father were dramatic and highlighted an option that could have been worth pursuing. Rather than romanticizing the rags-to-riches theme in American lore, however, Lucey worried about the plight of those who struggle to make a go of things. He supported American capitalism and free enterprise but with reasonable regulation and a safety net for those without resources.

## CHAPTER 2

# OUT AND BACK

When Patrick Lucey left the campus at St. Thomas to manage his father's store in Bloomington, he journeyed to a relatively tranquil corner of an increasingly tense and troubled world. Life in a small town in southwestern Wisconsin offered the comforts of being surrounded by family and neighbors. The nation's economy had recovered enough from the Great Depression that Lucey's father, GC Lucey, could purchase the store in Bloomington that he asked his son to run. On a personal level, Lucey had been doing well at a highly regarded school and felt confident that becoming a lawyer was a goal he could achieve. He envisioned his time in Bloomington as a temporary and pleasant diversion.

But there were serious threats to this Norman Rockwell portrait of life. The economy in the United States suffered a recession in 1937 and 1938 that evoked the memories of the recent Depression. In Wisconsin, labor unrest, farmer protests, and political uncertainty rattled prospects for a future of tranquility and prosperity. The growing power and aggressiveness of dictators in Germany, Italy, and Russia stoked fears of war and unrest.

Increasingly, pundits and politicians wondered if the US economic and governmental systems were capable of avoiding future depressions and keeping the country safe. They wondered whether the institutions of federalism and checks and balances could respond effectively to crises, especially when they occurred simultaneously.[1] Franklin D. Roosevelt asserted strong executive powers both to recover from the Great Depression and to respond to Nazi aggression in the early 1940s. Congress, and the country generally, did not want to send troops to Europe, but the president provided substantial military supply assistance to allies fighting fascism.

Importantly, he also began drafting young men and strengthening US Armed Forces even before the country declared war. Lucey felt at the time that military participation in the conflicts was all but inevitable.[2]

In Wisconsin, tensions felt by the country as a whole were intermingled with the conflict among Democrats, Republicans, and Progressives. Dairy farmers had demonstrated their frustration with low prices by engaging in milk strikes from 1932 to 1934. This was also a period of labor unrest in towns and cities throughout the state. The most visible example was a strike begun in 1934 against the Kohler Company in Sheboygan for higher wages and the right to bargain. That same year, Philip F. La Follette formed the Wisconsin Progressive Party, primarily by joining progressives from within the Republican Party with workers and farmers seeking a voice in state government.[3] In 1935, Governor La Follette proposed legislation aimed at providing jobs and boosting the state's economy through projects for highway construction, urban renewal, soil conservation, forestry, and fish and game management. In the 1935 legislature, however, the Progressive Party held only fourteen of the thirty-three seats in the state senate and nineteen of the one hundred assembly seats.[4]

The combination of Republicans and Democrats—who were conservative and not supporters of the New Deal or progressive causes—thwarted La Follette's initiatives. The Progressive Party tasted victory in 1936, reelecting La Follette as governor and winning majorities in both houses of the legislature and every statewide contest except for the US Senate seat, which Republican Alexander Wiley won. The Progressives also helped Roosevelt carry Wisconsin when he was reelected in 1936.

But the euphoria of 1936 was short lived. Benefits from the recovery efforts from the Depression were slow to reach farmers and industrial workers, fueling frustration and militancy.[5] The winning coalition anchored by the Progressive Party fractured. Wisconsin workers went on strike 190 times—a record number—in 1937, leading to fractures in the coalition between farmers and laborers. Farmers in Richland Center turned on creamery workers in their cooperative when they unionized, and farmers in Racine County no longer regarded unions as their allies when a strike shut down the local spinach cannery. Workers and farmers had substantially different interests, and getting them to cooperate required sensitive, careful effort, but La Follette's attention was on the

---

establishment of a national progressive party. In 1938, he openly broke his ties with President Roosevelt. Politics and governance, especially in Wisconsin, turned from coalitions to chaos.[6]

## MINDING THE STORE

Although Pat Lucey was aware of the international tensions, economic hardships, and political conflicts around him as he left St. Thomas, his focus was on his new job in Bloomington. GC obviously had confidence in his eldest son. He had purchased the store from his brother Gerald and gave management responsibilities to his son despite that Pat was only nineteen years old at the time. Pat enjoyed the challenge of being in a new community and being in charge of the store.[7]

Lucey's responsibilities included stocking the store, maintaining the building, keeping track of the finances, managing two employees, and writing ads for inclusion in the local newspaper, the *Bloomington Record*. He developed close relations with his customers. Journalist Neil Shively recalled that when he was covering the Wisconsin State High School Basketball Tournament as a reporter for the Dubuque *Telegraph Herald* in 1973, then-governor Lucey asked if he could watch with Neil from the press box. Bloomington was playing Crivitz for the Class C title. Governor Lucey explained, "Some of these kids are grandchildren of my Bloomington customers." He cheered and they won.[8]

While working in Bloomington, Lucey enjoyed an active social life. He was not a party animal or a regular at the taverns in town, but he did do some dating and got engaged to Rita Patterson.

Lucey did not earn a salary or put aside savings when he worked in Bloomington. GC paid for living expenses. Pat did, however, enjoy some perks. One was that he could get a beer at local taverns, even though he was under the legal drinking age at the time. Bartenders assumed that, as manager of the store, he had to be at least legal drinking age.[9]

The major competitor of the Lucey store was Porter's Grocery, right across the street. It was a serious but respectful and friendly rivalry. Both stores did well. Later, that competition would turn political. Foster Porter served as a Republican in the state senate while Lucey was a Democrat in the state assembly.[10]

Although the plan was for Lucey to interrupt his schooling only for one semester, the time away from the classroom stretched beyond that. After three years, Pat told his father that he was ready to return to school. He wanted to go to Madison to finish his undergraduate work and then pursue a law degree. Supportive of these goals, GC hired a couple to run the store and helped Pat with the move.

While a student in Madison, Lucey voted for the first time. Like many students, he listed his formal residence as his hometown—in Lucey's case, Bloomington—and he cast an absentee ballot. In the 1940 election, he voted for the reelection of Roosevelt and for Progressive Party candidates for state offices. His only choice for partisan county offices was Republican, since no Progressives or Democrats were on the ballot.[11]

## MILITARY SERVICE

Lucey intended to enroll in an undergraduate program at the University of Wisconsin that allowed students to take electives that would meet requirements for a law degree as well as a bachelor's degree. Essentially, this meant that he could simultaneously complete his bachelor's degree requirements and the first year of law school, assuming he was admitted. Then, after two more years of law school, he would be a lawyer. That was the plan.

In August 1941, however, Lucey received a draft notice. The United States was not yet at war, but President Roosevelt and Congress authorized a buildup of the military to prepare for the possibility of entering the conflict in Europe and Asia. Lucey's initial response was to petition for a deferment so that he could pursue his educational plans. He met with the secretary of the Crawford County Draft Board and argued that since the United States was not at war at that point, it made sense to issue a deferment so he could get his law degree. The secretary came from a family that included some lawyers, and he just laughed and said, "Lawyers only protect us from other lawyers. If we draft them all, we will have nothing to worry about!"[12] Petition denied.

Lucey reported to Camp Grant near Rockford, Illinois, where he took a test measuring aptitude and intelligence and apparently did quite well. He was told he could choose any branch of the service that he wanted. Lucey replied that he had run a grocery store for three years, so the

Quartermaster Corps would seem appropriate, and indicated that he would like to be sent to Hawaii, since he had never been there. The next day, he was told that there were no vacancies in Hawaii, but he could be assigned to the Quartermaster Corps in the Philippines. Lucey asked to see a map and afterward said he did not think he wanted to go there. It was too close to Japan. But he was willing to go almost anywhere else.[13]

Lucey was at Camp Grant for about six weeks. He became a favorite of the officers in part because his experience marching while in ROTC at Campion made him a natural choice to lead others. He was concerned about where all this might end, however. One Sunday while on guard duty, he happened to meet a second lieutenant who was married to a woman Lucey knew from his time at Campion, when she was at St. Mary's. She recognized Lucey, and as they talked, Lucey raised his concern about his placement in the army. Her husband counseled Lucey that he would end up in a dead-end job of some sort unless he went through officer training. He talked to Lucey's commanding officer, and within a few days, Lucey was in Fort Warren, Wyoming, enrolled in a series of four thirteen-week basic training programs. He finished as a second lieutenant.

While Lucey was at Fort Warren, Japan attacked Pearl Harbor. The following day, when President Roosevelt addressed a joint session of the US Congress, Lucey and everyone else at the base stood in formation at parade rest to listen to the "Day of Infamy" speech. It was obviously a sobering time. Training sessions resumed with a new sense of urgency.[14]

At the conclusion of his time at Fort Warren, the army sent Lucey home to Ferryville on leave for two weeks. While there, he received orders to report to New Orleans. He discovered that many of those in New Orleans were Puerto Rican and guessed correctly that he was headed to the Island of Enchantment.

It took twelve days for the convoy of ships to sail from New Orleans to San Juan, Puerto Rico. The protocol is for a military convoy to travel at the speed of the slowest ship, and that meant going at five knots, the top speed for the tankers in the convoy. In addition, the ships had to zigzag as they traveled as a defensive maneuver.[15]

Lucey was stationed at Losey Field, a newly established base on the southern coast of Puerto Rico with the initial mission of patrolling the Caribbean to be sure the Germans did not sabotage the Panama Canal. The

Pat in his army
uniform with his
parents, GC and Ella.
WHI IMAGE ID 143876

base was named after Captain Robert M. Losey, the first US combat casualty
in World War II.[16] Shortly after Lucey's arrival, the mission of the base
changed from monitoring submarine activity to providing aircraft to North
Africa and Europe and later to defending the US mainland. The Thirty-
Second Fighter Squadron used Losey until March 1943, sending Curtiss
P-40 Warhawks to the Mediterranean area. From May 1943 to March 1944,
the 417th Bombardment Squadron was stationed at Losey with outdated
semiretired Douglas B-18 Bolos. Their presence was for defense, and the
squadron never went into action. The base steadily lost personnel, which
meant fewer officers and more work for those who remained.

Lucey had an ever-growing list of responsibilities as the deputy quartermaster and also the commissary officer. In addition to these duties,
he was put in charge of the PX (Post Exchange), the bakery, and the officers' club.[17] He was also made a member of the intermediate court martial
board. When the base's legal staff was downsized to a single lawyer who
served as defense attorney, Lucey was assigned the role of prosecutor even
though he had not been to law school. Lucey prepared himself for litigation

by virtually memorizing the *Manual for Courts-Martial*. He tried a handful of minor disciplinary cases over a six-month period, and in each one, the board issued the maximum sentence of six months.[18]

After about a year at Losey Field, Lucey was promoted to the rank of captain and moved to the main base at San Juan. He went from, as he described it, "doing retail to wholesale work" in the Quartermaster Corps.[19]

While in Puerto Rico, Lucey enjoyed what he described as "a very serious romantic relationship" with Marmaleta Gabara Garcia. Indeed, he ended his engagement with Rita Patterson and got engaged to Garcia. Their engagement ended when Lucey left the military, although he and Garcia did remain in touch. She married and moved to Los Angeles, and Lucey contacted her when an article he wrote was published in the *Los Angeles Times*. The *Times* would not send him a copy of the essay, so he called Garcia and asked her if she had seen it. She said yes and that she had remarked to her husband, "I wonder if that is our Pat Lucey." Garcia collected several copies of the article from neighbors and sent them to Lucey. Later in life, when Lucey served as ambassador to Mexico, Garcia's mother visited him.[20]

Puerto Rico was not a bad place to serve during the war. The troops stationed there experienced anxieties over the disruption that German U-boats caused to supply lines for oil to Europe and bauxite to US aircraft manufacturers, and they were restrained by the personal restrictions that went with military routines and protocols. However, especially as the war progressed, they found ways to relax and even treat as comedic acts that would otherwise be reasons for discipline. Lucey, for example, talked about the drunken soldier who commandeered an officer's jeep and drove it into a swimming pool next to the officers' club before sobering up.[21] And there was a pilot who seemed to enjoy giving everyone fits by flying over the airstrip at a low altitude and upside down.[22]

While in the military, Lucey observed instances of racial discrimination. He had an assignment to take care of the food service needs of African American troops who were confined to separate base facilities. Not only was he shocked that these troops were being physically segregated, but he was appalled at the condition of their facilities and equipment. This experience made him, like many other veterans, a strong supporter of the postwar civil rights movement.[23]

## BACK TO WISCONSIN

As 1945 came to an end, Lucey, after four and a half years of military service, donned civilian clothes. His discharge was on Christmas Day, and he prepared for this transition by visiting Madison while on leave in November of that year. Before attending the homecoming game against Northwestern, he went to the registrar's office at the University of Wisconsin and talked about what he needed to do to finish his bachelor's degree. The Badgers lost the football game, but Lucey felt he scored a victory. He needed only seventeen more credits to graduate. With hard work, he could do that in one more semester. He returned to Madison in January looking forward to framing his degree.

Pat with his siblings, Roger, Kathleen, and Greg (back row), and Eleanor and Verona (seated), in a photo taken on April 29, 1988. COURTESY OF GREGORY LUCEY, SJ

Lucey majored in philosophy and remembered in particular the classes he took from Professor Max Carl Otto, who was also his adviser and chair of the Department of Philosophy.[24] Otto was a noted and visible member of the faculty. A member of the First Unitarian Society of Madison, he had been attacked by politicians and clergy for his teaching and writings that developed a nontheistic foundation for understanding the human condition.[25] Charles Van Hise, president of the University of Wisconsin, famously defended Otto and articulated the need to protect academic freedom in his 1912 commencement address, "The Spirit of the University." Otto distinguished himself as a pragmatist and humanist, akin to John Dewey and William James. His political sympathies were with Robert M. La Follette Sr. and the progressives, whom he saw as committed to improving the condition of individuals and families and to using science and evidence to design public policies.[26]

In a seminar that Lucey took from Otto, the two of them took the same side in a class debate. They argued for scientific humanism, and Lucey grew to respect and admire his partner. He appreciated Otto's acceptance of Lucey as a practicing Catholic and gained an understanding of Otto's atheism. They converged on their diagnoses and prescriptions for contemporary society and their support for progressives.[27] Lucey felt very fortunate that he was in Otto's class. Otto retired at the end of the next academic year.

While Lucey was studying, writing papers, and taking exams, the Wisconsin Progressive Party held its final convention. Delegates met on the Ides of March in 1946 in Portage, a small town forty-one miles north of Madison. The 412 people assembled there acknowledged the inherent handicaps of a third party, especially on a national level. The Progressive Party experienced success in many of the state elections, but it could not play a meaningful role in presidential politics as long as that scene was dominated by the Republican and Democratic Parties. Unable to send delegates to one of the two major parties' national nominating conventions, Progressives were outsiders, unable to directly affect whose name would appear on the ballot. The key question for Wisconsin Progressives was whether to join Republicans or Democrats.

Bob La Follette Jr. announced at the Portage convention that he would seek reelection as a US senator on the Republican ticket and urged delegates to disband the Progressive Party and join him in returning to the Republican fold. The vote was 284 to 131 to do just that. Of those dissenting, seventy-seven favored maintaining the Progressive Party, fifty-one felt it made much more sense to join the Democratic Party, and three opted to become members of the Socialist Party.[28]

Among the Progressives who followed La Follette to the Republican Party was Gaylord Nelson. Nelson ran unsuccessfully on the GOP ticket for a seat in the state assembly in 1946 and then switched to the Democratic Party, eventually becoming a state senator, governor, and US senator. John Reynolds followed a similar path and served as attorney general and governor in Wisconsin and then as a federal judge.[29]

Lucey was focused on being a student that spring and did not attend the Progressive Party convention but followed what was happening. He identified with those who supported FDR and the New Deal and felt the best course was to join the Wisconsin Democratic Party, transforming it to align with the more liberal national party. He knew that it would be necessary to grow the party, and he favored abandoning the traditional, conservative positions of the state Democrats.[30]

Lucey's parents, GC and Ella, went to Madison for Lucey's graduation. Lucey told them that he planned to stay at the university and earn a law degree. Since he was able to take courses while an undergraduate that would count toward law school requirements, Lucey calculated that he could earn the degree by taking a full load of courses for two more academic years plus two summer school sessions. Veterans' benefits would cover costs.

GC, however, said that the family business needed Pat at that point and observed that if the family needed a lawyer, they could hire one. Although Lucey had harbored a vision of becoming a lawyer for more than five years, he followed his parents home.[31]

Pat's father had built on his record as a successful entrepreneur while Lucey was in Puerto Rico. GC had acquired fourteen farms in the Ferryville area during the war and wanted Pat to manage them. Because the war effort required all available metal, a shortage in farm equipment developed. To meet this need, GC repaired old, discarded farm machinery and then sold it at an annual auction. To enable cash-strapped farmers to purchase the equipment, he partnered with Conway Finance to provide low-interest loans. He invested in area farms and then rented the farms,

GC Lucey's tenant farmers pose for a group photo. GC held an annual picnic for the farmers and their families. WHI IMAGE ID 143891

offering the tenants the opportunity to buy the farms on a land contract basis.[32] This earned him not only income but gratitude from farmers faced with tough times.[33] Each year, GC organized a "renters' picnic"—a festive family-oriented event.

In addition to being a successful entrepreneur himself, GC helped others succeed in business. Beyond selling his farms to renters, he gave those who had worked for him before the war valuable opportunities when they returned. He offered jobs to returning veterans and then made them partners, primarily in the grocery business and John Deere dealerships. Gradually, GC would withdraw from the business and let his partners become full owners. Eight people benefited from this arrangement.[34]

To prepare for his job of managing the farms, Pat went to several federal agencies and to the university's College of Agriculture to get briefed on agricultural issues and techniques relevant to southwestern Wisconsin. Most of the farmers had dairy cows but were also growing corn and tobacco. Lucey taught them about pasture renovation, contour stripping, terracing, and the use of new seeds and fertilizer.[35] He found the renters very receptive to ideas about how to improve productivity and efficiency.

Jack Gillespie, the banker in the village of De Soto, praised the results of Lucey's work. Gillespie owned several farms and remarked that, while he was losing money every year on each, Pat and GC were reaping profits. The results were quite impressive, he thought.[36]

When Lucey returned to Ferryville, he resumed his relationship with Rita Patterson, and they became reengaged. Once again, however, the engagement came to an end.[37]

In addition to tackling his new responsibilities managing the farms, Lucey was active in the political arena. Like others who had supported the New Deal and progressive policies, he felt torn about the candidacy of Joe McCarthy in the Republican primary for the US Senate. When McCarthy first ran, there was no indication that he would recklessly accuse people in the US State Department and elsewhere of being Communists or Communist sympathizers. His accusations began in 1950, four years later. The dilemma confronting Lucey and Democrats of like mind was that while a prominent progressive such as Bob La Follette Jr. might lose his bid for reelection by losing the GOP nomination for US Senate to McCarthy, a progressive Democratic candidate might have a better chance facing McCarthy rather than La Follette in the general election. To help their party, Democrats put forth only one candidate in their primary, thereby freeing Democrats to vote for McCarthy in the Republican primary. The sole Democratic candidate, Howard J. McMurray, pledged to bow out of the race and support La Follette if he later chose to run as a Democrat. Democrats hoped that if La Follette got beaten in the Republican primary, he and other Republican progressives would then side with Democrats in the general election—and beyond.[38]

To the chagrin of the Democrats, La Follette lost to McCarthy in the 1946 Republican primary and then not only refused to join the Democratic Party but encouraged his Republican supporters to stick with the GOP through the general election. At least in the short term, progressives remained split between the two major parties, and McCarthy went to Washington, DC, as Wisconsin's junior senator.

Lucey supported Democrats' national strategy in 1946, but his focus was on local politics. He worked on the campaign of his friend and former schoolmate, Frank Antwine, who ran as a Democrat and was a perennial losing candidate for the state assembly. The only Democrat who won in traditionally Republican Crawford County was Margarete Rogers, the register of deeds.[39] Antwine lost again in 1946, this time to Republican Donald C. McDowell, who was speaker of the Wisconsin State Assembly. After the ballots were counted, Antwine encouraged Lucey to run in his stead two years later, in 1948.

Lucey's first elective victories were examples of how local politics can be happenstance. When he returned to Ferryville in the spring of 1946, a good friend, Jean Garvey, jokingly organized a write-in campaign to elect Lucey as justice of the peace. Lucey added to the humor by pledging that he would not charge anything but a modest fee to anyone who wanted to get married. No other candidates ran for the position, and Lucey won with the seven votes that were cast![40]

No couple ever took Lucey up on his offer to marry them at a bargain fee, and his caseload as justice of the peace was very light. The only case he recalled involved a man who became intoxicated at one of Ferryville's taverns and was arrested and jailed by one of the deputized tavern keepers. The next morning, the man was brought before Justice Lucey, who in accordance with the statutes released him when his wife paid the court costs of $2.75. As the couple left, Lucey thought of the hardships faced by the woman, who had to go back to the farm and milk the cows, collect eggs, care for the other livestock, till the soil, weed the garden, cook and clean house, in addition to rescuing her husband when he went off to enjoy himself in the bars. It didn't seem at all like the right person was being punished.[41]

At the same time that he served as justice of the peace,[42] Lucey served on two local school boards. He was elected to the Ferryville School Board by the fifteen people who attended the annual board meeting in 1947. Previously, Ferryville and other school districts that had only an elementary school sent their students to a high school in Seneca, but many parents were dissatisfied with the Seneca school. Gillespie, the De Soto banker who had been impressed with Lucey's success as a farm manager, initiated the creation of a separate school district that would operate a high school to be located in De Soto to serve as an alternative to the Seneca school. In the mid-twentieth century, Wisconsin state government authorized the creation of special districts to operate a single school. This was in essence a precursor to the charter school movement begun in 1993.

Lucey went along with Gillespie and was rewarded with being named as a charter board member for the new high school district. This position did not conflict with his service on the Ferryville School District, since Ferryville had no high school.

In the aftermath of the 1946 elections, Lucey busied himself with both the family businesses and politics. GC, Pat, and cousin Eddie McNamara developed a close and successful working relationship. They gave serious consideration to becoming partners in a formal way. Politics is a part-time endeavor for all but a relatively few officeholders, so political involvement did not preclude business activity as long as politicians avoided conflicts of interest. Initially, it looked like Pat would pursue careers in both arenas, but it soon became clear that politics had the stronger allure and was going to consume the bulk of Lucey's time and attention. GC would have preferred another scenario, but he was gracious and supportive as his son focused on the ballot box and a public policy agenda.[43]

## CHAPTER 3

# POLITICS CALLS

P atrick J. Lucey was a giant killer. His first venture into electoral politics was against the speaker of the Wisconsin State Assembly. Donald C. McDowell represented the Crawford County district from his initial election in 1936 until his defeat by Lucey in 1948. His Republican colleagues chose him as speaker in the 1945 and 1947 legislative sessions. He was well known in the district, having served as postmaster in Soldiers Grove for twelve years, and he had been on the school board, the county board, and a number of commissions. Crawford County had maintained its Republican tradition by casting 57.1 percent of its vote in 1944 for Thomas E. Dewey while the rest of the country gave landslide support for Franklin D. Roosevelt. McDowell ran without opposition in 1944. In 1946, with little effort, he beat Democrat Frank Antoine. Understandably, McDowell did not expect to lose in 1948. But, surprisingly, Lucey expected to win.

With virtually no party organization or help from Democrats, Lucey relied on face-to-face, door-to-door campaigning. Lucey received a fifty-dollar check from the Railway Brotherhoods, a loose federation of unions representing various railway employees, but he financed his campaign primarily himself.[1] He spent only one thousand dollars, most of which was from his personal savings from his military salary.[2] No burning issues called for a change in representation in the capital. Voters in Crawford County generally based their choice on their comfort with and confidence in the person they sent to Madison, so Lucey knew that meeting as many voters as possible was key to winning.

## THE DISTRICT

Like most states in the 1940s and 1950s, Wisconsin state legislative districts were malapportioned in favor of rural areas. Lucey had fewer doors to knock on and fewer hands to shake than his counterparts running in urban areas. Despite a state constitutional provision mandating reapportionment based on the decennial report of the US Census Bureau, Wisconsin's legislature had not redrawn district boundaries since 1911. Every ten years, the legislature appointed a joint committee on reapportionment, but either the committee never reported or the legislature took no floor action on the report. In 1946, the State Supreme Court in *State ex rel. Martin v. Zimmerman* acknowledged this but, in issuing its frustrated opinion, ruled that the Court could do nothing about it.[3]

The basic unit for drawing assembly district boundaries was the county. Until 1964, the state constitution was interpreted as barring the creation of districts by taking part of a county and combining it with another county or part of another county.[4] Typically, a single county constituted an assembly district. If the population was very small, two or three counties would be combined. If the population was large, the county would be divided into two or more districts. The occasional legislative action redrawing boundaries throughout most of the twentieth century was to make minor adjustments that accommodated annexations.

According to census data, 18,328 people lived in Crawford County in 1940 and 17,652 in 1950. Table 3.1 compares Crawford County with a sample of other rural and urban districts.

TABLE 3.1. Population of Selected Assembly Districts

| District | 1940 | 1950 |
|---|---|---|
| Crawford | 18,328 | 17,652 |
| Richland | 20,381 | 19,245 |
| Vernon | 29,940 | 27,906 |
| Grant (2 districts) | 20,320 avg. | 20,730 avg. |
| Milwaukee (20 then 24 districts) | 38,344 avg. | 36,294 avg. |
| Dane (3 then 5 districts) | 43,553 avg. | 33,871 avg. |
| Kenosha (2 districts) | 31,753 avg. | 37,619 avg. |

Source: *The State of Wisconsin Blue Book 1948* (Madison: Wisconsin Legislative Reference Bureau, 1948), 485; *The State of Wisconsin Blue Book 1950* (Madison: Wisconsin Legislative Reference Bureau, 1948), 492.

When Lucey ran for the assembly, his district had the smallest population in the state. And the number was declining. Neighboring districts of Richland and Vernon Counties likewise had relatively small and declining populations. Grant County was populous enough to be split into two districts, but each averaged fewer than twenty-one thousand residents. In contrast, the urban areas of the state, illustrated in Table 3.1 by Milwaukee, Dane, and Kenosha Counties, had relatively large and growing populations. The average number of people in Milwaukee and Dane County districts was about double the number in the Crawford County district.

Crawford County is one of the oldest in Wisconsin. It was created by the legislature of the Michigan territory in 1818 and included the western half of what is currently Wisconsin. The county is named after William H. Crawford, who was US treasurer when James Monroe was president. After Wisconsin became a separate territory from Michigan and eventually a state, legislatures repeatedly subdivided the county and the current boundaries took shape.

Crawford County was and is home to farms and small towns and villages—such as Ferryville. The largest town is the county seat, Prairie du Chien, which had a population of 4,622 in 1940 and 5,392 in 1950, representing 25.2 percent and 30.5 percent respectively of the county population. While many of the other towns, villages, and unincorporated communities are nestled against the Mississippi and Wisconsin Rivers that form the western and southern boundaries of the county, most are scattered throughout. Thus, despite the county's relatively small population, a candidate campaigning door to door and farmhouse to farmhouse has some traveling to do.

## THE CAMPAIGN

Lucey relied primarily on shoe-leather campaigning. He was upbeat about his chances of unseating McDowell for two reasons. First, McDowell had beaten Democratic candidate Frank Antoine in 1946 by a margin of only 211 votes, not impressive in a Republican-leaning district. Second, in the aftermath of Antoine's defeat, Lucey had been busy organizing a local Democratic Party and felt good about his success in recruiting candidates to run for a wide variety of village and county offices and precinct captains to help get out the vote. The feedback he was getting from these recruits was encouraging, and no major controversies or challenges were polarizing voters. The main concern was that people had a general sense that elected officials, including McDowell, were not listening to or caring about their concerns.[5]

Lucey had a simple pledge: "No fantastic promises—just the best representation I can possibly give the people of Crawford County. No special privileged interest—just the best interests of all the people first, last and always."[6]

Lucey was the chief strategist and organizer for the campaign, but he persuaded John Moses to be listed as his campaign manager. Moses was well known and respected in the community. Later, Moses would serve as the head of the state's Department of Veterans Affairs. When Lucey was governor, he and Moses fought on opposite sides over whether the department head should serve at the pleasure of the governor or be chosen by a board.

On a typical day of campaigning, Lucey would drive with his mother, Ella, to a town or village. His mother would go from house to house, and Lucey would visit the neighboring farms. After the election, the *Wisconsin State Journal* observed:

> Some mothers keep the baby shoes in which Junior took his first steps. Assemblyman Pat Lucey's mother has a more novel memento of the young Ferryville Democrat's first venture into the political arena. She's keeping a right-hand suede glove, in excellent condition except for a hole over the knuckles—she wore it out rapping on Crawford County front doors on behalf of her son's successful race last fall.[7]

Lucey and his mother would engage in brief conversations with the people they met, encouraging support for Lucey and citing the details of when and where to vote. They left a small pamphlet, and if voters were not home, they included a handwritten note about their visit.

Pat and his mother were not, of course, always talking with strangers. The Lucey name was well known in the area. The family—including grandparents, aunts, uncles, cousins, and other relatives—had lived in several communities in Crawford County. They owned grocery stores and farm equipment dealerships, and Lucey was out and about managing the fourteen farms his father owned. Both Pat and his father had been active in local government and politics, and Lucey had been busy building a party organization.

Most of Lucey's limited campaign funds paid for direct mail to residents.[8] Parties in the district did not have records of their supporters, and Wisconsin does not record party affiliation when people register to vote, so it was not possible to target voters. Mailings went to everyone, and this effort increased costs.

Lucey also ran classified advertisements in the county's five weekly newspapers. One ad was titled "Handyman for Hire." It presented Lucey as someone who would work hard in the state assembly for the people of Crawford County. The cleverness of the ad garnered Lucey considerable applause, according to Eliese Howe of the *Prairie du Chien Courier*.[9]

This description of campaigning makes it sound like a full-time job. But Lucey, as well as most other candidates for the state legislature, had to somehow fit wooing voters into a schedule that included work at a regular job and time for family life. Lucey had two advantages: his work managing farms provided flexibility, and he was still a bachelor.

Lucey also had the good fortune to be in a three-way race. Ted Reddick ran against McDowell in the Republican Party primary and, when he lost, filed as an independent candidate in the general election. Not only did he split the Republican vote, but his campaign was almost entirely a constant, harsh attack on McDowell. The negative banter between the two GOP candidates allowed Lucey to emerge as a positive, civil, and optimistic alternative. When the votes were counted on November 2, 1948, Lucey received 3,465 votes, McDowell garnered 2,920 votes, and Reddick trailed with 794 votes. Lucey won with 48.3 percent of the vote. He would have preferred something over 50 percent, but he won, and he beat the speaker of the assembly. His upset victory garnered him instant visibility throughout the state, and some of the Republican legislators joined in welcoming him to the chamber. Republicans were split between conservative Stalwarts and refugees from the disbanded Progressive Party, and the latter were happy to see McDowell go.[10]

## LINKS TO THE PARTY

Lucey initially did not have strong ties to any political party. When he began his political activity in Crawford County, he acted on his own. He was not recruited by the Democratic Party, but he did support the New Deal and President Roosevelt. His source of news was the *La Crosse Tribune*, not Madison's progressive *Capital Times*, and he followed syndicated columnist John Wyngaard, who supported neither Democrats nor Progressives.

Lucey felt isolated until he attended a meeting in June 1948 at what was then Central High School in Madison. He had learned that a group of individuals who wanted to change the Wisconsin Democratic Party to a progressive, viable organization would be gathering. Intrigued, he boarded a bus to find out what was happening. Democrats had been minor players in state politics ever since the birth of the Republican Party in Ripon in 1854. With a few exceptions, they performed woefully at the polls. In 1922, Democrats had so few people voting in their primary that they lost their status to have an automatic entry on the ballot.[11] From 1919 to 1933, except for 1929 and 1930, the Socialist Party held more seats than the Democrats in the state legislature. Conservatives were dominant in the state's Democratic Party and opposed the New Deal and Franklin Roosevelt's leadership. Roosevelt, in turn, eschewed his own party in Wisconsin and channeled federal patronage in the Badger State through the Progressive Party.[12]

A group of liberals within the Democratic Party got a boost when Dan Hoan joined them. Hoan had been the mayor of Milwaukee from 1916 to 1940 and a prominent leader of the state's Socialist Party. He had credited Roosevelt with moving in the right direction but criticized him for not attacking capitalism. In 1940, Hoan acknowledged the success of the New Deal and left the Socialist Party to join the Democrats. In 1944, he won the Democratic nomination for governor and, along with other liberals, succeeded in electing Robert Tehan, a state senator representing Milwaukee, as chair of the state party. Although that was a Republican year and Roosevelt lost the vote in Wisconsin, Hoan won 41 percent of the votes in the gubernatorial race—considerably more impressive than the 12 percent and 19 percent the Democratic candidates got in the 1942 and 1940 elections respectively. Hoan brought with him Socialists and Milwaukee labor support and hope for those trying to end conservative control of the party.[13]

Lucey visits Ripon, the birthplace of the Republican Party.
WHI IMAGE ID 143897

Hoan recognized the need to expand Democratic support beyond his base and began efforts to reach out to other parts of the state. He focused much of his energy on northwestern Wisconsin. Tehan worked on broadening support in Madison and Dane County. Liberal Democrats and former Progressives were encouraged when liberal Democrat Carl Thompson won 49 percent of the vote in a special election in 1946 for a seat in the US House of Representatives. He lost to Republican Glen Davis by fewer than 850 out of 47,000 votes.

In preparation for the 1948 meeting in Madison that Lucey attended, a small group, including Carl Thompson, Jim Doyle Sr., John Reynolds, and Henry Reuss, met in the Retlaw Hotel in Fond du Lac to lay the groundwork for formally establishing a new Democratic Party in Wisconsin. Rather than try to gain control of the existing party, they calculated it would be easier and quicker to replace it with a new organization. This effort would begin with the creation of a separate body that under Wisconsin law could accept members and campaign contributions. The next objective would be to secure recognition of the new organization by the Democratic National Committee (DNC) when delegates from Wisconsin were seated at presidential nominating conventions. Until the new party secured national recognition, it would be called the Democratic Organizing Committee (DOC).[14]

At the June meeting in Madison, Lucey met Doyle, Thompson, Reynolds, Reuss, Horace Wilkie, Gaylord Nelson, Thomas Fairchild, and Ruth Doyle. In Lucey's words, "That was the first time I realized that what I was doing out in Crawford County was really part of a movement and that I was very much in sync with what these people were doing, with whom I had had no communication at all."[15] This group, including Lucey, came to be called "the young Turks." Those who met in Madison laid the groundwork for supporters from throughout the state to adopt a constitution for the DOC.[16]

A convention was held in November 1949 at the Northland Hotel in Green Bay to adopt the proposed constitution. Gaylord Nelson presided, and the keynote speaker was US Senator Paul Douglas of Illinois. Those assembled adopted the constitution, which had been drafted by Doyle, and elected an administrative committee, chaired by Jerome Fox. Each congressional district had a vice chair, and Lucey was chosen for District 3. Delegates considered Lucey as their spokesperson for farmers in the state.[17] Other notable members of the administrative committee were Henry W. Maier, who would become mayor of Milwaukee; Thompson, who would run for governor; and Virginia Hart, who would later serve in the Lucey administration, becoming the first woman cabinet officer in Wisconsin state government.

By 1950, the DOC had earned recognition from the Truman administration and the DNC. The old Wisconsin Democratic Party lost recognition and went out of existence. The DOC received financial support from the national Democratic Party and in 1952, as the Democratic Party of Wisconsin, sent delegates to the presidential nominating convention. A major factor in national help to the reinvented Democratic Party in the Badger State was the desire to stop Joe McCarthy.

During his 1948 campaign for state assembly, Lucey agonized about whether to be seen with President Harry S. Truman, who was running for reelection as the Democratic nominee. Truman was on his famous whistle-stop campaign and would be traveling from Minneapolis to Milwaukee, which would bring him near but not into Lucey's district. Because of the president's apparent unpopularity at the time, Lucey feared being identified with Truman would not play well in Crawford County. Nonetheless, Lucey hesitantly made the trip to Minneapolis, where he met the mayor, Hubert H. Humphrey. Lucey then boarded Truman's campaign train, the *Ferdinand Magellan*, and appeared with him for the first third of the journey from the Twin Cities to Milwaukee. Like many observers, Lucey was surprised when Truman won the election and, in hindsight, regarded the decision to board the train as a good one.[18]

After taking his seat in the assembly chambers, Lucey engaged even more vigorously in efforts to strengthen the Democratic Party. During the 1949 session, he met every Monday morning with Bill Proxmire, a reporter for the *Capital Times* who engaged in Democratic politics during his off-hours.[19] The two identified an issue of the week, and Proxmire would then write a press release. He and Lucey would identify a Democratic legislator who should be quoted in the release. They then had the Democratic Party headquarters make copies of the release and used the Rural Electric Association's mailing list of state newspapers and addressograph machine. Proxmire and Lucey put them in the mail and began thinking of the next week's issue.[20]

## State Assembly

Lucey was one of twenty-six Democrats who, along with seventy-four Republicans, took their seats in the assembly after the 1948 elections. Republican Oscar Rennebohm was governor, and the state senate held a twenty-seven to six GOP majority. The legislature's most notable accomplishment was to adopt a plan that ostensibly aimed to equalize funding for public schools throughout the state. The formula provided more state aid to poorer than to wealthier school districts. Prior to this, districts received state funds in direct relation to how much their residents paid in state income taxes, so there had been no redistribution of resources. While the 1949 legislation adopted a new principle, it was applied imperfectly. Property values affected aid going to poorer districts, but the richest districts received a "flat aid" or standard fee per child, thus departing from the

Lucey joins President Harry Truman on the *Ferdinand Magellan*, the train Truman used in his presidential whistle-stop campaign in 1948. COURTESY OF LAUREL LUCEY

equalization formula and retaining an advantage for the wealthiest areas. When Lucey became governor more than twenty years later, the school aid formula underwent major changes to provide more effective equalization.

Urban issues were noticeably absent from the 1949 legislative agenda. Despite growing urbanization in the state, representation still favored rural areas, and neither the governor nor the legislature addressed the concerns of Milwaukee, Madison, and southeast Wisconsin. Urban housing shortages were severe, and streets in cities were overwhelmed with cars and buses. Neighborhoods and schools were racially segregated. The African American population in Milwaukee in 1910 had been only 980 but grew to more than 13,000 in 1945 and nearly 22,000—more than the entire population of Crawford County—by 1950.[21] But largely isolated and with few political ties to statewide parties, Milwaukee had to address its challenges without any significant help or even attention from the rest of the state. The needs and sympathies of the community aligned with progressives, but instead of being part of the now defunct Progressive Party or the New Deal Democrats, Milwaukee voters usually supported candidates associated with the Socialist Party.

As a member of the rural-dominated legislature and a representative of a rural district, Lucey, too, pursued a rural agenda. As a member of the minority party, Lucey, in any case, was unable to make much of a difference. His major legislative initiative, which he regarded as his pet project, was an attempt to establish a tobacco marketing board. Farmers in Crawford County complained bitterly that the major companies buying tobacco leaf would meet at the Fortney Hotel in Viroqua the day before they made purchases, and then they all offered the same price to the farmers. Democrat Thomas Fairchild, elected as Wisconsin's attorney general in 1948, started an antitrust suit, but Governor Rennebohm cut Fairchild's budget for antitrust action by 50 percent. The two-year term of the state's attorney general also handicapped litigation, and support increased for establishing a state board to provide oversight over tobacco leaf purchasing. Lucey worked with progressive Republicans in the assembly and got the bill passed, 45 to 43. However, Majority Leader Warren P. Knowles used a parliamentary maneuver to scuttle the proposal when it reached the senate.[22]

Lucey also took action to have the Wisconsin Department of Agriculture work with the University of Wisconsin College of Agriculture and the US Department of Agriculture to respond to an outbreak of Bang's disease (brucellosis) among dairy herds in Crawford County. This is a devastating, contagious disease caused by the bacterium *Brucella abortus* and resulting in aborted fetuses in cows (as well as sheep, pigs, and other livestock). Cows need to give birth to produce milk, so this disease obviously hurt productivity. When farmers approached Lucey about the outbreak, he organized a special task force and prompted Wisconsin's Department of Agriculture to slaughter affected animals and provide education on how to prevent Bang's disease.[23]

Lucey's long-term interest in tax reform began in the assembly. One of his earliest initiatives was to change who benefited from property taxes paid by rural electrical cooperatives. State law stipulated that a power plant pay property taxes to the jurisdiction where it was located. Lucey worked with the cooperatives to alter that law so the property taxes would be paid to all the communities served by a cooperative's power plant, regardless of the plant's location. He built support within both houses of the legislature but was unable to enact this reform until he became governor.[24]

Lucey realized that, although he represented a rural district, he also had a responsibility to serve the state as a whole. A harbinger of a major priority on his gubernatorial agenda more than twenty years later was a proposal to place the nine state teachers colleges under the University of Wisconsin.[25] Other bills that Lucey sponsored included racially integrating the National Guard, establishing a Human Rights Commission, consolidating school districts, mandating racial integration in public elementary and secondary schools, and establishing a commission to reorganize state government to make it more efficient.[26] None passed, but the efforts helped make Lucey more visible among legislators and politicians.

His newsletters to constituents provided information and served as messages of self-promotion, although they lacked shrill partisan rhetoric. He praised the efforts of Foster Porter, his political and business rival, to reorganize and improve public schools in the state. Porter, a Republican, served in the state senate while Lucey was in the assembly. He also gave credit to Governor Rennebohm on the few occasions when the Republican supported progressive measures. One newsletter consisted entirely of a speech by Ruth Doyle, a Democrat representing Madison, urging women to be active in politics and government.[27] Lucey and Doyle were close friends and collaborators in the assembly's Democratic caucus.

Since the legislature met only part-time, Lucey found he could take advantage of being near the University of Wisconsin campus. He completed a course in public finance while serving in the assembly.

Early in his term in the assembly, Lucey determined that he could not continue as a state legislator for long. The workload was limited, and members of the assembly earned only one hundred dollars per month. Even while sharing a room with other legislators when in Madison, living at home in Crawford County, and getting a part-time salary from his father, he struggled to make ends meet. If he were to stay in politics, he needed to move up. He decided to run for Congress.[28]

Lucey prepared for a 1950 campaign for a seat in the US House of Representatives by recruiting candidates for all of the partisan offices in his congressional district. The district consisted of ten counties, so that meant convincing ten lawyers to run for district attorney, ten individuals interested in law enforcement to run for sheriff, ten people to run for register of deeds, and so on down the line. He reasoned that he had to build from the bottom up as well as present himself as an attractive candidate on the top of the ballot. A key ingredient for victory at the polls is turnout, and having a full slate of candidates getting their friends and supporters to vote is a way to boost a party's chances for success.[29]

## RUN FOR CONGRESS

Wisconsin's congressional districts, like those for the state legislature, gave disproportionate weight to rural areas with lower populations. The population of congressional districts varied in 1950 from 249,654 in the Tenth District (northwestern Wisconsin) to 438,041 and 433,006 in the Fourth and Fifth (the two Milwaukee districts). Lucey ran in the district with the second-lowest number of people, 300,025. The largest city in the Third District was La Crosse with a population of 47,535. Only twelve other communities had more than 2,500 people, with Baraboo topping that list at 7,264.

The 1950 campaign occurred during a time of tension. The economy after World War II was plagued by high inflation and a recession that lasted from the third quarter of 1948 to the second quarter of 1950. The country as a whole was in the midst of a baby boom. As builders scrambled to address a serious shortage of housing, urban centers became surrounded by suburban sprawl.[30]

The relief that the war was over was replaced by the anxiety of the Cold War and the fear of Communist expansion. In 1948, the Soviet Union had blockaded the western sectors of Berlin, and the United States and its allies dramatically airlifted supplies, rescuing West Berlin but adding to international anxiety and fears that armed conflict would be inevitable. Russia had aggressively seized control over Eastern European countries and threatened takeovers of Greece and Turkey. Communists in North Korea, with the support of China and Russia, looked southward. The US House of Representatives ignored warnings from President Harry S. Truman and defeated a bill in January 1950 that would have provided aid to South Korea. Five months later, North Korea invaded South Korea. President Truman established a program demanding that federal employees pledge loyalty to the United States, adding to an atmosphere of fear and suspicion that McCarthy exploited.[31]

Estes Kefauver, a US Senator from Tennessee and aspirant for the Democratic presidential nomination, led a campaign against corruption that, although justified, also added to the collective angst and public distrust. Kefauver and his colleagues on the Special Committee to Investigate Crime in Interstate Commerce traveled the country in 1950 and 1951 and exposed corruption involving organized crime, government officials, and businesses throughout American society.

Prospects for Democrats were not good. Since they occupied the White House, they inevitably were blamed for the state of the union. Voters typically favor the party that is not in control in midterm elections, and Wisconsin's Third Congressional District had traditionally supported Republicans.

Nonetheless, Lucey thought he had a path to get to Washington, DC. The incumbent, Gardner Withrow, was a La Follette progressive but a Republican. Lucey calculated that if a conservative, or stalwart, Republican won the Republican primary, then a New Deal Democrat might win the general election. That scenario would have especially bright prospects if, as happened when Lucey ran for the assembly, the losing Republican candidate stayed in the race and ran as an independent in the general election.

Withrow did indeed face opposition in the GOP primary. The problem was that he faced two opponents. One was Porter, a conservative who had the support of Republican Party leaders in the state. The other candidate, Jay Walsh, was also conservative and opposed Porter primarily because of his initiative to consolidate school districts. Walsh favored traditional school district lines, even if it meant very small student populations. They split the conservative vote, and Withrow won the nomination. Meanwhile, Lucey was unopposed in the Democratic primary. Neither Porter nor Walsh chose to run as an independent, so the general election was between Lucey, Withrow, and a Socialist Party candidate.[32]

The two major party candidates, a progressive Republican and a New Deal, progressive Democrat, agreed on major issues. Withrow had the advantage of identification with the party that voters in the district traditionally supported. As a former railway conductor and union member, he also had the endorsement of organized labor. Labor began supporting him when he first ran in 1931 as a La Follette progressive Republican. The unions continued to endorse Withrow in 1950 even though he had supported the anti-labor Taft-Hartley bill in the Republican-dominated Eightieth Congress.

Lucey was in trouble. He again relied on door-to-door, face-to-face campaigning, but now the area he had to cover was much larger, and he was not well known outside Crawford County. This time, he spent ten thousand dollars, again mostly from his own savings. Bill Proxmire came out to La Crosse and worked with Lucey's campaign manager, Jean Garvey. Garvey had married and moved to La Crosse since organizing the write-in campaign that had elected Lucey as justice of the peace in Ferryville in 1946. Proxmire advised her on how to run a more conventional campaign.[33]

While campaigning for himself and for the candidates he had recruited to run for the partisan county offices, Lucey also promoted Thomas Fairchild, who headed the Democratic ticket in 1950 as a candidate for the US Senate, and Carl Thompson, candidate for governor. Fairchild had been elected in 1948 as attorney general. His opponent in the Senate race was the incumbent, Alexander Wiley. As part of his campaign, Fairchild held a rally at the La Crosse labor hall and lined up Walter Reuther, president of the United Automobile Workers, as the featured speaker. As part of his remarks, Reuther was to praise all of labor's endorsed candidates. Even though labor had endorsed Lucey's opponent and Lucey was not invited

A cartop sign promotes Lucey for Congress in 1950. WHI IMAGE ID 143819

to the rally, Fairchild insisted that Lucey come and sit front and center with him. When Reuther went down the list of candidates whom he urged voters to support, he did not endorse anyone for the Third Congressional District.[34]

Neither Lucey nor Fairchild won their 1950 bids for office. Lucey lost in each of the ten counties in the district, including Crawford County. The results (see table 3.2) were not surprising, but they were disappointing.

**TABLE 3.2.** General Election Results, Third Congressional District, 1950

| County | Lucey (D) | Withrow (R) | Alexander (S) |
|---|---|---|---|
| Crawford | 3,410 | 3,745 | 3 |
| Grant | 5,046 | 7,661 | 8 |
| Iowa | 2,691 | 3,885 | 4 |
| Juneau | 1,979 | 3,719 | 3 |
| La Crosse | 8,557 | 11,260 | 64 |
| Lafayette | 3,193 | 3,413 | 1 |
| Monroe | 3,032 | 5,153 | 12 |
| Richland | 2,264 | 4,033 | 1 |
| Sauk | 4,616 | 7,714 | 80 |
| Vernon | 3,477 | 4,230 | 4 |
| Total | 38,265 | 54,783 | 180 |

Source: *The State of Wisconsin Blue Book 1952* (Madison: Wisconsin Legislative Reference Bureau, 1952), 745.

Democrats did not fare well in Wisconsin that year. Carl Thompson lost in the gubernatorial race, as did Democratic candidates for lieutenant governor, secretary of state, treasurer, and attorney general. Of seventeen state senate seats on the ballot, only five Democrats won, three of them from Milwaukee. Democrats numbered twenty-six in the assembly in 1948. After the 1950 election, that number dropped to twenty-two. In the 1950 election, Republicans outspent Democrats by $831,800 to $266,300.[35]

The Democratic Party—specifically the Democratic Organizing Committee—needed help, and Lucey had to decide whether he would heed the cry for assistance or return to Ferryville and participate more actively in the family businesses.

## CHAPTER 4

# PARTY BUILDER

"**H**e's a loser. Why are you rewarding a guy who lost an election?"
That was the reaction of Henry Maier to the proposal in
1950 by Jim Doyle Sr.[1] that Patrick Lucey be hired to build the reinvented
Democratic Party in Wisconsin.[2] Maier was a newly elected state senator
and would later become Milwaukee's longest serving mayor (1960–88).
Doyle was the chair of the Democratic Organizing Committee (DOC) of
Wisconsin.

Doyle wanted the executive committee of the DOC to appoint Lucey as
executive director. The job description would be simple, but the job itself
would be challenging. Lucey was to organize progressives in Wisconsin
into a viable, competitive political party. His salary was five hundred
dollars a month, and although payments would be delayed whenever fund-
raising lagged, Lucey preferred politics and public policymaking to retail
sales and farm management. Also, Lucey was deeply concerned about the
inflammatory rhetoric of Joe McCarthy.

At Maier's insistence, Doyle agreed that Lucey would not be paid from
any money raised in Wisconsin. Instead, Doyle solicited contributions
from people on the East Coast who wanted to nurture a robust and progressive political party to take on McCarthy.[3] The national anti-McCarthy
movement played a major supporting role in building the Democratic
Party of Wisconsin.

With the cash cow for the incipient progressive Wisconsin Democrats
out of state, Democrats struggled for support in America's Dairyland.
Indeed, in the early years, Lucey presided over losses. He was the campaign
manager for Thomas Fairchild in his unsuccessful 1952 race against

McCarthy. He managed the 1954 campaign for Doyle when he lost to Bill Proxmire in the Democratic gubernatorial primary. When someone who thought Doyle might one day be elected as US president asked Lucey what happened to derail Doyle's candidacy, Lucey responded, "Some stupid SOB ran his campaign for governor."[4]

Reflecting back over almost half a century, former newspaper publisher and member of the UW Board of Regents John Lavine said of Lucey: "Wisconsin would have been the poorer if he had quit when he lost."[5]

Instead, Lucey built on the achievements of Dan Hoan and Robert Tehan and worked with Doyle, Fairchild, Gaylord Nelson, John Reynolds, and other progressives to transform the state's moribund, conservative Democratic Party into a competitive, viable organization. Through their efforts, Wisconsin became a competitive two-party state. Proxmire's victory in 1957 in the special election for McCarthy's US Senate seat both symbolized the strength the party had acquired and gave it a boost for further growth.

## MODELS FOR BUILDING A PARTY IN WISCONSIN

Political parties have two major functions. One is electoral. The concern is to recruit candidates and then provide them with the assistance needed to prevail against candidates from other parties. Parties rely on professionals and volunteers for this function. Activity and involvement ebbs and flows with the rhythm of elections. The other function of parties is governance. The core actors are elected officials rather than voters, and the dynamic to watch is how those officials enact and implement public policy. The two dimensions are, of course, related, but the dynamics are distinct. Lucey's work spanned both of these functions.

One classic model of an electoral political party is a machine, controlled by a boss or, in the case of Wisconsin in the aftermath of the Civil War, a triumvirate of bosses. The bosses determine who will represent the party on the ballot and dispense patronage to those responsible for getting voters to the polls. Machines in the United States have been based largely on ethnic bloc voting—residents of a neighborhood or town that is ethnically fairly homogeneous will get services and jobs if they cast their ballots in support of the party that puts mayors, governors, and legislators into office. In Wisconsin in the late nineteenth century, Philetus Sawyer, John

Spooner, and Henry Payne presided over the Republican Party machine that controlled government and major sectors of the state's economy. Robert M. La Follette Sr. led the Progressive movement that destroyed this machine. The legacy of that struggle made it virtually impossible for Lucey or anyone else to build a party in the state that followed the machine model.[6]

The progressive reforms led by La Follette and Francis E. McGovern at the dawn of the twentieth century consciously provided that Wisconsin would have political parties with very limited powers. Specifically, the constraints on party organizations included the following:

- Open primaries: This requirement empowers voters, rather than bosses, to determine the nominees of a party. To get their names on the ballot as nominees of a particular party, candidates must win a primary contest against others seeking that party's nomination. In Wisconsin, the open primary means electors can vote in a party's primary without ever having joined or been affiliated with that party.

- Party endorsements prior to primaries: Although party endorsements in advance of a primary are allowed in Wisconsin, the Progressive and Democratic Parties have refused to follow the practice, further reducing the role of their respective parties in elections. Republicans in Wisconsin have endorsed candidates prior to the primary, but even so, the nonendorsed candidates have occasionally won.

- Nonpartisan elections: Elections to judicial positions and most local government positions—including school board members— do not list the candidates' party affiliation. The elections to these offices are scheduled in Wisconsin for the spring instead of November, when partisan contests occur. This is another obstacle to those who would base politics on patronage.

- No party registration: When individuals register to vote, they do not indicate a party affiliation or preference, and so parties cannot get lists of their respective supporters. This handicaps not only would-be bosses but also candidates who would like to target their campaign efforts. It is possible to get information on who voted in what elections—but not, of course, for whom they voted—and this practice allows for the construction of lists of likely voters and, using primary election data, likely partisans.

- Limited patronage: To combat patronage, it is illegal to ask for the party affiliation of applicants for most government jobs and contracts.[7]

An alternative model to a machine is to form a coalition of interest groups. Neighboring Minnesota used this approach. Progressives in that state began separating themselves from the Republican Party, which, according to Russel B. Nye, was more completely under the grip of organized business than in any other Midwestern state in the late nineteenth century.[8] Eventually, they became the Nonpartisan League and then the Farmer–Labor Party, which brought together farm groups and labor unions committed to agrarian reform, worker protection, social security, and public ownership of railroads, utilities, and natural resources. The Farmer–Labor Party, like the Progressive Party in Wisconsin, won several gubernatorial elections and contests for state and federal legislative positions in the period from 1921 to 1941. Under the leadership of Hubert H. Humphrey, the Farmer–Labor Party and the Democratic Party merged in 1944 and secured recognition by the Democratic National Committee. Lucey and Philleo Nash—both of whom would later serve as chairs of the Democratic Party of Wisconsin—differed over whether to follow the Minnesota model which Nash favored and Lucey opposed.

Lucey favored a more grassroots model. He favored policies that were generally supportive of rural and labor interests but was leery of having the party become an instrument of labor unions. Lucey wanted to build a party based primarily on mass membership rather than a formal coalition of interest groups.[9] Party organization would use the boundaries established for administering elections and voting for local government officials (i.e., counties, wards, and precincts). He welcomed—and even sought—help from labor and other groups but based on a convergence of goals rather than on institutional affiliation or control. Party building in this way was a daunting task. It would have been much easier to use existing interest group organizations as the constructs. Persuading individuals to become members instead of working with groups requires considerable time, energy, and shoe leather.

Membership is not, of course, synonymous with being a supporter, even a loyal supporter. Although members presumably are supporters, all supporters are not necessarily members. Especially in Wisconsin, party membership is primarily symbolic, an indication of commitment to a brand and a platform. Membership is not required for appearing on a ballot as a candidate of a particular party or, as mentioned previously, of those voting in a primary. Membership does not entitle someone to patronage or any particular benefit. Certainly, membership is expected of delegates to conventions and participants at county- or ward-level meetings, but becoming a member of a political party is a statement of support, and little more than that. Paying dues, no matter how modest, psychologically enhances commitment and a feeling that someone has an investment and a stake in the game. For Lucey, membership helped identify who he could go to in a particular community when recruiting candidates and getting them elected. And that was what the Democratic Party needed to do.

To produce more electoral success, Lucey and others trying to build the Democratic Party in the 1950s needed to change the image of the organization in the state. Democrats in Wisconsin had not supported President Roosevelt and the New Deal or President Truman and the Fair Deal. They sided with Republicans on most major issues. The party's brand had to take on new meaning. It was uniting a disparate conglomeration of progressive refugees from the Republican Party, young and liberal veterans home from World War II, immigrants from Eastern Europe, and socialists and unionized labor from Milwaukee.[10] It was not an easy task to define who the Democrats were.

In addition, Wisconsin was far from homogeneous in its political traditions. As political scientist Leon Epstein pointed out in his analysis, place has been a critical factor in understanding Wisconsin politics. He pointed to the divisions between urban and rural areas that were salient in the 1950s.[11] These divisions were made more visible by rural overrepresentation in the legislature and the resulting relative neglect of urban issues.[12]

In his study of Wisconsin voting patterns, R. Booth Fowler noted how white ethnic and religious identities added a complicating dimension to approaching politics on the basis of where voters live. Ethnicity frequently trumped place. For example, whereas in 1910 German Lutherans in small towns and villages split their partisan loyalties and German Catholics who lived primarily in urban areas leaned Democratic, in the 1950s almost all Wisconsin voters of German descent were Republican. Polish areas, both urban and rural, were solidly Democratic throughout the first half of the twentieth century. Norwegians in 1910 overwhelmingly voted Republican, although they were part of the progressive wing. After the breakup of the Progressive Party, Norwegians supported Democrats. Swedish areas were for Republicans until the 1950s, when they split their allegiances.[13]

## EARLY ORGANIZATION

Clearly, Lucey faced a complicated task. One size would not fit all the potential elements of a party that needed to win elections both statewide and in local districts. He would have to pull together progressives who had ties to Milwaukee and those who identified with Madison. Some potential Democrats were in rural areas dominated by Norwegians and some in places where German and Polish immigrants had settled. Labor and farm groups identified with populist ideas, but they had different and sometimes conflicting agendas.

In addition, Lucey had to operate with relatively few resources. In 1950, the Republican Party outspent the Democratic Party by $831,800 to $266,300, a ratio of more than 3 to 1. Lucey's work helped reduce the gap to $1,297,400 to $520,100, a ratio of 2.49 to 1, by 1958, but the GOP still had a considerable edge.[14] The primary source of funds for Republicans was, by far, corporations and wealthy businesspeople. For the Democrats, it was labor unions and party members. Lucey's efforts to build party membership, in other words, were important both to soliciting needed cash and to establishing a base of supporters. The party established modest annual dues of two dollars, or three dollars for a married couple. County units collected payments and forwarded $1.30 to state headquarters.[15] Under Lucey's leadership, membership steadily increased from fewer than fifteen hundred in 1950 to fifteen thousand in 1958.[16] The Republican Party did not require members to pay dues, although it allowed local units to do so.

When Lucey began his work as executive director, not all counties had a Democratic Party organization. Given his goal to build a mass membership party, one of his first tasks was to make sure that each county and ward had at least a chair. The chair usually was a former member of the Progressive Party, a labor leader, or head of a farm organization. Lucey, Doyle, or another leader personally visited the county leaders and encouraged them to hold an organizational meeting and to compile a mailing list of probable supporters.

The initial response in some counties was disappointing. As late as 1953, only three people attended a Brown County meeting and only two in Pierce County. Lucey, Thompson, and Doyle sometimes drove great distances only to find an empty meeting hall. Even county chairs did not always show up.[17]

County chairs were important in recruiting candidates to run for office. Lucey firmly believed that the party should run a full slate of candidates, even if the prospect of winning a particular local race was slim. He reasoned that candidates were key to increasing voter turnout. At a minimum, a candidate for sheriff or county coroner or clerk of courts would almost inevitably get his or her family and friends to the polls. While in the booth voting for their friend or relative, the thinking went, they would also probably vote for other Democrats on the ballot.[18] The counterargument that such candidacies might be wasteful carried little weight. Prior to the end of the twentieth century, not much money was spent in most campaigns, so few resources were at risk.[19] The major approach to soliciting support was meeting people individually and in small groups, much like Lucey did when he ran for the assembly in 1948.

Lucey's message to county chairs was that if they could not recruit someone to run for a particular office, they should run themselves.[20] Many a sheriff or clerk of courts was a former county chair.

## FEAR IN THE FIFTIES

The political atmosphere in which Lucey worked was one of fear and tension. The Cold War struggle between the United States and the Soviet Union was at its height and sent people to bed with nightmares of a nuclear holocaust. Soviet domination over Eastern Europe led to concerns about further expansion of communism at the expense of democracy and freedom.

In Asia and Africa, independence movements challenged the colonial empires of England, France, Italy, the Netherlands, Portugal, and Belgium. The Soviet Union provided support to a few of the independence fighters—most visibly to Ho Chi Minh in Vietnam. The French fought "Uncle Ho" from 1950 to 1954, when they lost badly at Dien Bien Phu. The United States, driven by the fear of communism, sided with Ho Chi Minh's opponents in Vietnam and took up where the French left off.

The list of struggles was long and included other countries in Asia, many colonies in Africa, and even some countries in the Western Hemisphere. Many of the independence struggles only threatened violence, but the pattern was clear and, to some, worrisome.[21]

The year 1953 seemed to be especially tense for many in Europe and the United States. Nikita Khrushchev, who succeeded Joseph Stalin after his death, seemed like he would loosen the tight hold of the Kremlin over its own society and over the Eastern European countries. People in East Germany and Hungary misread the signals. Their uprisings were ruthlessly put down in 1953 and 1956 respectively. The Cuban Revolution also began in 1953 and ended in 1959 with the installation of Fidel Castro and the first Communist government in the Western Hemisphere.

The conflicts around the globe understandably generated anxiety. When McCarthy charged that prominent individuals within the US government itself were engaged in conspiracies and were soft on communism, he stoked existing fears. When he was irresponsible and acted as a demagogue, he himself became a source of fear. Lucey said that, at the time, he viewed McCarthy "as a potential American Hitler."[22] He was not alone.

## JOE MUST GO

Lucey cited his concerns about the effects of McCarthyism as the major reason for accepting Doyle's offer to hire him in 1950 as executive director of the DOC.[23] The goal of defeating McCarthy was central for Lucey and for Democrats.

Whether or not to endorse candidates prior to primary elections was an ongoing debate at this time in the DOC. The fear as the DOC geared up to take on McCarthy was that a divisive primary might severely hamper the efforts of the new organization to establish itself. Some worried that the winner of the primary might not be the strongest candidate for the general election.

On June 10, 1951, a who's who group of notable Democrats secretly met at the Park Hotel in Madison. As executive director, Lucey sent a confidential memo to the invited, which included Doyle, Proxmire, Nelson, Hoan, Fairchild, Maier, Henry Reuss, George Molinaro, Horace Wilkie, John Nestingen, Jerome Fox, and Miles McMillan. The memo defined the agenda as a "preliminary discussion of candidates for United States Senator, Congressman, and Governor for 1952."[24] The meeting did not result in agreement on support for any particular slate of candidates or on the general principle of endorsement. At the annual state convention held in Wausau the following October, delegates reaffirmed the progressive principle of not endorsing.[25]

After the 1951 convention, Lucey continued his organizing work. He traveled the state and whenever possible held down costs by staying at the home of a party member. He built a membership base, recruited candidates, and organized rallies. The party maintained a modest second-floor headquarters on the Capitol Square in Madison, where Lucey spent time writing and publishing a monthly newsletter that was sent to dues-paying members.[26]

Reuss, a Milwaukee County prosecutor, was also traveling around Wisconsin. Formerly a Republican, Reuss joined the Democrats in reaction to McCarthy. Democrats had made an overture to Robert La Follette Jr. to support him as the anti-McCarthy candidate if he ran as their nominee, but La Follette refused to run as a Democrat, leaving Reuss as the probable nominee.[27] Reuss spent much of 1951 and 1952 campaigning for the nomination. However, Doyle, Nelson, and McMillan led a group in the DOC that considered him a weak and ineffective candidate. Shortly before the filing deadline in July 1952, they persuaded Fairchild to seek the nomination. Fairchild was considered more likely to win because he had been elected statewide as attorney general in 1948, and he had the experience of running against Alexander Wiley for a US Senate seat in 1950.[28] Because of his position as executive director and the DOC's nonendorsement policy, Lucey stayed neutral in the Reuss versus Fairchild contest.

Fairchild won the 1952 primary (and Reuss went on to serve as Milwaukee's congressman from 1953 to 1983). Fairchild's campaign manager in the Senate primary was Warren Sawall, the first husband of Proxmire's wife, Ellen. The day after the votes were counted, Philip Marshall, one of Fairchild's key supporters, called a meeting to plan for the general election against McCarthy. Marshall insisted that Lucey attend the meeting, and Sawall drove him to Marshall's house in Milwaukee. The first item on the agenda was to persuade Lucey to replace Sawall. Despite Fairchild's primary win, Marshall felt that Lucey could do a better job running the general election campaign. Lucey agreed to accept the position, pending Doyle's approval of a leave of absence from Lucey's DOC job. Lucey and Sawall had a long and awkward drive back to Madison.[29]

The next morning, Lucey met with Doyle at Doyle's law office. Lucey explained that he wanted to do whatever he could to get McCarthy out of office but recognized that he had agreed to be executive director of the party. Doyle agreed that because Lucey's main reason for working for the party was to defeat McCarthy, becoming Fairchild's campaign manager was a natural progression on that path. He approved the leave of absence, and Lucey became the manager of Fairchild's campaign.[30]

Doyle asked Lucey to pick his replacement. Lucey went to the DOC office and shared what had happened with Esther Kaplan, treasurer of the DOC. Kaplan suggested John Gronouski, who had worked on Wilkie's congressional campaign in 1950. Kaplan said Gronouski was exceptionally competent and could probably interrupt his graduate work for a couple of months. Without ever having met Gronouski, Lucey called him and offered him the job. Gronouski said, "Well, I'm working on my doctoral dissertation, but I guess I can shove that into the middle drawer of my desk for two months, and I'll take the job."[31]

Gronouski would later be appointed by President John F. Kennedy as postmaster general and by President Lyndon B. Johnson as ambassador to Poland. In 1976, as a federal judge, John Reynolds ruled school segregation in Milwaukee unconstitutional and appointed Gronouski to serve as special master to shape corrections. The Lucey and Gronouski families became very close friends.

Lucey immediately began his work managing the Fairchild campaign, and Doyle left for the East Coast to raise funds. Doyle relied primarily

Jim Doyle Sr., chair of the Democratic Organizing Committee, John Gronouski, and Pat Lucey confer. Gronouski temporarily replaced Lucey as executive secretary of the DOC when Lucey took a leave of absence to run Tom Fairchild's campaign against Joe McCarthy in 1952. COURTESY OF LAUREL LUCEY

on two sources: the Americans for Democratic Action and the National Committee for an Effective Congress. Doyle was an active member of the Americans for Democratic Action and in 1953 was cochair with Arthur Schlesinger Jr. His main contact with the National Committee for an Effective Congress was Maurice Rosenblatt, whom he had known since their time together as undergraduates at the University of Wisconsin–Madison. Both organizations had wealthy liberals as members, and both provided Doyle with leads to other donors.[32]

The first problem that Lucey and Fairchild faced was how to respond to an invitation from President Truman to attend a meeting at the White House. At the time, Truman had only a 23 percent approval rating, so association with him was not considered as desirable. Doyle was firmly opposed to starting out the campaign with this meeting. As a compromise, Fairchild and Lucey arranged to meet first with Illinois Governor Adlai Stevenson, who was the Democratic presidential candidate, and then with Truman.

Lucey and Fairchild drove to meet Stevenson in Springfield. As they approached the Illinois capital, they noticed the gas gauge was low. A few miles from Stevenson's office, the tank was empty. A stickler for being on time, Fairchild persuaded his campaign manager to join him in pushing the car to the nearest gas station. Luckily, it was mostly downhill.

They were greeted at Stevenson's office by Newton "Newt" Minnow, who was from Milwaukee and would later distinguish himself as chair of the Federal Communications Commission. After a pleasant visit, Fairchild went to the airport for his flight to Washington, DC, and Lucey returned to Madison.[33]

Lucey ended up with a campaign budget for Fairchild of about forty thousand dollars, which he spent mostly for radio spots. He also paid for a half hour program on WTMJ, a Milwaukee television station, that ran at eight o'clock the Sunday night before the election. Lucey featured Edward P. Morgan, a retired Federal Bureau of Investigation analyst, who argued that McCarthy was actually hampering anti-communist efforts. Morgan said that despite sweeping allegations, McCarthy had not identified one Communist who could be prosecuted. In addition, Morgan revealed that McCarthy used a forged civil service commission report when he attacked alleged Communists in government in a Senate speech. WTMJ staff required that they be given a typewritten copy of what Morgan would say before airtime. Morgan went to his hotel room and dictated his speech. The station never asked for it, but the speech was ready. Lucey received anecdotal feedback that Morgan's talk was very persuasive, and McCarthy felt threatened enough that he scrambled to try to discredit Morgan.[34]

After the election, Lucey blamed himself for not getting a public endorsement of Fairchild from a prominent Republican. Lucey had convinced Fred Zimmerman, a progressive Republican running for reelection as secretary of state, to issue the following statement: "I hope you'll vote for me next Tuesday, but also I hope you'll cross over and vote for my good friend, Tom Fairchild, running for the US Senate." On the way to the printer, Lucey called Zimmerman to read him the final wording. When Zimmerman answered the phone, he told Lucey that friends told him the endorsement was a dumb idea, and he backed down. Lucey firmly believed that if he had taken a written copy of the ad to Zimmerman instead of reading it over the phone, Zimmerman would have given the thumbs up.[35]

McCarthy's margin of victory in 1952 was narrow enough to prompt some second-guessing, although it seems unlikely that what Lucey considered as his personal mistake had cost Fairchild the election. McCarthy did indeed run behind all the other Republicans running statewide in Wisconsin. His total was 870,444, and Fairchild's was 731,482—a difference of 138,962. In the presidential contest, Dwight Eisenhower got 357,569 more votes than Adlai Stevenson. In the race for governor, Proxmire lost to Republican Walter J. Kohler Jr. by 407,866 votes.[36]

In 1954, Leroy Gore initiated a recall campaign that adopted and popularized the slogan "Joe Must Go." Gore was the editor of the *Sauk Prairie Star*, a weekly newspaper serving a village of about two thousand on the banks of the Wisconsin River. He was a longtime Republican and supported McCarthy in his successful bid for reelection but then was appalled at the attacks lobbed by the senator. Democratic Party and labor union leaders were suspicious of Gore and doubted he would be successful. Moreover, there would be troublesome legal challenges because state recall laws do not apply to federal offices. Despite their agreement with the objective of Joe Must Go, it did not seem wise to invest resources or reputations in the campaign. While Lucey and other leading Democrats were not active in the campaign, they cheered Gore from the sidelines.[37]

Gore needed 413,000 petitioners, but collected only 330,000—83,000 signatures shy of the requirement to schedule a recall election. Although he fell short, he succeeded in generating considerable attention in Wisconsin and throughout the nation. Gore and his paper suffered retribution from McCarthy supporters. He was harassed, and the *Star* lost advertisers. Months after the campaign, Gore sold the paper for fifty thousand dollars—a casualty of the fear and anxiety of this period.[38]

## More Campaigns

After the 1952 general election, Lucey returned to his organization-building work for the DOC, and Gronouski went back to working on his dissertation. Lucey met with the administrative committee in December and proposed a budget for 1953. To meet the rather Spartan revenue side of the ledger, Lucey proposed that he no longer receive a salary. Instead, he began selling real estate and, for a six-month period, partnering in a lumberyard.[39]

Lucey's organizational work for the Democratic Party of Wisconsin—no longer known as the DOC after a vote to change the name at the 1954 state convention—focused on small towns and rural areas, courting the farm vote. He was particularly eager to elect Democrats to the eight county offices—sheriff, district attorney, clerk of circuit court, county clerk, county treasurer, coroner, register of deeds, and county surveyor—that were filled through partisan elections. In 1954, Democrats held only seventy of the more than five hundred partisan-elected county jobs. They did not run a single candidate for any of these positions in thirteen of the then seventy-one counties, and only one in ten more counties. Within four years, a record 411 Democrats were running for county jobs filled in partisan elections, ninety-seven candidates for the then one hundred assembly seats, and a candidate for each of the state senate seats up for election. In 1958, more Democrats than Republicans were running for assembly seats—a pattern not seen since the advent of the GOP.[40]

In addition to his work growing the Democratic Party organization, Lucey managed additional campaigns, including Doyle's campaign for governor in 1954. Lucey had the highest level of respect and admiration for Doyle but regarded him as an ineffective campaigner. He was awkward when glad-handing voters and did not raise much enthusiasm when giving speeches. Lucey had Doyle's car adorned with a big, triangular sign on top saying Doyle for Governor. The candidate took one look and demanded that the sign be removed, saying, "I'm not going to drive around with that silly sign on there." Lucey responded, "In other words, you're going through the northern counties incognito?" But Doyle won the argument, and the car did not advertise who the passenger was or what he was pursuing.[41]

Although Doyle was the favorite of many leaders in the Democratic Party, he was soundly beaten by Proxmire in the September 14, 1954, primary—85,187 to 141,548.[42] Proxmire would in turn suffer defeat by Kohler in the November 4 general election—560,747 to 596,158.[43] This narrower-than-expected margin indicated the growing strength of the Democratic Party.

In 1956, Lucey signed on as campaign manager for Elliott Walstead, who competed with Maier for the Democratic nomination for US senator. Walstead had been an attorney and executive director of the Wisconsin

Real Estate Brokers Board from 1938 to 1951, and he served as chair of the Democratic Party in the state from 1953 to 1955, succeeding Doyle. Walstead had been one of the founders of the DOC, and Maier was the state senate minority leader when he filed papers for his bid to go to Washington. Maier, as noted earlier, opposed Lucey's appointment as the party's executive director on the grounds that Lucey had a record of losing elections. Maier may well have felt vindicated: he defeated Walstead 169,903 to 83,801.[44] In the general election, Alexander Wiley was reelected, winning over Maier 892,473 to 627,903.[45]

## 1957 SPECIAL ELECTION: PROXMIRE VS. KOHLER

After McCarthy died on May 2, 1957, the special election to fill his unexpired term was a threshold event. Two perennial losers, Proxmire as the candidate and Lucey as the chair of Proxmire's campaign committee, teamed up to beat former governor Walter J. Kohler Jr. and usher in an era of increased electoral success for Democrats in Wisconsin. A number of prominent Democrats initially expressed interest in running for the seat. These included state senators Maier and Nelson, congressional representatives Reuss and Clement Zablocki, and of course Proxmire. Lucey called Proxmire as soon as McCarthy's death was announced and urged him to run. Lucey followed the call by sending a campaign donation of five hundred dollars.[46]

Philleo Nash, who was the chair of the state party, wanted somebody—anybody—other than Proxmire to be the Democratic candidate.[47] Nash worked with the administrative committee to design a process that would eliminate Proxmire from consideration but failed. Lucey argued that Proxmire's name recognition would be invaluable, especially given the short campaign. The primary was scheduled for July, less than three months after McCarthy died, and the general election for August.

Within the Democratic Party, two sentiments were expressed: the usual argument that a contested party primary would expend resources and weaken the eventual nominee and a specific concern that Proxmire had already lost three statewide races, two of which were to Kohler, the probable Republican candidate. Responding to the first concern, everyone except Zablocki dropped out of the race. Proxmire won the primary handily,

86,341 to 56,817, winning in every county except Milwaukee and Portage. Kohler won the Republican nomination following a tough primary battle with Congressman Glen Davis.[48] Davis, along with Melvin Laird and John Byrnes, was considered within the Republican Party as a Young Turk. The Young Turks had been opponents of McCarthy. Davis's constituency included Madison, which provided some hope that he would appeal to a diverse statewide electorate, but conservatives in the Republican Party preferred Kohler, who prevailed.[49]

Although Lucey was the titular head of Proxmire's election bid, Proxmire and his wife, Ellen, ran the campaign. They did the scheduling and made the strategic and tactical decisions.[50] This approach contrasted with the more common campaign model, in which professional managers and consultants determine in detail what a candidate does and says.

Lucey contributed by drawing on his connections to benefit Proxmire. He was successful in getting John F. Kennedy, then a US senator, to stump for Proxmire in the Fox Valley. Generally Republican territory and fairly Catholic, the Fox Valley had been McCarthy's home base. Kennedy had been under serious consideration as a vice-presidential running mate for Adlai Stevenson at the 1956 Democratic nominating convention. After avoiding the taint of going down on Stevenson's ticket, Kennedy had his eye on the presidency at the time he helped Proxmire in the 1957 special election.[51] Lucey was impressed by Kennedy's effectiveness on the campaign trail and believed he helped Proxmire.

Like most, Lucey anticipated another defeat for Proxmire and the Democrats. A few days before the election, he called to warn Ellen Proxmire, "This is like all the other campaigns you and I have been in. There's just one difference. This time you're the wife of the candidate. And I'm just calling you to tell you that I don't see an outcome any different than we've had in previous campaigns, and you just ought to adjust to that result."

She responded by shouting, "Pat! You don't understand! We're going to win!"[52] And she was right. Proxmire won with almost 57 percent of the vote.

Kohler's problems probably contributed to Proxmire's victory. When Davis lost the Republican nomination, many of his supporters stayed home rather than vote for Kohler. Kohler received 4,357 fewer votes in the general election than the total number of votes that had been cast in the GOP primary. Proxmire, by contrast, won 292,827 more votes than he and Zablocki combined got in the primary.[53]

Another problem was of Kohler's own making. Having beaten Proxmire twice for governor, he assumed a third win was assured and did not campaign hard.[54] This was in contrast to Proxmire's tireless effort, building on more than half a dozen years of nonstop campaigning and handshaking. John Patrick Hunter of the *Capital Times* quipped that Proxmire had been on the campaign trail so often that people thought they were voting for an incumbent.[55]

A signature feature of Lucey's organizational activities was to generate high voter turnout, and that was evident in the Proxmire victory. Lucey mobilized farmers, many of whom were unhappy with the agricultural policies of President Eisenhower. In addition, Lucey worked with labor unions to institute, for the first time in Wisconsin history, a massive phone bank operation to get out the vote.[56]

## STATE PARTY CHAIR

As soon as the ballots in the special election were counted, Proxmire vowed to replace Nash as state party chair. His choice was Lucey.

The state Democratic Party Convention was held in Madison in October, three months after the special election. One of the items on the agenda was the election of state chair. Nash had been elected as chair in 1955 with the strong support of Maier. He was open and vocal about his opposition to Proxmire and his criticism of the mass membership model pursued by Lucey. He was also quite negative about Doyle, Fairchild, Reynolds, Nelson, and others he regarded as part of what he dubbed "the Madison group."[57] Nonetheless, he sought another term.

Prior to the convention, Proxmire, Doyle, Reynolds, Nelson, and Madison attorney Roland Day (whom Lucey, as governor, would appoint to the state supreme court) began gathering support for replacing Nash with Lucey. Day was particularly active in lining up support from the chairs of county organizations around the state. Lucey noted that under Nash, party membership had declined and twenty counties had no paid members at all. He also charged that the party's treasury declined from a five-thousand-dollar surplus to a ten-thousand-dollar deficit. A controversy had also arisen over a ten-thousand-dollar contribution from the AFL-CIO's Committee on Political Education that was supposed to go to Proxmire's campaign in the special election but mysteriously disappeared. Nash claimed that the contribution never existed and the controversy was due to a rumor started by someone at a Democratic Party event in Janesville who passed a cryptic note to Ellen Proxmire that alleged the mishandling.[58]

Ella Lucey, Lucey's mother, attended the convention and helped generate votes for her son. A delegate approached her and said he wasn't sure whom he was going to support. Ella covered her nametag and said, "Well, I've known Pat Lucey since he was a child. He's got my vote."[59]

The balloting was close. Lucey won the support of 692 delegates, and Nash had 687. Lucey went on to serve for six years, a longer period than any of his predecessors. Despite the bitter campaign for chair, Lucey encouraged Nash to run in 1958 as the party's nominee for lieutenant governor. Nash did and won. Years later, he praised Lucey for this gesture and for his record as governor. He continued, however, to think that Lucey was wrong to use a grassroots approach to build the party. And he blamed Maier for being ineffective when Nash sought reelection as chair.[60]

Another key issue at the 1957 convention was whether the party should be reorganized along the same lines as the Minnesota Democratic Farmer–Labor Party. Nash, the Congress of Industrial Organizations (CIO), and the Wisconsin Farmers Union had begun an effort at the 1955 convention and met in Milwaukee one month before the 1957 convention to plot action. They got Paul Siciliano, the Tenth District Democratic chair, to bring the proposal to the Democratic Administrative Committee, which placed the proposal on the convention agenda. Despite the support they had enjoyed from labor and farmer groups, Proxmire and Lucey vigorously opposed the move to create a party that was an institutional coalition of interest groups. Their preference was the more grassroots model that Lucey had toiled to build.[61] Proxmire and Lucey prevailed. In the words of columnist John Wyngaard:

> Organized labor forces have been significantly repulsed in their evident desire to take over and remold the Democratic Party and its machinery in this state. Some observers believe that the defeat of some of the designs of labor leaders was the most significant long-range result of the recent Democratic state convention.[62]

The proposal offered by Nash and the labor leaders was buried when delegates referred it to the Democratic Administrative Committee for further study.

Another question before the 1957 convention was the oft-visited issue of party endorsements before primaries. As chair, Nash had appointed a committee to bring a recommendation to the delegates that they repeal the party's constitutional prohibition of candidate endorsement. Doyle was among those favoring a change. Proxmire, Lucey, and Day opposed preprimary endorsement and, once again, Nash lost.[63]

## BUILDING A TWO-PARTY STATE

The Democratic Party enjoyed several notable achievements during Lucey's tenure as state chair. Democrats won three successive gubernatorial elections, both US Senate seats, and four of the ten congressional districts. In 1958, Democrats won fifty-five of the then one hundred seats in the state assembly, the party's first majority since 1933. The party established organizations in each of the state's then seventy-one counties. After winning only 70 of the 540 county offices up for election in 1954, Democrats were victorious in 152 contests in 1964. Paid membership increased from six thousand in 1957 to twenty-five thousand in 1963. And the party treasury went from a negative balance of ten thousand dollars to a positive one of fifty thousand dollars.[64] Under Lucey's leadership, Democrats did not displace Republicans as the dominant party, but Wisconsin clearly became a competitive two-party state.

Party leaders are to varying degrees engaged in recruiting candidates, and Lucey was especially active. Party labels matter, especially for those segments of the electorate that rely on party identity as a cue. But the meaning of labels change, as the history of progressives and parties in America's Dairyland demonstrates. Party organizations can help a candidate but, as a result of progressive reforms of the early twentieth century, no longer can draw upon a system of bosses and patronage networks to deliver the blocs of votes to virtually guarantee victory. A key issue, therefore, is what resources a party has and how they are allocated to support candidates. Lucey employed an approach that had a dual focus on individual candidates and on Democrats generally. His goal was to get individuals who shared progressive values elected at all levels of government, and he pursued a number of approaches to make the Democratic Party of Wisconsin the vehicle to achieve that goal.

As the party grew, Lucey recognized he needed help to achieve these goals. In 1959, he persuaded the administrative committee to double the budget of party headquarters and to hire two full-time field directors. With administrative committee approval, Lucey hired Norman Clapp, a former secretary to Senator La Follette, and James Megellas, a decorated war hero and unsuccessful congressional candidate, as the field directors. Their duties were like a description of what Lucey had been doing for the party when serving as its executive director:

- Foster local and area membership meetings and drives;

- Help precinct organizations get started and function well;

- Promote full slates of candidates;

- Conduct candidate training programs; and

- Encourage party activity and visibility generally.[65]

Although the administrative committee and the party as a whole could not endorse candidates prior to primaries, Lucey asserted that the prohibition did not apply to him as chair. He considered his public backing as an important tool in his efforts to recruit candidates who were progressive and who could get elected. In May 1958, he precipitated a controversy when he publicly endorsed John Reynolds over Christ Seraphim as the Democratic candidate for attorney general. Nash introduced a motion in the administrative committee to muzzle Lucey, which the committee rejected by a ten to nine vote. Lucey explained that he had "never been neutral about anything, and I don't intend to be now. I'm aware that it is a tradition in the party that the state chairman should remain neutral. It's also a tradition that we usually lose elections."[66]

Lucey wanted to win elections, and he acted to help the candidates he considered most attractive. Sometimes it appeared that his endorsements were strategically designed to help his friends. The most prominent example was in 1961 when Gaylord Nelson was considering whether to run for another term as governor or to take on Alexander Wiley for a US

Senate seat. Nelson had not announced a decision. In the midst of this uncertainty, Lucey made a public endorsement of Nelson for the Senate and Reynolds for governor, seemingly opening an opportunity in Madison for his ally and encouraging Nelson, who was an intraparty rival, to head to Washington, DC.[67]

One of Lucey's initiatives as state chair was to provide training for candidates and party officials. Wyngaard reported on this initiative in the *Green Bay Press Gazette*:

> [Candidates] were hapless amateurs, with respect to the mechanical and quasi-professional details of running a campaign.
>
> The Democratic brain-trusters had thought of that and acted accordingly. Each of the local district nominees was given a packet of instructional materials, including a professionally prepared sample "news release," which they were encouraged to appropriate for their own purposes in their own localities.
>
> Nor was this the academic example that is found in textbooks, relating to nothing of immediate importance.
>
> It was carefully designed not only to instruct the beginner in the techniques of handling local publicity, but also to encourage him to use as his own the kind of issues the Democratic headquarters thinkers have concluded are the most effective in getting the voters' ears.[68]

More than one hundred one-day training sessions for candidates were conducted throughout the state in 1960 alone. Instructors were experienced campaigners, party officers, and candidates for statewide offices. The sessions included briefing on policy issues, and each participant was given a "mutual assistance pamphlet" that included detailed positions on major issues, biographical sketches, photographs of state and congressional candidates, and recommended techniques for getting the best public exposure.[69] Chairs of county organizations attended weekend-long meetings on fund-raising, getting out the vote, and generating publicity.

It took three years for Lucey to make the Democratic Party financially solvent after he became state chair. When he ended his tenure, the party had a surplus of fifty thousand dollars despite having hired more full-time staff and paid for training programs and publicity materials. The sums involved would pale in comparison to the vastly higher spending levels of parties, candidates, and political action committees at the turn of the twenty-first century, but they were significant substantively and symbolically in the 1950s and early 1960s.

Five months after Lucey was elected as state chair, he was at a Waukesha County Democratic dinner and demonstrated he could be effective at raising money. The five hundred people in attendance were in a good mood, still celebrating Proxmire's special election victory. At one point, the band played the party anthem, "Happy Days Are Here Again," and everyone went wild, cheering and singing and banging the tables. Lucey seized the moment and asked for pledges of $2.50 per month for the 1958 campaign. In ten minutes, he raised one thousand dollars.[70]

Lucey placed emphasis on paid membership in his grassroots building efforts and grew the roster to twenty thousand by 1962. He initiated a Dollars for Democrats campaign, which was essentially a door-to-door charity drive. In 1958, he also began a Pledge Plan, encouraging party members to contribute more than the annual membership fee. Dollars for Democrats brought in pennies and nickels, but the Pledge Plan netted fourteen thousand dollars in 1958 and twenty-three thousand dollars in 1959.[71]

Annual Jefferson–Jackson Day dinners—a creation of the Democratic National Committee—have been a traditional event of speeches and partying that also serve as an important fund-raiser for state parties. In 1962, Lucey unilaterally raised the price of a ticket to the dinners from twenty-five to one hundred dollars. If someone was content to watch while others ate, the fee was five dollars. The dinner raised $150,000 for the state party in 1962 ($1.3 million in 2019). Some labor union leaders opposed the increase in fees because it might have raised enough money to reduce dependence on labor money.[72]

Lucey, however, continued to welcome financial support from labor unions. He, coincidentally, gave major credit to David Rabinovitz for the financial health that the party acquired when Lucey was chair.[73] Rabinovitz was party treasurer and also the attorney for the United Auto Workers.

Lucey emphasized voter registration and turnout. Higher turnout among Democrats certainly was an important factor in Proxmire's victory in the 1957 special election. Within a year after he became chair, Lucey commissioned a study of voting patterns. The study examined every precinct, town, city, and village in the state. Lucey shared the findings with candidates for assembly seats in 1958 and noted that with a higher percentage of people voting, it was probable that Democrats could win in districts that traditionally sent Republicans to Madison. He made the same point in a revised version of handbooks for county chairs and incorporated voter registration processes in party training programs. Efforts were not targeted in any precise manner, but everyone understood that, for statewide races, Milwaukee was obviously important, especially with the state becoming increasingly urbanized. Labor unions worked closely with the Democratic Party both in voter registration and in turnout efforts.[74] In addition, Lucey was successful in getting the National Association for the Advancement of Colored People, the Congress of Racial Equality, the Elks Club, and a number of churches to contribute volunteers and funds to voter registration drives. One of the most effective approaches he promoted was to deputize volunteers so they could go door to door and register people.[75] As governor, Lucey followed through on his effort to get more people to participate in elections when the state legislature enacted a law enabling eligible voters to register at the polls just prior to casting their ballots.

Lucey obviously was not solely responsible for the phenomenal growth of the Democratic Party of Wisconsin in the 1950s, but his leadership certainly was key. He gained support for his vision of a party based on grassroots organization. He was instrumental in recruiting attractive candidates who shared basic progressive values and policy goals. He built a party that provided effective services to candidates and was financially sound. The brand of the Democratic Party became valuable.

With the party's success came the emergence of factions. An early division was over the Lucey grassroots model versus the Nash preference for a coalition of interest groups. Subsequent splits, however, were primarily over who received the party nomination—which had become a prize worth winning.

The most visible intraparty conflict among Wisconsin's Democrats was between Pat Lucey and Gaylord Nelson, two of the state's and the nation's most prominent progressives. Something like a feud was evident when Lucey was state chair and Nelson was governor. Their disagreements were—as summed up by Nelson's biographer, Bill Christofferson—over personal ambitions, not policy or politics.[76] As the party moved forward, intraparty conflict had consequences for who held the steering wheel, not—despite occasional turbulence—where the boat was going.

## CHAPTER 5

# LUCEY MEANS BUSINESS

Politics at the state and local levels is mostly part-time work. Only a few party and elected positions are full-time jobs. Most who are active in politics rely on careers and businesses in the private sector for income to support themselves and their families. Inevitably, this raises the potential for conflicts of interest in which politicians use or even only appear to use a public office to enhance personal wealth. Contracts for public projects might go to companies that are owned partially or entirely by a public official. Land might be purchased or zoned by a city in schemes that directly or indirectly enrich public officials who own that land. Relatives or political supporters are sometimes hired for government jobs.

Lucey made his living in real estate, a field especially vulnerable to conflicts of interest. Zoning decisions and city expansion plans can favor specific developers, especially when developers have special access to information and to decision-makers. The enforcement of building codes can be uneven, advantaging some landlords. Public funds can be spent in ways that enrich certain firms, and those firms can be owned by individuals active in politics. Scandals involving real estate are as old as the Republic and seem to be a part of every era.[1]

Lucey got into real estate so he would have the flexibility and time to build the Democratic Party, manage statewide campaigns, and serve as chair of the Democratic Party of Wisconsin. He did not get into politics so he could succeed as an entrepreneur.

He grew his business through the 1960s, sold it when he was elected governor, and then resumed real estate activity after his last campaign. Lucey knew he would be vulnerable to charges of having conflicts of

80

interest. He in fact was accused. But the charges clearly lacked substance and led to no scandals. To the contrary, Lucey became known as a person with integrity and high ethical standards, and he earned prestige for his success as a businessperson. The slogan "Lucey means business"—which emerged from a family brainstorming session while at the dinner table—served him well in his campaigns.[2] His stature in the real estate business also allowed him to play a significant role in persuading Madison to adopt an ordinance prohibiting discrimination in housing.

## Teaming Up with Jean

Lucey complied only partially with his father's criteria for an ideal mate: Democrat, Catholic, and Irish. He found someone who was very much a Democrat, but she was Greek Orthodox. He met Jean Vlasis shortly after his upset 1948 victory for a seat in the state assembly. Jean's given name was Angelica, which was shortened to Agnes before she was nicknamed Jean. Pat and Jean both were at the meeting at the Northland Hotel in Green Bay that formally launched the Democratic Organizing Committee (DOC).

Jean Vlasis was born to Greek immigrants who settled on the east side of Milwaukee. She had three sisters and five brothers, and her father successfully ran several dry-cleaning establishments. Greek was spoken in the home, and Jean did not learn English until she went to school. She learned how to read and write English in the first grade and then passed the reading test required before students could advance to the second grade. She excelled as a student and was one of the first graduates of the new Lincoln High School in Milwaukee, which was initially staffed by teachers from throughout Milwaukee who were considered to be the "cream of the crop."[3]

After high school, Jean served in the Navy WAVES (Women Accepted for Voluntary Emergency Services) during World War II and was posted in Washington, DC. In 1949, several people, including Thomas Fairchild and Bob Tehan (with whom she served on a veterans committee), urged Jean to apply for a job on the staff of Congressman Andrew Biemiller. She was initially reluctant because she did not want to return to Washington, but she applied and was hired to work in his Milwaukee office. Biemiller had been active in the Socialist and the Progressive Parties and was elected to Congress as a Democrat. He represented Milwaukee's Fifth District, which at the time included fifteen wards in Milwaukee, Fox Point, Shorewood, and Whitefish Bay. In addition to working for Biemiller, Jean took courses at the University of Wisconsin–Milwaukee.[4]

Although Pat and Jean first met at the constitutional convention of the DOC in Green Bay, they did not start dating until the following year. When they were working together to make arrangements for the annual Jefferson–Jackson dinner fund-raiser in 1950, they decided to have a dinner or two on their own, and began dating. Lucey was traveling the state frequently at that time, organizing for the party. He recalled that during their dates, they spent much of their time discussing politics, a shared passion. On their marriage license, Lucey listed "politician" as his occupation.[5]

Pat and Jean were married in Milwaukee in 1951 at Gesu Catholic Church, a centerpiece of Marquette University, a Jesuit university. Jim

Jean and Pat Lucey,
circa the late 1970s.
WHI IMAGE ID 143871

Doyle, Lucey's mentor, was best man, and Ruth Doyle was matron of honor. Lucey was pleasantly surprised that his rival in the party, Henry Maier, came to the wedding and offered his best wishes.[6]

The Luceys moved to Madison, and their first child, Paul, was born in 1952. Their two other children, Laurel (called Laurie) and David, were born in 1954 and 1956 respectively. When Lucey managed the campaign of Thomas Fairchild in his effort to unseat Joe McCarthy from the US Senate, Jean often brought infant Paul with her to campaign headquarters while she worked.

After Election Day, Lucey told Doyle that he needed to resign his position with the party because they could not pay Lucey what he needed to support his new family. Lucey would continue to do what he could to help the party, but he had to get a job or start a business. Doyle suggested that he consider getting a license to work as a real estate broker. He sent Lucey to see Phil Seagull to find out if Badger Realty could use another broker. Lucey immediately recognized that by selling real estate, he could earn the money he needed and still have the flexibility to remain active in politics.[7]

Seagull offered Lucey a two-year contract, which Lucey thought was odd. He asked if others on the staff were on a fixed term instead of a commission. "No, but I know when I am training my competition," Seagull said.[8] This turned out to be a good prediction. After Lucey earned his real estate license, he worked for Badger Realty for only seven months. He then bought out his contract, and the Luceys started their own business. Pat handled advertising and sales, Jean took responsibility for arranging the closings and keeping records, and Doyle was their attorney.

While launching the real estate business, Pat ventured briefly into the lumber business. Robert Brooks, who was a student at Campion with Lucey, had bought a lumberyard on a shoestring and was struggling to turn a profit. The former classmates reunited when Lucey rented space to run the Fairchild campaign in a building owned by Brooks and his partner. Brooks asked Lucey to become president of the lumber company, but Lucey had already committed to manage Doyle's campaign for governor, and the primary against Proxmire was only months away. Brooks proposed that Lucey go ahead with the campaign and receive five hundred dollars per month until the election was over and then one thousand dollars per month after that. This was an attractive arrangement, and Lucey accepted.

Lucey left after only seven months when he learned that most of the checks he was signing as president were not covered—they were sent with the hope that funds would be available by the time the check was cashed by the recipient. Brooks asked Lucey to approach his father about putting $40,000 ($394,000 in 2019) into the company, but Lucey was not confident enough in the business and realized that check kiting was illegal and unethical. He did the obvious and resigned.[9]

In contrast to the lumber experience, the Luceys had phenomenal success in the real estate business. They initially ran Lucey Real Estate Service from their home. Within two months, they began hiring staff and established a separate office. In three years, they surpassed Stark Realty as the major realty firm in Dane County and had five million dollars in annual sales.[10] After the first decade, Lucey Real Estate Service had twenty salespersons, one accountant, two receptionists/secretaries, and two offices. Annual sales were slightly more than nine million dollars (more than seventy-seven million in 2019), and the Luceys had acquired a diverse portfolio of investments.[11]

They took steps to develop a loyal and highly motivated workforce by sharing profits with their employees and offering incentives for hard work. As one entered the main office, there was a chart on a wall that prominently displayed the name of each salesperson next to two columns: one showing the number of homes each person sold each month and the other detailing the total monthly value of sales. The top performers at the end of the month earned prizes. In addition, bonuses were awarded annually.[12]

The Luceys received invaluable assistance from Lucey's father, GC Lucey. GC visited them in January 1953 and announced that he had just sold the fourteen farms that Lucey had been managing. He sold them to tenants on a land contract, requiring them to pay only one dollar down. He explained that he was hedging his bets because Dwight Eisenhower was elected president in 1952 and "farmers never make much money during Republican administrations."[13] By selling the farms on a land contract basis, GC could count on steady payments even if federal agricultural policies had adverse effects on farmers. Only one of the fourteen farmers was unable to keep up with his payments. The others paid their obligations in full.

The relevance of land contract arrangements to Lucey Real Estate Service was linked to another experience of the entrepreneurial GC.

He helped farmers who were not eligible for bank loans by partnering with financial firms to provide an alternative source of loans for purchasing farm equipment. GC and Pat established the Lucey Investment Company to duplicate this model for those seeking to buy homes through Lucey Real Estate Service. GC invested $200,000 ($1.9 million in 2019) of his own money to help get Lucey Investment Company off the ground. He and Pat worked out a schedule in which GC received payments in cash and stock.[14]

Providing an opportunity to potential buyers in the housing market was especially important in the mid-1950s. For those who could not afford the down payments and mortgage required by financial institutions, the Department of Veterans Affairs (VA) and the Federal Housing Authority (FHA) had good lending arrangements. One could get a VA loan with no down payment, and the FHA required only 5 to 10 percent down. However, these loans were hard to procure. Qualification requirements were restrictive, paperwork was exhaustive, and the process was long and frustrating. Lucey Investment Company bought from sellers at discounts from asking prices, but sellers were happy to get their homes off the market. Buyers had

GC Lucey, father of Pat Lucey, helped get Lucey Real Estate Service started.
WHI IMAGE ID 143883

to pay Lucey Investment interest rates that were somewhat higher than
those offered by savings and loan associations, but at least they could get
a loan—and a house. And, of course, the sales force at Lucey Real Estate
Service was happy because they were making sales, earning commissions,
and, for the most successful, getting bonuses.[15]

The Lucey approach to real estate was ahead of the general industry.
Land contracts did not become popular until the late 1970s and early
1980s. Relationships between real estate agents, lenders, and insurance
companies then became complex and sometimes worked against the best
interests of sellers and buyers. In 1974, Congress passed the Real Estate
Settlement Procedures Act (RESA) to mandate disclosure of relationships
and costs to consumers. RESA also created firewalls between the various
institutions involved in the buying and selling of homes. For example,
lenders could no longer require someone buying a home to work with a
particular real estate agency or get their insurance from a particular company. There were no allegations or charges of improper behavior against
Lucey Investment Company or Lucey Real Estate Service. Nonetheless,
RESA drew the relationship between the two to an end. At the same time,
the VA, FHA, and financial institutions generally changed their policies
and procedures to make home loans more available. Homebuyers no longer needed land contracts through Lucey Investment.[16]

## CONFLICT OF INTEREST?

Governor John Reynolds precipitated debate over potential conflict of
interest issues when he named Lucey to the State of Wisconsin Investment
Board (SWIB) on August 1, 1963. The governor and state legislature created
SWIB in 1951 when they consolidated more than seventy-five separate and
often small pension funds for public employees working in local jurisdictions and in state government. The five trustees of the board provide
general policy direction and oversight over the employees who make the
investment decisions, and in 1963, they received fifty dollars per diem
when they attended meetings.

Governor Reynolds appointed Lucey to fill the unexpired term of
C. Hayden Jamison. Although Republican opponents to Reynolds and
Lucey later charged that there was a conflict of interest between Lucey's

involvement in Lucey Investment Company and service on SWIB, the initial focus was on whether he could join the board prior to Senate confirmation. Attorney General George Thompson, a Republican, told the board that Lucey could not be seated until confirmed by the state senate, which had declined to act on almost all of Reynolds's appointments. The board followed the attorney general's advice but permitted Lucey to join its deliberations as a guest.[17]

Reynolds reacted with a press conference criticizing the attorney general for trying to limit the authority of the governor and directed him to bring the matter to the courts. Thompson, as expected, refused the governor's order. State law allowed the governor to hire a special counsel to represent the chief executive in court, and Reynolds appointed two Milwaukee attorneys: Max Raskin and Philip Padden.[18]

Reynolds made the initial appointment on August 1, when the state senate was in session. On August 2, the senate adjourned until November 4. Acting on legal advice, Reynolds reappointed Lucey to SWIB on September 26, when the senate was not in session, thus creating a technically different circumstance. When the board met on September 27, it accepted Lucey as a member without discussion and without a formal vote.[19]

When the senate reconvened in November, it confirmed Lucey's appointment by a 24-to-5 vote. Majority Leader Robert P. Knowles, a Republican, stated that he felt Lucey was certainly qualified to be a trustee on SWIB, and "Senate Republicans were not going to vote against him merely because of his leadership in the opposition party. We hope that Democratic senators will remember that in future votes on confirmation of appointments."[20]

Less than two weeks after the state senate vote, Attorney General Thompson again challenged Lucey's appointment to SWIB. This time, the concern was conflict of interest, because Lucey was president and treasurer of Lucey Investment Company. The attorney general cited Section 8.25.155 of the Wisconsin statutes: "Any person who has any financial interest in, or is employed by, a person who, or a firm which, is primarily a dealer or broker in securities, or in mortgages or real estate investments, shall not be eligible to be appointed as a trustee."[21]

Before Reynolds appointed Lucey to SWIB, Lucey had sought legal advice from Robert C. Voss, a real estate attorney. Voss advised, "From my experience with Lucey Investment Corp., you are using this organization solely for the purpose of putting together financing of low down payment housing, wherein and whereby you are able to sell one or more houses in order to collect a real estate commission for Lucey Realty Service, Inc. I cannot conceive where the activities of Lucey Investment Corp. would be such as to show a conflict of interest from the inside information which you might obtain in the Investment Board functions."[22]

Reynolds added that on August 22, 1963, Attorney General Thompson had issued a memo stating that the kinds of holdings Lucey owned and the focus of Lucey Investment Corp. on land contracts would not make him ineligible to serve as trustee. Thompson, in other words, was contradicting himself.

The charges prompted two Republican senators, Louis Romell of Adams and Nile Soik of Whitefish Bay, to introduce a resolution asking the attorney general to seek Lucey's ouster.[23] The senate did not take action on the Romell–Soik resolution, and Lucey took his seat on the board.

In 1965, the year after Lucey was elected lieutenant governor, he was again accused of inappropriate ties. Unidentified persons went to the Madison newspapers to raise concern about possible conflict between Lucey's elected position, his part ownership in a real estate firm (separate from Lucey Real Estate Service), and a state government program to acquire lake property and lake and river access. The state had initiated a ten-year conservation program, financed by a penny increase in the cigarette tax, before Lucey ran for lieutenant governor. Spending totaled $4.5 to $5 million per year. The governor and the heads of five affected state agencies were responsible for selecting the land to be bought. The lieutenant governor, who generally had very little authority, played no role. In addition, this was a time when governor and lieutenant governor were elected separately, and Lucey served with a Republican, Warren P. Knowles, in the governor's office. Lucey had neither authority nor influence over state land purchases.

The basis for the charges of a conflict of interest was that Lucey was president and 30 percent owner of Doolittle-Barden, a firm that sold lake property in northern Wisconsin. M. William Gerrard invited Lucey to make the investment. Gerrard and James R. Grueninger each had 30 percent shares, and the remaining 10 percent was retained by the original owners. The 30 percent ownership cost Lucey, Gerrard, and Grueninger six thousand dollars each. Gerrard, a Republican, and Lucey had become friends as well as business associates, and Gerrard was a major fund-raiser for Lucey despite their different party affiliations.

Lucey had anticipated accusations when he became president and part owner of Doolittle-Barden. He warned his business partners and designated Madison attorney Maurice Pasch as trustee for any common stock he held in any closed corporation regulated by the state. Most of this stock was in insurance companies. He also talked with Lester Voight, director of the State Conservation Department, and arranged that Doolittle-Barden would contact the department before obtaining property to be sure the state had no interest in the land involved.

When questioned by the newspapers, Lucey explained the details.[24] Neither the newspapers nor the state's politicians pursued the issue any further.

## REACHING OUT

Profits made from the real estate business and other investments allowed Pat and Jean Lucey to become developers. Their biggest project was on the far west side of Madison. Throughout the 1960s, the Luceys bought farms anticipating expansion of the city to the west. In the spring of 1969, prior to running for governor, Lucey submitted a proposal for development of 683 acres of land that would take ten to fifteen years to complete. The price tag was $67.1 million ($468.3 million in 2019). Of the total plan, 130 acres were located in Middleton and 553 in Madison. The City of Madison was the major jurisdiction that had to approve the proposal. Lucey had not held or run for a city or county office, so he had no conflict of interest. This project had the effect of enhancing Lucey's image as a successful businessperson. For some, he was almost inherently suspect and warranted scrutiny, like any developer.[25]

Lucey worked with William L. Nelson and Associates of Milwaukee to design a planned unit development, which included a wide variety of functional features. Seventy-three lots would be allocated for duplexes and 974 for single-family dwellings. Permanent open space covering 192 acres was designated for parks, ponds, greenways, and pedestrian walks.

The plan included thirty-eight acres for industrial office space, seven for shopping centers, seven for a church complex, four for a nursing home, nine for professional office space, and two and a half acres for three gas stations. The plan as a whole was considered cutting edge. Lucey explained that he chose the Nelson firm because it had represented both private developers and municipalities. "I didn't want a planner who had only the developer's point of view," he said.[26]

Madison has been notorious for deliberative processes and contentious reactions to development plans. However, Ray Burt, the city building inspector, raised the only substantial objection to Lucey's plans, concerning ease of snow removal, a resolvable issue. Most of the reaction was positive, especially about the green space and relatively low density. Duane Hinz, the city's principal planner, and Madison Plan Director Kenneth Clark praised the project and correctly predicted swift and smooth approval.[27]

## OPEN HOUSING

Lucey did not sacrifice his commitment to public values to gain standing in the private sector. He drew the ire of peers in the real estate business for his public stance against housing discrimination. The Madison Board of Realtors vigorously opposed a city proposal for open housing. The board ran an advertisement in the *Wisconsin State Journal* and the *Capital Times* opposing a proposed ordinance that would prohibit racial and religious discrimination in the sale, rental, and lease of housing and public accommodations. Full-page ads appeared in the December 2 editions of the papers. The next day, Lucey issued a statement disagreeing with the board. He made it clear that it certainly did not speak for him or for Lucey Real Estate Service.[28]

Three days later, Lucey issued a statement endorsing the proposed ordinance. He argued that one could not uphold the US Constitution and at the same time oppose an ordinance designed to ensure that housing is open to people of all races and creeds. He spoke to the Madison Common Council at its December 6, 1963, meeting.[29] Lucey told the Common Council members that Lucey Real Estate Service had a nondiscrimination policy and that he had made it clear to his staff that they were to serve everyone, regardless of race, creed, or national origin. He added emphasis by telling his agents that they would be fired if they ever discriminated. His appearance was especially notable because he was among the most prominent real estate brokers in Madison and because of his lone stand in opposition to the position of the Board of Realtors.

Shirley Abrahamson, an attorney who played a major role in drafting the fair housing ordinance, was at the December 6 meeting. The advocates had a list of individuals to testify in favor of the open housing proposal. Lucey was not on that list. Abrahamson and others were pleased when Lucey stepped forward to offer his support. Abrahamson was in the same law firm as Jim Doyle and occasionally saw Lucey there, but she had not worked with him and did not know him well. She recalled being impressed with how firm and articulate Lucey was in testifying in support of the proposal.[30]

After hearing testimony and engaging in debate, the council members voted, splitting evenly. Mayor Henry Reynolds, a Republican in what is nominally a nonpartisan office, had the authority to break the tie. He explained that he had grown up in Madison with friends and neighbors from a wide diversity of ethnic and religious backgrounds. He said he was genuinely surprised and confused by all the fuss. He cast his vote in favor of the proposal and open housing became law.[31]

The Luceys feared that real estate agents, buyers, sellers, and others might express their displeasure with the new ordinance by protesting and boycotting Lucey Real Estate Service. That did not happen. Instead, Lucey earned respect from many in the industry as well as in the community.[32]

## PEOPLE'S PARK

The campus of the University of Wisconsin–Madison was the scene of frequent protests throughout the 1960s. In 1961, students objected to threats to freedom of expression and association from the US House Un-American Activities Committee (HUAC). Madison's open housing ordinance was adopted in the midst of civil rights demonstrations that reached high levels in 1963 and 1964 and then resumed in 1968, in part in response to the assassination of Dr. Martin Luther King Jr. Protests against American military involvement in Vietnam began in earnest in 1965, and students on the Madison campus disrupted the recruitment activities of Dow Chemical Company and the Central Intelligence Agency in 1966 and 1967.

The year 1968 was marked by considerable tension. Students objected to requirements that men enroll in Reserved Officer Training Corps programs and to the lack of an African American studies department. They joined the grape boycott in support of migrant farm workers. In response to the demonstrations, Governor Warren Knowles deployed the National Guard on campus from February 12 to 21, 1968. Prior to the presence of the National Guard, local police engaged in violent clashes with students.

On May 3, 1969, a block party on Mifflin Street, near campus, began as a combination celebration of spring and protest against the war in Vietnam. Police considered the activity as noisy and out of control and again clashed with students. Interactions between police and students were generally hostile, and students responded to what they regarded as excessive force by rioting. The confrontations lasted three days.

In the aftermath of the Mifflin Street riots, rumors circulated that guns and explosives were going to be brought from Chicago to Madison for another round of violence. William Dyke, known for his hostility toward students, had been elected mayor. Residents around campus lacked confidence that city leadership would dampen the prospects for more violence.

A group of citizens approached Abrahamson, who was president of the Wisconsin Civil Liberties Union, to divert student energies. Their idea was to use two adjacent vacant lots in downtown Madison for a garden to grow vegetables for low-income residents in the community. Pat and Jean Lucey owned the lots.

Abrahamson did not know Lucey outside of seeing him at the open housing hearing but agreed to encourage him to let the students use the lots. She went to his house in Maple Bluff, a Madison suburb, and arrived at dinner time. After apologizing for interrupting the family meal, she explained the proposal. As an attorney, she felt obliged to caution him on the risks of letting someone use the property, regardless of how worthy the cause might be, and explained that getting students to leave the property could be difficult and might involve legal costs and negative publicity.[33]

Lucey listened and without hesitation gave his approval. He leased the property to the West Mifflin Street Co-op, the major grocery store in the area, for one dollar. The co-op was owned collectively by area residents.

Students dubbed the lots People's Park and enthusiastically grabbed hoes and rakes, planted seeds, and took pride in their gardens. The violence ceased. After two growing seasons, students quietly went on to other things, and the lots were used for another housing project.[34]

Not surprisingly, although Lucey and Abrahamson did not have a continued working relationship, they developed considerable mutual respect. When Lucey was governor, he appointed Abrahamson to the Wisconsin Supreme Court, making her the first woman on the court.

## SALE AND TRUST

The Luceys sold Lucey Real Estate Service to Wauwatosa Realty (which became Shorewest Realty) when Pat was elected governor, and he put his assets and investments into a blind trust, which was administered by Robert Voss. Trusts are used by almost all elected chief executives to avoid conflicts of interest.

Lucey could have followed an alternative path and disclosed all of his holdings and then recused himself from any decision-making role that might have affected or involved any of his investments. Given the broad range of responsibilities of a governor, recusal would have been frequent and cumbersome, at best, and unlike his previous public positions, being governor was a full-time job. It deserved his undivided attention, free of entanglements or suspicions.

## CHAPTER 6

# CAMPAIGNS, CONFLICTS, AND CIVILITY

I n the 1960s, Wisconsin evolved into a clearly competitive two-party state. Republicans in the state enjoyed success throughout the twentieth century, but from 1957 onward, the party built by the Democratic Organizing Committee (DOC) also had victory celebrations. Democrats did not always win elections, but the party label now held value. To appear on a ballot as a Democrat gave a candidate a chance of being elected—especially in certain communities and in statewide races. Candidates found it was worth fighting for the party's nomination, and as a result, Democrats found themselves fighting with one another as well as battling Republicans. Intraparty struggles were common—and sometimes bitter.

Tension between Patrick Lucey and Gaylord Nelson was a persistent theme during this period. Distrust between the two had simmered since 1951, when as a state senator Nelson did not support a motion of censure against Joseph McCarthy. Lucey called Nelson a coward.[1] When Nelson won election as governor in 1958, he assumed that he would be able to name the chair of the state party, but Lucey and newly elected US Senator Bill Proxmire had other ideas. Lucey's strength came from the grassroots support he built while organizing the party. Nelson fostered his own support, relying on individual ties rather than on the party. He was an attractive and articulate campaigner. Lucey got the job done, but he wasn't especially flashy or entertaining. Although their styles differed, they were almost ideological twins—like siblings quarreling for a dominant position in the family. They came together when the family needed unity, but the rivalry persisted.

Wisconsin's delegates to the Democratic National Convention became major players in the presidential sweepstakes, and the open primary used to determine the state's delegates became a barometer of how candidates might fare in the November general election. Struggles between presidential contenders in Wisconsin both reflected and exacerbated existing divisions within the state's Democratic Party, and the divisions had lifespans beyond Election Day. As party chair and as an important player in state and national campaigns, Lucey had a major impact on the processes and the outcomes of elections. He was also instrumental in determining whether discourse and deliberation would be civil.

## PICKING A PRESIDENTIAL NOMINEE

In 1960, only sixteen states had primaries to determine delegate support for candidates seeking the Democratic nomination. Party bosses continued to dominate the nomination process. Moreover, in twelve of the states with primaries, Democrats chose to support a "favorite son"—usually their governor—rather than host a contest between national candidates. In favorite son delegations, votes were not usually pledged, leading to a particular national contender. Rather freewheeling conventions could result. In 1960, Hubert Humphrey entered only five primaries and John F. Kennedy seven. Their first head-on clash was in Wisconsin on April 5.

Because Kennedy confronted the question of whether a Catholic could be elected president, he needed to demonstrate in primaries that he had the level of support required to win in the November general election. That made Wisconsin and then West Virginia critical.[2]

When Lucey first met Kennedy at the 1952 Democratic National Convention, his assessment was that the young man from Boston was too much of a northeastern aristocrat to get elected president. Lucey met Kennedy again at the 1956 convention, and this time Lucey had a different assessment. He admired Kennedy's intellect and winning personality, although he had some questions about Kennedy's commitment to progressive values. Those concerns were initially addressed not by Kennedy but by Ted Sorensen, a top aide and later speechwriter for the president.

At the 1959 meeting in Milwaukee of the Mid-West Conference of the Democratic Party, Sorensen chatted with Lucey after a banquet where Humphrey was the speaker. Sorensen, who was representing Kennedy in the candidate's absence, asked Lucey point blank if he would commit to supporting

Kennedy for president. Lucey shared his concerns about how liberal the senator from Massachusetts was. Sorensen assured Lucey that Kennedy was genuinely progressive and argued that anyone more liberal than Kennedy probably could not get elected. Lucey was anxious to see a Catholic who was progressive elected as president and committed to the Kennedy team.[3]

While Lucey favored Kennedy, his rival supported Adlai Stevenson. Since Stevenson was not a declared candidate, Nelson aimed for a victory by Humphrey with the idea that a deadlock between Kennedy and Humphrey would probably prompt delegates at the convention to turn to Stevenson. Stevenson had unsuccessfully run for president twice in the 1950s, but Nelson hoped that Stevenson's third try would be a charm. An important subplot to this drama was the position of Jim Doyle, Lucey's long-term mentor. Doyle was the national chair of the effort—funded by friends in Chicago—to secure the nomination for Stevenson.[4]

Lucey's position as chair of the Democratic Party of Wisconsin in 1960 was both an advantage and a disadvantage. As chair, he felt he had to remain publicly neutral in the presidential primary and carefully avoid giving Kennedy an advantage when the party scheduled events or encouraged voter turnout. At the same time, Lucey's position enhanced his value to the Kennedy campaign. Sorensen and Robert Kennedy knew that Lucey had used a grassroots organizational approach to building the state's Democratic Party. Lucey knew county party leaders and had even recruited most of them. His relationships with these officials throughout the state was a valuable asset to East Coast folks—especially since their major competition for Wisconsin delegates was Humphrey, from neighboring Minnesota. Many Badgers considered this Gopher their third US Senator.

In the midst of the primary fight, Lucey sought an unprecedented second term as chair and ran into opposition from Nelson. The governor wanted Svarre Roang, from Edgerton, to take over from Lucey. When Roang indicated he was not interested, Nelson supported Herman Jessen, a mink farmer from Phelps who sought to oust Lucey and assume the helm of the party. Jessen had sided with Philleo Nash when Lucey was elected chair in 1957, and he continued to be upset that Lucey had supported John Reynolds over Christ Seraphim for attorney general in the 1958 election. Jessen charged Lucey with juggling party financial figures to look good.[5]

Lucey responded with a statement listing the doubling of paid members, the record number of Democrats running for office, the record donations, and the party's electoral successes.[6] On his side, Lucey had Doyle, Proxmire, Reynolds, Robert Kastenmeier, Frank Nikolay, Owen Monfils, John Lynch, and most of the county chairs. Lucey defeated Jessen, 896 to 301.[7]

A highlight of the 1959 state convention was that both John Kennedy and Humphrey addressed the delegates. They gave separate speeches rather than engage in a debate. Stevenson continued to have support within the state, but he was not a declared candidate, so he did not mount the podium at the convention.

Because the strategy of Stevenson backers in Wisconsin was to support Humphrey as a way of preventing Kennedy from wrapping up the majority of delegates before the first ballot was cast at the national convention, it was difficult to disentangle Stevenson backers from those who genuinely preferred Humphrey. Clearly, the strategic Humphrey backers included Nelson and Doyle, but most of the labor union leaders genuinely wanted Humphrey. These included Wisconsin AFL-CIO President George Haberman, UAW Regional Director Sam Rizzo of Racine, Wisconsin Machinists' Union President John Heidenreich, and UAW Regional Director Harvey Kitzman. Seraphim, Jessen, Henry Reuss, and a narrow majority on the Wisconsin Democratic Administrative Committee were in the Humphrey camp—some strategic and others genuine supporters.[8] Within Milwaukee, the southside Polish Catholics and the Jewish community allied with Kennedy, while the north side favored Humphrey.[9]

In Madison, a prominent group of fifty-nine faculty members at the University of Wisconsin signed a statement endorsing Humphrey. The list included Jack Barbash (a former member of Humphrey's staff), Merle Curti, Max Otto (Lucey's former philosophy professor), Ralph Huitt (an adviser to Proxmire), and Llewellyn Pfankuchen (spouse of Gretchen Pfankuchen, a founder of the DOC). David Carley, a rising figure in the party and a protégé of Nelson, also urged support for Humphrey. Like Nelson, many in the university community promoting Humphrey were primarily interested in derailing Kennedy to help Stevenson.[10]

In addition to Lucey, the team supporting Kennedy included Reynolds, Vel Phillips (a leader in Milwaukee's African American community), Madison Mayor Ivan Nestingen, Milwaukee's Fourth District Congressional

Representative Clement Zablocki, Democratic Party Treasurer David Rabinovitz, Wisconsin Farmers' Union Leader Robert Moses, Madison Federation of Labor Executive Secretary Marvin Brickman, and Gerald Bruno (former member of Senator Proxmire's staff). Humphrey had a larger lineup, but both candidates drew support from major constituencies.

Nelson agreed with Lucey that, as governor, Nelson should not publicly endorse any of the presidential candidates. He initially suggested that he would run as a favorite son. Lucey discovered from a conversation with Jerry Heany, someone he knew from his student days at St. Thomas College, that Humphrey and Nelson concurred that Nelson should run as a favorite son and then lead a delegation that would support Humphrey and eventually Stevenson at the nominating convention. Heany was living in Minnesota and trying to get Lucey to support Humphrey or, at a minimum, to be inactive.

Lucey, however, wanted to help end the "stop Kennedy" movement promoted by those supporting other candidates. He went to the administrative committee and got them to invite all liberal Democratic candidates,

Presidential candidate John F. Kennedy at the Madison airport on October 23, 1960, with state Democratic leaders: Madison Mayor Ivan Nestingen, Madison Federation of Labor leader Marvin Brickson, Governor Gaylord Nelson, state Democratic Party head Patrick J. Lucey, and Heidi Licht, secretary at Democratic Party headquarters.
WHI IMAGE ID 45434

including Kennedy, to participate in the Wisconsin primary. Nelson resisted. Lucey then persuaded Proxmire to declare that he would also run as a favorite son if Nelson persisted. Both Nelson and Proxmire backed down, and the administrative committee issued its invitation.[11]

Most of the senior advisers and officials in the Kennedy campaign opposed accepting the invitation. Their major argument was that Wisconsin was probably Humphrey territory and a primary loss would be very costly so early in the campaign. Three people favored entering the Wisconsin primary: Lucey, Joseph Kennedy Sr. (the candidate's father), and the candidate himself. Lucey recognized the risks but argued that Kennedy could win, which would be a major blow to Humphrey and to the pro-Stevenson efforts.

Lucey was with Kennedy when he announced his decision, waiting for his plane to fly to Nebraska, where he would publicly enter that state's primary, too. After his public statement, Kennedy turned to Lucey and said: "Well, now that you've conned me into this thing, how do you feel about it?"

Lucey replied, "Well, that I would feel pretty terrible if you lost."

After teasing Lucey a little, Kennedy said, "Well, don't feel that way about it. As of today, my chances of getting the nomination are a lot less than fifty–fifty. If I win the Wisconsin primary, they'll be slightly better than fifty–fifty. So, if you look at it that way, I'm not gambling very much."[12]

While the governor did not officially endorse anyone during the campaign, Nelson notably praised Humphrey and his stands on issues, remaining silent on Kennedy. The governor loaned members of his staff to the Humphrey campaign. When both Kennedy and Humphrey were in Wisconsin in June 1959, Nelson had Humphrey stay as a guest in the governor's residence, while Kennedy was on his own to find a hotel room.[13]

As party chair, Lucey made staff and services available to both the Humphrey and the Kennedy campaigns. He instructed field directors James Megellas and Norman Clapp to be impartial in helping candidates meet people, organize rallies, and generally make their case to voters.[14] At state headquarters, paid personnel were meticulously neutral. They supplied the organizations of both candidates with lists of party members and county chairs. Office equipment and addressing services were equally available and charged at the same rates. Those who visited the office could pick up leaflets, buttons, and other campaign material promoting both candidates.[15]

To prevent schedule conflicts and resolve administrative issues, Lucey established a coordinating committee consisting of Nestingen (state chair for the Kennedy campaign), Rizzo (state chair of the Humphrey campaign), and himself. Although the committee could be charged with being stacked two to one in favor of Kennedy, no controversies ensued over scheduling.[16]

Meanwhile, Lucey worked with the Kennedy campaign and with Kennedy himself to tailor the Massachusetts senator's campaign to match Wisconsin's political profile. Bobby Kennedy and Ted Sorensen called Lucey "our most effective ally" in Wisconsin.[17]

Lucey traveled with John Kennedy during his twenty-nine visits to the state from January to April 1960, driving up to two hundred miles a day, briefing the candidate on the small towns they visited, and encouraging him to interact directly with voters in the style of Proxmire—walk the streets, greet workers at plant gates, and shake hands. Lucey calculated that Kennedy made about 250 individual speeches.[18] At one point, an exhausted Kennedy asked how things looked. When Lucey responded that he thought Kennedy was ahead of Humphrey, Kennedy looked at him and said, "Well, then—couldn't we stop this Proxmire formula?"[19]

Bobby Kennedy told Lucey that he should schedule Rose, mother of the Kennedy brothers, for some campaign appearances. However, Lucey also received a message from Kenneth O'Donnell, one of the top lieutenants, to disregard this suggestion. O'Donnell said, "If anything we don't need it is to have Rose Kennedy come to Wisconsin. She looks like she is forty and here we are trying to convince voters that her son is old enough to be president."

Lucey reported that Bobby Kennedy called a few days later, at seven in the morning, asking about the schedule for his mother. Lucey said he did not have one, and Kennedy said, "Well, get at it. Get at it!" Lucey told O'Donnell he was going to arrange a visit, and if O'Donnell still felt Rose should stay out of Wisconsin, he should take it up with Bobby.

Lucey asked his original campaign assistant, his mother, to help. Ella Lucey was living in Prairie du Chien at the time. She rented space at the Fort Crawford Hotel for a tea with Rose Kennedy and sent out invitations, beginning with her bridge-playing friends. Ella included Gregory, Lucey's youngest brother and a Jesuit priest, on the invitation list. As part of his service prior to ordination, he was teaching nearby at the Campion school that Lucey had attended. Father Greg attended the tea in his clerical attire. When Ella introduced him to Rose and noted that Roger, brother of Greg and Pat, was also a Jesuit priest, Rose smiled and said, "I have always said that I would trade a congressman for a priest and a senator for a bishop."[20]

It was an enjoyable and successful event. When Ella told her son that she felt sorry for Rose because of all the work she had to do to help her son get elected, Pat reminded his mother of all that she had done helping her own son.[21]

Lucey also worked to arrange coffee meetings around the state for Kennedy's sisters. His sister, Verona, hosted one of these meetings for Jean Kennedy Smith, who visited Ferryville on a campaign stop for her brother. Jean asked Verona whether the farmers' wives who gathered really got up early every morning to milk the cows.[22]

## DELEGATE ALLOCATION

While candidates and their supporters were campaigning, the administrative committee of the party was embroiled in a dispute over how to distribute the state's thirty-one delegates according to primary election results for the purposes of the national convention. The rules of the game at the start were that the winner of the statewide popular vote would get ten pledged delegates, the winner of each of the ten congressional districts would get two, and the remaining vote would be split between the state's national committeewoman and national committeeman (who were free to vote for whomever they chose). During the last week in January 1960— nine weeks before the April 5 primary—Rizzo, chair of the Humphrey for President organization, proposed that the administrative committee revise the delegate distribution pattern. He wanted to reduce from ten to five the number of delegates the statewide winner would get and increase congressional district delegates from 2 to 2.5.[23] Lucey led the resistance to this proposal. In part, Lucey objected to changing the rules of the game in the middle of the campaign. The objection also was based on his expectation that Kennedy would win the statewide vote and that Humphrey's best chance for getting delegates was at the congressional district level.[24] Lucey lost this battle. After heated and prolonged debate, the administrative committee voted 14 to 12 to adopt the Rizzo proposal.[25]

Nelson publicly agreed with Lucey that the rules should not be changed midstream, but he later criticized Lucey, Nestingen, and John Kennedy for continuing to voice displeasure after the vote. Others who had agreed with Lucey also thought it was time to let it drop, among them Robert Moses, a Kennedy staff member who as a member of the administrative committee had voted against the rule change.[26] The issue did not go away, however, and Kennedy himself incorporated the complaint about delegate redistribution into his stump speech.[27] Most of the newspapers sympathized with him. The issue was a major source of conflict and mistrust in the state party for the next decade.[28]

The revised formula, of course, made a difference. Kennedy won the statewide vote in the primary: 476,024 to Humphrey's 366,753. Kennedy also won in six of the ten congressional districts. Table 6.1 presents a comparison of the impact on delegate distribution of the original and revised formulas. Not included is the single, shared vote of the national committee members. The potential impact was minimized because Kennedy won both the popular vote and the vote in most of the congressional districts. As the national convention approached and it became clear that Kennedy had enough support to win the nomination, Humphrey released delegates pledged to support him so that they could vote for whomever they wanted, thus negating the effects of the formula even further. Release of the delegates lowered the heat in the dispute but did not erase the memory of the maneuver by Rizzo and other Humphrey supporters.[29]

**TABLE 6.1:** Impact of Formulas on Distribution of Delegates Based on 1960 Wisconsin Primary Results

|  | Popular— Original | Popular— Revised | District— Original | District— Revised | Total— Original | Total— Revised |
|---|---|---|---|---|---|---|
| John F. Kennedy | 10 | 5 | 12 | 15 | 22 | 20 |
| Hubert H. Humphrey | 0 | 0 | 8 | 10 | 8 | 10 |

Source: Calculated from data in David Adamany, "1960 Elections in Wisconsin," (master's thesis, University of Wisconsin, 1963), 55–57.

## CAN A CATHOLIC WIN?

The Wisconsin primary provided a partial answer to whether Kennedy, as a Catholic, could be elected as president. Religion was very visible as an issue. Two groups were especially active in generating anti-Catholic and anti-Kennedy sentiment: Protestants and Other Americans United for Separation of Church and State (POAU) and the Fair Deal for Humphrey Committee (which was repudiated by Humphrey). The latter organization ran ads in newspapers throughout the state alleging that Republicans who were Catholic were organized to vote for Kennedy in the Democratic primary, giving him an unfair and misleading primary advantage over Humphrey.[30] Kennedy supporters, fearful that his identity as a Catholic was a political liability, criticized newspapers for emphasizing religion and frequently running photos of Kennedy with nuns.[31]

Paul Corbin, an ardent supporter of Kennedy, sent a campaign message to voters in the Fox River Valley, an area from Green Bay to Oshkosh known to be heavily populated by Catholics who voted Republican. The message warned that Kennedy would follow directions from the pope if elected and urged voters to support Humphrey. Corbin sent the mailing from Minneapolis so it appeared to be coming from the Humphrey campaign. The intent, of course, was to anger Catholic Republicans and encourage them to take advantage of Wisconsin's open primary to vote for Kennedy.[32]

In general, Kennedy ran well in the industrial, Catholic parts of the state, while Humphrey prevailed in the rural, Protestant areas. Kennedy carried each of the ten most heavily Catholic counties in the state. Analyses by a number of political scientists identified religion as a major factor in the minds of voters.[33] Leon Epstein and Harry Scoble found that a significant number of Republican Catholics, especially in the Fox River Valley area, voted for Kennedy, although they did not vote for other Democrats on the ballot.[34] Kennedy, of course, needed to demonstrate that he could get non-Catholics to vote for him. Ideally, religion would not matter.

The evidence was not decisive, as religion was often entangled with other factors. With the exception of the Second District, the districts Humphrey won not only were rural and Protestant but also all bordered Minnesota. The Second District was dominated by the Madison area and the University of Wisconsin where Stevenson—and secondarily

Humphrey—had strong support.[35] Kennedy had overwhelming support in Milwaukee's Fourth and Fifth Districts, where many of the residents were blue-collar industrial workers of Polish and German descent.[36] One could, in other words, see a pattern of voting along economic and ethnic as well as religious differences. While the Wisconsin victory was critical to Kennedy's journey to the White House, it left the religious question only partially answered. The campaign had to move to heavily Protestant West Virginia for a more definitive test.

Lucey received a call from Bobby Kennedy asking for help in West Virginia. The younger Kennedy did not feel that his brother was being scheduled properly in coal country. After meeting with the scheduling staff and making a speech for Kennedy in West Virginia, Lucey got a road atlas and drove around the state, stopping to talk with people at filling stations, stores, and restaurants. He wanted to get a feel for how things were going. An operator of one filling station told Lucey he was going to vote for Kennedy, explaining, "You know I can't vote for that fellow Humphrey, because he's a Catholic."[37] The salience of religion—despite confusion about who was and was not Catholic—worried Lucey. Nonetheless, Kennedy won West Virginia, demonstrating that his religious identity was not a make-or-break factor.

Lucey later recalled a conversation with President Kennedy during a visit Lucey made to the Oval Office in 1962. The two of them remembered that during the primary campaign, they stopped for lunch at Nelson's Café in Viroqua in western Wisconsin. Kennedy impressed Lucey by remembering the details of that particular campaign stop. Lucey had expected Kennedy to do well in Vernon County because of its Scandinavian heritage and its history of support for Robert M. La Follette and Progressives, but Kennedy lost there by one thousand votes. Lucey told the president he had just been to the café and had asked its owner how he thought Kennedy would do if he were running for reelection. Nelson, the café owner, said confidently that Kennedy would win. Surprised, the president asked Lucey what had changed. Lucey said that when he asked that question of Nelson, the reply was: "Well, the pope has not moved into the White House."[38]

## THE NOMINATING CONVENTION

Lucey was not a delegate to the 1960 Democratic National Convention, but his father was. When the state party officials met to choose a slate of delegates, Lucey thought it would be nice if GC had the honor of being on the list. Lucey got himself named as his father's alternate, thinking that GC would not be interested in going to Los Angeles and Lucey would move to delegate status. GC surprised his son, grabbed his sunglasses, and packed his bags. Lucey went as an alternate.[39]

His formal status mattering little, Lucey played a critical role at the convention. In addition to being a leader in the Wisconsin delegation, he provided direction to the Iowa delegation. Bobby Kennedy had designed a system of having a floor coordinator for each state to monitor developments and maintain communications. He chose someone who was not a member of the state delegation to be the coordinator to minimize the possibility that internal disagreements would complicate the flow of information. Lucey was the coordinator for Iowa, while Kirk LeMoyne "Lem" Billings, JFK's former roommate at Harvard, was the coordinator for Wisconsin.

Iowa delegates supported Kennedy but had pledged their delegates to their governor, Herschel C. Loveless, for the first round. This approach generally allowed a state to have a moment in the sun where they could make a speech celebrating their state's history and attractions as they cast their ballots for their favorite son. Lucey learned that Governor Loveless was looking forward to his delegation nominating him as a presidential candidate on the first ballot but understood the gesture to be symbolic. Like his delegates from the Hawkeye State, Loveless did not consider himself a serious candidate. Lucey was concerned, however. The projection was that the voting on the first ballot would be close, and not having the Iowa votes might result in a wide-open process that could deny Kennedy the nomination. Lucey raised this issue in the daily morning meeting that Bobby Kennedy had with all the state floor coordinators.

Archibald Cox (later noted for his bow tie and his role as special prosecutor in the Watergate scandal) met with Lucey right after the meeting, offering legal advice about the options available. Lucey went back to the Iowa delegation and orchestrated a scenario in which they satisfied

Governor Loveless with an initial nomination and then were immediately recognized to change and cast their first ballot votes for Kennedy.[40]

The Wisconsin delegation was split between Kennedy and Humphrey supporters. Before the convention, Lucey and O'Donnell had had lunch with Frank Nikolay, who was the head of the Humphrey supporters in the Wisconsin delegation. Nikolay agreed at the lunch that if Humphrey released his delegates, he would urge everyone to vote for Kennedy. In a show of unity and civility, Humphrey did release delegates pledged to him so they could cast their votes for Kennedy. At the convention, however, Nikolay reneged. He and other Humphrey supporters cast their votes for Humphrey, denying Kennedy, albeit temporarily, the ballots he needed for a first-ballot nomination. Wisconsin had been in a position to put Kennedy over the top on the first ballot but instead let that honor go to the next state in alphabetical order, Wyoming. Lucey just shook his head when, after JFK took office, Nikolay was dismayed that he was not appointed the federal US attorney for the Western District of Wisconsin.[41]

## THE 1960 ELECTION

Although Kennedy won important support from Wisconsin when he won the Democratic presidential nomination, the state's electoral college votes went to Richard Nixon on November 8, 1960. Polls and campaign crowds had indicated a Kennedy win in Wisconsin, so his loss was a surprise. As the final votes were tabulated, Lucey got a call from Bobby Kennedy, who asked, "What the hell happened?" Lucey had no answer.[42]

The Democratic Party had seemed to mobilize right after the presidential nomination convention to elect Kennedy and his running mate, Lyndon B. Johnson, and to reelect Nelson as governor, Nash as lieutenant governor, Reynolds as attorney general, and six of the state's members of Congress. They had a full slate of candidates for the state legislature for the first time and fielded 353 candidates for county positions, the highest number since the rebirth of the party.[43]

In cooperation with the Democratic National Committee, the state party had sponsored a series of precinct worker schools and mounted an aggressive effort to register voters. Jerry Clark, of Proxmire's office, coordinated the registration work and established an office in Milwaukee, where the largest number of unregistered and probable Democratic voters resided. Alders on the Milwaukee Common Council nixed door-to-door and mobile-unit registration, but volunteers nonetheless urged eligible voters to make their way to government offices. Door-to-door registration was most successful in Madison, Kenosha, Fond du Lac, Sheboygan, Oshkosh, Prairie du Chien, and Wausau. Mobile units registering voters ran up and down Green Bay streets.[44]

Lucey supervised the coordination of the Kennedy–Johnson and the Nelson campaigns. The state party established a speakers' bureau to handle the many requests for national figures to help rally local partisans. Those who visited the state in the fall included Eleanor Roosevelt, G. Mennen Williams, Estes Kefauver, Ed Muskie, James Symington, and, of course, Hubert Humphrey.[45] Kennedy continued to visit the state and drew enthusiastic crowds.[46] Lucey participated in arranging every visit and accompanied the future president each time.[47] The internal party differences that were so visible during the primary seemed to be healing. Nelson endorsed Kennedy without any hesitation. Doyle also voiced support for Kennedy and headed fund-raising for Nelson's reelection.

Despite signs of optimism, however, Kennedy's candidacy came with some important caveats. The longstanding rivalry between Lucey and Nelson haunted some of the attempts at unity and coordination. During the 1960 campaign, Nelson vetoed cooperation with the Kennedy–Johnson efforts in the western parts of the state because of the anti-Catholic sentiment there. Nelson feared that being associated too closely with Kennedy would harm his own bid for reelection. This angered Kennedy supporters in heavily Catholic areas in the Fox Valley and Milwaukee. They refused to campaign for Nelson.[48]

Complacency also bedeviled the Democrats. They were basking in the glow of their 1958 successes, thinking this was the beginning of a long trend, and they believed they had a presidential candidate who was clearly more attractive than Richard Nixon. Reynolds, running for another term as attorney general, sounded the alarm, but few heeded him. Reynolds noted that phone banks were not being fully utilized and volunteers were not as numerous or as energized as he had seen them in the past.[49]

In contrast, Republicans were mobilized and hungry for victory. Jack Olson, a successful business leader in Wisconsin Dells, led Nixon's campaign in Wisconsin. Focusing largely on the northern and western parts of the state, Olson built on the state's traditional pattern of voting for the GOP and on concerns about a young, elite, Catholic easterner moving into the White House. Claude Jasper, the new chair of the Republican Party of Wisconsin, was an able and vigorous fund-raiser.[50]

Lucey pondered Bobby Kennedy's question about why Wisconsin did not, as anticipated, vote for his brother. He speculated that a sizeable number of Republicans voted in the Democratic primary but then "returned home" in the general election. The total Democratic vote in the primary was 842,777, but the vote for Kennedy on November 8 was only 830,805. More than 543,000 more Badgers voted in November than had in April, so the decline in presidential voting by Democrats was not due to an overall decrease in the number going to the polls.[51]

While Kennedy lost Wisconsin's electoral college ballots, the state's voters split their preferences on down-ballot races. Nelson was reelected as governor and Reynolds was reelected attorney general, while Republicans beat Democratic incumbents in the offices of lieutenant governor and treasurer and Republican Robert C. Zimmerman won another term as secretary of state. Democrats lost one of their five members of Congress and ten seats in the state assembly. The state senate stayed the same, and Democrats gained in the total number of elected positions in county governments. Republicans did better than Democrats overall, but they did not dominate the way they once had. Wisconsin could reasonably be classified as a competitive two-party state.

## Party Politics

Governors naturally prefer to have someone from their own party in the White House. When Nelson was first elected governor in 1958, Republican Dwight Eisenhower was president, and Wisconsin's chief executive had no expectation of special access for federal patronage. However, when fellow Democrat John F. Kennedy was in the Oval Office, Governor Nelson had reason to anticipate calls when appointments were made and special treatment when funds for state programs were being distributed.

But Nelson had not supported Kennedy's quest for Wisconsin's delegates to the nominating convention. Lucey, as party chair, had been the one who worked to help Kennedy win the primary. And it was Lucey who was at the forefront of the campaign in the state to put Kennedy in the winning column in the general election. Lucey not only was an ally and trusted worker for Kennedy but also had become a friend of the president and the president's family, especially brother Bobby. When JFK was inaugurated, Lucey was assistant deputy grand marshal of the parade from the White House to the Capitol and had the honor of sitting in the presidential box while the president-elect took his oath of office.[52]

Weeks before the inauguration, Lucey was watching the 1961 Orange Bowl and noticed the television camera focused a few times on Kennedy in the stadium. About thirty minutes after the game ended, Lucey's phone rang. It was JFK. He said he was surprised that Lucey was not on any list of people seeking an appointment in his administration and asked Lucey why not. Didn't he want something? Lucey thanked the newly elected president but said he was not interested in a move to Washington, DC. He explained that he was making more money in his real estate business than a president could pay him, was focused on being with his children, and was comfortable with his life in Madison.[53]

Lucey as a marshal at the inaugural parade for John F. Kennedy. COURTESY OF LAUREL LUCEY

President John F. Kennedy and Patrick J. Lucey in the Oval Office on August 8, 1961.
JOHN F. KENNEDY PRESIDENTIAL LIBRARY AND MUSEUM

Although Lucey turned down a federal appointment for himself, he played a major role in getting positions in the Kennedy administration for others. He compiled three lists of people he recommended for appointment: individuals who had worked hard in the Kennedy–Johnson campaign and deserved at least a small reward, those who had made major contributions by running for an office and mobilizing support for Democrats generally, and people who quite simply were very talented. Politics played little role in Lucey's recommendations. Nash, who originally had supported Humphrey but was very active in supporting Kennedy after the convention, was on the second list. Lucey felt Nash risked his own reelection as lieutenant governor when he urged voters to cast their ballots for Kennedy. Lucey also recommended John Gronouski and Edwin Bagley, who was Gaylord Nelson's press secretary at the time.[54]

Some of the most prominent names who received their appointments at least in part because of Lucey's recommendations were Bagley as press information director for the Peace Corps; Nash as a consultant of Indian Affairs in the Department of the Interior; Gronouski as postmaster general; Nestingen (former Madison mayor and head of the Wisconsin Kennedy campaign) as undersecretary of Health, Education and Welfare; Carlisle Runge as Assistant Secretary of Defense for Manpower; Norman Clapp as director of the Rural Electrification Administration; Charles Stoddard as director of technical services in the Department of Interior; and Robert Lewis as deputy director of the Department of Agriculture's Commodity Stabilization Administration. Nelson was not consulted on any of these appointments.[55]

In June 1961, prior to the state's annual Democratic Party convention, Nelson privately asked Lucey to step aside at the completion of his second term as chair. Lucey fully intended to do just that, although he had not publicly announced his plans. Nelson and Howard Meister, the Milwaukee County Democratic chair, began aggressively moving to displace and discredit Lucey.[56] Meister accused Lucey of blocking former Humphrey supporters from federal jobs, although Bagley and Nash had been prominent backers of the senator from Minnesota. Meister also felt Lucey inappropriately endorsed Reynolds in the 1958 attorney general primary against Seraphim. Nelson had appointed Meister to the state real estate board in 1959—a move considered hostile to Lucey—and Nelson appointed Seraphim to a Milwaukee District Court judgeship. Meister lined up Herman Jessen, Janet Lee (Nelson's sister), Elizabeth Tarkow, and a handful of county chairs to support Lucey's departure.[57]

Before Lucey made any announcement about not running for another term, Nelson publicly endorsed Nikolay for the position.[58] Lucey was still smarting from Nikolay's failure to keep his word and get Humphrey delegates at the Democratic National Convention to vote for Kennedy after they had been released, and he resented Nelson's pressure and the plans to have him ousted. Lucey responded with a determination to serve a third term. He garnered support from an impressive lineup: Proxmire, Reynolds, Doyle, Gronouski, Kastenmeier, Phillips, Reuss, Rabinovitz,

Elliot Walstead, John Werner, and sixty-three county chairs. Lucey issued a four-page statement touting his record as chair and aggressively attacking Meister.[59]

The expected confrontation over who would serve as chair did not take place. Just prior to the convention, Nikolay was called to active duty in the Wisconsin Thirty-Second Red Arrow Division of the National Guard. Nikolay withdrew his candidacy.

Nelson and Lucey met for a private lunch in Madison at the Simon House, a restaurant and bar near the capitol. The agenda was to smooth ruffled feelings and pledge to work together. After lunch they issued a joint press statement:

> We have engaged in an extensive discussion of the various issues that gave rise to this contest for state chairman. We have also conferred with a representative group of party leaders.
>
> As a consequence, we have resolved all of the major differences of party policy, direction, organization and purpose at issue. With this agreement we are both confident that all factions can be reunited and that we can forget past differences.[60]

Delegates met in Eau Claire and, by a vote of 918 to 67, decided to have Lucey serve an unprecedented third term. The relationship between Lucey and Nelson continued to be uneasy, but it was civil.

The year 1962 began with Lucey praising Nelson and promoting him for election to the US Senate. His endorsement could have been interpreted as a sign that all was well between the two. It also could have been seen as an only slightly subtle strategy of pressuring Nelson to vacate the governor's office and pave the way for Reynolds, Lucey's friend and colleague, to become the state's chief executive. Lucey's statement that Nelson would be a great senator included a forecast that Reynolds would be a great governor. At the time Lucey made his endorsement, Nelson had not yet decided whether he would run for another term as governor or challenge Senator Alexander Wiley and head to the nation's capital. Wiley was widely considered vulnerable, so entering the Senate race was a reasonable alternative.[61]

The contentious side of the Lucey–Nelson relationship reemerged at a time when most Democrats were celebrating. President Kennedy agreed

Gaylord Nelson and Patrick J. Lucey. WHI IMAGE ID 143818

to be the keynote speaker at Wisconsin's 1962 Jefferson–Jackson dinner, the major gala and fund-raising event of the party. The invitation was issued by party chair and friend of the president Pat Lucey, notably not by the governor. Lucey took advantage of the president's popularity to raise dinner ticket prices from twenty-five to one hundred dollars per plate and to persuade at least fifty Democrats to sponsor a full table. Although Meister and Nelson had doubts, Lucey's gamble paid off, raising seventy-five thousand dollars for the National Democratic Party and two-hundred thousand dollars for state and local candidates.[62]

Nelson was pleased the president was coming. As governor, he expected he would introduce Kennedy at the dinner. Lucey rejected that idea and said that since he had made all the arrangements, he would introduce the president. Not happy, Nelson reluctantly agreed to give a brief general welcome before Lucey introduced Kennedy.[63] To laughter from the knowing audience, Nelson declared that he liked the Democratic Party because "there is so much fighting in it." Lucey did not gloat, delivering an introduction that was short and to the point. He simply announced, "Ladies and gentlemen, the president of the United States."[64]

Beforehand, Lucey had to do some spur-of-the-moment problem-solving. Just as people were being seated, Vince Lombardi unexpectedly appeared at Lucey's side. Lombardi held a telegram from President Kennedy inviting the coach of the newly crowned champion Packers to the Jefferson–Jackson Day dinner. Since the coach had no assigned seat, Lucey ushered him to the dais and told him he was sitting next to the president. That was actually Lucey's seat. After introducing the president, Lucey quietly slipped to the wings where the press corps was covering the event and enjoyed the evening from there—without a meal.[65]

## THE 1962 ELECTION

The sales tax, an issue that Lucey and Nelson had clashed over, became a key issue in the 1962 governor's race. In 1960, Nelson had appointed a gubernatorial Blue Ribbon Tax Revision Study Commission and named Doyle as vice chair. This was viewed as a preliminary step to the introduction of a sales tax, which was pushed by Republican leaders in the state senate and opposed by Lucey, Reynolds, and Nestingen on the grounds that it was a regressive approach to raising revenue. Individuals would not pay on the basis of their ability to pay but of their need to purchase goods and services, disproportionately impacting lower income brackets. Although Nelson felt uncomfortable about the regressive nature of the sales tax, he calculated that it was necessary to balance the state's budget.[66]

Seraphim and Reynolds, the 1958 rivals for the Democratic nomination for attorney general, collaborated on a resolution to keep a kind of peace. They urged delegates to the 1960 convention to oppose a general sales tax and to praise Governor Nelson for establishing the study commission.[67] The resolution was adopted. The following year, Nelson reached a compromise with Republicans to implement a 3 percent selective sales tax—made less regressive by exempting necessities such as food and shelter.

The issue came up again at the 1962 convention in Sheboygan. Nelson faced criticism within the party for having approved the introduction of the sales tax. Lucey and Reynolds were among the most prominent dissident voices. In response to the criticism of the governor, Doyle proposed that delegates adopt a plank that recognized a need for securing revenue from a balanced combination of income and sales taxes. His proposal was rejected by the platform committee and shouted down on the convention floor. Instead, those assembled adopted a resolution that in part read, "It is our objective to repeal the selective sales tax. Revenue needs can be met far more equitably through income rather than sales taxation."[68] Nelson acknowledged what the resolution meant: "The one person on our ticket in serious political trouble is I—and I am a realist in politics and I know it."[69]

Reynolds emphasized his commitment to repealing the sales tax when he ran for governor in 1962. The Republican candidate, Philip Kuehn, helped turn the gubernatorial contest into a referendum on the sales tax by advocating going from a selective to a general tax. Kuehn argued explicitly for relying more on a sales tax and less on the income tax. Lucey and Proxmire stumped hard for Reynolds. Lucey persuaded Bobby Kennedy, then US attorney general, to keynote a fund-raising dinner for Reynolds that netted more than thirty-five thousand dollars.[70] Reynolds also benefited from woes faced by Kuehn. Although Kuehn gained some momentum from his party's endorsement at their 1962 convention, he faced an unusual and demanding challenge in the primary from Wilbur Renk. This took money from his campaign treasury that he needed in the general election.[71] In addition, distractions from Kuehn's affair with his secretary cost some loyalty and enthusiasm from his Republican base.[72] Reynolds won 637,491 to 625,536.

Nelson focused on issues other than the sales tax in his 1962 quest for a seat in the US Senate—and he won. He concentrated on issues such as the environment, Medicare, and drug prices. A central message was that Senator Wiley was beyond his prime and should not serve another six-year term.[73] Nelson had his own campaign organization, independent of the party—a pattern he had followed in the past and one that was especially critical given his problems at the convention and his cool relationship with the party chair.

Lucey did help Nelson, the tensions with the governor notwithstanding. He arranged a trip to Milwaukee by President Kennedy to promote Nelson's candidacy. Kennedy was eager to replace Alexander Wiley, who had voted against Kennedy's Medicare proposal, which lost in the Senate by only two votes earlier in the year. Nelson had pledged to vote for the program.

The president, however, did not make it to Wisconsin to stump for Nelson. Kennedy campaigned for a Democratic Senate candidate in Illinois the day before his scheduled visit to Milwaukee. The night before Kennedy was to fly from Chicago to Milwaukee, presidential aide O'Donnell told Press Secretary Pierre Salinger that "the president may have to develop a cold tomorrow."[74] The president had learned that the Soviet Union was installing missiles with nuclear warheads in Cuba and rushed back to the White House to deal with the crisis. A crowd had already gathered at Milwaukee's Billy Mitchell Field when Salinger made the announcement canceling Kennedy's visit.

On October 25, the day when United Nations Ambassador Adlai Stevenson dramatically confronted Soviet Ambassador Valerian Zorin in the Security Council meeting on the Cuban missile crisis, Kennedy sent Nelson a letter apologizing for canceling his trip to Milwaukee and praising his leadership and record as governor.[75]

International events emphasized the importance of having able people in the US Senate. As the ranking Republican member of the Senate Foreign Relations Committee, Wiley was summoned back to Washington and left the campaign trail. His message to voters was that he was experienced and needed. However, those concerned about Wiley's age became all the more anxious for him to retire. Nelson suspended his campaign and did not resume until the crisis was over—less than a week before the election.[76] When the votes were tallied, Nelson handily defeated Wiley 662,342 to 594,846.

Pundits considered the results of the 1962 elections as evidence that the successes of the Democratic Party of Wisconsin that began with the election of Proxmire to the US Senate in 1957 were not flukes.[77] Nelson's victory meant Democrats had captured both Senate seats, and Reynolds's win was the third time in a row that Democratic candidates won the governor's office. Four of the ten congressional districts had sent Democrats to Washington. Although David Carley lost the race for lieutenant governor in 1962, the party was well represented in state constitutional offices, the legislature, and county positions.

As chair, Lucey continued to build the party using his grassroots approach and to emphasize its commitment to progressive ideals. He hired Lynn Ansfield, who had just graduated with a degree in journalism from

Northwestern University, to edit and distribute the party's newsletter, the *New Wisconsin Democrat*. Over a decade after the DOC had transitioned into the Democratic Party of Wisconsin, Lucey continued to emphasize that this was not the party that had opposed the New Deal and Franklin D. Roosevelt. Ansfield sent the newsletter to more than thirty-three thousand party members each month.[78]

Lucey had reason to feel good about the status of the Democratic Party. Deciding that he would not run in 1963 for a fourth term as chair, he joined with Nelson in endorsing J. Louis Hanson of Mellen as the next chair. Hanson was a friend and protégé of Nelson. Democrats met in La Crosse for their annual convention and voted for Hanson, 716 to 170.[79]

Lucey was feted at the convention. The 1963 Democratic Party Yearbook had a special section devoted to accolades for Lucey. In part, it read:

> This man is one for the record book. Men like him are rare. He has left an indelible imprint on the pages of Wisconsin's great political history. Lucey brought the most dedicated and inspiring leadership this state's Democratic Party has ever had. His tough-minded idealism has brought success to our party and has shown that the citizen in politics can seek out and have as great a role as he may wish to have and is capable of handling the forces that mold his political system.[80]

Miles McMillin sounded a discordant note amidst all these hymns of praise. In his column in the *Capital Times*, he complained that Lucey was the source of fighting and feuding in the Democratic Party. What others saw as firm commitments to progressive principles, McMillin viewed as stubbornness and self-centeredness. Instead of crediting Lucey for breaking down racial barriers, McMillan said the state chair "caused an uproar in the party by planning and successfully promoting the election of Vel Phillips of Milwaukee for national committeewoman, the first Negro to serve on the national committee." McMillan also found fault with Lucey for supporting Kennedy and for feuding with Nelson.[81]

The column criticizing Lucey prompted a detailed and articulate response from David Adamany, which the paper included in its issue eight days later. Adamany summarized all the accomplishments Lucey had made in developing the Democratic Party as an organization and described his effectiveness as a leader. Adamany pointed out that Lucey also grew an unusually successful business and that he was devoted to his family.[82]

As he left the office of state party chair, Lucey planned to focus on his real estate business, spend more time with his family, and help President Kennedy get reelected. The campaign organization used the same model it had in 1960 in which each state would have an outside coordinator. Lucey was assigned responsibility for the crucial state of Ohio. He was about to board a plane for Cleveland when he heard the shocking news that President Kennedy had been shot while visiting Dallas. Like the rest of the world, he wept.

## CHAPTER 7

# THE PRELUDE

The period that followed the assassination of President John F. Kennedy was challenging. The murder of the president was especially traumatic for a country in the midst of tensions from the Cold War, the civil rights movement, and technological changes in production and communication. Patrick Lucey felt he lost a friend as well as a president and party leader.

Like others close to the Kennedys, Lucey had reluctantly accepted the Texas senator Lyndon B. Johnson as a vice-presidential running mate when JFK had first chosen him. But when tragedy put Johnson in the White House, Lucey and others rallied behind him as the leader of their party and their country. Initial support was cordial, although tentative.

Lucey flew with Wisconsin Governor John Reynolds and Minnesota Governor Karl Rolvaag to Kennedy's funeral on November 25, 1963. On the way, he called the White House and immediately was put through to President Johnson. Lucey wished the new president well, and they had a genial conversation. They both recalled Johnson's trip to Wisconsin in 1962 to be the keynote speaker at the annual Jefferson–Jackson dinner. Lucey had wanted to match the crowd that had gathered the previous year for Kennedy. The enthusiasm level for Johnson was much lower, however, and Lucey gave out two hundred free tickets to inflate the crowd and make the vice president feel welcome. Lucey was open about what he was doing, which took some of the luster off the celebration of Johnson's visit.[1]

Going forward, Lucey's interactions with President Johnson were neither as many nor as personal as they had been with President Kennedy. The primary focus of Lucey's energy and activity in the mid-1960s was

Wisconsin. The mid-1960s for Lucey were a prelude to the conflict and the success that would usher in the decade of the 1970s. He learned both positive and negative lessons in his first experiences as a statewide candidate, winning his bid for lieutenant governor in 1964 and losing his first run for governor in 1966. During this time, Lucey discovered the differences between campaigning and governing. Although the role of lieutenant governor was limited, he had the opportunity to help make public policy as he presided over the state senate. The process of working with other elected officials, including those of another party, was quite different from working with members of his own party to win elections.

Lucey continued to be a national player. As a progressive, he found it easy to support President Johnson on civil rights legislation and Great Society programs. But he abandoned party loyalty to oppose the increasing involvement of the United States in Vietnam.

## APPOINTMENT OF JUDGES

The appointments of John Reynolds and Jim Doyle Sr. as federal judges illustrate the blending of success and tension that Lucey and Wisconsin Democrats experienced in the mid-1960s. Wisconsin has two federal judicial districts: Eastern (which includes Milwaukee) and Western (which includes Madison). On January 13, 1963, Judge Patrick J. Stone died, leaving the Western District bench vacant. A committee of Wisconsin Democratic Party leaders met to recommend candidates to Attorney General Robert F. Kennedy, who would then make a recommendation to his brother, the president. The members of the committee were Governor Reynolds, Party Chair Lucey, Senators Gaylord Nelson and Bill Proxmire, and Congressional Representatives Robert Kastenmeier, Lester Johnson, Henry Reuss, and Clement Zablocki. They provided a list of five, in order of priority: Jim Doyle Sr., David Rabinovitz, Jack DeWitt, Robert Dean, and Frank Nikolay. The Wisconsin Bar Association submitted a list of eleven that included Doyle, but none of the others on the Democratic leaders' list.[2]

Bobby Kennedy's favorite was Rabinovitz. His least favorite was Doyle, whom he objected to because of Doyle's leadership in the 1960 effort to get Adlai Stevenson the Democratic nomination for president. Rabinovitz, on the other hand, was an early JFK supporter and had worked with Bobby on investigations for the US Senate Rackets Committee. Lucey and Reynolds had very positive working relationships with Rabinovitz but urged President Kennedy to appoint Doyle. President Kennedy, however, sided with his brother and nominated Rabinovitz on August 30, 1963.[3]

The state Democratic Party leaders communicated their support for confirmation of Rabinovitz to the Senate Judiciary Committee. Senators Nelson and Proxmire both appeared at the confirmation hearing and voiced support. However, the State Bar of Wisconsin voted two to one in a poll against Rabinovitz. They said he was not qualified because he did not live in the Western District. In addition, the state bar committee opposed Rabinovitz because of his role as attorney for the union in the historic 1954 strike against the Kohler Company. Committee members recognized the obligation of attorneys to provide clients with representation, but they didn't like the idea of having someone associated with the strikers on the federal judicial bench.[4] Influential newspaper columnist John Wyngaard made the same arguments.[5] Nelson backed away from Rabinovitz, exercising his right as one of Wisconsin's senators to force the Judiciary Committee to delay its vote by not returning his blue slip. Senate rules at the time allowed senators from the state of a judicial nominee to send a blue slip to the Judiciary Committee with a recommendation for or against approval. A failure to return the blue slip had the effect of stopping action on the nomination. Congress adjourned without acting on the nomination, and Rabinovitz began serving without having been confirmed.

After the assassination of Kennedy, Johnson renominated Rabinovitz. Senators Nelson and Proxmire reiterated their support, but Nelson again halted Judiciary Committee action by not returning his blue slip. Johnson gave up on the Rabinovitz appointment and told Nelson and Proxmire to submit new names. Proxmire recommended Reynolds. Nelson submitted both Reynolds and Doyle but pointed out that only Doyle was a resident of the Western District. While indecision continued in the nation's capital, Judge Kenneth Grubb announced that he would retire from the federal bench in the Eastern District. With two vacancies, it would seem appointments could easily be made.

Not really. Lucey, who was serving as lieutenant governor at the time, was interrupted by a call from Johnson while presiding over the Wisconsin State Senate. Johnson complained to him, "Oh, about these two judicial appointments in your state—the two senators each have a candidate, and they are a couple of losers. They couldn't get elected,* and now they want me to appoint them judge. I think there are some other qualified people up there, maybe there's a black lawyer. I want you to make up a list of people that you think are really qualified to be on the federal bench and send them to me."

Lucey responded, "Yes, Mr. President. Yes, Mr. President. Yes, Mr. President."

Then Lucey turned to his aide, David Adamany, and said, "What the hell do I do?"

Adamany advised, "Nothing. That's the President of the United States! That fellow makes about three hundred calls a day. Do you think he keeps a checklist on who calls him back and who doesn't?"[6]

They laughed, and Lucey followed Adamany's advice.

Meanwhile, Adlai Stevenson intervened. Stevenson and Johnson were very different political figures, but they had developed a close relationship when the former was the Democratic presidential nominee and the latter was Senate majority leader. Stevenson knew Doyle would distinguish himself as a federal judge and encouraged LBJ to go ahead with the appointment.[7] That nudge was all that was needed.

Johnson appointed Doyle, who was confirmed on May 20, 1965, more than twenty-seven months after the death of Judge Stone. Reynolds, on the other hand, received his appointment quickly and smoothly. He was appointed as federal judge of the Eastern District on November 13, 1965, just three months after the formal retirement of Judge Grubb.[8]

The lengthy and awkward process of appointing Doyle was embarrassing to everyone involved. After all, he had been first on the list of everyone except Bobby Kennedy. Conspiracy theories emerged. One was that President Johnson initially demonstrated deference to the Kennedy brothers in the immediate aftermath of the assassination but then abandoned Rabinovitz when given the chance to show independence. Others theorized that Lucey wanted to replace Rabinovitz as Wisconsin's committee member on the Democratic National Committee (DNC) and worked behind the scenes against Doyle and for Rabinovitz. Lucey,

---

*Reynolds had lost his bid to be reelected as governor in 1964, and Doyle had lost elections to be governor and to be a state judge.

according to this explanation, counted on Rabinovitz resigning his position on the National Committee to accept the federal judgeship, thus creating an opportunity for Lucey to join the DNC.[9] Indeed, Lucey did replace Rabinovitz in 1963 and remained on the DNC until he resigned to run for lieutenant governor. Like many conspiracy theories, the ones attempting to explain the awkward appointment of Doyle were impossible to prove, but their mere existence contributed to discord among the Democrats.

## CAMPAIGN FOR LIEUTENANT GOVERNOR

In 1964, Reynolds prepared for his bid to be reelected as governor. As part of that preparation, he suggested to Lucey, his close friend and colleague, that the two of them would make a great executive team. At that time, candidates for governor and for lieutenant governor in Wisconsin ran on separate tickets. Even though Lucey and Reynolds had to run separately, they could certainly present a united front, and if they both won, they could govern together. Lucey's response was positive, although he joked that two Irish Catholics running together wasn't exactly what he would call a balanced ticket.[10]

Lucey made the decision to run for lieutenant governor with some misgivings. The idea of serving with Reynolds was certainly a positive, and serving as lieutenant governor could be a step toward being elected as governor. But the annual salary of lieutenant governor in 1964 was only seventy-five hundred dollars ($62,000 in 2019). The responsibilities of the office in 1964 were to preside over debates and deliberations in the state senate, vote in cases of a tie, and act as governor if the incumbent could not fulfill the duties of that office.[11] Despite the drawbacks, Lucey filed nomination papers and ran a serious campaign, determined to win.[12]

No other Democrat entered the race, so Lucey from the outset focused on introducing himself to Wisconsin voters and convincing them to choose him instead of his Republican opponent, Jack Olson. Heading into the race, Olson had substantial strengths. To begin with, Olson was the incumbent lieutenant governor. He was known for the success of his businesses in the Wisconsin Dells: Dells Boat Tours and Amphibious Duck Rides. In addition, Olson had chaired the presidential campaign committee in Wisconsin for Richard Nixon. Lucey introduced his campaign plan with several assumptions, including a view that Olson was a popular incumbent. Lucey also believed that a straight party vote favored Republicans, so he would have to win support beyond the Democratic base. Finally, he asserted that he intended to either win or retire from politics.[13]

Lucey adopted as a campaign slogan one that emerged from family brainstorming at the kitchen table: "Lucey Means Business." Invariably, when Lucey was cited in a news article, he was referred to as a successful businessperson, a credential that was not normally associated with a Democrat. And, of course, the slogan also depicted Lucey as someone who was serious and would get things done.

Lucey formulated a detailed campaign plan, designed to help Reynolds and the Democratic Party generally in addition to getting himself into the lieutenant governor's office. He articulated a threefold strategy: convince opinion leaders that he knew something about state government, present an image of a successful entrepreneur who would bring business sense to a Democratic administration, and concentrate heavily on villages and small cities. The latter included developing a program to revitalize smaller communities, stressing property tax relief, and presenting antimonopoly, pro–small retailer positions.[14] Lucey noted that the Democratic Party was doing well in Milwaukee, Superior, Madison, Kenosha, and Racine, as well as with farmers. But, he observed, the party "was taking a real beating in villages and smaller cities."[15]

The plan emphasized organization. Lucey aimed to have a campaign committee in every county and specified that he needed two full-time workers, a secretary, and an aide. The secretary would work with local campaign committees, schedule events and appearances, and send press releases to all weekly and daily newspapers and to radio and television stations. The aide would drive Lucey around the state, distribute literature at various campaign events, and be of general assistance.

The campaign plan prescribed an itinerary of plant gate appearances at every major industrial company in the state and at least one appearance in every county that had a Lucey for Lieutenant Governor Committee. He wrote that in the early part of the campaign he would deliver four speeches per week, all within easy driving distance from Madison. He would return home every evening unless he was going to greet an early shift of workers and it made more sense to stay overnight near the plant. He wanted to get to his real estate office by midafternoon at the latest on as many days as possible. In the last three or four weeks of the campaign, he would have a heavier schedule allowing for several appearances every day. Lucey directed his secretary to schedule joint appearances with other Democratic candidates for local offices and to arrange as many joint appearances and debates as possible with Olson.

Lucey's plan included tasks for his two older children, Paul and Laurie. He assigned Laurie—ten years old at the time—the job of maintaining a scrapbook of press clippings. At twelve, Paul was to keep a map with colored pins that indicated where county committees existed, where Lucey made appearances, and where news stories about his father were published.[16]

As the campaign developed, Lucey found a way of involving his family in an even more active and memorable way. The entire Lucey family traveled to every county in the state. Days were sometimes packed with

Pat and Jean Lucey pose with their children, Laurie, Paul, and David, in 1966, when Pat was lieutenant governor.
WHI IMAGE ID 118672

as many as five events in as many locations. Paul, Laurie, and David (who was eight years old at the time) recalled the tour of the state with fondness despite long days and many hours in the car.[17] They enjoyed being together and learned from their father as he briefed them about the history and the leaders of each community they visited.

The year 1964 was generally a good one for Democrats, including Lucey. He beat Jack Olson: 841,970 to 801,141. In addition, Bronson La Follette was elected attorney general, Proxmire was reelected to the US Senate, and Johnson won in a landslide over Barry Goldwater, nationally as well as in Wisconsin. Wisconsin Democrats increased their numbers in both houses of the state legislature and in the delegation to the US House of Representatives. The total Democratic vote statewide for congressional seats was over sixty thousand more than that garnered by Republicans.

The big disappointment was that Reynolds lost his bid for reelection as governor. Reynolds had suffered from bitter clashes with the legislature over budget, taxes, reapportionment, and highway construction. The sales tax, in particular, was a major issue that worked against the governor. Despite his longstanding and vocal opposition to the sales tax, Reynolds felt he had to compromise with GOP senators and continue it. The abandonment of a key plank in the party platform—regardless of the reasons—was not well received by some of the most dedicated party loyalists.[18] Reynolds tagged his campaign material with "Repeal the Republican Sales Tax," but that just seemed to add to his reputation for waffling on the issue. The Republican gubernatorial candidate, Warren Knowles, hammered away at the contradictory positions Reynolds took, a strategy that won him the governorship.[19]

## LIEUTENANT GOVERNOR

Instead of a Reynolds–Lucey team providing leadership from the east wing of the Wisconsin State Capitol, Lucey would be serving with a Republican chief executive. Lucey had hoped he would be governing. Instead, he would be campaigning—as chief spokesperson for the Democratic Party and as a candidate himself for governor in 1966. In his inauguration speech, Lucey made it clear that he would be an active, visible lieutenant governor, advocating for progressive values and programs. He also made it clear that he wished Knowles well and that he would work with him as much as possible.[20] And Knowles reciprocated. The first gesture by the new governor was to suggest that Lucey represent the state at the inaugural festivities for Lyndon B. Johnson in Washington, DC. Lucey gladly accepted the offer.[21]

The role of presiding over the state senate and ruling on parliamentary procedure motions gave Lucey an opportunity to have some impact—albeit marginal—on policymaking. Whether a motion was in order could be critical to the defeat or passage of a proposal. Lucey developed working relationships and some friendships with senators on both sides of the aisle while wielding the gavel.

Lucey presided over only one tie vote in the state senate, and that was whether to create two new university campuses—one in Green Bay and the other in Kenosha, known as Parkside. Lucey broke the tie in favor of university expansion.

Wisconsin's lieutenant governor is the first person in the order of succession when the governor dies, resigns, or is removed from office. In addition, he or she becomes acting governor when the chief executive is absent from the state or too ill to perform the duties of governor. On several occasions, Knowles traveled out of state and Lucey temporarily was acting governor. Lucey was firm that when he was acting governor, he would not do anything without the explicit consent of the governor.[22] The most substantive decision Lucey made as acting governor was to call a special election in 1965 when Knowles was in Europe on a three-week trade mission. Before he left, Knowles appointed Robert Haase, the Republican minority leader in the state assembly, to be the state commissioner of insurance. Haase resigned his seat in the legislature in September, and Knowles was planning to call a special election to fill the vacancy the following April when spring elections were scheduled. Lucey, however, thought the people of Florence and Marinette Counties were entitled to representation without having to wait for half a year. He told Knowles and his staff that he wanted to announce a special election for November 16. Knowles said he disagreed with Lucey but would not object. Lucey proceeded, and the special election was held.[23] Democrats had a five-seat margin as majority party, so the special election had no impact on who controlled the assembly.

## CONFLICT OF INTEREST

Shortly after his election as lieutenant governor, Lucey resigned as a director of Continental Mortgage Insurance and placed his stock holdings in trust. The *Capital Times* had reported that both Lucey and governor-elect Knowles had investments in insurance companies that were regulated by Wisconsin's State Insurance Department and the state's Securities Department. The governor-elect and his brother, Robert, who was in the state senate and scheduled to become majority leader, owned stock in the Mortgage Guaranty Insurance Corporation of Milwaukee. That company had been at the center of a national scandal in which Bobby Baker arranged for bribes and sexual favors in return for votes in the Senate and federal contracts.[24] Baker had been an aide and adviser to Johnson when Johnson was Senate majority leader.

The *Capital Times* report was accompanied by an editorial calling on Lucey and the Knowles brothers to avoid a conflict of interest by separating themselves from involvement in those companies. Lucey did, but the Knowles brothers did not.[25]

## STAFF

It is not unusual for governors and legislators to attract the services of bright and energetic young people who treasure the opportunity to rub shoulders with prominent officials and build their résumés. What such young people lack in experience they make up for in idealism and hard work. And as lieutenant governor and later as governor, Lucey had interns and volunteers who fit this description.

Lucey attracted and mentored individuals who were especially capable of doing thoughtful analyses and who enjoyed participating in policymaking. As lieutenant governor, he established a pattern of challenging those who helped him with complex problems and important issues. He listened carefully, absorbing every detail and asking insightful, probing questions. He was demanding but also caring and nurturing.

One of those promising young people was David Adamany, who would become Lucey's chief analyst, adviser, and confidant during his years as lieutenant governor and later governor. Born in Janesville,

Wisconsin, Adamany spent much of his youth in Green Bay. He was involved in politics even before he could vote, initially as a member of Young Republicans. When he pleaded with other Young Republicans to take a stand against Joe McCarthy, however, he was booed and shunned. Disheartened, Adamany joined other progressives and left the GOP for the reinvented Democratic Party.

When Proxmire ran in the 1957 Special Election for the US Senate seat vacated by the death of McCarthy, Adamany was home for the summer from his undergraduate studies at Harvard and decided to volunteer for the campaign. He got permission to use his family's big black Oldsmobile, put a loudspeaker on the top of the car, and drove around downtown Green Bay and in nearby villages broadcasting "Vote for Proxmire."

Adamany invited his sister Doreen to help campaign. She agreed, and the next morning they got up at dawn and crossed the bridge over the Fox River to the Fort Howard paper mill. They put campaign literature on the windshields of the cars of night shift workers and then handed out material to those arriving for the first day shift. Brother and sister were back home for breakfast at seven o'clock. Then they made literature drops at the homes of voters in Brown County.[26]

Reynolds, also from Green Bay, was impressed by Adamany's enthusiasm and commitment to progressive ideas. Adamany was a regular at political gatherings and debates and invariably contributed insightful comments or asked probing questions, according to Reynolds. In 1958, Reynolds hired Adamany to work in his law office. Adamany's major role was to write press releases and generally to help Reynolds in his 1958 run against Christ Seraphim for the Democratic nomination for attorney general. When Reynolds campaigned in a particular town, his routine was to meet with the editor of the weekly newspaper and leave copies of the press releases composed for him by Adamany.

In mid-August 1958, the primary race looked very tight, and Reynolds told Adamany to work on the campaign from Madison. Reynolds arranged for Adamany to work under the supervision of Lucey, whom Adamany had not met yet. Reynolds also arranged for Adamany to stay with the Luceys. Adamany packed his bags, moved into a bedroom at the Lucey home, ate with the family (meals frequently included the Reynoldses), wrote press releases, and did whatever Lucey put on the to-do list.[27] That was the beginning of a lifelong personal and professional relationship between Adamany and Lucey—and Reynolds won both the primary and the general election.

In 1960, Adamany, at the age of twenty-four, was the national chair of Students for Kennedy. At that point, few states allowed eighteen-year-olds to vote, and the Kennedy campaign did not rely extensively on the support of young people. Nevertheless, Adamany worked closely with Lucey on the campaign in Wisconsin, and the two men got to know each other even better.[28]

Adamany graduated from Harvard Law School in 1961, passed the state bar examination, and went to work for Reynolds in the attorney general's office. Adamany and Lucey also worked together on Reynolds's successful campaign for governor in 1962. They conferred several times a week on issues, strategy, and organization, and Adamany, again, wrote many of the speeches and press releases.

Lucey and David Adamany, a close friend and longtime aid. COURTESY OF JOE SENSENBRENNER

Adamany served as Governor Reynolds's pardon counsel from January 7 to September 20, 1963. At age twenty-six, he resigned to accept an appointment by the governor to the state's three-person Public Service Commission (PSC). The PSC regulates the operations and rates of public and private power, water, and telephone utilities. Republicans objected to the appointment of such a young person to such a responsible position. They also thought he was too involved in partisan politics.[29] The state senate never confirmed his appointment, but Adamany continued serving, raising the question of whether state law required confirmation before a commissioner could take office.

Adamany resigned from the PSC to work on the 1964 campaign, devoting most of his efforts to helping Lucey in his quest to become lieutenant governor. In 1964, the lieutenant governor's office was allowed to hire only a part-time administrative assistant and a clerk. When he won, Lucey hired Adamany as his assistant. Adamany continued drafting speeches and press releases, and he advised Lucey on opinions and rulings from his chair presiding over the state senate. Lucey liked to point out that the Republican majority never rejected one of his rulings, saying, "Of course, I had a Harvard lawyer writing them."[30]

Adamany's annual salary as an aide to Lieutenant Governor Lucey was only seventy-five hundred dollars, half of what he earned on the PSC. Senator Richard Zaborski, a Democrat from Milwaukee, introduced a bill to require that the salary be raised to an amount set in accordance with policies of the state's Bureau of Personnel. Senator Walter Hollander, a Republican from Rosendale, amended the bill to allow Lucey to set the salary as he saw fit—a move widely interpreted not as a generous gesture but as a way of making Lucey vulnerable to criticism no matter what he paid Adamany.[31] Governor Knowles vetoed the bill—his first veto of the session—on the grounds that the salary should be set within limits set by state personnel rules.[32] The state senate voted 18 to 13 (with two members abstaining) to override the veto. The governor's brother, Senator Robert Knowles, joined those supporting the override, but the vote was short of the two-thirds required, and the veto was sustained.[33]

By using his pen to nix the bill, Governor Knowles rescued Lucey from an embarrassing situation. Adamany's salary, however, remained at a low level. Adamany was completing his PhD at the University of Wisconsin,

As lieutenant
governor (1965–67),
Lucey presided
over the Wisconsin
State Senate.
COURTESY OF
LAUREL LUCEY

and he secured a faculty position at Wisconsin State University in Whitewater (renamed University of Wisconsin–Whitewater in 1971) to help him
pay bills as well as to advance professionally.

Jenann Olsen filled the Lucey's clerical office position. She was hired
on Adamany's recommendation. Olsen had been working in Senator
Proxmire's Milwaukee campaign office while completing her undergraduate work at Marquette University and then in Proxmire's Senate office
in Washington, DC, after graduation. When Lucey discovered Olsen was
Catholic, he jokingly protested, saying he thought he was getting a Lutheran and that he was Catholic enough for both of them.[34]

Olsen came to Adamany's attention primarily because she was very
active in helping Democrats get elected and advocating for open housing
in Milwaukee. Olsen had a desk in the lieutenant governor's office and
worked with Adamany on press releases and scheduling. She was struck
immediately by how committed Lucey was to social justice issues and to
public ethics. Soon after she began work, Lucey had her send a campaign

contribution back to a donor because he suspected the check was part of an effort to secure appointment as a judge.

Republican state senators frequently objected to the noise that seeped into the senate chambers from Olsen's mimeograph machine, which seemed to be in constant use duplicating Lucey press releases. Under Adamany's direction, Olsen helped write the press releases as well as reproduce and distribute them.

Another noise coming from the lieutenant governor's office was the telephone. Frequently, the call was from Lucey's wife, Jean, who shared her views on any negative press coverage of her husband. Jean was particularly vocal about criticism in the *Capital Times*, which she called the "*Crap Times*," Olsen recalled. She also called Olsen occasionally for babysitting help.

For a time, Olsen also helped with driving Lucey to party meetings and campaign events. She remembered Lucey as a rather reluctant campaigner—more interested in policy issues and strategies than anything else. Lucey read a lot in the car and would sometimes talk about what he was reading, processing it in his mind. He also rehearsed for his visits by talking about the communities they were visiting and the people he would meet.[35] Jean Lucey later thought that having Olsen drive might prompt scandalous rumors and insisted that her husband have a male driver.[36] That man was David Lasker.

Lasker's first time staffing Lucey was when he filled in at the last minute for a friend and fellow student at the University of Wisconsin in Madison who was supposed to drive Lucey to a labor meeting in Milwaukee. The friend was a graduate student completing an internship in Lucey's campaign office. On the way to Milwaukee, Lasker mentioned that he and his parents had been very active in Democratic politics in New York. The two men shared stories about the Kennedy brothers and immediately formed a bond. After the meeting, Lucey had Lasker drive to the home of Reynolds, who was living in Milwaukee. Not only did Lasker enjoy the banter and the humor of the former governor and the current lieutenant governor, but he was instructed in how to make a brandy old-fashioned and how best to introduce himself to people. From the start, Lasker felt mentored and valued.[37]

Lucey shared his positive evaluation of Lasker with Adamany, who agreed and trusted Lasker with increased responsibilities. As Lucey geared up for his run for governor in 1966, Lasker organized another family tour of the state. He designed a schedule to visit all seventy-two counties in a four-week period and then accepted the invitation to do the driving and staffing.[38]

During his time as lieutenant governor, Lucey also brought two students into his office under a federally sponsored work-study program designed to give part-time employment to students from low-income families. A federal requirement was that 10 percent of the $1.50 per hour salary had to be paid from state funds. The state budget included funds for this match in the offices of governor, attorney general, secretary of state, and treasurer, but not lieutenant governor. To participate in the program, Lucey used his own private funds. The University of Wisconsin's director of student financial aid, Wallace H. Douma, however, ruled that the required match had to come from state funds and told Lucey to terminate the employment of work-study students in his office.[39] Lucey complied, but he and Adamany continued to find ways to give students opportunities to assist the lieutenant governor.

## DEVELOPMENT OF AN AGENDA

As lieutenant governor, Lucey was giving speeches and making public appearances about five times a week. Newspapers—especially the weekly ones in small towns—came to expect the seemingly constant flow of press releases. While some of Lucey's pronouncements were partisan criticisms of Governor Knowles and Republicans in the state legislature, most were proposals for change. In effect, Lucey was developing an agenda for when he would become governor.

The standard procedure was that Lucey would talk with Adamany about a problem or issue and then have Adamany write a position paper on the subject. Typically, that meant contacting an expert at the University of Wisconsin or conferring with a specialist located elsewhere. Adamany and Lucey would review the paper and discuss approaches to the issue. Adamany would then edit the paper so it could be understood easily by a wide audience and finally draft press releases and speeches, which Lucey reviewed and approved.[40]

The topics covered ways to improve the way government operated and to improve life for the citizens of Wisconsin. Lucey's agenda addressed the goals of creating a fairer approach to taxation, supporting the University of Wisconsin, guaranteeing civil rights, assisting the poor, expanding highways, and running state government more efficiently. More specifically, his plan sought to

- Lower local property taxes by increasing state aid to school districts.

- Make taxes more equitable across various income levels.

- Improve care for the mentally ill and the blind.

- Guarantee quality education for all children.

- Strengthen civil rights.

- Improve care for the poor.

- Continue commitment to conservation programs.

- Expand highways.

- Lower the legal blood alcohol level for drivers.

- Require the use of seat belts.

- Establish four-year terms for governor and lieutenant governor.

- Elect governor and lieutenant governor on the same party ticket.

- Authorize the governor to reorganize the executive branch.

- Preserve academic freedom at the state universities.

- Establish new university campuses in southeastern and northeastern Wisconsin.

- Hold Republican legislators to their 1963 promise to keep university tuition at the same level for four years.

- Use a nonpartisan commission to draw electoral district lines.

- Protect and expand the rights of workers to bargain collectively.

- Promote the unionization of dairy farmers.[41]

It seemed that from day one as lieutenant governor, Lucey was preparing for a run for governor. Lucey was active and visible in criticizing
Knowles and Republicans and advocating for an agenda of change. He was
not in the shadows checking the pulse of Knowles. Nonetheless, he had
considerable respect for Knowles and genuinely liked him. The two had a
very civil relationship.

## 1966 CAMPAIGN FOR GOVERNOR

As the 1966 elections approached, Lucey weighed the possibility of running
for reelection as lieutenant governor. After considering the amount of
time he was spending away from his real estate business to earn a very low
salary on a job with few responsibilities, he concluded that he definitely
would not seek another term. Then he thought about whether to run
for governor. Knowles was very popular and planned to seek reelection.
Democrats generally were suffering under Johnson's presidential
leadership because of growing urban unrest and opposition to the war
in Vietnam. The chances of winning were not good. However, Lucey's
success in running for lieutenant governor in 1964 demonstrated he had a
formula for winning a statewide office. Also, he was concerned that some
other Democrat might run for governor and, even if unsuccessful, gain
the kind of name recognition that would help secure a win in 1968.[42] That
scenario would keep Lucey from being governor for the foreseeable future.
He decided to go for it.

An informal start to Lucey's candidacy was a testimonial and fund-
raiser at Milwaukee's Pfister Hotel on August 13, 1965. Bobby Kennedy,
now a US senator representing New York, provided luster and helped raise
ninety thousand dollars ($711,500 in 2019) for Lucey's campaign treasury.
Les Aspin, Wisconsin's future First Congressional District representative,
chaired the event, which was attended by a capacity crowd of fourteen
hundred in the hotel's new ballroom. Kennedy did not want to take sides
at that early stage in the jockeying for Wisconsin's Democratic nomination
for governor. David Carley, a protégé of Nelson, had made it known that
he planned to run. Like Lucey, he had not made a formal announcement.
To avoid the impression that he had a favorite, Kennedy agreed to meet
Carley, with press coverage, at Milwaukee's General Mitchell Field when he

Bobby Kennedy and Patrick J. Lucey at a testimonial dinner for Lucey on August 13, 1965.
COURTESY OF DOREEN ADAMANY

flew in for the Lucey testimonial. About fifty reporters and photographers waited for a plane that never landed. After what seemed like an eternity, the group discovered that Kennedy's plane had been diverted to Timmerman Airport. Despite the awkwardness of the senator's change in plans, Carley smiled and said, "That's part of the game."[43] Lucey had engineered the diversion and told Kennedy's staff it was necessary because Timmerman was ten minutes closer to downtown Milwaukee and Kennedy was on a tight schedule.[44]

Carley rushed from Mitchell airport to the Pfister for the Lucey testimonial. Before the dinner, Carley met privately with Kennedy for about twenty minutes in his hotel suite, and Kennedy apologized for the mix-up. Afterward, Carley was seated at the far end of the long head table. The senator's remarks were clearly a tribute to Lucey, describing him as a capable progressive, but stopped short of a formal endorsement. He said, "Nobody in Wisconsin was a stronger or more important friend of [Jack] Kennedy than Pat Lucey. I'm sure his career will go on for a long time in Wisconsin. He is an outstanding public servant and friend."[45]

Carley was slighted by the Kennedy event, but he did not throw in the towel. He formally declared his candidacy on November 4, 1965, six months before Lucey took that step. Carley and his brother James were partners in Carley Capital Group, which in the 1960s to 1980s built huge projects in Madison and then in major urban centers around the United States. David Carley was close to Nelson. As governor, Nelson had appointed Carley as director of the Wisconsin Department of Resource Development. The Republican-controlled state senate repeatedly refused to confirm Carley, but Nelson kept reappointing him.[46] When Nelson went on to the US Senate, Carley wrote speeches and prepared issue papers for him. In 1962, against Nelson's advice, Carley ran for lieutenant governor and lost to Jack Olson.[47] Carley went on to become a member of the Democratic National Committee.

When Carley announced his candidacy in 1965, the common assumption in the press was that Lucey would also seek the governorship and would win the Democratic nomination.[48] Accordingly, Carley began his quest with attacks on Lucey, complaining that Lucey was a political hack and had no concern for policy issues.[49] Lucey chose to ignore the attacks but teased those who asked whether he was going to enter the race with nonanswers. A memo by Citizens for Lucey circulated in December 1965 announced that a poll showed Lucey would be the strongest Democratic candidate for governor, drawing Carley's ire. His attacks might have served to make Lucey's probable candidacy more visible.[50]

## THE 1966 CONVENTION

It wasn't until May 23, 1966, three weeks before the annual state party convention, that Lucey formally announced his candidacy. Lucey launched his official campaign with press conferences at six airports around the state.[51] Milwaukee criminal defense lawyer Dominic Frinzi and Milwaukee industrialist Abe Swed also threw their hats in the ring.

All of the candidates had the services of young, progressive, and highly educated assistants. Lucey continued to work with Adamany, who was then twenty-nine, for the 1966 race. Carley hired twenty-eight-year-old David Klingenstein to run his campaign. A native of New York and graduate of the University of Wisconsin, Klingenstein was a field director for the Democratic Party of Wisconsin when Carley appointed him. Frinzi relied on Frank Campenni, a native of Pennsylvania who had graduated with a master's degree from the University of Iowa. He had been on the staffs of Senator Proxmire and Milwaukee Mayor Henry Maier and was an instructor at the University of Wisconsin–Milwaukee when tapped by Frinzi to head his bid for the governor's office.[52]

The line between official and campaign activities of an elected official blurs at times. This is particularly true for the many part-time positions—such as lieutenant governor—in state and local governments. Lasker, for example, was an unpaid intern who worked primarily out of Lucey's campaign office, where he teamed with William Drew, Lucey's campaign manager for the 1966 run for governor. But Lasker's staff work served Lucey as lieutenant governor as well as candidate for the chief executive spot.

Linda Reivitz likewise worked out of the campaign office but supported Lucey no matter what hat he was wearing. Reivitz, who began her public service career as a student working for both Lucey and Adamany, did both routine tasks and substantive analyses. She helped with policy development and press releases and assisted Adamany with his PhD research on campaign finance. Lucey impressed her with how highly he prized good research and analysis. He responded to a comment that Reivitz made about a proposal that might be good policy but would probably not be popular by saying, "Young lady, you focus on the policy. I can take care of the politics."[53] Reivitz went on to staff US Representative David Obey and then made her mark as a policy analyst, agency manager, campaign organizer, cabinet member, and public health academic.

One of Lucey's strategies was to avoid major engagement with his rivals and to assume the posture of frontrunner. The organizers of the annual Democratic Party convention scheduled for June 11–12 in the Orpheum Theater in Madison planned for an opening session at which each of the prime gubernatorial candidates would give a keynote speech. Lucey, however, demurred, claiming that he had made a prior commitment to appear at a civic celebration in Prairie du Chien. He said he planned to be at the convention the second day and hoped planners would allow him some time then to address delegates. Carley, indignant, accused Lucey of arrogance and objected to Lucey acting like he was party boss.[54] After the public squabble was aired, Lucey, in fact, spoke at the opening session, and Carley and the other candidates spoke the next day.[55]

Much of the drama at the convention was a reprise of the Lucey–Nelson rivalry. Senator Nelson never formally endorsed Carley, but his preference was clear, and he allowed Carley to use his photo on campaign literature. Proxmire also did not make a public declaration of his choice, but most delegates assumed that his preference was Lucey.[56]

Lucey tried to blunt opposition from the Nelson camp by naming Carl Thompson as his campaign manager. A state senator from Stoughton and a previous Democratic candidate for governor, Thompson had staunchly supported Hubert Humphrey in the 1960 presidential primary. Carley countered by lining up support from George Molinaro, an assembly representative from Kenosha, who had served as speaker. Frinzi had the backing of his former boss, Mayor Maier.[57] The party adhered to its policy of not endorsing candidates.

The question of whether to support President Johnson's policies in Vietnam emerged as a major issue at the convention. The platform committee proposed that delegates support the president's policies. Proxmire spoke in favor and Nelson against. Some argued that this was not a state issue and delegates should be publicly neutral. Carley had announced his opposition to US involvement in Vietnam two weeks prior to the convention. Lucey agreed, contending in his address and in a detailed statement that delegates should not dodge the issue but instead express strong opposition to continued military action in Southeast Asia.[58] Lucey did, however, criticize Carley for exploiting the misery of US troops to gain political advantage. Lucey urged a united and clear stand without the distractions of carping against one another.

News coverage of the convention was favorable to Lucey. John Wyngaard labeled Lucey as the clear frontrunner and praised him both for his positions and for his civil, working relationship with Republican Governor Knowles. Wyngaard cautioned that Democrats might suffer because of their internal divisions, although in any case they would have a very difficult time unseating the popular Knowles.[59] Lucey also scored with the *Capital Times*. The progressive Madison newspaper had treated him with skepticism and favored Carley. Nonetheless, Lucey's position on Vietnam notably earned editorial commendation.[60]

## THE PRIMARY

After the delegates adjourned, Lucey resumed campaigning in earnest. He set a frenetic pace and again emphasized a grassroots approach to earning voter support. The days were filled with traveling the state visiting plant gates and meeting with people. He adopted "Lucey Means Leadership," another slogan generated by family brainstorming, as the major theme.[61] The slogan was part of a message that Knowles was a nice guy but not an effective leader.

The family did another tour of the state, much like the one featured in the 1964 campaign for lieutenant governor. This time, Lasker organized the visits and did the driving and staffing. He designed an intense and sometimes grueling schedule that included all seventy-two counties in a four-week period. Jean Lucey was concerned about everyone's health and sanity. According to Lasker, she could be very hard on staff and second-guess their work, but she deferred to him on the trip logistics, and they developed a good working relationship.[62] Lasker and the children enjoyed each other's company and developed lifelong friendships. They got a running commentary from their father about politics in the state—and sampled lots of pie.[63]

After a number of trips, each of the children was able to give their father's stump speech almost word for word. When Lucey realized this, he occasionally invited them to give the speech while he looked on with pride.[64]

Lucey's campaign focused on the agenda he had been outlining since his inauguration as lieutenant governor. He also criticized Knowles for his lack of leadership and initiative. He made a parody of the campaign slogan Knowles used in 1964: "Had Enough?"[65] He spent little time responding to attacks from Carley, Swed, and Frinzi.

In August, the month before the primary, Frinzi leveled ethics charges against both Carley and Lucey. He alleged that the two top Democrats running for governor had conflicts of interest from insurance investments and real estate involvement. Adamany responded for Lucey, noting that Lucey had resigned as a director of Continental Mortgage Insurance Company and placed all his stock in that company into a blind trust. Adamany also pointed out that Lucey had ordered his real estate firm to avoid handling any purchases or sales that involved state property. Adamany went on to note that Carley, in contrast, did continue to serve as a director of Continental Mortgage and a Milwaukee bank. Also, Carley was vulnerable to attack because he was purchasing more stock in Continental Mortgage.[66]

Carley responded to both Frinzi and Adamany. He charged that his accusers ignored his statement that he would divest himself of all holdings in regulated companies if he were elected governor. Carley also said Adamany was wrong when he wrote that Carley was purchasing more stock in the mortgage insurance company. He threatened to sue Lucey for libel.[67] The flap created headlines but nothing more.

As anticipated, Lucey won the September 13 primary (see results in table 7.1). Lucey was strongest in Milwaukee, Waukesha, Racine, Kenosha, small towns, and rural areas. Carley beat Lucey handily in the Madison area, winning 40 percent of the vote in Dane County compared to Lucey's 18 percent.[68] In the contest for the Democratic nomination for lieutenant governor, State Senator Martin J. Schreiber bested Jerome Grant, 172,245 to 78,226.

**TABLE 7.1.** Democratic Primary Results for Governor, 1966

| | |
|---|---|
| Patrick Lucey | 128,359 |
| David Carley | 95,803 |
| Dominic Frinzi | 44,344 |
| Abe Swed | 15,362 |

Source: *The Wisconsin Blue Book 1968* (Madison: Wisconsin Legislative Reference Bureau, 1968), 703.

The winning Lucey campaign spent more than eighty-five thousand dollars, and runner-up Carley spent almost forty-five thousand dollars in the primary.[69] (In 2019 dollars, those amounts are $672,000 and $356,000.)

Frinzi and Swed joined the celebration at Lucey headquarters in Milwaukee to pledge their support as soon as it was apparent that Lucey had won the nomination. The next morning, Frinzi joined Lucey at plant gates. Carley was slower to throw his support behind his opponent. He complained of Lucey's close ties to the Kennedys—calling it "Kennedyitis"— and was unhappy that Nelson had not been more active in his support, especially since Proxmire did campaign for Lucey. Carley said, "I'm not miffed, but apparently Senator Proxmire has more regard for his supporters than Senator Nelson does for his."[70]

Carley did make a public statement supporting Lucey after meeting with him for an hour and a half at Lucey's residence. Carley went to the meeting with a set of conditions. He sought a pledge that Lucey would support Nelson in his expected bid in 1968 for reelection and refrain from directing or controlling the selection of delegates to the 1968 Democratic National Convention to nominate a presidential candidate. He also asked Lucey to promise to work to eliminate the dummy building corporation method of circumventing the state debt limit, develop a strong urban affairs program, and investigate automobile insurance rates and policy cancellations. Carley said he hoped that he would be calling Lucey governor after November 8.

## GENERAL ELECTION

Lucey thanked Carley for his endorsement and made it clear that he made no commitments to his former opponent. Lucey also received a telegram from Nelson pledging to actively campaign for him. In an important show of party unity, Humphrey, Lawrence O'Brien, Bobby Kennedy, and Ted Kennedy also scheduled visits to the state to promote Lucey's candidacy.[71] These appearances also sought to energize voters. Only 20 percent of eligible voters had participated in the primary.[72]

Ted Kennedy's visit presented a challenge. He was scheduled to speak on October 27, 1966, on the University of Wisconsin campus in Madison, where students were likely to lead protests against American military involvement in Vietnam. University policies required that a student organization sponsor activities of outside groups on campus. Keith Clifford had approached Lucey to offer the assistance of UW Young Democrats for his gubernatorial campaign. Lucey was surprised because the UW Young Democrats had a reputation as more of a debating club than an active political organization. Lucey responded with two requests: that they sponsor Ted Kennedy's appearance on campus and that they contact Reivitz for assignments to engage in some shoe-leather campaigning by distributing bumper stickers and campaign literature. Clifford, whose family had been very active as Democratic Progressives, accepted on behalf of his club.[73]

The protocol was for the sponsoring campus organization to introduce the visiting celebrity or program. Lucey shared his concern about possible

Lucey, Ted Kennedy, and Keith Clifford at a rally at the Stock Pavilion at the University of Wisconsin–Madison on October 27, 1966. COURTESY OF KEITH CLIFFORD

protest activity and wanted to be sure that whoever introduced Kennedy and the other Democratic dignitaries would help neutralize rather than inflame any disruptive activity. Given his close ties to Clifford's family, Lucey was confident in Keith. The Stock Pavilion, where the Kennedy event took place, was filled beyond capacity with supporters and protesters. What was not fully anticipated was how loud and disruptive the protesters' heckling would be. The crowd was quiet and respectful for their fellow student, Clifford, but no one else on the dais could complete a sentence before being shouted down. Kennedy invited one of the protesters to come on stage and speak. The student voiced the protesters' anti-war views, but the tactic did not quiet the protest. Kennedy was unable to resume, and everyone left.[74]

This was a new and shocking instance in which anti-war protesters had made it impossible for a speaker to address a crowd. The event was featured in headline news on national television as well as in major newspapers around the country. It was all the more jarring because the major speaker was Ted Kennedy, himself an opponent of US military activity in Vietnam.

Clifford and the Young Democrats got more than ten thousand student signatures on a letter issuing a public apology for the disruption.[75] Even though Lucey, Kennedy, and other officials agreed that the United States should get out of Vietnam, their message was lost because all the attention was given to the behavior of the protesters. Lucey publicly and in private discussions with his children made a distinction between dissent and how it is expressed. He opposed Johnson's policy, but he also opposed disruption and, especially, violence.[76]

Lucey assessed his chances of beating Knowles as a long shot.[77] The year 1966 was generally not a good one for Democrats. President Johnson no longer enjoyed the support that fueled his landslide victory in 1964. Uneasiness with Vietnam was growing. As racial tensions flared, the country reeled from riots in Harlem, Philadelphia, Watts, Cleveland, and Omaha.

Superficially, Wisconsin seemed isolated from the unrest rocking other parts of the country. Unemployment was low, and the economy was doing well. Not too far below the surface, however, anxieties and tensions simmered. Those would be manifest in the summer of 1967, when Milwaukee and 159 other cities would reel from violence, burning, looting, and shootings. In the lead-up to the election of 1966, Knowles was a source of calm and security. He would not enflame. He was liked and appeared distinguished and in control.

Patrick J. Lucey and Warren Knowles on June 22, 1971.
*CAPITAL TIMES*

Lucey was among those who liked Knowles, but his job was to find fault and give voters reason to elect a new governor. Lucey recalled bumping into Knowles in the state capitol in the midst of the campaign and Knowles saying, "Well, I suppose you've been out giving me hell." And Lucey replied, "Well, gosh, Warren, isn't that what I'm supposed to do?"[78]

Knowles was vulnerable to Lucey's charge that he had not demonstrated much leadership in his two years in office. He neither introduced major initiatives nor addressed any crises, taking the approach that it was up to the legislature to consider and pass new laws and programs. The role of the governor, in his mind, was to decide whether to sign or to veto. Lucey played on a common image of Knowles by emphasizing his penchant for ribbon cutting.[79] When Lucey emphasized issues in his own campaign and challenged Knowles to debate, Knowles refused. To dramatize Knowles's avoidance of policy discussion and debate, Lucey placed an empty chair next to himself at speaking engagements.[80]

Lucey had to combine his general criticism of Knowles with more specifics. An improbable issue—but only in retrospect—was colored oleomargarine. Emotions ran high in 1966 when residents in America's Dairyland debated whether to lift the ban on selling colored oleo. It was legal in Wisconsin to sell margarine that was an unattractive and unappetizing white blob accompanied by a yellow substance that one could mix with the margarine to make it look like butter. But if you wanted already colored oleo, you had to cross the border and purchase it in a neighboring state. Lucey broke with his background in agriculture and incurred the wrath of dairy farmers by supporting the right to purchase fake butter in Wisconsin grocery stores. Knowles took no position on the issue, leaving it up to the legislature to decide. Milwaukee Common Council Member Vel Phillips quipped: "Whoever is going to win this election is going to do so by the slimmest of margarines."[81]

Lucey also argued for more state regulation over automobile insurance rates and policy cancellations. Again, Knowles did not declare himself. Lucey pointed out that the rate increases were based on a formula conceived in 1921, and state law put no limits on the cancellation of policies. Lucey called for a thorough investigation of the automobile insurance industry and the enactment of protections for consumers. He favored no-fault insurance in which payments did not depend on the determination of fault in an accident. In polls, concerns about insurance ranked second in voters' minds to colored oleo. Despite protests, neither racial tensions nor the war in Vietnam ranked among the top issues in Wisconsin in 1966.[82]

Ethics was another major topic in Lucey's campaign speeches and literature. He reminded voters that Warren and Robert Knowles continued to profit from stock they owned in a mortgage insurance company regulated by state government. They refused to follow his example of avoiding a conflict of interest by placing stock in a blind trust.

Knowles blunted Lucey's attacks on water pollution, open housing, and technical and vocational education. The governor had initially opposed accepting federal funds to control water pollution but then successfully worked with the Democratic majority in the state assembly to pass a bill that Secretary of the Interior Stewart Udall called model legislation. Knowles responded to a Democratic bill on open housing by agreeing to a weaker measure. He then diverted possible white backlash by calling out the National Guard to end street demonstrations objecting to public officials joining the whites-only Eagles Club in Milwaukee. Similarly, Knowles dodged Lucey barbs on deficiencies in Wisconsin's vocational education options by proposing nineteen bills making improvements.[83] In short, Knowles was primarily reactive as a leader. He shored up his image as a moderate Republican more interested in calming the public than in bold problem-solving, robbing Lucey of campaign targets.

Knowles and Lucey publicly agreed on a number of issues. They both, for example, opposed merging the state's two public university systems. Wisconsin had one system, started in 1866, that had evolved from teacher training schools. It included nine colleges and in 1964 was dubbed the Wisconsin State University System. In addition, the University of Wisconsin existed as an entirely separate higher education system with campuses at Madison and Milwaukee and new ones at Green Bay and Kenosha (known as Parkside). The state had two boards of regents, one for the state universities and one for the University of Wisconsin. The state's Coordinating Committee for Higher Education was supposed to oversee the two systems and their respective boards. Both Lucey and Knowles expressed satisfaction with this arrangement, although Lucey would change his mind later in his career.[84]

Although Lucey had distinguished himself as a leading advocate for open housing and civil rights generally, leaders in Milwaukee's African American community criticized him. In the waning days of the 1966 campaign, Jean Lucey attended a meeting sponsored by the Sixth Ward Political Education Committee to encourage African Americans to vote for her husband. It seemed like it would be an easy sell. The Milwaukee Youth Council of the National Association for the Advancement of Colored People (NAACP) had sponsored weekly civil rights demonstrations since August and voiced its objection to remarks by Knowles that the Youth Council was misguided. But when Jean Lucey reminded those at the meeting about Lucey's civil rights record, she was rebuffed by Milwaukee County Supervisor Isaac N. Coggs, who said that Lucey "failed to recognize the Negro political leadership in this community" and demanded that Lucey issue a policy statement on civil rights. Coggs went on to challenge Lucey to lead a NAACP demonstration scheduled for Sunday, November 6.[85]

Jean Lucey and County Supervisor Coggs traded accusations, and the decibel level went up. Others at the meeting joined the discussion. Jean was not normally intimidated easily, but she left the meeting in tears. Newspapers featured a photo of an angry Coggs pointing his finger at Jean, who is looking away, seemingly in defeat.[86] The confrontation was not helpful. When the Youth Council contacted Lucey while he was campaigning in Sheboygan, he said he would have to check his schedule before responding to the invitation to lead the demonstration. He did not accept.

Lucey had little to cheer about as the campaign drew to an end. Knowles had received the endorsement of every newspaper in the state, except for the *Capital Times*, which refused to endorse any candidate.[87] And Lucey was strapped for cash. He could not afford more than a token media buy in the last weeks. Knowles, however, had a surge of favorable ads and news coverage in the weeks just prior to Election Day.[88]

## The Last Day

Lucey ran hard but continually encountered frustrations. The day prior to the election was a microcosm of the challenges. After little more than two hours of sleep, Lucey arose at four thirty in Manitowoc to greet workers at plant gates. He and Bronson La Follette, who was running for attorney general, arrived at the side entrance of a small hydraulic coupling firm. La Follette shook hands with the relatively few workers who arrived and passed each on to Lucey, whom he introduced as "your next governor."

Meanwhile, campaign volunteers put bumper stickers on the twenty-five cars in the parking lot.

Lucey and La Follette then rushed to the Mirro aluminum plant but missed the bulk of those showing up for their shift because they were at the wrong door. In Two Rivers, Lucey was shown to the management gate at Schwartz Manufacturing, a maker of milk filters. In other words, he greeted Republicans!

Back in Manitowoc, at a breakfast with party workers and other candidates, Lucey noted a generally high level of apathy. Issues had not caught the attention of most voters. When Lucey met people on the street or at plant gates, few recognized him. After a quick taped interview with a reporter from a radio station, Lucey walked around downtown hoping to greet more voters. The streets and shops were almost deserted. Again, he had focused his time in the wrong place. On the way out of town, he was driven through an area where the streets were crowded.

Lucey then went to Ripon, the town that boasts the birthplace of the Republican Party. Due to a miscalculation in the scheduling, he arrived so late at Ripon College that a segment of his audience had to leave for afternoon classes shortly after he started to speak. As was his nature, Lucey remained cheerful and relaxed, despite the day's developments—or lack thereof. He was due in Milwaukee but spent time walking through Ripon greeting the few people who were on the sidewalks.

When he arrived in Milwaukee, he went straight to his hotel room to rest, bathe, and shave. He looked refreshed as he addressed a group of mobile home owners. They wanted to hear his views on zoning ordinances that restricted the location of trailer parks. Lucey took a pass, explaining that he did not know enough about the issue and therefore should not make any promises. Instead, he called for consumer protection generally and repeated his stand against the ban on colored oleo.

Lucey left for a Democratic rally, where Carley introduced him and urged support for his erstwhile rival. Father Roger Lucey, one of Lucey's Jesuit brothers, was also at the rally. In a short, private moment, Roger told his brother, "You have to work harder."

"I got two and a half hours sleep last night," Lucey responded.

"Quit crying about yourself," his unsympathetic sibling said. "There will be plenty of time to sleep after the election."[89]

Lucey's twenty-two-hour day ended at a Madison television station, where he and La Follette fielded questions from around the state. He ended the half-hour program with a blast against Knowles for his ties to insurance companies and a call for a thorough review of the state's insurance laws and regulations.

## The Results

Knowles defeated Lucey 626,250 to 538,797. Despite the results, Lucey began the day after the election greeting workers as they arrived at American Motors and Allis Chalmers to thank them for their support.

As anticipated, 1966 was a very good year for Republicans. They won all of the statewide constitutional offices except for attorney general. La Follette handily beat Louis Ceci. Schreiber, who would run again in 1970—and win—lost his bid for lieutenant governor to Jack Olson, who then became the Republican candidate for governor in 1970. Democrats lost two of their five representatives in Congress and lost their majority in the state assembly.

Lucey did well in medium-sized towns around the state, but he lost normally Democratic Dane County by an astonishingly large margin. The Madison-area voters favored Knowles 43,249 to 27,976 (64.7 percent), which Lucey blamed on the lack of support for his candidacy from the *Capital Times*. Voter turnout statewide was generally low, and Lucey was especially disappointed that more residents of Milwaukee did not go to the polls. The suspicion was that poor weather and the confrontation between Jean Lucey and Isaac Coggs were factors.[90]

Lucey identified several other reasons for his defeat and for the overall poor showing of Democrats. Clearly, the unhappiness with President Johnson clouded Democratic chances. Closer to home, he cited the lack of Democratic candidates for many offices and the financial drain of his primary battle against Carley. Lucey probably lost farm votes due to his support for the sale of colored oleo, while Knowles had success avoiding issues.[91]

Lucey dodged questions about whether he would run again, but he had already decided he would not run in 1968. He wanted to focus on his family and the real estate business that he and Jean had been growing so

successfully, and he anticipated being occupied in some way in presidential politics. Also, Lucey anticipated that Knowles might run again, and
losing to him a second time would probably doom Lucey's chances of ever
becoming governor. Lucey knew that La Follette was interested in running
for governor in 1968, and he was happy to let him go for it. Lucey would
consider his options again as the 1960s came to a close.[92]

## CHAPTER 8

# TRAGEDIES AND REFLECTION

V iolence and death were ever present in the late 1960s. They haunted the entire country and, on a personal level, Pat Lucey. The Cold War and the threat of nuclear war continued to cause general anxiety. Thousands of Americans and Vietnamese died as the United States escalated conflict in Southeast Asia. Protests intensified and spread. As David Maraniss demonstrated in *They Marched into Sunlight*, violence in the peace movement paralleled violence in the combat areas.[1]

Riots and shootings made parts of American cities, including Milwaukee, seem like war zones themselves at times. For the most part, urban unrest pitted African American neighborhoods, frustrated with racial injustice, against white police forces and white city and state officials.

Amidst the unrest, several assassinations of political and civil rights leaders rocked the country and affected Lucey personally. These events created a tense backdrop for the Democratic primary season, culminating in a notoriously chaotic and violent scene at the nominating convention in Chicago.

## RUN, BOBBY, RUN!

In the fall of 1967, Allard Lowenstein, Curtis Gans, and Midge Miller led a Dump Johnson movement. This trio, led primarily by Lowenstein, was appalled by President Lyndon B. Johnson's continued escalation of US military action in Vietnam. They wanted Democrats at their 1968 National Convention to refuse to nominate Johnson for another term, and they wanted US troops out of Vietnam. Miller was from Madison, Wisconsin, and would be elected to the state assembly in 1970. Gans was on the faculty of American University and a political activist. Lowenstein had been president of the US National Student Association and wrote Robert F. Kennedy's famous "Day of Affirmation Address" delivered to the National Union of South African Students at the University of Cape Town in 1966—a courageous statement in then-apartheid South Africa.[2]

Lowenstein formed the Committee of Concerned Democrats to serve as the clearinghouse for anti-Johnson activities. He, Gans, and Miller believed that the Dump Johnson effort needed to have an alternative candidate. Their first choice, by far, was Senator Bobby Kennedy.[3]

Kennedy shared their opposition to Johnson's policies in Vietnam, and he was very concerned about the rioting in cities. But he considered it more than a long shot that anyone, including him, could deny a sitting president the chance to run for reelection. He knew that some considered him a ruthless Machiavellian politician. They would not understand his principled reasons for running but instead would assume he was selfishly taking advantage of his kinship to a martyred president. In addition, Kennedy had a deep-seated, serious fear that he, like his brother, would be the target of an assassin.[4] He suggested that Senator George McGovern be approached. McGovern in turn suggested Senator Eugene McCarthy.

Kennedy struggled with what he should do, even after suggesting McGovern should run. Kennedy convened several sessions of family, friends, and members of his staff to discuss the pros and cons of becoming a presidential candidate. He received conflicting advice.[5] Lucey was among those who initially discouraged him from tossing his hat in the ring. Lucey argued that the odds of beating an incumbent president of your own party were low, and a run against Johnson might doom Kennedy's long-term chances of getting into the White House.[6]

The surprise attacks launched by North Vietnamese forces on January 31, 1968, played a major role in persuading Kennedy to do battle with the president. The Tet Offensive, as it was called because it began as the Vietnamese celebrated the beginning of the lunar new year, exacted a huge human cost on all sides and exposed major US and South Vietnamese vulnerabilities. Kennedy was especially upset with Johnson and his military chiefs for downplaying the seriousness of the North Vietnamese offensive and escalating American involvement even more. He had been critical of Johnson's policies before. After Tet, Kennedy's opposition was sharp and clear.[7]

Richard Daley, mayor of Chicago and kingmaker in the Democratic Party, acted to forestall a nomination contest between Johnson and Kennedy. He suggested that the president establish a task force with a broad mandate to review US policies and options in Vietnam, with Kennedy as a member. Ted Sorensen, speechwriter and a top aide to President John F. Kennedy, facilitated Daley's suggestion. Although both Johnson and Bobby Kennedy initially supported the task force idea, they were slow to agree on the details.

Meanwhile, in November of 1967, McCarthy had launched his campaign for the Democratic presidential nomination. Most regarded McCarthy's quest as quixotic, and a major part of his campaign strategy was to keep expectations low.[8] Shockingly, McCarthy garnered 42 percent of the vote in the March 12, 1968, New Hampshire primary. Johnson got 48 percent—way too close for a sitting president.

Bobby Kennedy grew frustrated with negotiations with Johnson over the mission and makeup of the proposed task force. Increasingly, it seemed that the president was scheming to get a report that endorsed his policies of militancy and escalation. It was time for Kennedy to run or to announce his support for McCarthy.[9]

At the same time, Lucey was changing his mind about whether Kennedy should run. Lucey, too, was frustrated with Johnson. The president's response to every development was to escalate US involvement in Vietnam, and he was not being honest with the American people. While riding home from Mass one day, Lucey discussed the issue with his daughter, Laurie, a high school student who opposed the war. She asked her dad, "Well, if you're against the war and there's only one guy running against Johnson, why don't you support him?" Lucey agreed but felt that McCarthy was not the candidate who could succeed. It was time to get Kennedy to topple the president.[10]

Bobby Kennedy sent his brother Ted to the Northland Hotel in Green Bay—scene of the constitutional meeting of Wisconsin's Democratic Organizing Committee in 1949—where McCarthy and his staff were planning a push for support in the April 2 Wisconsin primary. Ted Kennedy arrived on March 15 with a briefcase and a proposal. McCarthy, however, refused to see what was in the briefcase and did not want to entertain any proposal. He said he had learned that Bobby had scheduled a press conference for the next day. McCarthy said he planned to stay in the race, and that if Bobby Kennedy wanted to run, he should limit himself to primaries that McCarthy had not entered. If both Kennedy and McCarthy did well, Johnson might bow out.[11]

That night, Bobby Kennedy called Lucey. He told him that the next day he was going to announce his candidacy for the Democratic presidential nomination. Kennedy wanted to talk to Lucey about what he should say in the announcement. Lucey tracked down David Lasker to ask his advice before getting back to Kennedy. Lasker recalled being flabbergasted by the news. He could not remember what he suggested, only that Lucey thanked him and said he would share it with Kennedy.[12] On March 16, 1968, Bobby Kennedy made it official: He was running for president.

A few days later, at a dinner party, Jackie Kennedy took Arthur Schlesinger aside and said, "Do you know what I think will happen to Bobby? The same thing that happened to Jack."[13]

Johnson regarded Kennedy as a formidable foe and had feared the senator would run against him. He decided to drop out of the presidential race rather than be unceremoniously ousted.[14] On March 31—three days before the Wisconsin primary—Johnson addressed the nation on television and said he would retire to Texas at the end of his term.

The contenders for the Democratic nomination were now McCarthy, Kennedy, and Vice President Hubert Humphrey. Only one-third of the states had primaries in 1968, and Humphrey decided that he would not enter any of them, instead counting on support from party bosses and elected officials. McCarthy and Kennedy would get delegates by scoring primary victories and demonstrating they had the level of voter support needed to win in November.[15]

Kennedy was too late to get on the ballot for the Wisconsin primary and encouraged voters to cast their ballots for McCarthy. McCarthy did very well, receiving 56 percent of the votes. Johnson, whose name was still on the ballot, got 35 percent. Write-in ballots for Kennedy accounted for the remaining six percent.

After he declared as a candidate, Kennedy headed to Indiana for its primary on May 7. He asked Lucey to join him. The contest there was between Kennedy, McCarthy, and Indiana Governor Roger Branigin, who was running as a favorite son.

While Kennedy was stumping in the Hoosier State, the Reverend Martin Luther King Jr. was making trips to Memphis, Tennessee. After devastating riots in Newark, New Jersey, and Detroit, Michigan, in 1967, King devoted his attention to the pursuit of economic justice. He initiated the Poor People's Campaign to focus on eliminating race-based discrimination in employment and housing. The Poor People's Campaign was to be an alternative to riots for those frustrated and angered by conditions in cities.

King met several times with sanitation workers who were striking for better working conditions, grievance procedures, and compensation, and spoke at community rallies supporting them. On April 4, James Earl Ray shot and killed the civil rights leader as he stood on the second balcony of the Lorraine Motel. King had just delivered a speech at Mason Temple in which at one point he seemed to be prophesizing his death.

Kennedy and Lucey learned of King's assassination on the way to a rally in an African American neighborhood of Indianapolis. Those gathered had not yet learned the terrible news. Police officers cautioned against going ahead with the event, but Kennedy insisted on speaking to the crowd briefly. Police left Kennedy to proceed on his own. The rally site didn't have a stage, so Kennedy, Lucey, and several others climbed onto a nearby flatbed truck.[16]

Kennedy tossed aside the speech he was going to give. As he began, the crowd cheered loudly and waved signs high. He said, "Ladies and gentlemen, I'm only going to talk to you for a minute or so this evening because I have some very sad news for all of you. Could you lower those signs please?" The crowd was quiet, very quiet.

He continued, "I have some very sad news for all of you and I think sad news for all of our fellow citizens and people who love peace all over the world. And that is that Martin Luther King was shot and was killed tonight in Memphis, Tennessee."

Kennedy was silent as he tried to contain his emotion. He had never made a public comment about what happened in Dallas on November 22, 1963, until that moment. He said he still grieved for the loss of his brother and acknowledged that some may feel anger as well as sadness. He urged everyone to honor King by renouncing violence and lawlessness and instead turning to prayer.

The would-be rally had taken on the atmosphere of a funeral, as the crowd stood quiet and crying. They soon dispersed.

As Kennedy left, he told Lucey and others around him, "That could have been me."[17]

Around the country, people reacted to King's assassination with rioting, burning, and looting, causing numerous arrests, injuries, and killings. In Washington, DC, alone, police arrested more than six thousand rioters, and ten people were killed. Indianapolis, which reacted with anger and mourning but no violence, was an exception.

Kennedy ran hard in Indiana. He competed with McCarthy for the college student vote and reached out to African American communities and to low-income whites in rural areas. Lucey organized a get-out-the-vote drive that included sound trucks meandering on streets in the cities broadcasting Kennedy's pleas for support.[18] When the votes were counted, Kennedy won with 42 percent, Branigin got 31 percent, and McCarthy got 27 percent. A poll conducted by Newsweek indicated that if Branigin had not been in the race, Kennedy would have beaten McCarthy 61 to 39 percent.[19]

Kennedy had little time to celebrate. Nebraska had its primary the next week. In Nebraska, the secretary of state lists on the primary ballot the names of those he or she identifies as likely to run. Those who do not want to run have to so declare to have their names removed. While some advisers thought Kennedy would lose in conservative Nebraska and counseled him to stay out of the state, Sorensen, a native Cornhusker, persuaded Kennedy to leave his name on the ballot. Humphrey was not included because, at the time the ballot was constructed, Johnson was still in the race. The secretary of state deleted Johnson's name when he announced he was not seeking reelection. Consequently, Nebraska was a head-to-head contest between McCarthy and Kennedy.[20]

Lucey had been splitting his time between Indiana and Nebraska and headed to the latter in an intense—almost frantic—effort to get voter support. He was helped by Les Aspin, Linda Reivitz, and others from Wisconsin, as well as by Mark Shields, who was a legislative assistant to Senator Bill Proxmire. Shields went on to become a nationally syndicated columnist and commentator.

Also working with Lucey was Don O'Brien, an activist from Iowa, and Ted Sorensen's brother, Phil Sorensen, who had served as Nebraska's lieutenant governor from 1965 to 1967. Kennedy did not make clear who was in charge of the Nebraska campaign, thinking that several people would assume responsibility and they would all work hard. Lucey knew of this approach and suggested to O'Brien, "Let's let Phil think he's running the thing, but if we see him doing something stupid, we'll counteract it."[21]

To make good use of the short amount of time available to campaign in Nebraska, Kennedy wanted to do a whistle stop tour of the state. Phil Sorensen focused on that project. He arranged for a train that started in Cheyenne, Wyoming, and crossed Nebraska, stopping at every station along the way. Lucey took charge of getting as many people as possible to see and cheer the candidate.

Lucey assigned Shields the task of going to every courthouse along the route and getting the names of every registered Democrat in the county. Securing these names was possible because in Nebraska, unlike in Wisconsin, voters indicated their party affiliation when they registered to vote. Lucey then had Bobby Kennedy sign a letter encouraging attendance at the whistle stop. Lucey sent the letter and addresses to Steve Smith, Kennedy's brother-in-law, in the Washington, DC, campaign office to duplicate and mail. After three days, Smith called Lucey and said that the volunteers stuffing the envelopes had made a mistake, and the home addresses on the letters did not match the home addresses on the envelopes. It would obviously be embarrassing for recipients to get letters that were meant for someone else. Lucey told Smith to extract the letters and put them in window envelopes to make sure they went to the right people.[22]

The effort was worth it. The attendance at each stop was impressive and drew enthusiastic crowds from entire counties rather than just the immediate community. Kennedy won the Nebraska primary with 53 percent of the vote. McCarthy got 31 percent, and Humphrey earned 9 percent as a write-in candidate.

The campaign moved on to Oregon, South Dakota, and California. Lucey, Reivitz, Shields, and others packed their bags and continued to advance Kennedy's candidacy. Oregon, one of the strongest anti-war states in the country, was a disappointment although not a surprise. Oregonian Wayne Morse had been the first senator to oppose US military action in Vietnam. McCarthy had an early and sound lead in the state, and Kennedy was derided as "Bobby Come Lately." Kennedy would have skipped that primary, but Oregon put candidates on the ballot without their consent. Candidates could not remove their names unless they renounced their candidacies nationally, not just in Oregon.[23] McCarthy beat Kennedy 44.7 percent to 38.8 percent—the first defeat in a primary suffered by any Kennedy.

The South Dakota and California primaries were both on June 4, and California in particular was considered essential both for delegates and for momentum.[24] Lucey helped in northern California, where he sensed that things were going well. On Sunday, June 2, Kennedy was with Lucey and asked if he would talk strategy with him the day after the two primaries. They would meet at the Ambassador Hotel in Los Angeles, where Kennedy would be on election night. Lucey spent the next two days going door to door in San Francisco and flew to Los Angeles late on Tuesday, June 4. When he landed, he took an airport limousine instead of a cab to save a little money, even though it would take longer to get to the hotel. Lucey thought it would be fine to be a little late for what he presumed would be a victory party.

Lucey arrived at the Ambassador to find bedlam and chaos. Several women rushed by him in tears. He wondered if Kennedy had just announced he was withdrawing from the race in favor of McCarthy.[25] As he entered the ballroom where people had gathered to celebrate the primary wins in both California and South Dakota, Lucey heard Steve Smith asking everyone to stay calm and to please leave. Bobby Kennedy had just been shot.[26]

Kennedy died at 1:44 a.m. on June 6 after valiant but futile efforts to save him. Devastated once again by the loss of a political ally and friend, Lucey returned to Wisconsin.

On July 19, Lucey addressed two thousand delegates assembled in Milwaukee at the annual state Democratic Party convention. He shared his sorrow and dismay in one of the most moving speeches of his life, noting that everyone would have been inspired and energized by Kennedy if he had been able to deliver the keynote at the convention as planned. "But the magic is gone. The demand that we do better is silenced. The voice of conscience is stilled," Lucey said.[27]

Lucey was in a "blue funk" regarding politics generally, as *Wisconsin State Journal* writer John Wyngaard described it. He was sorely tempted to sit on the sidelines, at least temporarily, and turned back efforts to get him to be a candidate for governor or party chair.[28] But Lucey was increasingly incensed by Johnson's policies in Vietnam, and that prompted him to get back into action. On August 7, he announced his support for the remaining major anti-war candidate, Eugene McCarthy.[29] To express his gratitude, McCarthy said that if he won the presidency, he would appoint Lucey as postmaster general.[30]

## CHAOS IN CHICAGO

Lucey was a Wisconsin delegate to the 1968 Democratic National Convention, held in Chicago August 26–29. As the floor leader for the McCarthy campaign, he was responsible for bringing together all of the McCarthy supporters at the convention and then growing that base as much and as fast as possible.[31] He knew victory was a long shot, but he was determined to work diligently and creatively to get the presidential nomination for McCarthy.

Lucey took a moment from his convention work on August 24 to call Lasker, who was getting married that day. Lucey apologized for not being able to make it to the festivities and promised to pick up some delegates for McCarthy as a wedding present.[32]

Lucey approached Richard Goodwin, who had worked as a speechwriter for both John F. Kennedy and Lyndon B. Johnson, and proposed that Goodwin have dinner with John Connally to see if he would be interested in running for vice president, as McCarthy's running mate. Connally had been governor of Texas and was in the limousine with President Kennedy when he was shot. Lucey's plan was to get Connally's support, thereby bringing delegates from southern states into McCarthy's camp. With other delegates who were either committed or persuadable, McCarthy might have a chance at getting the nomination.

Goodwin reported back to Lucey that Connally was indeed interested. Lucey went to O'Hare Airport to greet McCarthy as he arrived in Chicago and rode with him to the International Amphitheatre, where the convention was being held. Lucey explained his plan to McCarthy and asked for his approval. The response was a flat and definite "No!" Lucey continued with the effort to get delegates to support McCarthy, but he was very pessimistic about the outcome.[33]

The Wisconsin delegation was among the most strident against the war. It was headed by Donald O. Peterson, who had been active in the Democratic–Farmer–Labor Party in Minnesota and the Democratic Party in South Dakota before moving to Eau Claire, Wisconsin, and working as a pizza distributor. In 1967, the Wisconsin legislature passed a law providing an option to vote no if those going to the polls did not like any of the candidates listed on the ballot. Peterson had been the leader of a vote-no campaign to register opposition to President Johnson in the 1968 Wisconsin Democratic primary. When Senator McCarthy announced his run for the presidency, the vote-no effort became the Wisconsin McCarthy for President Committee, and Peterson served as a cochair.

The Chicago convention began with a heated and time-consuming fight over credentials. The disputes and maneuvers threatened to push a discussion of the peace plank of the platform into the early morning hours, when delegates would be exhausted and media coverage would be almost nonexistent. Peterson initiated a boisterous demonstration by the Wisconsin delegates that forced a recess so that deliberations over the peace plank would take place the next day. When convention delegates voted 1,567.75 to 1,041.25 to reject the plank, the Wisconsin, California, Indiana, Oregon, South Dakota, and New York delegations loudly objected and demonstrated on the floor. Their protests paralleled those by tens of thousands of demonstrators outside the convention hall. An undisciplined and violent Chicago police force inflamed the situation. The media covered the chaos, and Chicago Mayor Daley was furious.[34]

On the convention floor, the favorite sons and party establishment prevailed. Although many of the delegates who had been elected to support Bobby Kennedy switched to side with McCarthy, there just were not enough of them. Anti-war and anti-Johnson delegates encouraged Senators George McGovern or Ted Kennedy to agree to be a candidate, but neither one obliged.

The majority of delegates ignored the results of presidential primaries and dutifully crowned Johnson's vice president as their nominee. Humphrey won on the first ballot, more as the default candidate than as an enthusiastic choice. He got 1,759.25 ballots, McCarthy got 601, and six other candidates picked up the remaining 246.75 votes. One of those six was Paul "Bear" Bryant, the legendary coach of the University of Alabama football team, who got 1.5 votes.

Lucey did not endorse Humphrey until October 11, six weeks after he had been nominated. Lucey was reluctant but acknowledged that voting for the Democratic ticket was better than voting for Richard Nixon or George Wallace or staying home on Election Day. Lucey hoped that Humphrey would return to advocating for civil rights, economic justice, and international cooperation, as he had done before partnering with Johnson.[35]

McCarthy refused to endorse Humphrey until October 29, exactly one week before the November 5 election. McCarthy coupled his endorsement with a statement of his disappointment with Humphrey's position on Vietnam.[36] Peterson had endorsed Humphrey shortly after the conclusion of the Chicago convention. Like many others who had worked for McCarthy's candidacy, Peterson continued to decry the convention and its decision.

In response to what happened in the Windy City, Democrats decided to change the rules of the game. Although the chaotic convention in 1968 was largely because of the opposition to Johnson's policies in Vietnam, the delegate selection process was also an issue. The delegates lacked ethnic and gender diversity, and some states continued to be dominated by party bosses and what was loosely referred to as "the establishment."[37] The Democratic National Committee appointed the Commission on Party Structure and Delegate Selection and designated Senator McGovern and Representative Donald M. Fraser to serve as cochairs.

Simultaneously, some of the delegates who had backed McCarthy joined with some who had supported Kennedy to form the New Democratic Coalition (NDC), an internal reform movement in the Democratic Party. Donald Peterson was a cochair along with Paul Schrade, a United Auto Workers official from Los Angeles who was wounded when the shots that killed Bobby Kennedy were fired. Lucey joined and took responsibility for developing a policy agenda. He established study groups to propose responses to urban and racial problems and to suggest reforms to the process for selecting delegates. He told the groups to complete their work in time for a conference in the spring of 1969.[38]

From Humphrey's perspective, the November 5, 1968, election was held about five days too soon. He was gaining on Nixon.[39] Although polls showed the Humphrey–Muskie ticket behind by almost twenty points in the immediate aftermath of the convention, the final tally of the popular vote was Nixon 43.4 percent, Humphrey 42.7 percent, and Wallace (on the American Independent ticket) 13.5 percent. The margin in the electoral college vote was much more decisive: Nixon won thirty-two states for 301 electoral college votes, Humphrey won thirteen states and Washington, DC, for 191 votes, and Wallace won five Deep South states for 46 votes. Wallace had a margin in several other states that could have made Humphrey the winner—but that, of course, is math divorced from reality. Lucey was surprised that the popular vote was so close. Republicans' electoral success extended to Wisconsin, where Knowles easily won reelection.

Lucey provided a postmortem of the election in a keynote address he gave to the NDC meeting in Omaha on December 7, 1968. He blamed Johnson's escalation of military force in Vietnam and said that Humphrey had "the impossible chore" of remaining loyal to LBJ while trying to reestablish his identity as a progressive civil rights advocate. Lucey went on to observe that the Roosevelt coalition of big-city machines, Southern Democrats, farmers, and labor unions no longer existed. He called for a new alliance of progressives committed to peace and social justice, a coalition of the concerned that would transform the Democratic Party much like the Democratic Organizing Committee did in Wisconsin.[40]

As calendars were turned to 1969, it was clear that it was time for change, but it was not clear what the direction should be. One reaction was the "law and order" mantra chanted by politicians to end both anti-war protests and urban riots. Moving in quite another direction was the growth of the peace movement. Activists found new resolve to pursue social justice issues. The Poor People's Campaign, begun by King just before his murder, continued, although it struggled to gain its share of attention.

President Nixon and Governor Knowles both struggled to craft an effective response to the problems and concerns of the times. As 1970 approached, progressives such as Lucey had an opportunity to provide leadership.

## CHAPTER 9

# THE 1970 RACE FOR GOVERNOR

As preparations began for Richard M. Nixon's inauguration, Patrick
Lucey turned his attention to the Wisconsin gubernatorial race that
was only two years away. The tragedies that characterized the late 1960s
were sad reminders of how important politics and public policy were.
Defeats provided lessons and motivation. Lucey was determined to lead
his state as its next governor.

The prize was now more valuable than it had ever been. Wisconsin
voters changed their state constitution in 1967 to provide that, effective
in 1971, the terms for governor, lieutenant governor, attorney general,
secretary of state, and treasurer would be increased from two to four years.
Voters also agreed that candidates for governor and lieutenant governor
from the same party be listed together on the ballot. Party primaries,
however, would continue to be separate for the two offices. In other words,
the state would not follow the national model whereby a gubernatorial
candidate would choose his or her running mate. Although candidates for
the two top executive positions would share the same party label and win
or lose together in the final November election, they would not necessarily
act as a team.

In a radio interview with Jay G. Sykes on Milwaukee station WMVS on
November 25, 1968, Lucey said that he might run for governor in 1970.
Lucey considered the time to be right, and, as is often observed about
politics, timing is everything. The popular Warren Knowles said after his
reelection in 1968 that six years in the office were enough for him, and
he would not run again. Another timing factor was that Lucey and other
Democrats were no longer saddled with an unpopular president from their

party. Lucey had developed an agenda since his election as lieutenant governor. It was an ambitious, progressive agenda that would take at least four
years to accomplish. It was time to get started.[1]

Lucey speculated that others who might pursue the Democratic nomination were Milwaukee Mayor Henry Maier, Attorney General Bronson
La Follette, and David Carley, Lucey's opponent in the 1966 primary for
the Democratic nomination for governor.[2] Lucey did not include in his
list of potential candidates Donald Peterson, the head of Wisconsin's delegation to the Chicago convention and cochair of the New Democratic
Coalition (NDC). Peterson, it turned out, would become his main rival
for the nomination.

Lucey considered making a formal announcement just before the June
13–16, 1969, state Democratic convention, held that year in Stevens Point.
The strategy was to declare early and ward off other potential candidates,
thus allowing for an uncontested primary. Carley learned about the plans
and let people in the party and the media know that he was also interested
in running. To inject some drama and maximize press coverage, Lucey
decided he would not formally declare his candidacy until late summer or
early fall 1969. He had a group of supporters informally talk to delegates to
tell them his plan. Lucey established a place at the convention where either
he or a representative was always present to talk with delegates, one on one
or in small groups. Supporters distributed stickers and buttons designed
by Lucey's youngest son, David, saying, "Happiness Is a New Governor"
and "Lucey for Governor."[3]

On September 26, 1969, Lucey made it official: he was running for governor. Prior to the announcement, Lucey began laying the organizational
foundation for his bid. He traveled throughout the state giving speeches
and meeting with potential campaign workers. He launched a statewide
Friends of Pat Lucey for Governor Committee, chaired by M. William
Gerrard, the founder of Gerrard Realty Corporation in La Crosse and a
former Republican. Lucey had recruited Gerrard to raise money for the
Democratic Party of Wisconsin when Lucey was chair of the party in 1961.

Lucey was especially eager to build support in Dane County, which
he had lost to Carley and then to Knowles in 1966. The announced
supporters of Lucey in Dane County included a number of leaders in
previous campaigns waged by Carley. Robert Levine, who chaired Gaylord

Nelson's successful reelection for US Senate in 1968, served as head of the Dane County Friends of Pat Lucey for Governor. Nelson and Carley were allies. The list of announced Lucey supporters included seven former Dane County Democratic Party chairs, prominent University of Wisconsin faculty, and longtime party activists.[4]

Peterson did not formally announce his candidacy until much later. On October 27, 1969, he told a group of supporters at a breakfast meeting in Madison that he would run but would not formally declare for several months. He scheduled a fund-raising program featuring Julian Bond, a Georgia legislator and civil rights leader, for December 13 at the University of Wisconsin Stock Pavilion in Madison.[5] Peterson made his formal announcement that he was a candidate on April 24, 1970, at press conferences in Milwaukee and Madison. He acknowledged that he was an underdog and pledged to support Lucey if Lucey won the primary. At the Stevens Point convention, both Lucey and Peterson pledged to support the winner of the primary.[6]

Senator Eugene McCarthy was grateful to both Peterson and Lucey for their support when he ran for the Democratic presidential nomination. McCarthy accepted an invitation from Peterson to keynote a fund-raising event for him on August 9. While he was raising money for the Peterson campaign, McCarthy said in his remarks that he could easily support Lucey for governor as well.[7]

Lucey faced brief opposition from Carley, who had criticized Lucey for his role in the NDC. Carley charged that the NDC had cost Hubert Humphrey the presidency in 1968 and continued to split the Democratic Party. Milwaukee Democrats and labor leaders were upset with Lucey over this. Lucey disagreed with their reasoning but acknowledged the dangers of factions. He quit his involvement with the NDC in June, prior to the state party convention.[8]

On November 21, two months after Lucey formally declared his candidacy, Carley announced that he would not seek the Democratic nomination for governor. He cited heavy commitments in his real estate business as the reason. Carley, his brother Jim, and Green Bay Packer Coach Vince Lombardi had formed Public Facilities Associates in 1967 to design and develop low-cost housing in urban areas. In May 1969, they had begun working on a merger with an Ohio prefabricated housing manufacturer,

Scholz Homes, and with Inland Steel Company. Carley said he had to complete arrangements for the merger and could not run for office.[9]

Carley formally endorsed Lucey on March 8, 1970. He urged Democrats to unite and announced that he was heading fund-raising for the Lucey campaign.

Lucey was more concerned about the potential candidacy of Milwaukee Mayor Maier, who had an obvious base of support in any run he might make for a statewide office. Milwaukee was home to more people and, importantly, more Democrats than any other city in Wisconsin. Moreover, the state's largest labor unions were in Milwaukee and southeastern Wisconsin.

In 1968, Maier established the Have-Not Conference to highlight the need for state and federal assistance to urban areas in Wisconsin. Maier also played an active role in the National League of Cities and became a visible spokesperson for urban issues at a time of summer disturbances in metropolitan areas. He seemed well positioned to run for governor and address major concerns of the time.

Lucey thought that Maier would not run unless he was sure he would win. Lucey had a clear edge in statewide support and needed to sow doubt in Maier's mind about the level of backing he would get from Milwaukee.[10] Lucey sought support from at least some of the labor leaders and prominent political figures in Milwaukee.

## ENDORSEMENTS

John Schmitt, the head of the Wisconsin AFL-CIO, had urged Maier to enter the 1970 gubernatorial race. Maier indicated that he indeed was considering becoming a candidate but wanted to wait for a "real draft" from the unions.[11] The AFL-CIO leadership agreed to conduct a statewide poll among union members to measure preferences among potential Democratic candidates for governor.[12]

While Maier hesitated and pressed for an indication of support from labor, Lucey and his supporters publicly built pressure to discourage the mayor. On March 19, 1970, Lucey triggered a bandwagon effect by lining up support from twenty-six of the forty-seven Democrats in the state assembly. Of special interest on the list were Milwaukee representatives William A. Johnson, chair of the assembly's Milwaukee caucus and a legislator with strong labor ties, and two representatives who had been widely expected to support Maier: John McCormick and Daniel Hanna. Lucey also got backing from Dennis Conta, newly elected assembly representative from Milwaukee and widely recognized as an able and rising star in the legislature.[13] The announcement of support from legislators was accompanied by endorsements by fifty-seven Democratic county chairs from throughout the state. The United Auto Workers, which at the time was not part of the AFL-CIO, favored Lucey.[14] Lucey followed those and other endorsements with a public statement that he himself would solicit the support of Maier.[15]

While working in his campaign headquarters in Madison, Lucey received a phone call from Frank Zeidler, a Socialist and Maier's predecessor as mayor of Milwaukee. Zeidler told Lucey that he was wholeheartedly for him and would like to do anything he could to help. He then asked, "So, Pat, do you want me to come out for you or against you?" Lucey laughed and said a public endorsement from the famous Socialist would be great. And Zeidler followed through.[16]

In the midst of these developments, the executive committee of the National Farmers Organization in Wisconsin agreed to back Lucey and secure a formal endorsement at their convention in August. Although Schmitt had been an early supporter of Maier, he liked the idea of a farmer–labor coalition. David Obey credited support from a coalition between farmers and workers for his winning the 1969 special election to the US House of Representatives.[17]

Eager to get action out of his board at the AFL-CIO, Schmitt agreed to a one-on-one meeting with Lucey that was arranged by Richard Weening, Lucey's campaign manager. Lucey was losing some weight to get in shape for the rigors of the campaign, but he put aside restrictions on food and drink to wine and dine Schmitt. The labor leader and the candidate had a good time, and Schmitt felt very comfortable switching his support from Maier to Lucey.[18] Shortly after meeting with Lucey, Schmitt told Maier that many of the top- and second-level labor leaders in the state thought Maier had waited too long to decide on his candidacy and were going to back Lucey.

On April 13, the executive board of the AFL-CIO met in Milwaukee and passed a resolution endorsing Lucey and urging other Democrats to unite behind him. Schmitt summarized, "I think we have a great chance of electing a liberal as governor this year. Why spend a lot of money on a primary race when we will need it for the general election?"[19]

Maier was not happy. He sent a letter to Schmitt saying,

> I have tried throughout all of our talks to demonstrate that I would probably only yield to the first and only true "draft" that I have ever heard of in my nearly 25 years in politics, the draft showing the will of the people in the form of the results of the poll. . . . Things apparently have changed and your united opinion of a few weeks ago apparently has shifted. . . . Since the basic reason for my holding the door open at all—your urging—has dissolved, I can see no reason on my part to wait for a poll or to delay closing the door.[20]

Maier withdrew from consideration but did not endorse either Lucey or Peterson.

An impressive list of people and organizations endorsed Lucey prior to the September 7, 1970, primary. John Gronouski, former postmaster general under Presidents Kennedy and Johnson and US ambassador to Poland, was one of the first to express support.[21] John Kenneth Galbraith, the famed Harvard economist and Kennedy's ambassador to India, traveled to Milwaukee and Madison to boost the Lucey campaign. The United Auto Workers, the AFL-CIO's Committee on Political Education, and the Wisconsin Professional Firefighters Association also gave Lucey and lieutenant governor candidate State Senator Martin J. Schreiber the nod in June. Officers of the Young Democrats of Wisconsin around the state formed a committee to voice their support.

Lucey was unsuccessful in securing the endorsement of Clement Zablocki, the congressional representative from Milwaukee's South Side. The two met several times and publicly exchanged friendly banter, but Zablocki was firm on not taking sides before the primary. He acknowledged to Lucey that he continued to hold a grudge because Lucey had not endorsed Humphrey in 1968 until just before Election Day.[22] Zablocki did suggest, however, that he thought Lucey would get the nomination by asking him, "You're not afraid of Peterson, are you?"[23]

## CAMPAIGN ORGANIZATION

Lucey applied his extensive experience in running campaigns—his own and others'—to his run for governor in 1970. But he did not want to manage his own campaign. Lucey felt that he had made a mistake in his unsuccessful run in 1966 by being too involved.[24] This time, he would focus on being the candidate and let others do the scheduling, organizing, press releases, and myriad other tasks necessary to wage a winning effort. The decision meant that Lucey had to recruit a campaign team and manager who were competent and could be trusted.

Lucey followed the advice of Dennis Conta and asked Richard Weening to find a good, energetic campaign manager. Weening and Conta were friends, and Weening had orchestrated Conta's successful 1968 contest against the incumbent, Republican Joseph Bellante, for the state assembly seat representing Milwaukee's Third District. It had been a tough race in a year when Democrats struggled, but Conta won 8,798 to 6,795. After the election, Weening worked for US Representative Henry Reuss on Milwaukee housing rehabilitation projects.[25]

When Weening approached people about their interest in working as Lucey's campaign manager, he usually got the question tossed back at him. Maybe Weening should do the job. James Wimmer, chair of the Democratic Party of Wisconsin in 1970, joined that chorus. After the two had dinner together, Wimmer handed his phone to Weening and encouraged him to give Lucey a call and offer his services. He did and Lucey accepted the offer.[26]

David Lasker was the campaign's field director, a logical appointment because Lasker had traveled the state with Lucey in the 1966 campaign. He had scheduled and organized the Lucey family tour, knew local party loyalists, and enjoyed Lucey's trust.

Stephen Holmgren was schedule director. Holmgren was happy to have the opportunity but was concerned because he did not have the experience he felt was needed. Lucey nonetheless had confidence in Holmgren and said he would teach him how to do the job. He invited Holmgren to have dinner, laid out a map of Wisconsin, gave a description of every county, and then told Holmgren how to arrange meetings with community leaders, local newspaper editors, and various groups. Lucey suggested how Holmgren might feed questions to reporters so that they could make the most of their sessions. This was especially important for Minnesota media that had Wisconsin customers but were not well versed on issues facing their neighbor. Each day on the campaign trail would include six or seven stops. After the crash course, Lucey stepped back and let Holmgren make arrangements and inform the candidate where they were going and whom they would see.[27]

David Adamany continued to be confidant and counsel to Lucey. Adamany's title was research director, and Lucey frequently referred to him as the brains of the campaign. Lucey relied heavily on Adamany for advice on policy issues and political strategy. Bill Schutt was press relations director and worked closely with Adamany. Schutt's assistant was Elizabeth Allen, a recent graduate of Wisconsin State University at Eau Claire.

Esther Kaplan, who had a long history of keeping track of spending and raising money in the state Democratic Party, served that same role in the 1970 Lucey campaign. She was the comptroller. In the primary, Lucey spent $111,747 ($738,000 in 2019), and Peterson shelled out $41,017 ($230,000 in 2019). The annual salary for Wisconsin's governor in 1970 was $25,000 ($165,000 in 2019). Martin J. Schreiber, who won the lieutenant governor nomination in a five-way race, spent $18,280 ($121,000 in 2019).[28]

The Boiler Room was a key feature of the campaign. This was borrowed from the Kennedy approach to campaign organization and was a way of directing the energy and enthusiasm of volunteer workers. Individuals were assigned counties and given a variety of tasks that included disseminating information, identifying supporters, organizing and advancing events, and generating support on a door-to-door, face-to-face basis.[29]

## THE PRIMARY CONTEST

Lucey and Peterson campaigned vigorously, but maintained a civil and almost cordial relationship. Lucey was always considered the frontrunner, but he did not take victory for granted. Neither Lucey nor Peterson resorted to personal attacks.

Lucey and Peterson had a debate at Memorial Union on the University of Wisconsin campus in Madison. The term *debate* was, however, misleading,

Donald Peterson and Lucey debate at University of Wisconsin–Madison during the Democratic primary for governor in 1970. WHI IMAGE ID 143813

since the two candidates did not differ on issues. When asked by a student to identify where they differed, the candidates simply smiled and the crowd laughed.[30] Peterson had the advantage on campus because of his early and strong identification with McCarthy and the anti-war cause, but he drew groans when he was not as strident as had been expected by activists in the crowd. He also alienated some with a sexist joke. Lucey had a style described as pedantic and clinical—like students saw in their classrooms—but he applied his progressive philosophy to issues and shored up the support he had had before the debate began.[31]

The Madison campus was the scene of an act of violence that sobered people in and outside the anti-war movement. In the early morning hours of August 24, 1970, four protestors drove a stolen van filled with a ton of ammonium nitrate and fuel oil and parked it next to Sterling Hall. Their specific target was the Army Mathematics Research Center, which was linked to military efforts in Vietnam. The explosion not only damaged the building but also killed Robert Fassnacht, a graduate student working that night.

The Sterling Hall bombing profoundly shocked not only the Madison community but the entire country. It was a new and disturbing level of violence. Anti-war protests paused. Protestors emphasized new ways of voicing pleas for peace.

Politicians increased their calls for law and order. Some blamed everyone who questioned US policy and cast university students as irresponsible. Jack Olson, seeking the Republican gubernatorial nomination, told a meeting of veterans that campus violence was "the work of a revolutionary cult." Lucey worked with Adamany and carefully crafted a statement that firmly denounced the use of violence but called for upholding First Amendment rights and for understanding rather than condemning those who opposed the war. Separately, Lucey criticized Governor Knowles for proceeding with a "goodwill mission" to Ireland in the wake of the bombing. Knowles seemed detached when, Lucey contended, he should have provided leadership.[32]

As the September primary neared, Lucey and his campaign team felt cautiously optimistic. The major causes for uncertainty and concern were projections for a low voter turnout and rumblings about Republicans crossing over in Wisconsin's open primary to vote for Peterson. There was not much of a contest in the Republican primary between Olson and Roman R. Blenski. The latter was not well known and did not campaign aggressively. For that reason, GOP voters might act as spoilers and cast their ballots for Peterson, widely perceived as the Democrat least likely to prevail in the general election in November.[33]

Voter turnout was low, as usual in a primary contest. Only 28 percent of Wisconsin's 1.8 million eligible voters in 1970 bothered to cast a ballot. Lucey and Olson won their respective primaries (see tables 9.1 and 9.2).

**TABLE 9.1.** Democratic Primary Results for Governor, 1970

| | |
|---|---|
| Patrick J. Lucey | 176,067 |
| Donald O. Peterson | 106,049 |
| Edward Ihlenfeldt | 10,008 |

Source: *The Wisconsin Blue Book 1971* (Madison: Wisconsin Legislative Reference Bureau, 1971), 290.

**TABLE 9.2.** Republican Primary Results for Governor, 1970

| | |
|---|---|
| Jack Olson | 202,420 |
| Roman R. Blenski | 9,279 |

Source: *The Wisconsin Blue Book 1971* (Madison: Wisconsin Legislative Reference Bureau, 1971), 290.

Lucey did well on a statewide basis and achieved impressive margins in Milwaukee and Kenosha Counties, where he garnered 63 percent and 74 percent of the vote respectively. However, Lucey again found victory in Dane County elusive. Peterson beat Lucey in the Madison area 19,140 to 10,706. Lucey could take some consolation from his 2,742 to 1,780 victory over Peterson in Eau Claire County, Peterson's home.[34]

The day after balloting, Peterson urged his supporters to back Lucey. He congratulated his rival and noted that the two candidates did not differ on the issues and had maintained respect for one another. Peterson vowed that he would campaign actively for Lucey and encouraged others to do the same.[35] In an editorial, the *Appleton Post-Crescent* also cited the civil nature of the competition between Lucey and Peterson.[36]

Separately, candidates came forward for the Democratic nomination for lieutenant governor. They included State Senator Schreiber, who, like Lucey, ran and lost in 1966. At age twenty-three, Schreiber had been the youngest person in Wisconsin elected to the state senate. He served there from 1963 to 1971 and was most closely identified with labor and education issues as well as concerns about the elderly. During his first year in the senate, he completed his law degree from Marquette University. His father, Martin E. Schreiber, had been a Republican member of the assembly from 1941 to 1944 and served on the Milwaukee Common Council until 1976.

The younger Schreiber faced four others in the race for the Democratic nomination for lieutenant governor. He had the advantage of strong backing from Milwaukee-based unions. Even though whoever won would appear on the November ballot as his running mate, Lucey carefully avoided expressing his preference. He got along well with Schreiber and was pleased that primary voters selected him (see table 9.3).[37] State Representative David O. Martin was unopposed for the Republican nomination.

**TABLE 9.3.** Democratic Primary Results for Lieutenant Governor

| | |
|---|---|
| Martin J. Schreiber | 123,365 |
| Frank L. Nikolay | 51,832 |
| John F. O'Malley | 34,999 |
| Jay G. Sykes | 34,282 |
| Harry Halloway | 16,106 |

*The Wisconsin Blue Book 1971* (Madison: Wisconsin Legislative Reference Bureau, 1971), 290.

Although the winners of the primaries for governor and lieutenant governor for each party would appear on the general election ballot together, the campaign organizations for Lucey and Schreiber remained separate. They each continued with their own campaign staffs and finances, and their schedules were not coordinated, with only rare joint appearances.[38] But both candidates had progressive agendas and shared positions on issues.

The results of the primary for secretary of state were less to Lucey's liking. Incumbent Robert C. Zimmerman, who had held the position since 1957, was endorsed by the Republican Party at its convention and had no primary opposition. The Democratic candidates included Robert A. Zimmermann and Thomas P. Fox. Whereas Fox had been an active and prominent leader in the state's Democratic Party, Zimmermann had no background as a Democrat but instead had been a supporter of George Wallace and his far-right American Independent Party.

Lucey had urged support for Fox during the primary campaign but to no avail.[39] Zimmermann took advantage of the similarity of his name with that of the long-serving Republican and beat Fox 164,085 to 85,961. Zimmermann's win put Lucey and Schreiber in the awkward position of having to urge voters in November to support the Republican, not the Democratic, candidate.[40]

## THE GENERAL ELECTION

The primary election provided Lucey a good foundation for his quest for the governor's office. The contest with Peterson had not been acrimonious or divisive. Democrats in Wisconsin sensed an opportunity for victory and united behind Lucey's leadership.

Lucey and Jack Olson speak at Wisconsin State University–Stevens Point during the 1970 campaign for governor. WHI IMAGE ID 143814

As the campaign began, Lucey challenged Olson to eight debates. He proposed that the two meet in Janesville, Madison, La Crosse, Oshkosh, Stevens Point, Green Bay, Superior, and Milwaukee and that they ask a panel of newspaper reporters and columnists to pose questions. Lucey also suggested that at least some of the debates be televised.[41] Olson chose not to debate. He said he would not be able to fit debates into his schedule and noted that the two candidates were scheduled to appear at the same events several times before Election Day. Olson argued that media coverage would be sufficient to let voters know about policy differences between the candidates.[42]

As the incumbent lieutenant governor, Olson generally played defense. Governor Knowles continued to be popular, and President Nixon had not yet been tarred by the Watergate scandal. The strategy of defending the status quo was risky, however. Economic growth of the post–World War II era had ended in the late 1960s, and the term *stagflation*—high unemployment and high inflation occurring simultaneously—entered the lexicon of analysts and reporters. The economy had started to show signs of the impending recession of 1973–75.

The state fiscal situation had deteriorated, and property taxes had risen steadily since 1967. Olson sided with conservatives in the state legislature as they slashed deeper into the cuts in education, welfare, and transportation proposed by the more moderate Knowles.[43]

## Taxes

Lucey hit hard on the need for property tax reform. Property taxes provided the lion's share of support for public schools. State government was paying 38 percent of school costs in 1967. But as costs had risen, state dollars remained at a constant level. Thus, local school districts had to increase property taxes to make up the difference, placing a growing burden on local farmers, homeowners, and businesses and creating a growing funding disparity between wealthy and less wealthy school districts around the state.[44] The average property tax increase in 1969 was 10 percent and came on top of significant rises of the previous two years, prompting Lucey to label the issue a top priority.[45] He charged that the implications of continuing existing state policies would be an additional burden of sixty-eight million dollars ($448.8 million in 2019) in property taxes for the city of Milwaukee alone.[46]

Property taxes emerged as the major topic at a statewide Have-Not Conference organized by Milwaukee Mayor Maier. The "have-nots" were jurisdictions in the state concerned about their lack of resources and lack of authority due to policies and budgets formulated by state officials in Madison. Maier invited both Lucey and Olson to address the conference and succeeded in hosting a joint appearance that became the only major debate in the campaign between the two candidates. Lucey went first and pledged to increase the state's share of school costs to help address the financial woes of the have-nots. He endorsed the recommendations of the Task Force on Local Government on Finance and Operation (known as the Tarr Task Force), which had been created by the Republican-controlled state legislature in 1967. Olson made a general statement supporting property tax relief but said he did not want to get "locked in" to any specifics. He said he favored relief "whenever revenue conditions permit."[47]

One could not discuss property taxes without considering the other major sources of public revenue: income taxes and sales taxes. Despite the opposition that he and his party historically expressed to the sales tax, Lucey did not advocate its repeal. He did, however, pledge that he would not extend it to cover all goods and services. He wanted exemptions on necessities. The Republican-controlled legislature had just expanded application of the 4 percent sales tax to apply to clothing and other items some considered essential.[48]

Lucey and his staff did the math. The level of financial commitments made by the Republican legislature and governor was significantly higher than any reasonable projection of revenues. The Metropolitan Milwaukee Association of Commerce invited both Olson and Lucey to speak and address taxation issues. As usual, Adamany was assigned the task of drafting Lucey's speech. Adamany called Lucey and said, "Well, it's pretty hard to get elected governor if you are running in favor of raising taxes. What do you want me to put in the speech?"

Lucey replied, "Tell 'em the truth. We're going to have to raise taxes."[49]

Then Governor Knowles dropped a bomb. In an interview with Neil Shively of the *Milwaukee Sentinel*, Knowles said that there was "no way" the governor and legislators elected in November could avoid increasing taxes. The governor told Shively that if he were to continue in office, he would propose a "balanced" tax program that included income, sales, and excise taxes and would use the additional revenue to pay for property tax relief and for funding state programs.[50]

This acknowledgment by Knowles contrasted with the statements by Olson that a tax increase was not necessary.[51] In a position paper, "A Sound State Fiscal Policy," Olson claimed that Lucey would raise state income taxes 60 percent if elected governor. As an alternative, Olson emphasized holding down expenses and touted zero-base budgeting as the way to do that.[52] Zero-base budgeting is an approach to public budgeting developed by the Rand Corporation and publicized by Jimmy Carter when he was governor of Georgia. The name is misleading. Rather than beginning with a base of zero for each department's budget, as the name suggests, this method requires analysts to propose spending under three scenarios that typically include increases, decreases, and no change. In any case, it says nothing about raising or lowering taxes.[53]

Syndicated columnist John Wyngaard summarized the effects of the Knowles statement that taxes had to be raised:

> What the governor had done, in effect, was to undermine the key theme of the campaign of the Republican nominee for the succession to the governorship and to give the camp of Patrick Lucey, the Democratic challenger, the best ammunition it has had thus far.[54]

That such an assessment was made by a columnist known for his Republican preferences was especially telling. Knowles engaged in some damage control by making several appearances with Olson and echoing the GOP candidate's theme that Lucey was a big spender.[55]

Lucey continued to present himself as being realistic and truthful. His wife, Jean, worried that he would lose the election by saying he would raise taxes.[56] But Lucey reiterated the need for additional revenue to implement property tax reform and to fund needed programs and services. He voiced the importance of the principles of fair and equitable taxation and left the specifics to deliberation after inauguration.

## Vietnam

Lucey tried to get Olson to take a public position on US involvement in Vietnam. Olson and the Republican candidate for lieutenant governor, Martin, tried to recast the issue as a demonstration of inconsistency by Lucey. They said he could not be trusted. Instead of addressing the substantive question about whether the US military should be in Southeast Asia, the Republican team reminded voters that during the 1966 gubernatorial contest, Lucey had said that Vietnam was a foreign policy issue that should not be considered in a state campaign.

The Lucey quote was from June 10, 1966. Later that month at the Wisconsin Democratic Party Convention, however, Lucey acknowledged that the war in Vietnam had become central and was vital to every part of the American polity and identity. In the 1970 race, Lucey acknowledged that his early statement on the relevance of the war demonstrated "too little foresight," and he persisted in getting the Republican candidates to take a stand. Eventually, Olson declared that he supported President Nixon's policies in Southeast Asia.[57]

## Law and Order

The call for law and order was an example of how Vietnam affected domestic affairs in the United States. Peaceful demonstrations against the war and in promotion of racial justice, and the violence into which they occasionally degenerated, stimulated a reaction calling for a restoration of order and a recommitment to lawful behavior. Reactions to protests converged with concern for reducing traditional crime, muddling the two issues.

Lucey recognized the distinctions. He addressed traditional criminal justice issues and made a detailed statement on campus unrest and protest activities.[58] Lucey's position paper on crime included proposals for enhancing training and funding for police, compensating victims, expanding rehabilitation programs for criminals, providing more options for dealing with juvenile offenders, and reforming state courts to relieve backlogs of cases. He advocated generally for both law enforcement and social cures. Lucey presented a carefully balanced response to protest activity. He noted the dangers of extremism of any stripe that turned to violence.

Olson responded by accusing Lucey of only lately discovering the need to address crime. He did not quarrel with Lucey's positions but instead suggested a focus on ways to improve highway safety.[59]

## State Universities

Lucey and Olson differed on how to define the issue central to the public universities in the state. Lucey focused on access to quality higher education and an efficiently run set of institutions. Early in his campaign, Lucey suggested that the state's two systems of public universities (University of Wisconsin and Wisconsin State Universities) be merged. Shortly after the June 1970 Democratic state convention, Lucey outlined how a 1955 proposal by Republican Governor Walter Kohler Jr. might be modified to have a single board of regents govern the state's universities. At the time, he made clear that he was not necessarily endorsing the idea but thought it deserved serious consideration.[60] Subsequently, Lucey emphasized the need to keep tuition costs affordable, compensate faculty at competitive rates, and fund higher education to provide adequate instructional opportunities.

Olson did not engage Lucey on university merger or on other substantive matters regarding higher education but drew Lucey into a back-
and-forth over campus unrest, which he and other Republicans viewed
as a more pressing concern. Disturbances at Wisconsin State University
–Whitewater and the University of Wisconsin in Madison garnered attention. Republican legislators, led by Assembly Speaker Harold Froehlich,
Milo Knutson, and Gordon Roseleip amplified Olson's attacks. Lucey
reminded critics that very few students engaged in violence. He narrowed
his own criticism to that minority and spent most of his time and energy
defending students and faculty.[61]

*Environment*
Lucey tried but failed to get Olson to engage in a debate or discussion about
environmental issues. He issued position papers and had press conferences on water pollution, pesticide control, natural resource planning,
and electric power needs. An attack directed at Kimberly-Clark Corporation and other paper mills for polluting Wisconsin rivers drew responses
from Speaker Froehlich and lieutenant governor candidate Martin but not
from Olson. Froehlich and Martin represented areas where the mills were
located, and Martin was employed by Kimberly-Clark. As he had done on
other issues, Olson responded to claim Lucey's concern was not evident
earlier in his career and was therefore just political expediency.[62] There
was no substantive counterargument.

## Smear Campaign

The campaign for governor in 1970 had few sparks flying. The major exception was a smear campaign hatched in September by Republican strategists and launched three weeks prior to Election Day. The objective was
to associate Lucey with campus radicals and to portray him as a slumlord.

The *Capital Times* obtained and printed a confidential memorandum
written by Jim Harff that had been sent to Olson, Martin, Reed Coleman
(chair of the Wisconsin Republican Party), John MacIver (chair of the
Olson campaign), and Charlie Davis (partner in the McDonald-Davis-
Schmidt advertising agency) on September 8, 1970. Harff had been the
national youth chair of the Goldwater for President Committee in 1964

and was employed as assistant to the president of Plastics Engineering Company of Sheboygan. The owners of Plastics Engineering were longtime supporters of conservative Republicans in Wisconsin.[63]

The memorandum outlined a plot to distribute an article on student housing that alleged Lucey was linked to the Madison "hippie-student community" and to troubles on Mifflin Street adjacent to the University of Wisconsin campus. The article was to appear first in the *Badger Herald*, a student newspaper, and then would be provided to the *Wisconsin State Journal* and other newspapers around the state. In addition, one thousand reprints of the article were to be distributed to Republican candidates, legislative staff, and activists.

On September 14, the *Badger Herald*, started as a conservative alternative to the *Daily Cardinal* student newspaper, ran a full-page story on Lucey and Mifflin Street and provided one thousand reprints of the article to Republicans. Harff and Bud Gourlie, the public information officer for the Republican Senate Caucus, prepared press releases to accompany the *Badger Herald* article that referred to Lucey as "coddling and catering to the pot-smoking, free-loving student radicals who are behind every UW campus riot which results in fire-bombing, window-breaking and endangers the lives and safety of every law-abiding student and resident of Madison."[64]

The plot fizzled when Bill Robbins, managing editor of the *Wisconsin State Journal*, rebuffed Harff and refused to run or to expand on the material provided by the *Badger Herald*. In addition, Charles R. Field and Steven M. Frank, who had been listed as officers of the "Ad Hoc Committee for Decent Housing" that was a sponsor of the reprints, publicly said they were misled by an Olson campaign worker and wanted no part in an anti-Lucey campaign.[65] The coverage in the media quickly turned to the smear attempt instead of the allegations. Efforts to imply guilt by association, however, continued. A theme in Olson radio and television ads during the last weeks of the campaign was to associate Lucey with student radicals and with the New Democratic Coalition.[66]

Several other attempts were made to attack Lucey with "scandal sheets" that were printed and distributed without attribution to either author or sponsor. One example that was handed out in Milwaukee follows (emphasis per original):

Fact 1. Patrick J. Lucey is a <u>radical extremist</u>. Lucey assisted in the
founding of the New Democratic Coalition (NDC). As a member of
the NDC's Executive Board, Lucey was committed to this extremist
organization's goal of revamping society "through <u>radical</u> political
education" and the support of violent radicals such as the Black
Panthers and the Chicago Seven.

Fact 2. Patrick J. is a "<u>Lucey Come-Lately</u>" whose pronouncements
of moderation were politically timed and calculated to appeal to
dissident Democrats.

Fact 3. Patrick Lucey is a <u>staunch supporter of Federal Judge
James Doyle</u>. Both men have served as state chairman of the
Democrat Party.* Lucey served as Doyle's campaign manager
when Doyle unsuccessfully sought the Democrat nomination for
governor in 1954. Lucey has publically commended Doyle's abilities
on the bench.

Note: Doyle is a liberal jurist who has repeatedly ruled in favor
of campus demonstrators, has exonerated invaders of the State
Assembly and has opined that desecration of the flag cannot be
considered in violation of the law. Judge Doyle's decisions can be
termed "a legal invitation to permissiveness, radical behavior and in
some cases, misconduct and violence."

Fact 4. Patrick Lucey is a <u>former-hippy landlord</u>. Lucey, until mid-
June of this year owned numerous houses and apartments in the
hippy community of Madison. On three of his properties, marijuana
was found growing.

Fact 5. Patrick Lucey is an <u>irresponsible spender</u>. Lucey <u>has
promised Wisconsin an automatic tax increase</u>.[67]

Except for commenting that he thought the smear campaigns back-
fired on Olson and Republicans generally, Lucey did not respond to them.[68]
The media covered these attempts minimally rather than giving them
voice or legitimacy.

---

*Lucey was state party chair, while Doyle chaired the Democratic Organizing Committee.

## ADVERTISING

The Lucey campaign used the Charles Guggenheim firm of Washington, DC, to produce advertisements for television. Guggenheim had produced two Academy Award–winning memorial films on John and Bobby Kennedy. A policy of Guggenheim was to work only for candidates whom he could actually support.[69]

Fifteen television spots ran during the last six weeks of the campaign. To convey the image of a candidate concerned with issues faced by Wisconsin residents, the ads relied on candid shots of Lucey talking to and, importantly, listening to workers, farmers, conservationists, and residents of small towns. Eight of the spots were about economic worries. In one ad, Lucey listens to a lift driver on a dock in Milwaukee complain about taxes whittling the size of his take-home pay, then responds, "The sales and property taxes are regressive taxes and tax those who are least able to pay." Another ad shows him listening to a group of people who are fishing and talking about how pollution upstream has affected their catch. In some of the ads, Lucey is shown primarily as someone quietly reflecting and thinking rather than as a politician with a simple solution.[70]

Lucey hired Mitchell Fromstein, a Milwaukee advertising agency that had the Milwaukee Bucks as a client, to purchase radio and television time and to offer advice generally. After Guggenheim produced ads, they were sent to Fromstein for booking. Olson spent twice as much as the Lucey campaign did on television—$450,000 to $271,000 ($2.9 million to $1.8 million in 2019). Olson ads were filmed at coffees and meetings where everyone was wearing "Olson for Wisconsin" buttons.[71] Olson was talking, not listening, and conveyed a different image from that of the candidate in the Lucey ads. The bulk of Olson's spending was for daytime advertising, while Fromstein focused on prime time. Evening buys were more expensive, but they had more impact.

Olson featured two ads that attacked Lucey on the law-and-order issue. One used a clip from a visit to Green Bay by President Nixon in which he rebuked campus demonstrators and urged voters to support Olson. Another used a Slinky toy going down an incline with the warning:

Last year, Patrick Lucey was an organizer of the left-wing New
Democratic Coalition, a radical organization that supported student
demands. This year, he's all for law and order. What about next year?
Don't play the Lucey flip-flop. Vote for Jack Olson for Governor. You
know where he stands.[72]

Lucey ignored standard advice to avoid telling voters bad news. He
used an ad that repeated his conclusion that the state's fiscal situation
required increases in taxes, gambling that viewers would credit him for
being honest and realistic.

Lucey relied heavily on small-town newspapers, dailies and weeklies,
to help get his messages out to the electorate. That continued a practice
begun during his first days in politics and his organizing work for the
Democratic Party. When he visited communities around the state, he
made sure to stop in the office of the local paper, even when the paper
had been supporting Republicans. Lucey appeared unannounced in the
Chippewa Falls office of John Lavine, who owned and was editor of the
*Chippewa Herald, Shawano Leader, Baraboo News Republic*, and *Portage
Daily Register*. Lavine was in his twenties when he acquired the papers,
starting with the *Portage Daily Register* and the *Chippewa Herald* which
he bought from his father. He had interviewed Olson and had run luke-
warm endorsements in the Portage and Baraboo papers. Then he met
Lucey, and the two had a discussion, not just an interview. Lavine was
highly impressed. He thought Lucey came across as principled, honest,
and substantive. He clearly knew the issues and cared.[73]

Lavine ran endorsements of Lucey in the Chippewa Falls and Shawano
papers despite the tradition of support for Republicans from readers in
those communities. Lucey in turn was impressed with Lavine, whom he
would later appoint to the University of Wisconsin Board of Regents.[74]

## CAMPAIGN FINANCE

One of the lessons of the 1966 race was that it was critical to have sufficient
financial resources, especially at the end. Television advertisements and
the need for cash were not as much a priority as they would soon become
for political candidates, but money was certainly an important factor.

Lucey determined that this time he would not be outspent. His campaign would put forth a robust effort to raise funds. But if the well was running dry, Lucey was prepared to write checks on his own account.[75]

Lucey and Olson raised about the same amount of money for their respective campaigns, but Olson accumulated a debt by spending about twice as much as Lucey. According to financial reports, Olson raised $245,000 and Lucey $237,000 ($1.6 million and $1.5 million respectively in 2019). Olson listed a debt of $296,000 ($1.9 million in 2019 dollars) owed to McDonald-Davis-Schmidt, the Republican ad agency.[76]

The major source of support for Lucey came from labor unions. The total from all of the unions was $110,000, including $14,600 from out-of-state labor organizations. State laws placed limits on donors and required disclosure. One check received by the Friends of Pat Lucey for Governor was for $250 from Mr. and Mrs. Roland B. Day. Day was a registered lobbyist at the time and would be appointed by Lucey to the state supreme court. That donation became an issue in 1974 when reporters examined the records. The check was actually written by Day's wife, Mary Jane Purcell, which raised questions generally about vagueness and loopholes in campaign finance rules.[77]

Kennedy family members raised about fifty thousand dollars ($330,000 in 2019) to add to Lucey's campaign funds. On October 7, about two hundred people gathered at the McLean, Virginia, home of Senator Ted Kennedy and his wife, Joan. Senators Bill Proxmire and Gaylord Nelson joined in sponsoring the reception, although because of a late-night session, neither senator was able to attend. Joan Kennedy, Ethel Kennedy (widow of Bobby Kennedy), and Eunice Kennedy Shriver served as hostesses. At a press conference before the event, Lucey expressed optimism about being elected Wisconsin's next chief executive.[78]

Observers and analysts who reflected on Lucey's campaigning as Election Day neared agreed that he had learned from his past experiences and had built on his shoe-leather approach.[79] Lucey was busy. He typically began each day with greetings at plant gates. Then he had discussions with small groups of voters, gave interviews and cut tapes for newspaper and radio reporters, and conferred with staffers. Lucey always made time to visit the volunteers—who included his children—and soak up the buzz and excitement in the Madison campaign headquarters, located in

Lucey talks with voters in Columbus, Wisconsin while running for governor in 1970.
EDWIN STEIN, *WISCONSIN STATE JOURNAL*

space adjoining Lucey Realty. He was busy, but he was efficient, and he always took time to listen. There was a polish and confidence that had not been evident in his 1966 bid for the governor's office. He wasn't cocky or arrogant. But he conveyed a sense that what he was about not only was possible but was within reach.

The victory margin of the Lucey–Schreiber ticket was impressive. Statewide, they won 55 percent of the vote. They carried forty-five of Wisconsin's seventy-two counties, many of which had been solidly Republican. Lucey was only the sixth Democrat to be elected governor since the Republican Party was founded in the state in the events leading to the Civil War. Of the total vote for governor, 76 percent was cast in a triangle that runs from Racine County in the southeast to Brown County (the Green Bay area) to Dane County (the Madison area). The Lucey–Schreiber ticket prevailed in fifteen of the twenty-three counties in that area and garnered 560,000 of their statewide total of 728,000 votes. That was just 40,000 short of the Olson–Miller statewide total of 602,000. The five counties of Milwaukee, Racine, Kenosha, Douglas and Dane were particularly vote-rich. Lucey got 117,000 more votes than Olson in those counties. His total margin over Olson was 126,000. Despite such numbers, Lucey's campaign worked hard in rural areas throughout the state, not just as a strategy for ensuring victory but also because of Lucey's longtime commitment to small towns and to farmers.[80]

Election Day itself, described in the introduction, was both a microcosm of Lucey's campaign and the achievement of years of working, planning, and learning. Winning was not, however, the ultimate goal. Lucey was eager to improve governance and to enact progressive policies in the Badger State.

## CHAPTER 10

# LAUNCHING PROGRESSIVE REFORMS

After the successful and exhausting campaign for governor, Pat and Jean Lucey enjoyed a brief vacation in the Caribbean. When they returned to Madison, Pat moved into a newly furnished office on the ground floor of the capitol, directly below the offices of Governor Warren Knowles. The outgoing Republican governor wanted the transition to be as smooth as possible.

Lucey shared that goal. Knowles had made some appointments that had not been ratified by the state senate when Lucey was elected. Democrats were tempted to try to delay action until after Lucey took office so that he could fill the positions. The governor-elect, however, urged members of his party to stand aside and not object to the nominations.

This gesture was not an indication that Lucey was going to be a ceremonial head of government. He had an ambitious agenda, which he had written on a plain piece of paper and carried with him until it found a place in a drawer of his desk in the governor's office. Lucey was about to usher in a new era. His agenda was not just a list of preferred policies. It was a progressive plan to reframe fundamental approaches to governance to emphasize serving the common good and providing accountability to the electorate. Lucey's focus was on reformulating the funding of public education and welfare, taxing the income rather than the assets of businesses, consolidating public universities, and bringing heads of state agencies more directly and transparently under the direction of elected officials.

Lucey did not—and could not—accomplish these goals by himself. He had the support of key, committed leaders in the legislature, and he had the assistance of a talented, energetic staff and cabinet.

## Assembling a Team

Lucey continued working with those who played key roles during the campaign. His first major appointment was to name his campaign manager, Richard W. Weening, chief of staff. Weening's first tasks were to coordinate the transition between administrations and then to captain the effort to persuade the Republican-controlled senate to support Lucey's controversial proposals for tax reform and for restructuring public universities.[1]

Lucey asked Stephen Holmgren, who had been the campaign's schedule director, to serve in a similar capacity after the election. Holmgren was the appointments secretary, the governor's main scheduler and gatekeeper. Esther Kaplan, the comptroller in the Lucey campaign and a longtime player in the Democratic Party, pushed for Holmgren's appointment. She had been impressed with Holmgren when he insisted that Lucey refuse to accept the offer of David Martin, the GOP candidate for lieutenant governor, to be a last-minute substitute for Jack Olson in a debate scheduled for the gubernatorial candidates. Kaplan suggested to Lucey that Holmgren's style and judgment indicated he would be good in the job.

Weening offered Holmgren an annual salary of twelve thousand dollars, and Holmgren immediately accepted. Lucey then sat down with Holmgren and observed that the governor's salary was only twenty-five thousand dollars. Would Holmgren settle for less than his original offer—say, ten thousand five hundred dollars? Without hesitation or regret, Holmgren agreed that would be fair.[2]

David Lasker, the campaign's field director, had expected that he, too, would be offered a position. But Lucey, who served as a mentor to many who worked for him, reminded Lasker that he had planned to go to law school. Lucey had always considered a law degree valuable—even for himself at one point—and he urged Lasker to pursue his original plans.

Robert H. Dunn was new to Wisconsin when he was appointed to be the director of the executive office, reporting to Weening. David Adamany was the matchmaker between Lucey and Dunn. Adamany was dean and Dunn was associate dean at Wesleyan University when Lucey was elected. When Adamany returned to campus after the election, he convinced Dunn to meet with the governor-elect. He had no specific job in mind but rather a belief that Dunn would enjoy the opportunity to work with Lucey and that Lucey would be well served by Dunn.

Dunn traveled to Madison. After twiddling his thumbs for two days while waiting for a meeting, he had lunch with several people, including Weening, Kaplan, and Lucey. After lunch, Lucey told Dunn to meet him at his home, after which the governor-elect drove him to the airport. During the ride, Lucey asked if Dunn was going to be working for him. Dunn said he didn't know that he had an offer, and Lucey assured him that he did. Dunn resigned his position at Wesleyan effective at the end of the semester and then drove to Wisconsin. He went to Green Bay on a snowy Christmas Eve to stay with Adamany and his family. On the way, he saw his first snowmobile.[3]

Lucey persuaded Blake Kellogg to be his press secretary. Lucey got to know Kellogg during the nine years he was the news director for the WKOW television channel in Madison. At the time of his appointment to Lucey's staff, Kellogg was working as news director for KWWL, a television and radio station in Waterloo, Iowa.

Allen W. "Sandy" Williams Jr. was brought into the governor's office to be the pardon counsel. The plan was to hire someone else to be legal counsel to the governor. However, Lucey was so impressed with Williams after two days that he appointed him as legal counsel as well.[4] Williams did his undergraduate work at Harvard University and had just earned his law degree at Columbia University.

Joseph E. Nusbaum got the first cabinet appointment. Nusbaum was the secretary of the Department of Administration (DOA) when the agency was first created in 1959 under Governor Nelson. DOA helps the governor craft and manage the state budget. Kaplan once again played a key role. She persuaded both Lucey and Nusbaum that they would make a great team.

Lucey gave the people he appointed considerable discretion, and Nusbaum immediately put that to the test. He told Lucey he wanted to name Wayne McGown as his deputy secretary. McGown had served as secretary of DOA for Knowles. Lucey noted that some Democrats might raise their eyebrows but gave Nusbaum a green light. An advantage, Lucey reasoned, was that this would reassure Republicans that he was more concerned about competence and civility than about partisanship.[5]

Lucey appointed Edward Wiegner to head the Department of Revenue. Wiegner was on the economics faculty at Marquette University and had earned his PhD at the University of Wisconsin. Lucey had consulted Wiegner during the campaign and would rely on him to help fulfill the pledge to collect enough taxes to balance the budget but to do so in a progressive way.

Lucey asked his staff to research his options in assigning responsibilities to lieutenant governor–elect Martin J. Schreiber. Lucey remembered his own experiences in that office and wanted better opportunities for Schreiber. Lucey considered appointing Schreiber as secretary of the Department of Regulation and Licensing. Staff research concluded that doing so would, however, require a statutory change and perhaps even a constitutional amendment—neither of which seemed likely to pass the Republican-controlled senate.[6] Instead, staff suggested that Lucey give Schreiber some policy issue to pursue.[7] Schreiber focused on elder care.[8]

Lucey generally chose to surround himself with bright, young, inspired people. Members of the press referred to his staff as the Kiddie Corps. The elders were Nusbaum and Kellogg, who were forty-six and forty, respectively, at the time of their appointments. Wiegner was thirty-one. The rest were in their twenties, as was the common pattern for those who joined the staff throughout the Lucey years. In interviews with the author, many said John F. Kennedy had inspired them to go into public service. Everyone said they appreciated the opportunity to work with Lucey, who challenged them to think, to analyze, and to work hard.

For his part, Lucey said he valued advisers who were smarter than he was.[9] Lon Sprecher and Dan Wisniewski, members of the Kiddie Corps, understood his reasoning, but they considered Lucey to be "the smartest person in the room."[10]

Lucey relied heavily on task forces. During his tenure as Wisconsin's chief executive, he appointed forty such teams focusing on a variety of issues, including agriculture and rural affairs, health planning, voter registration and elections, environmental protection and natural resources, and offender rehabilitation.[11] Executive orders establishing task forces defined missions in general terms and did not foreclose particular findings or recommendations.

Creating task forces is agenda setting. It can be merely symbolic, but Lucey made appointments to those commissions seriously and relied

A cartoon sketch by Larry Sanders of the *Milwaukee Journal* depicts Lucey's young staff, nicknamed the Kiddie Corps by members of the press. COURTESY OF STEPHEN HOLMGREN

on them for both analysis and support. Typically, a task force included legislators from both political parties, advocates, experts, and citizens who had expressed interest in the issue. Lucey expected the commissions to hold hearings around the state to solicit ideas and reactions. It was left up to each commission whether to use these hearings to identify problems, gather suggestions, and/or get reactions to draft recommendations. Task force members would usually help generate legislative support for the recommendations that grew out of their work.[12]

Task forces and study commissions can become liabilities if they lose grounding in what is realistic or practical.[13] Lucey's commissions, however, generally provided studies and recommendations that he found useful.[14] Many of his initiatives were informed by task forces, some of which had been appointed by his Republican predecessor. The recommendation of his task force on prison reform to close state correctional institutions was clearly the most controversial and radical. Lucey expressed respect for task force members, but he did not pursue the idea of general prison closure, although he did agree that the reformatory in Green Bay was not needed.[15]

## WISCONSIN'S FIRST LADY

Jean Lucey hardly fit the mold of a supportive political wife of her era. Dunn recalled meeting her on his first visit to the governor's mansion, where he was supposed to meet the governor about a potential job in the administration. Standing at the front door, he heard yelling coming from inside and rang the doorbell with some trepidation. When Jean opened the door and asked who he was and what he wanted, Dunn answered that he had been asked to come and meet with Lucey and that they were discussing a position on the governor's staff.

She reportedly told him to come in and said, "Well, if you're going to work for Pat, you are going to have to get used to me!"

Dunn learned that was a fair prediction. Jean was independent, outspoken, and often had vocal disagreements with Lucey's staff. She was protective of her husband and had difficulty adjusting to being a public figure and to handling the demands Lucey faced as governor. "They want a governor's wife to sit around and have teas. Well, I don't like tea parties. I'm not a tea party dame," Jean Lucey said in a 1977 interview.[16]

While Jean was widely regarded as an excellent cook and could be gracious and charming as a hostess, she sometimes chafed at the limelight that came with being the governor's wife. Although she took steps to protect her family's privacy, her marriage was a topic of interest to the public and the media. While many couples might have spats, theirs were front-page news. Such was the case when Jean called the police at 11:09 p.m. on a St. Patrick's Day to complain that Pat refused to open their bedroom door at the governor's mansion. When the police arrived, they found her "kicking the door to their bedroom, shouting and swearing at Mr. Lucey." The police reported that alcohol was a factor. They waited until the situation calmed and Jean was able to retrieve some things from the bedroom and leave for their private residence.[17]

Pat Lucey made light in interviews of the suggestion that his wife was a political liability. As governor, Lucey spoke of not wanting an inner circle that would tell him only what he wanted to hear. That was already the case at home. "Certainly, if there was any possibility that I would develop the kind of ego that makes it difficult to make day-to-day decisions in the context of the real world, I can't think of anybody that would do a better job of deflating one's ego than my wife does on a daily basis," he said, laughing.[18]

## BUDGET AND AGENDA SETTING

Lucey had three months from the day he was elected to send a two-billion-dollar biennial budget proposal to the legislature. Budgets inherently make policy choices and establish priorities. Wisconsin's approach to budgeting provided Lucey with a particularly valuable opportunity for pursuing his agenda. Unlike the federal process, which requires separate actions to authorize and then appropriate money for various programs, Wisconsin authorizes and appropriates simultaneously. The state budget includes narratives as well as dollar figures.

One strategy for getting a new policy adopted is to include it in the budget. Being part of a broader package and a bill that must be passed enhances the chances of passage. More than his predecessors, Lucey used the budget to enact new policies.

In addition, Wisconsin's constitution empowers governors to veto parts of legislation that appropriate funds. To override a veto requires a two-thirds majority in both chambers—a very high bar that is rarely met. Lucey expanded the governor's authority through extensive use of the partial veto. He altered policies as well as sums in budgets sent to his desk.

Wisconsin state government begins the development of its biennial budget in even-numbered years. By early summer, governors provide executive agencies with revenue estimates and instructions. Agencies submit requests for spending authority by fall. (See Appendix A for an outline of the budget process.) Thus, when Lucey was elected in November 1970, he had in hand revenue estimates and agency spending requests for the July 1, 1971, through June 30, 1973, budget period. Lucey started the formulation of his first budget proposal with a five-hundred-million-dollar deficit. He had to address the gap between spending requests and expected revenue to comply with the constitutional mandate for a balanced budget.

Lucey was supposed to submit his budget proposal to the legislature by February 1, 1971. Nonetheless, he was very deliberative and refused to be rushed. Lucey, in fact, inserted a new step in the process. He got approval

A cartoon by Larry Sanders that appeared in the *Milwaukee Journal* depicts Lucey and the fiscal crisis he faced when elected governor in 1970. WHI IMAGE ID 143902

from the legislature to delay submission of his budget by one month and held seven hearings at locations around the state so that the public could have direct input. Some of the hearings encouraged comments on a particular theme or issue. The last one, held on December 23, 1970, in Stevens Point, for example, focused on rural concerns. Lucey was so pleased with the results of the hearings that he announced he would repeat this step when the biennial budget for 1973–75 was developed.[19]

Lucey was not happy with the bleak fiscal forecasts. His initial assessment was that the property tax relief he promised during the campaign might have to wait until the 1973–75 biennium and that because of the sluggish economy he might have to propose a six-month delay in any tax increases.[20] On December 11, three weeks before his inauguration, Lucey asked agency heads to begin austerity measures by freezing all hiring, cutting outside consulting services, and minimizing out-of-state travel. After he took the oath of office, the governor extended those austerity measures to June 30, 1971, the end of the fiscal year.[21]

Lucey had a personal goal of keeping the budget total below $2 billion and succeeded with a total of $1.98 billion. Despite the projection of tough times, Lucey provided one hundred million dollars in property tax relief. Lucey's budget proposed major policy initiatives:

- Merge the University of Wisconsin and the Wisconsin State University System.

- Change the basis for sharing state funds with local governments from where tax revenues originate to where populations and needs were the highest.

- Increase the state's share of funding for schools.

- Raise tax rates for higher incomes and rely more on the progressive income tax and less on regressive sales and property taxes.

- Restore cuts in funding for programs for the poor and develop programs that help families achieve financial independence.

- Focus on community approaches instead of emphasizing institutions to care for the mentally ill, blind, deaf, elderly veterans, and convicted criminals.

Reactions to the proposals varied in large part along party lines. The Democratic majority in the assembly applauded, while the Republicans who controlled the state senate declared, "Lucey's honeymoon with the legislature is over."[22]

Republicans in the senate caucused and decided to remove policy changes from Lucey's budget. They were particularly insistent that initiatives on shared revenue and the university merger be considered as separate legislation. That gave them a better chance to reject the proposals and, if they should pass, to keep Lucey from altering their bills with his partial veto pen, since only legislation that appropriates funds is subject to the partial veto. Lucey eventually agreed to separate them from the budget but vowed he would not entertain signing the overall budget until he first had acceptable merger and revenue redistribution bills on his desk. The merger issue was separated, but revenue redistribution eventually made its way back into the budget bill as a whole.

## University Merger

Although the GOP controlled the senate, Democrats had some hope for getting enough Republicans to join them to pass the merger proposal. After all, Republican fingerprints were all over that bill. The Committee for Educational Reform (commonly referred to as the Kellett Commission, after its chair William R. Kellett) appointed by Governor Knowles had proposed combining the Wisconsin State University System campuses around the state with the University of Wisconsin, which included the Madison, Milwaukee, Green Bay, and Parkside campuses, as well as an extension program. Each system had its own board of regents. The Coordinating Committee for Higher Education (CCHE) was supposed to provide central direction over all the campuses, but it had limited authority. The Kellett Commission cited the obvious inefficiencies and redundancies in this arrangement. Lucey wanted to make government more efficient, and the university was, in his mind, the most visible example of a state institution needing reform. Republican leaders in the state senate were eager to deny Lucey an important achievement at the start of his term. They identified university merger as the issue on which to take their stand, thus making the issue politically important for both Lucey and Republicans, as Lucey saw an opportunity to demonstrate he could bridge the partisan divide. Despite his Republican ties, Kellett himself endorsed Lucey's merger proposal. Joining Kellett when he announced his support was William Kraus, who was a member and then staff to the CCHE and who had been associate campaign manager for Knowles's campaigns.[23] In addition, Republican Senator Raymond Heinzen of Marshfield had separately authored a bill to accomplish merger, and several other Republicans in the senate voiced support.[24]

Lucey took steps toward merger even before the legislature acted. On March 30, 1971, he announced at a press conference that he was filling two vacancies on the Board of Regents for the Wisconsin State University System with labor leader Bert McNamara and regional newspaper publisher John Lavine. He also filled a vacancy on the University of Wisconsin Board of Regents with his former rival, David Carley. Lucey announced that those three would be appointed to the Board of Regents of the merged University of Wisconsin as soon as legislators approved the proposal.

Senator Milo Knutson, a Republican from La Crosse, was particularly eager to see Lucey fail to achieve a high-profile victory. He got the senate to invite Lucey to defend the merger in an appearance before the senate meeting as a committee of the whole. Having a governor testify before the senate was unprecedented. Knutson calculated that Lucey either would embarrass himself by not accepting the invitation or would accept and then wither before a barrage of attacks. Lucey conferred with Republican Majority Leader Bob Knowles of New Richmond, with whom he had maintained a personal friendship. Knowles said he thought Lucey could use it to his advantage. Lucey's staff split on their advice.[25] He accepted the invitation.

Lucey prepared by digesting volumes of background material prepared by Department of Administration analysts. Lucey spoke for twenty minutes and then answered questions. Knutson's gamble failed. The questions were hostile and challenging, but Lucey had anticipated them and was ready. As Lucey was leaving the senate chamber, Knowles said, "Thanks for coming, Governor. I don't think we will be doing this again soon."[26] Lucey received favorable press coverage and earned pledges of support from several moderate Republicans.[27]

While Lucey was in the senate, the legislature's Joint Committee on Finance met to consider supporting the merger. That committee is responsible for reviewing budget proposals and recommending action to each of the legislative chambers. It has commonly been regarded as the single-most powerful committee in the legislature. Democratic Representative George Molinaro of Kenosha chaired the Joint Finance meeting. Molinaro had successfully pushed the creation of the University of Wisconsin–Parkside campus in his district, fondly referred to as "Molinaro U." He was concerned that merger would have the effect of relegating the relatively new Parkside campus to a low position in a large system.[28] At the same time, Madison campus leaders and faculty were concerned about their status slipping and bitterly opposed the merger. Esther Kaplan was closely associated with Madison faculty and staff and argued to Norm Anderson, the assembly majority leader: "If Platteville could call itself the University of Wisconsin, the name will forever be besmirched."[29] Tensions were high.

Joint Finance in this session consisted of nine assembly representatives (seven Democrats and two Republicans) and five senators (four Republicans and one Democrat). The six Republicans voted against merger, seven Democrats in favor, and Molinaro, voting last, cast his ballot against, resulting in a seven-to-seven tie. The measure failed. Molinaro grumbled that if Lucey wanted his vote, he should come and discuss it. Lucey had a policy of not making deals to get votes, believing that it opens a never-ending process.[30]

Democratic Representative Dennis Conta of Milwaukee immediately called for a ten-minute recess, and Democrats assembled in Molinaro's office as Republicans sat back and grinned and the press corps sharpened their pencils. Conta notified Lucey, who dispatched Weening. Through the closed doors of Molinaro's office, one could hear Conta, Democratic Representative Anthony Earl of Wausau, and Democratic Senator Henry Dorman of Racine shouting. Weening burst in and announced, "The governor's mad as a hornet."[31]

The decibel level went down, and everyone left the office except for Molinaro and Weening. After the recess, Democratic Representative Ray Tobiasz of Milwaukee, the vice chair of Joint Finance, reconvened the committee and recognized Conta, who moved to reconsider the tie vote. Republican Senator Nile Soik of Fox Point asked, "Where's George?" and then answered his own question with the obvious: "George has been muzzled!"[32]

About fifty lobbyists and spectators laughed and enjoyed the tense but comedic exchange. The committee voted seven to six in favor of merger, with Molinaro recorded as absent. The drama in Joint Finance raised the visibility of the proposal and was credited with generating momentum.[33]

Ody Fish, a Knowles appointee to the University of Wisconsin Board of Regents and former chair of the Republican Party, worked with Senator Jim Devitt, a Republican from Greenfield, to scuttle the merger proposal. Most, but not all, GOP senators fell in line.

Weening visited key Republican senators in their districts to convince them to support the bill. He visited with one senator, Arthur Cirilli, at his home in Superior in far northwestern Wisconsin and came away with the impression that Cirilli favored the merger but was under pressure from his caucus to oppose it. Weening invited Cirilli to meet in Madison and have dinner with him and Lee Dreyfus, who had been a neighbor of Lucey before assuming the position of president of Wisconsin State University–Stevens Point. Dreyfus, who would be elected governor as a Republican in 1978, was a strong and articulate supporter of merger. His backing seemed to help recruit Cirilli to the camp of Republican supporters, but Cirilli made no commitment. Weening also made no commitment during a side discussion of Cirilli's interest in being appointed by the governor to a vacancy on the court in Douglas County, aware that Lucey would not make such a deal. Cirilli knew this, too, although he also realized that voting against the merger would not advance his cause.

Lucey met with Earl, Conta, and Weening for an update about the bill's prospects as the senate was about to vote. Earl told him that they were very close and probably needed the vote of Cirilli to ensure victory. When discussing Cirilli's judicial aspirations, Weening told the governor that Cirilli was probably going to ask for an appointment but was highly principled and, like the governor, unlikely to suggest a deal. He shared his assessment that Cirilli was probably going to vote in favor of the merger. Lucey looked at Earl and Weening and said, "I think Art Cirilli would look good in a robe, don't you?" They all laughed and left with fingers crossed. Indeed, Cirilli voted aye and several weeks after the session ended asked Lucey for the court appointment. Having anticipated the request, Lucey was very happy to grant it.[34]

Another key Republican vote was that of Clifford "Tiny" Krueger from Merrill. Dreyfus was a key constituent of his and helped secure Tiny Krueger's vote.

On September 17, the senate passed Heinzen's bill, as amended to be consistent with Lucey's vision. Six Republican senators (Bidwell, Cirilli, Heinzen, Johnson, Krueger, and Lorge) voted aye. Democratic Senator Fred Risser of Madison initially voted no but then switched in favor. On October 5, the assembly gave its approval, 55 to 42, with all thirty-four Republicans voting in opposition. Five days later, Lucey signed the bill.

The merger proposal that passed in 1971 included a provision for a subsequent implementation bill that would address issues of governance, campus autonomy, and the role and authority of a central administration and a single board of regents. Lucey and university administrators appointed a Merger Implementation Study Committee that produced a report recommending that each campus have a distinct mission and strong faculty control and that the central board of regents use a formula for allocating money to universities that emphasized enrollment. The

Governor Lucey signs the university merger implementation bill with UW President John Weaver, Lieutenant Governor Martin Schreiber, and other officials.
WHI IMAGE ID 143900

committee also urged recognition and support for the unique importance of research at Madison.

It took three years to pass implementation legislation. In part, the process was lengthy because it was so important. It also took so long because opponents sought to undo the 1971 act. In the meantime, Lucey grew frustrated, and university administrators complained that they were unable to make hires and pursue programs that depended on long-term certainty of how higher education in the state would be run. On January 9, 1974, Lucey threatened to call a special session of the legislature if the implementation legislation was not passed before the end of March.[35] When a governor calls a special session, he or she specifies and limits the agenda. Legislators, of course, do not have to approve the governor's proposal, but they must focus on the issue for which the session was called and may not act on other proposals. The threat prompted action, and a special session was not necessary. When Lucey signed the bill on July 2, 1974, the University of Wisconsin System became the country's third largest, behind New York and California.

The significance of the merger for the Lucey legacy was fundamentally twofold. Foremost, the merger reframed the state's approach toward higher education and emphasized efficiency, accessibility, and quality over the competitiveness and political jockeying that had dominated Wisconsin's disjointed higher education system. Also significant, partisanship took a back seat to civility and problem-solving. Lucey took an idea born and bred by a Republican administration and willed it into reality. While some Republican leaders were loath to let Lucey begin with a win and opposed university merger in spite of GOP identification with the idea, others pursued the merits of the issue and joined Lucey in arriving at a resolution.

## TAX AND REVENUE-SHARING REFORM

Lucey's 1971–73 budget pursued fundamental progressive principles of taxation based on the ability to pay and expenditures that provide for the common good and that helped the disadvantaged. As Wisniewski, one of Lucey's aides, observed, "Almost all of the major issues he pushed dealt with income equality. He felt strongly that people who happened to live in poorer communities or school districts or university communities outside Madison should have 'equalized' support from state government. That was the heart of his efforts."[36]

Lucey's budget replaced point of origin as the basis for sharing state revenues with local governments with formulas that distributed funds on the basis of population and need. The state's policy had been to send money to school districts and local government in accordance with how much their residents paid to the state in income taxes. That, of course, advantaged the already advantaged. River Hills became the symbol of relatively wealthy suburban communities that benefited from the point-of-origin approach. The bucolic village of fifteen hundred residents living in comfortable homes on five-plus acre lots along the Milwaukee River became the oft-cited target in the legislative debate of Lucey's redistribution plan.[37]

As with the university systems merger, revenue redistribution had initially been proposed by the Knowles administration via the Task Force on Local Government Affairs, known as the Tarr Task Force. However, the Republican-controlled legislature rejected the task force recommendations in 1969, objecting to sending relatively less money to wealthy areas of the state. Lucey altered the proposals to soften short-term blows to these communities by holding state funding to them relatively constant while channeling more resources to poorer areas. In addition, he delayed tax increases to upper-income individuals and to corporations, reasoning that it would be bad timing to do that when the economy was not doing well.

Even while compromising, Lucey insisted on the general concepts of progressive tax reform and revenue distribution. His program included increasing the state share of school costs, extending the homestead tax for the elderly to include the poor, expanding personal property tax relief, redistributing shared taxes, and not adding a sales tax on necessities of life.[38]

Lucey's objective was to fundamentally reformulate fiscal relations in the state. The formula he proposed was dubbed "the equalization formula." One expectation was that if the state increased its share of school costs and shared revenue based on population and need instead of point of origin, the migration of businesses and the middle class from cities to suburbs might be halted or at least slowed. Municipalities statewide could provide more and better services without massive increases in property taxes.

Lucey reached across the partisan aisle to achieve tax reform. He nurtured working relationships with moderate Republicans, especially in the senate, who had supported the Tarr Task Force, and he endorsed President Richard Nixon's federal revenue-sharing initiative. Lucey noted with approval the provision in Nixon's plan that at least 44 percent of federal money returned to states go to local municipalities, without any strings attached. Lucey saw that as an important component in his own plan for property tax relief.[39]

Joint Finance approved Lucey's submission, with few changes, on May 21, 1971, and sent it to the assembly. In addition to the policy changes offered by Lucey, the committee approved an amendment offered by Conta to fund urban mass transit partially from some of the money generated by the gasoline tax and auto registration fees. This amendment changed the policy of using this revenue only for roads.[40]

On June 12, the assembly passed Lucey's budget and sent it to the senate. Instead of voting on the bill passed by the assembly, however, the senate passed its own budget, giving Republicans their best chance at influencing the final product. An impasse between the assembly and the senate forced the establishment of a conference committee with equal representation from each house to try to devise a compromise. According to legislative rules, a bill that is agreed to in a conference committee must go back to each chamber for approval or rejection. It cannot be amended.

Deliberations and accusations dragged far beyond the July 1 date on which a new budget is supposed to take effect. According to Wisconsin law, taxing and spending continues in accordance with the most recently passed budget. Government does not shut down, but the absence of a new budget frustrates individuals, businesses, and local governments who need to know what to expect so they can develop their own plans.

Two conference committees—one for revenue redistribution and one for the budget as a whole—convened. The three Republican senators appointed to the redistribution committee were outspoken opponents of Lucey's proposal. After three weeks of unproductive talks, the three Democratic assembly members walked out, complaining that their counterparts were not interested in compromise.[41] School districts needed to set tax rates for 1972 by October 18, 1971. Pressure on the conference committee increased.

Weening and other aides worked on shoring up Democrats and getting the support of Republicans. Lucey met individually with senators of both parties.[42]

Lucey also made grassroots efforts to get senators on board. He gave speeches and held press conferences in the districts represented by those on the fence or on the wrong side of the fence. He was helped by his longtime rival Milwaukee Mayor Henry Maier, who represented the coalition he founded of have-not municipalities and was particularly concerned about the fate of revenue sharing.[43] Lucey met with officials from cities throughout the state and urged them to join him in pressing for fundamental change. He said, "The chance to get long-term reform is before us. Whether we succeed or we fail, the short-term problems will remain."[44] The governor suggested that city representatives back the proposal before the legislature and then bring in a special request in January for relief from any transition problems.

After a number of strategic legislative maneuvers, the senate passed a budget bill with the redistribution initiative. Seven Republican senators joined twelve Democrats to send it to the assembly. A coalition of six Republicans (including Senator Robert Knowles) and all thirteen Democrats was critical in rejecting hostile amendments. Republican Senator Myron Lotto of Green Bay threatened the Republicans who sided with Lucey and the Democrats, saying, "I want to congratulate the governor, his whiz kids, and the unholy six for this. It's going to take a while to regain your position with us."[45]

The only amendment Republican opponents in the senate were able to get adopted in their battle with the winning coalition was a provision that allowed nine communities where large utility plants were located to keep a sizeable share of the taxes on those plants. Lucey, however, used his partial veto authority to strike that clause from the final bill.[46]

Lucey reframed the fundamentals of his tax and revenue-sharing reforms and then built on them in future budgets. He increased funding from income, sales, and excise taxes for education and for property tax relief. The equalization formula was amended from time to time, but future governors and legislatures did not return to using point of origin as a basis for revenue sharing. In addition, the assumption that the state has responsibility for a major share of K–12 education has continued. The question has been how much.

While the ink was still drying on the 1971–73 budget, the governor prepared to submit a revision. In 1972, Lucey became the first governor to present a budget review report to the legislature. In part, the four-year term made reviews both possible and desirable.

Lucey told a joint session of the legislature on January 19, 1972, that revenue estimates had increased by $30.5 million due to an improving economy and because of the cuts he had mandated in agency spending. He downplayed the improved outlook for revenue, however, and argued the need for continued frugality. This provided him with an opportunity to invest more in fundamental changes while staving off pressures for increased spending on existing programs. His plan was to increase financial payments to school districts, using the recently passed reforms, and to raise the minimum standard deduction for the state personal income tax by three hundred dollars, effective on 1973 earnings. Lucey also proposed a more rapid depreciation allowance for businesses, saving Wisconsin businesses $2.9 million in the 1972–73 budget year.[47] Lucey did not include any policy changes in the budget review bill.

## PROGRESSIVE LEADERSHIP IN THE ASSEMBLY

Steve Holmgren was pulled aside by Norm Anderson at a party of Democratic legislators ushering in 1973. Holmgren was back on Lucey's staff after a stint with Ed Muskie's failed presidential campaign. The Democratic Assembly Caucus, meeting after the 1972 November elections, had elected Anderson to be speaker. Anderson, who was Lucey's preferred candidate to be speaker, told Holmgren, "Tell your boss he will be very happy with the appointment I made to cochair the Joint Finance committee. Happy New Year!"[48]

This was an announcement of enormous significance. Lucey had just secured the legislative leadership that would enable him to achieve the major progressive reforms on his agenda. Prior to the postelection caucus meeting, Anderson, Earl, and Conta met to consider leadership positions. The agreement: Anderson would be speaker, Earl would be majority leader, and Conta would be the assembly's cochair of Joint Finance. They did not actively campaign among their Democratic colleagues, however, and were surprised by a rival slate of more conservative legislators. Joseph Sweda and John McCormick led the alternative slate and had the active support of Bert Grover and the current cochair of Joint Finance, Molinaro, who was eager to continue in that position. The more conservative leaders almost won. Had they prevailed, Lucey would not have enjoyed the success that he experienced.[49]

Even after the election of Anderson as speaker, Molinaro's supporters almost dismantled the team supporting progressive reforms. Anderson faced considerable pressure from conservatives in the Democratic caucus and met with Conta to persuade him to agree to withdraw his candidacy for the Joint Finance position. Labor union leaders who backed Molinaro promised Conta support for a run at a seat in the US House of Representatives if he demurred. Conta, however, held firm. He saw an opportunity to have a major impact on public policy if he stayed home.[50] Lucey was not inclined to intervene, but realizing what was at stake, he met with Anderson and made his case for adhering to the arrangement Anderson agreed to with Conta and Earl. The governor was persuasive and was glad to get the New Year's greeting.

Conta had been in close contact with Lucey and his staff even before he served as cochair of Joint Finance. That intensified once he assumed

leadership. He met almost daily with Nusbaum and Holmgren in particular. He considered Holmgren like the tenth member of the committee.[51]

## 1973–75 BUDGET

Lucey was in a good position to include bold changes in his $2.8 billion
1973–75 budget. Not only did he have the support from legislative leaders
that he needed, he had almost $800 million in funds that were not already
allocated because of previous commitments or formulas or because of
federal requirements. The unallocated funds were due in part to savings
from productivity improvement plans and limits on travel and hiring.
In addition, there was a surplus of $139 million in unspent funds from
1972, a windfall of $464 million in tax revenue in a better-than-expected
economy, and $170 million in federal revenue-sharing funds.[52]

Lucey used an analytical, deliberative approach to shaping the 1973–75
state budget. Incremental decision-making typically drives budgets. Agencies, governors, and legislators begin with the existing budget and focus on
whether to make changes in levels of spending and taxing. Comprehensive
planning and reordering of programs and priorities are rare.[53] The four-
year gubernatorial term allowed Lucey to counter the tendencies toward
incrementalism and make more sweeping changes.

His process started with a review of priorities. Lucey instructed agencies to list their programs and services in order of importance with special
attention to the lowest 10 percent. He cautioned against playing games,
such as listing highly visible and sensitive programs at the bottom on the
assumption that it was unlikely those would be cut. Lucey wanted agency
lists by April and indicated it was likely he would cut or eliminate half of
the lowest priority programs and services.[54] Lucey explained, "We must
identify and terminate lower priority and obsolete programs to pay for
critical new needs that remain unsatisfied."[55]

Another key element of Lucey's budget process was to instruct agencies
to submit productivity improvement plans for his review and approval.
Lucey set a productivity savings target of 3 percent for 1973–75. The agencies' plans were then incorporated into the general review and analysis of
each agency's budget request. Lucey excluded aid to individuals from the
saving targets.[56]

Public hearings once again played an important role. Pleased with the public hearings on the 1971–72 budget that he held around the state after he was elected, Lucey directed that they be repeated in the spring of 1972 to solicit public input at an early stage of the process. The hearings focused on five topics: regional planning, educational opportunities, job opportunities, government accessibility, and environmental concerns. In addition, Lucey informed task forces that he had created that they should also hold public hearings and forward budget recommendations in a timely manner.[57]

Lucey's approach toward budgeting and, especially, productivity garnered positive attention in the academic world as well as the policy arena. Scholars had critiqued the traditional incremental approach to budgeting and suggested lawmakers make a more systematic analysis of public spending. Lucey himself contributed to the academic literature on public-sector productivity. With assistance from his speech writer, Harold Wilde, he wrote two essays that were published in the top journal in public management and another in a new journal devoted to productivity in government.[58] The emphases were on measuring inputs and outputs in public management, on using analyses in budgeting, and on generating savings. His approach was cited in other scholarly works and became part of the more general discussion of government reforms.[59]

Lucey's budget bill was almost three hundred pages. It was based on more than seventy distinct analyses and accompanied by a thirteen-hundred-page document explaining proposals. Analysts in the Bureau of the Budget organized into four teams: education, health and social services, natural resources, and general government. Each team had five members, each one of them logging up to seventy hours each week. Lucey met with them at the executive residence to avoid inevitable interruptions in the governor's office.[60]

Lucey's first priority was to increase spending on property tax relief by $490 million. He also allocated $30.8 million for income and sales tax relief and built on the school funding formula passed the previous year. Republican legislators argued that instead of expanding on equalization, Wisconsin's citizens should simply get a refund check in the mail. Assembly Majority Leader Earl countered, "A one-time check is a gimmick as far as I'm concerned" and encouraged support for Lucey's long-term policy-based approach.[61]

Lucey meets with budget analysts at the capitol in January 1971.

Lucey enhanced his approach to property tax relief by including in his budget three fundamental changes. First, to ensure statewide uniformity, the state would train and pay half the cost of county assessors and take over the assessment of all manufacturing property. Second, the state would assume costs of critical health, welfare, and social service programs, which had been supported by property taxes levied by counties and local governments. Lucey felt the more appropriate source of funding was state income and sales taxes. The state took full responsibility for Supplemental Security Income, Medical Assistance, and Aid to Families with Dependent Children. In addition, Lucey recommended that the state pay 75 percent, rather than 55 percent, of most other mental health and welfare programs. Third, the state would place limits on taxation and spending by school districts. Lucey feared that without levy limits school districts might use increased state assistance for new expenditures rather than for property tax relief. He referred to these approaches to property taxes as "double duty dollars"— offering both tax relief and financial support for more effective policies.

Another key component of Lucey's tax restructuring was to exempt manufacturers' machinery and equipment from property taxes. While some progressives objected to such a break for businesses, Lucey argued the state should tax businesses' income, not their property. This was also important to encourage the growth of the state's economy. However, the M&E exemption, as it was called, deprived local governments of an estimated $51.1 million in property tax revenue in 1974. Lucey's proposal included state aid to local governments to make up for that loss.[62] The proposal became a major point of contention in the budget review bill in 1973, and implementation was postponed to 1975.[63]

Lucey's budget included increasing personal exemptions in the state income tax and reducing by half the inheritance tax on transfers between spouses. He also increased the homestead tax credit and, importantly, broadened eligibility from the elderly to include the poor. And Lucey called for a repeal of the 5.25 cents a pound tax on oleomargarine (the ban on which had been lifted in 1967).

In addition to comprehensive, progressive tax reforms, Lucey used his 1973–75 budget to pursue major policy and productivity measures. Analyses demonstrated, for example, that some state institutions were underutilized. That prompted Lucey to propose closing the juvenile prison in Green Bay, the children's treatment center in Sparta, and a hospital at the prison in Waupun. When legislators objected, he compromised and agreed to close only one cell block at Green Bay and reduce the number of prison employees by one hundred.[64]

Much to the chagrin of future governor Tommy Thompson, Lucey sold a newly built but not yet opened correctional facility in Adams County to the federal government for the bargain price of one crisp new dollar bill.[65] That prison was in Thompson's assembly district. The federal government assumed the debt the state incurred to build the prison.

Lucey agreed to a pay increase for elected state officials but only if the legislature agreed to adopt an ethics code. The new law prohibited taking remuneration from private sources for public duties and asking or receiving anything of value for influencing official duties. The measure outlawed business and professional work that conflicted with public duties, either in substance or appearance. Legislators tied their pay to salaries of senior civil servants so that from 1975 onward they would not vote on their own compensation, a move that was politically sensitive.

Lucey pushed to replace part-time citizen boards established as part of the progressive reforms of Governors Robert M. La Follette and

Francis E. McGovern with secretaries who would serve at the pleasure of the governor, a system commonly referred to in the United States as *cabinet government*. Lucey reasoned that state agency responsibilities had grown and required a more accountable form of management. His budget focused on two of the largest state agencies: the Department of Health and Human Services and the Department of Industry, Labor and Human Relations.

The *Milwaukee Journal* editorialized in favor of Lucey's budget. It called the proposal "a brilliant document" and opined:

> As the first Wisconsin budget to benefit fully from a four year executive term, it is enabled to be the most thorough and comprehensive one ever laid before a legislature. . . . It grasps the opportunity to reallocate funds where they will do the most good, with lasting impact, in the most responsible way.
>
> Lucey . . . has drafted his 1973–75 executive budget just as he said he would, to shift a significantly large portion of total taxes from regressive sources to more equitable ones, and to make these so-called tax relief funds work constructively in the process—mainly to make the state-wide concern felt more effectively in welfare and education policies. His term for these fund reallocations—"double duty dollars"—is not just a catchy slogan.[66]

Both chambers passed the budget essentially as Lucey first proposed it. On July 24, 1973, the senate voted 16 to 13, with four Republicans joining twelve Democrats, to approve the measure. Two days later, the assembly approved the budget 58 to 38, with three Republicans voting in favor, and placed the document on the governor's desk. Lucey used his partial veto pen to delete the "2" from "$25 million," thereby reducing borrowing for highway construction to $5 million. That drew attention to how powerful and creative the partial veto could be. He made few other changes before signing the budget bill.

The final act in the drama of the 1973–75 budget legislation was the 1974 budget review bill, which primarily made modest adjustments based on updated forecasts of revenue and expenditures. The major substantive issue addressed fears that the fund for revenue sharing would be skimmed to reimburse local governments for property tax revenue lost because of the recently enacted machinery and equipment exemption. Lobbyists for municipalities and legislators from the Milwaukee area calculated that the net result would be less money available overall for local governments. The cost to Milwaukee, for example, would have been $600,000 in 1974–75 and about $3.9 million in the future. Milwaukee Mayor Maier and his aides met with Lucey, Secretary of Revenue Adamany, and Department of Administration Executive Assistant Robert Milbourne for almost an hour on April 10, 1974, and then Lucey and Maier met alone for another thirty minutes to discuss the issue. Maier was reassured, anxieties subsided, and Lucey proceeded with his work on the budget.[67]

Lucey called the legislature into a special session on April 29. The agenda included the budget review bill plus nine other items. The senate rejected a special session bill that would have reorganized the Department of Transportation into a cabinet agency. Republicans also defeated a bill granting the state regulatory powers over the cable television industry and a proposal to emphasize rehabilitation of youth offenders.

## CHAPTER 11

# RULES OF THE GAME

The Democratic Party has struggled with being democratic, and Pat Lucey was at the center of some of the major struggles. Several fundamental questions came to the fore in the 1970s:

- Should the party be open to any and all, or should it be limited to those with long-term and serious commitments to the party?

- Should the party be a loose confederation of state organizations, or should it be a unitary national institution?

- Is the party a private organization that gathers like-minded people, or is it so integral to representative government that it should be regulated?

Lucey was a key actor in large part because of his general stature in the party nationally as well as in Wisconsin. His record in organizing and energizing the Democratic Party of Wisconsin favored an open, grassroots organization. He adhered to the antimachine philosophy of the Progressive movement of the early twentieth century, and he applied those principles to battles in the party.[1]

## THE 1972 ELECTION

In February 1969, Fred Harris, the chair of the Democratic National Committee (DNC), appointed the Commission on Party Structure and Delegate Selection, often referred to as the McGovern–Fraser Commission after leaders Senator George McGovern and Representative Donald Fraser. The DNC instructed the twenty-eight commission members to establish guidelines for state parties that provided open and transparent processes for selecting delegates to future Democratic conventions and ensured representation of women, minorities, and young people.[2] McGovern resigned from the commission in 1971 to run for president, taking advantage of the new rules as well as the growing opposition to US military involvement in Vietnam.

Lucey was neutral during the 1972 Wisconsin primary. The initial field of candidates for the 1972 Democratic nomination was crowded, and their respective fortunes changed frequently and dramatically. McGovern's win in Wisconsin over Hubert Humphrey, Edmund Muskie, George Wallace, and eight others established him as a strong, viable candidate with momentum that virtually ensured him nomination on the first ballot when Democrats met in Miami.[3] After McGovern's win in Wisconsin, Lucey was active and energetic in building support for the South Dakota senator. Lucey served as a floor leader at the convention.

When McGovern won the nomination, his clear preference for the vice-presidential slot was Ted Kennedy, but Kennedy had no appetite for seeking a national office in 1972. He was still reeling from the 1969 incident when the car he was driving plunged into Poucha Pond on Chappaquiddick Island, killing his passenger, Mary Jo Kopechne. With Kennedy out of the picture, McGovern had his national political director, Frank Mankiewicz, assemble a twenty-four-person committee to provide advice on choosing a running mate. The committee had only three hours to sort through almost forty-five names.

Lucey had actively campaigned for the vice-presidential nomination. He and his supporters distributed buttons that read "McGovern–Lucey. Together We Win," and they circulated a pamphlet presenting Lucey's credentials and arguing that he was a progressive who could help McGovern win the election.[4] Lucey had told reporters that he would be honored to run with the South Dakota senator.[5] A cadre of Lucey supporters and staff— Bob Dunn, Jim Wood, Sandy Williams, and Paul Corbin—worked at the convention to build pressure to make the Wisconsin governor McGovern's running mate. They maintained contact with Steve Holmgren, who had worked on the Muskie campaign.[6]

The Mankiewicz committee gave McGovern a list that had Boston Mayor Kevin White at the top, followed by former press secretary to

President John F. Kennedy Pierre Salinger, Senator Abraham Ribicoff, Senator Gaylord Nelson, Governor Patrick Lucey, and Senator Thomas Eagleton. Kennedy and John Kenneth Galbraith vetoed White. Nelson said he was not interested and suggested Eagleton.[7] McGovern agreed and introduced Eagleton as his choice to cheering delegates.

After the ticket was set, McGovern learned that Eagleton had been hospitalized with severe depression. Initially, McGovern was going to stick with Eagleton as his running mate but then had second thoughts.[8] He called Lucey, among others, to seek advice. Lucey conferred with Keith Clifford, who was working on his legal staff, and requested that he ask county chairs in the Democratic Party of Wisconsin whether McGovern should drop Eagleton. That evening, with the assistance of Keith Johnson, a volunteer in Lucey's office, Clifford succeeded in reaching about one-half of the county chairs and found that most of them thought Eagleton should be dropped. Lucey reported the results to McGovern, who, after a brief conversation, told Lucey that he decided to drop Eagleton.[9] He was replaced by Sargent Shriver, the husband of Eunice Kennedy and the first director of the Peace Corps.

Lucey had mixed feelings about not being selected by McGovern, and it was awkward that he was involved in the decision to drop Eagleton. Although he had sought the nomination, not campaigning nationally freed him up to check off more on his to-do list in Wisconsin.[10]

McGovern lost the presidential contest to Richard M. Nixon—badly. He won only Massachusetts. At a press conference the day after the election, Lucey was asked if he thought McGovern might have won had he been the running mate. Lucey responded that McGovern would have won two states instead of just one. When then asked to name the second state, Lucey first raised his eyebrows and then joined in the laughter.[11]

Despite the debacle at the top of the ticket, Democrats in Wisconsin fared relatively well in 1972. Democrats retained control of the assembly and picked up two seats in the state senate. The party also achieved an edge in the congressional delegation. After the 1970 census, Wisconsin had its delegation in the House of Representatives reduced from ten to nine and had to redistrict. Prior to the 1972 election, the Wisconsin delegation was evenly divided between Democrats and Republicans. After the votes were counted, Democrats occupied five of the nine seats.

## Saving the Open Primary

The response of the Democratic Party to McGovern's overwhelming defeat—like the response to the disastrous 1968 convention in Chicago—was to change its rules for selecting delegates to the presidential nominating convention. The feeling was that the McGovern–Fraser reforms had contributed to the selection of a weak candidate. One concern was that the quota system guaranteeing that delegates include women, minorities, and young people had allowed so-called outsiders to play an outsized role. The other concern was that Republicans took advantage of open primaries in states such as Wisconsin by crossing over to vote in the Democratic primary for candidates unlikely to prevail in the general election—despite evidence to the contrary found in studies by political scientists.[12] The conclusion was that the party needed to have more control over its nominating process.

The solution was 1976 rule 2A. The DNC required state parties to restrict participation in the delegate selection process to Democratic voters only. It charged its Compliance Review Committee (CRC) with enforcing the rule. Delegates chosen in open primaries would no longer be recognized and seated at national conventions. States would have to record the party affiliation of voters and close their primaries to anyone not registered as a Democrat or use party caucuses to select delegates. In addition, 1976 rule 2A prohibited winner-take-all systems. States would have to send delegates pledged to candidates in accordance with the percentage of support each candidate got from Democrats in that state. Wisconsin's law ran afoul of 1976 rule 2A both because it required an open primary and because it allotted pledged delegates on a winner-take-all basis.

The new rule ran contrary to the letter and the spirit of Wisconsin law and progressive principles. Badger State traditions assumed it is not appropriate to require voters to state their party affiliation to exercise their right to vote. This principle was essential to thwart any effort to establish a political machine. Lucey felt that the DNC had thrown down the gauntlet. He was caught between his state's progressive principles and the party he had labored for his whole political life. It was not difficult for him to identify where his primary loyalty belonged.

Using the political and organizational skills for which he was famous, Lucey strategically maneuvered through the maze of state legislative procedures and DNC rules. A loophole provided a way out of the dilemma. The CRC had authority to waive 1976 rule 2A if a state party made a good-faith effort to comply but could not. State laws govern party primaries, so good-faith effort would be an attempt to change the laws in a state. Whether an effort that failed was nonetheless sufficiently in "good faith" to get a waiver was up to the CRC. Lucey strategized to get the waiver without abandoning Wisconsin's open primary.

On February 4, 1975, CRC Chair Robert F. Wagner sent Herb Kohl, the chair of the Democratic Party of Wisconsin, a memorandum establishing July 1, 1975, as the deadline for the state to submit its revised process for selecting delegates. Wagner also told Kohl to keep the CRC informed of progress as proposals were considered by the state legislature.[13]

Lucey, Kohl, and legislative leaders proceeded without a sense of urgency. Linda Reivitz was the executive assistant to Tony Earl, then secretary of the Department of Administration. One of her duties was to discuss departmental issues with legislators. Reivitz added the open primary concern of the CRC to her list. She understood that the real agenda was to establish a record to use in getting the CRC to waive the rule and seat Wisconsin's delegation. The objective was to make it look like Wisconsin was making a good-faith effort but without actually closing the primary. Reivitz inadvertently became a point person for media inquiries and became identified with a proposal to ask voters if they wanted to use a partisan ballot or an independent ballot.[14] The former would be used for delegate selection, and the latter would be only advisory. The proposal became known as "the Reivitz bill."[15]

Simultaneously to the discussions with legislators, Kohl had the administrative committee of the Democratic Party of Wisconsin formulate a way forward. Kohl's committee gave tentative approval to a plan, but the legislature never saw that plan.

While all this was (or was not) going on, Lucey and Kohl asked Wisconsin Attorney General Bronson La Follette to sue the CRC and the DNC to prevent them from rejecting Wisconsin's delegation to the national convention if the state retained the open primary. The suit argued the primacy of First Amendment protections against efforts to restrict how voters express themselves.

Wisconsin did not meet the July 1 deadline to report a new delegate selection process to the CRC. Rather than simply acknowledge that the state party intended to retain the open primary, party officers continued to act as though they were trying to change their rules. Party officials successfully applied for an extension of the CRC deadline from July 1 to July 15, then to August 15, and then to November 23.

Lucey called a special session of the legislature for the first week in December. Senator Carl Thompson, a Democrat from Stoughton, submitted SS SB-4, a proposal to sponsor an advisory presidential preference poll and then ask all voters participating in that poll if they also wanted to record their party affiliation and cast a ballot in a closed primary, which would be open only to registered Democrats. Republican Senator F. James Sensenbrenner (who would later be elected to Congress) criticized the bill as a "one-person-two-votes" scheme.[16]

National Democratic Party officials flew to Madison to lobby for ending Wisconsin's open primary. The delegation was led by National Democratic Chair Bob Strauss, who had been elected to purge the party of McGovern influence. He was supported primarily by southern and border-state officials and the AFL-CIO unionists who had opposed McGovern's nomination. Lucey was not a fan of Strauss, and the feeling was mutual. Strauss tried to make his reception in Madison somewhat welcoming by including in his delegation National Deputy Chair Mary Lou Burg, who was from West Bend, Wisconsin. Strauss first met with the Democratic caucus in the assembly. The reception was a chorus of loud and firm objections to the idea of closing the primary, which the senate caucus echoed.

As Strauss and company departed, the assembly—without debate—tabled the Reivitz bill. The senate voted 17 to 16 to postpone Thompson's proposal indefinitely.

On January 14, 1976, the executive committee of the DNC voted unanimously to find Wisconsin out of compliance with 1976 rule 2A. The committee ordered the state's Democratic Party to submit a plan to use caucuses unless by February 15 the legislature passed a bill closing the primary. On February 11, the senate took up Thompson's bill again, defeating it by a larger margin (21 to 11) than in the December special session.[17] The Dairyland's legislature would not be cowed.

Lucey was satisfied. His major objective in calling the special session was to provide evidence of a good-faith effort to get a waiver of 1976 Rule 2A, and legislators were on board with this.[18] He was counting on at least one of two outcomes: securing a waiver from the CRC or winning the lawsuit filed by La Follette.[19]

On February 16, Lucey made an official request to Strauss to appear at the next CRC meeting and seek a waiver. Lucey knew eighteen of the twenty-five CRC members and expressed confidence he could get the commission to set aside its ruling. Lucey worked with one of his aides, Brady Williamson, who listed on notecards personal information about each of the CRC members, including previous contacts with Lucey. Lucey then pursued a fourfold strategy to secure the votes needed for a waiver:

- Making personal telephone calls to the eighteen CRC members with whom he had previous experiences

- Asking Lucey's network of contacts in the party to argue for a waiver, focusing on CRC members who had ambitions to move up in the party ranks

- Having the campaign organizations of candidates supported by CRC members argue that they would do better in an open primary in Wisconsin than in caucuses (a particularly effective strategy in cases where the candidate did not have the organizational presence in the state that a caucus system requires)

- Getting the support of trusted peers or associates of the CRC member who also happened to be friends or political allies of Lucey to pressure for a waiver

Typically, the phone call was sufficient.[20] Lucey was able to make a reasonable argument that Wisconsin had made a good-faith effort. On March 5, the CRC met and heard Lucey's presentation, after which it voted 18 to 5 to overturn the finding that Wisconsin was not in compliance and grant the waiver.

The 1976 Wisconsin presidential primary was open and binding, although it no longer awarded delegates on a winner-take-all basis. Lucey reached an informal understanding with the DNC that Wisconsin's open primary would be followed by caucuses to select delegates in accordance with the results of the primary. Ten presidential candidates competed in the April 6 primary, and half of them garnered enough votes to be allocated delegates. Jimmy Carter and Morris Udall were the top vote-getters, with 271,220 and 263,771 respectively. Applying a proportionality formula, they were each allocated twenty-five delegates. The other candidates who qualified for delegates were Wallace (92,460 votes and ten delegates), Henry Jackson (47,605 votes and seven delegates), and Ellen McCormack (26,982 votes and one delegate).[21] Caucuses met on May 15 in each congressional district to elect delegates who would attend the upcoming Democratic convention in New York. A special caucus was held in Madison to select at-large delegates: four pledged to Carter, four to Udall, one to Wallace, and one to Jackson.

Lucey had voted for Udall, although he remained publicly neutral. He was not a delegate but, as governor, had privileges on the convention floor and served as chair of the Wisconsin delegation. James Sykes, coordinator of Wisconsin Carter for President and leader of the state's delegates pledged to Carter, supported naming Lucey as chair after being reassured of his neutrality. Sykes argued, "Frankly, we need and want Pat Lucey's support. . . . There is no question in our minds that a united Democratic effort will place Wisconsin in the Carter column in November."[22]

At the convention, Lucey was very active in persuading delegates to support Walter Mondale for the vice-presidential nomination. Carter agreed he would be a good choice, and the Carter–Mondale ticket won Wisconsin as part of winning the national election.

## Court Rulings

Wisconsin's open primary fared well in the Wisconsin Supreme Court but not in the US Supreme Court. Attorney General La Follette argued that the main issue was the right of voters to express their preference for a candidate without having to disclose publicly their party affiliation. He also contended that states, not a national organization, should continue to determine electoral law. Writing for a unanimous Wisconsin Supreme Court, on January 19, 1980, Associate Justice Shirley Abrahamson agreed with La Follette. In her thirty-four-page opinion, she pointed out that restricting participants in a primary election to those willing to state their party affiliation did not effectively prevent crossover voting. Voters could easily change their registration from one party to another as they voted in each primary election. She and her colleagues were not persuaded that Wisconsin's laws denied the Democratic National Party its First Amendment right of association.[23]

The US Supreme Court, however, reversed the Wisconsin ruling. In a 6 to 3 opinion, that court concluded that a state cannot compel a national party to seat a delegation that was chosen in a way that violates the rules of the party. Wisconsin could still have an open primary, the court reasoned, but that need not be the mechanism for selecting delegates.[24] In other words, the primary could be advisory. The national party had the right to stipulate that a caucus system be used to determine who represents the state at the nominating convention.

Lucey's victory in getting the DNC to accept delegates chosen through Wisconsin's open primary established a precedent and a general principle, even though it did not result in a new party rule at the time. The DNC informally accepted the pattern established in 1976 in which an open primary was followed by caucuses that customarily followed the results of the primary. The primary was technically nonbinding through 1984. Gary Hart won the Wisconsin primary that year, but those who participated in caucuses did not follow the primary results and instead favored Mondale. That was awkward, and state officials pressed for a rule change. In 1986, the DNC formally agreed that Wisconsin and Montana, effective in 1988, could have an open primary, and caucuses that followed to name actual delegates were bound by the results of the primary.

## 1974 REELECTION

Lucey had an impressive beginning to his tenure as governor. He achieved progressive tax reform and revenue sharing, restructured higher education, and adopted budget procedures that emphasized analysis and productivity. But he was eager to do more—much more. Lucey had that to-do list in his desk drawer. With a twinkle in his eye, he told a caucus of Republicans who controlled the state senate that he would not run for reelection if he got approval for everything on his agenda.[25] Not surprisingly, they balked. Lucey needed another term.

The Watergate scandal, which began with the break-in at the DNC offices on June 17, 1972, and resulted in the resignation of President Nixon on August 9, 1974, provided a challenging setting for Republicans running for almost any office.[26] The election of 1974 promised good fortune for Democrats.

Lucey wanted to be reelected, but he did not need—or expect—a landslide. Lucey knew that not everyone appreciated his style of leadership, and he felt it was more important to pursue change than popularity. If he got 51 percent of the vote, he would be happy.[27]

Lucey asked Jim Wood to run the reelection campaign. Wood and Lucey had worked on Bobby Kennedy's presidential campaign in Indiana, although they did not actually meet each other. Then a professor at Purdue University, Wood had been told to expect a busload of campaign workers from Wisconsin that Lucey had recruited to help with canvassing. Due to a staff miscommunication, however, the bus went to a different location, and Wood was left stranded. The wayward bus incident led to a heated exchange by phone between the two.

Four years later, Robert H. Friebert suggested to Wood—who had moved to Wisconsin and joined the faculty of Carroll College in Waukesha—that he might want to apply for a position as director of constituent relations in the governor's office. After discussions with members of Lucey's staff, Wood met with Lucey at the Pfister Hotel in Milwaukee. This was their first face-to-face meeting. Although Wood worried that their previous interaction might cost him the job, the call about the bus incident did not come up during the interview. Instead, Lucey probed Wood's background, experience, and interest, concluding somewhat oddly, Wood thought, with Lucey asking him if he knew what a predicate was. Wood assumed the question was asked in jest and responded, "No, but I know what a Democrat is." Lucey laughed, and Wood got the job. Only then, as Wood was leaving with his hand on the doorknob, did Lucey say: "Jim, I want you to know I haven't forgotten our phone conversation in Indiana."[28]

Wood began his constituent relations job by interviewing party officials and community leaders around the state. He held "office hours" around the state to solicit concerns and suggestions that he could convey to staff and agencies in Madison and follow up with case work. After examining the schedule kept by Claudia Dennis, Lucey's secretary, Wood concluded that Lucey was so immersed in his work as policy leader and chief executive that he risked losing touch with those who helped put him in office. Lucey was no longer attending party events or meeting with people outside the capitol. He had been unusually effective as a listener, but it seemed he had become too busy to continue to do that. Wood negotiated to set aside time for Lucey to get on the road and talk with people, calling the events "blue days" because they were marked on Dennis's calendar in blue ink.[29]

Wood resigned from the governor's staff in January 1974 to begin his work as campaign manager. He developed a campaign organization using the grassroots approach that Lucey had pioneered when building the Democratic Party of Wisconsin. He enjoyed his face-to-face interactions out on the campaign trail. While shaking hands and asking for support from those gathered in one village bar, Wood recalled encountering one person who loudly announced that there was no way he would vote for Lucey. When the tirade was over, Lucey turned to Wood and said, "Mark him down as 'undecided.'"

It was important to reach out to people throughout the state but essential to get support and high voter turnout in the twenty counties with the highest concentration of Democratic voters. Milwaukee, Dane County, and southeast Wisconsin were critical.

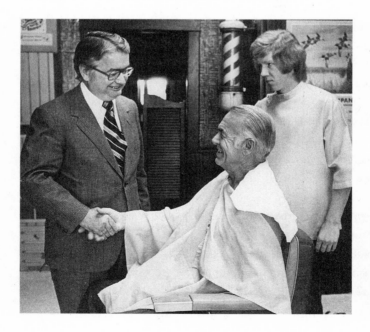

Lucey visits a barbershop in Horicon in April 1977. EDWIN STEIN, *WISCONSIN STATE JOURNAL*

The slogan and theme for the campaign was "Lucey Works for Wisconsin." Wood initiated discussions with speech writers and others on Lucey's staff on how to craft messages that were clear and understandable. Campaign messaging highlighted the governor's accomplishments and priorities, focusing on the following:

- Economic development—touting both Lucey's actions to promote the growth of businesses (such as the machinery and equipment property tax exemption) and his support for labor unions

- Education—pointing out the assumption by the state of a larger share of the costs of K–12 schools and the adoption of changes in property taxes to provide for more equity in funding public education

- Efficiency—explaining the use of productivity and austerity measures to pare state agency spending

- Environment—pursuing policies abating pollution and conserving natural resources[30]

When asked what the most important part of a campaign was, Lucey quipped, "Choosing your opponent."[31] He would not choose to run against some of the potential Republican candidates in 1974. Melvin Laird and Robert Warren, for example, would have been formidable opponents. Voters in central Wisconsin had elected Laird to the US House of Representatives. Laird went on to serve as Secretary of Defense under President Nixon. At his first meeting with his staff, Laird made it clear that his priority was to end US presence in Vietnam.[32] Laird was popular in his home state but in 1974 was happy as senior counselor for national and international affairs at *Reader's Digest*. He politely turned aside requests to run against Lucey.[33]

Warren was attorney general in Wisconsin and had been posturing to run for governor, but Nixon saved Lucey from a potentially difficult race by appointing Warren to a federal judgeship. Other possible candidates included Robert Kasten and Robert Knowles, both state senators at the time. They also demurred. William Dyke, a former mayor of Madison, wanted to run against Lucey, and Republicans were relieved to have a candidate.[34]

Dyke acknowledged that he entered the race as a distinct underdog.[35] State Representative John Alberts was the Republican candidate for lieutenant governor running against the incumbent Martin J. Schreiber.

Usually, incumbents running for reelection do not favor debates that might give their challengers the appearance of being on equal footing. Lucey, however, felt confident enough to begin the formal campaign by challenging Dyke to a debate. While he awaited a response, Lucey embarked on a five-day, twelve-hundred-mile campaign trip that took him into thirty-three Wisconsin communities.[36] Dyke did not commit to debating until October, and to his chagrin, the debates included independent and minor party candidates seeking to sit behind the desk in the east wing of the Wisconsin State Capitol.

One of Dyke's challenges was the lack of support he had from the business community, which usually backed Republicans. Lucey had convinced business owners that he understood their needs when he exempted machinery and equipment from the property tax. Lucey believed businesses should be taxed on their profits, not their property. He had increased income tax rates for the wealthy, and business owners seemed to accept that, although they didn't uncork champagne. Dyke was understandably not pleased with the business elite for supporting Lucey and spent much of his campaign railing against "fat cats."[37]

Lucey's popularity led him to outpace Dyke in fund-raising, as well. He outspent Dyke by about four to one: $370,000 to $94,000 ($1.9 million to $488,000 in 2019).[38] Come November, Wisconsin voters favored Lucey by 53.2 percent to Dyke's 42.1 percent. It was, as expected, a Democratic year, although Lucey had not anticipated a double-digit victory margin. To put it into perspective, Nelson won reelection that year to the US Senate beating Thomas Petri 61.8 percent to 35.8 percent. Democratic candidates won the other statewide contests—attorney general, treasurer, and secretary of state—and won control of both houses of the state legislature—the assembly 64 to 35 and the state senate 19 to 14. Democrats increased their margin in the assembly by two seats and picked up four GOP state senate seats to go from minority to majority status—the first time Democrats were in the majority in the senate since 1892!

At the victory party, Lucey invited legislators to join him in pursuing an agenda of reforming campaign finance, transportation policies, and automobile insurance regulation. Lucey also urged reorganization of agencies to pare costs and improve accountability.[39]

Having Democratic majorities in both chambers was a major asset for Lucey. But Democratic control of the legislature did not provide him with a blank check. For example, Tim Cullen was one of the Democrats elected to the state senate in 1974, and he indicated that he could not support the governor's 1975–77 budget proposal. Cullen supported equalization but took issue with a provision to transfer property tax revenue from wealthy to poor districts, referred to as *negative aid*. The proposal was to amend the equalization formula passed in the first term so that the richest districts collected more in property taxes than they were allowed to spend, with the remainder redistributed to the poorest school districts.

Dan Wisniewski, Lucey's senate relations assistant, ushered Cullen into Lucey's office. After giving Cullen his pitch, Lucey asked how he intended to vote. When Cullen repeated that he was casting his ballot with the opposition, Lucey let loose with an expletive, slammed his hands on his desk, and turned to stare out the window. After a long silence, Cullen and Wisniewski looked at each other, realized the meeting was over, and left the office.[40] The negative aid proposal passed in spite of Cullen's opposition, but in 1976, the Wisconsin Supreme Court ruled in *Busé v. Smith* that the policy violated the state constitution.

Lucey got a bit of revenge. Cullen authored an amendment that cut out-of-state travel by state employees by 25 percent—a move that was politically popular but tread on executive prerogatives. He fully expected Lucey to veto this provision. Lucey let it stand, however, and then quietly suggested to the press corps that the Cullen amendment hampered the ability of the state Department of Revenue to collect taxes owed by businesses headquartered outside of Wisconsin.[41]

Eventually, Cullen and Lucey patched over their differences and became good political and personal friends. When Lucey was putting together the 1977–79 budget, Senators Cullen and John Maurer asked if the governor would include an item they wanted, and Lucey agreed without hesitation. Then he reached into his coat pocket and pulled out a list to ask if he could count on their support for the six items on it. Cullen and Maurer agreed that all six were good initiatives. As they left the governor's office, the two senators sheepishly realized that they had just dealt with a master.[42]

Cullen went on to become senate majority leader, a member of Republican Governor Tommy Thompson's cabinet, and a prominent player in the state's political turmoil in 2010.[43]

Although Democratic legislators did not march in lockstep behind Lucey, he did lead them through an unusually productive period. Nationally respected analysts Neal R. Peirce and John Keefe wrote, "Governor Patrick J. Lucey produced a plethora of new initiatives the like of which has been unseen since 1911 (the La Follette-Progressive era)."[44] Those initiatives altered how Wisconsin governed itself and how it defined and addressed policy issues. Appendix B lists the most significant achievements.

## CHAPTER 12

# LEAVING A LEGACY

The portrait of Governor Francis W. McGovern hung prominently on a wall in Patrick Lucey's office. He admired McGovern because of all that he had accomplished.[1] As Wisconsin's twenty-second governor (1911–14), McGovern followed Robert M. La Follette Sr. as occupant of the state's executive office. The fiery La Follette, nicknamed Fighting Bob, is commonly identified with the progressive agenda. McGovern deserves credit for translating most of the agenda into actual achievements.[2]

Like McGovern, Lucey valued getting things done. He said that he got elected to accomplish changes.[3] And Lucey had a long list of impressive accomplishments. He introduced structural and procedural management reforms that made state government more professional and efficient. His progressive policy reforms were aimed at improving the common good, providing opportunities to all individuals, and ensuring a healthy environment.

## GOVERNANCE

### Cabinet Government

The Progressive movement of Fighting Bob La Follette had sought to eliminate political machines and rule by party bosses. One way of doing that was to limit the appointment powers and patronage opportunities of governors. Wisconsin's constitution had already limited chief executives by creating some agencies headed by independently elected officials, such as attorney general and superintendent of public instruction. Part-time citizen boards controlled agencies including transportation and health and social services. And some appointments—such as to the University of Wisconsin Board of Regents and the Public Service Commission—were for fixed, limited terms instead of having individuals serve at the pleasure of the governor.[4]

Republican Governor Warren Knowles had created a task force, the Kellett Commission, in 1965 to recommend ways to improve the operation of state government. Commissioners favored a system of cabinet government in which part-time citizen boards were replaced with full-time secretaries who would serve at the pleasure of the governor. Despite early support from within the Republican party, when advocated by Lucey, some GOP lawmakers chose to characterize the proposal as nothing more than a "Lucey power grab."[5]

Lucey began his push for cabinet government with his first budget, but the legislature rejected his proposals. He continued to advocate and eventually won approval for cabinet government for the following departments (in some cases as the result of proposals initiated by Lucey but authorized in legislation signed by Martin J. Schreiber when he became acting governor):

- Agriculture, Trade and Consumer Protection

- Business Development

- Employment Relations

- Health and Social Services

- Industry, Labor and Human Relations

- Local Affairs and Development

- Regulation and Licensing

When Lucey transformed the Department of Health and Social Services into a cabinet agency, he went out of his way to stress professionalism over patronage. Health and Social Services was the second-largest unit in state government after the university. It included welfare programs, family services, Medicaid, public health, and prisons. When the part-time board was replaced, Representative Dennis Conta seemed the obvious choice to be named as secretary. As cochair of the legislature's Joint Finance

Committee, Conta had dealt with the complex issues of the agency. He had earned a reputation of being unusually able and hardworking. He and Lucey had a high level of respect for one another. But instead of appointing Conta, Lucey and his staff did a national search. Lucey chose Manuel Carballo, who had degrees from Princeton and Harvard and distinguished himself on the staffs of New Jersey Governor Richard Hughes and New York City Mayor John Lindsay. Ironically, while Lucey avoided a charge of patronage, Republican legislative leaders criticized him for going outside of Wisconsin.[6] Lucey later appointed Conta as secretary of the Department of Revenue.

Lucey tried but failed to make the Department of Veterans Affairs a cabinet agency. John Moses was secretary of the department when Lucey took office in 1971. As governor, Gaylord Nelson appointed Moses to head Veterans Affairs in 1961. Nelson gave Moses lifetime tenure and had him report to a seven-person advisory board. This arrangement was unique. Other department heads were accountable either to the governor or to a board that had appointment and dismissal authority.

Moses had chaired Lucey's assembly campaign in 1948, but that did not insulate him from Lucey's critiques. Lucey objected when Moses eliminated an $11.9 million appropriation for housing loans for veterans from the department's 1973–75 budget request. He also took Moses to task for not providing support for educational programs for returning Vietnam veterans. In addition, Lucey raised concerns about the low collection rate on loans and apparent favoritism in providing loans for department employees.[7]

In 1977, Lucey supported a bill adding $175 million in borrowing authority for housing loans for veterans and insisted that the bill include a provision converting the advisory Veterans Affairs board to one with authority to dismiss the department secretary. The bill passed, and Moses was fired.

Moses, however, had the last word. In 1978, after Lucey had left office, the Wisconsin Supreme Court nullified the dismissal and ordered his reinstatement. The justices said the board's authority to dismiss applied to Moses's successors but not to him.[8] Moses continued as secretary until his retirement in 1984, and the Department of Veterans Affairs did not become a cabinet agency until 2011.

Lucey also had the Department of Natural Resources on his wish list for cabinet government but did not prevail against those arguing that environmental protection had unique concerns and should be somewhat isolated from the governor.

### Groundbreaking Appointments

Lucey valued opportunities to make appointments. He made almost seventeen hundred appointments and reappointments as governor.[9] As a policymaker, he sought expertise, and as a manager, he wanted accountability. He sometimes made surprising choices to send a message. For example, Lucey surprised the Board of Veterans Affairs when he appointed twenty-seven-year-old Theodore Fetting to be a member. Fetting had been awarded the Star of Gallantry, the Bronze Star, the Purple Heart, and two Meritorious Service Medals denoted by bronze oak leaf clusters. Fetting was also active in protests against US involvement in Vietnam, where he had earned his medals. He wore a blue service cap, a symbol of Veterans for Peace.[10]

Lucey wanted to break barriers and include women and minority group members in the ranks of senior state government officials. He was eager to tap an existing pool of talent and wisdom, and he wanted to make a statement by being inclusive. Lucey's first appointment to the Wisconsin Supreme Court, however, was classic old school. Justice E. Harold Hallows left the bench when he had reached what was then the mandatory retirement age of seventy. Although judges and justices are elected positions in Wisconsin, the governor has the power to appoint a replacement, without senate confirmation, when a vacancy occurs midterm. On July 22, 1974, Lucey named his friend and political compatriot Roland Day to fill the vacancy left by Hallows. Day had worked with Lucey in building the Democratic Party and chaired Wisconsin's Robert F. Kennedy for President organization in 1968. Lucey had previously appointed Day to the University of Wisconsin Board of Regents.

A group of prominent lawyers met to compile a list of others whom they felt deserved consideration if another vacancy occurred on the court. That group met with Shirley Abrahamson and asked if they could include her on the list. She was flattered but replied that she did not want to interrupt her teaching at the University of Wisconsin Law School or her legal work.[11]

When Chief Justice Horace Wilkie died in 1974, Lucey examined the list that had been created. Despite Abrahamson's disavowal of interest, her name was included. Lucey's contact with Abrahamson had been limited. They met when he testified for Madison's open housing ordinance in 1963 and when Abrahamson visited him at his house in 1969 to suggest he let students develop People's Park. On occasion, Lucey and Abrahamson exchanged greetings when Lucey visited his friend and lawyer Jim Doyle at the law offices of La Follette, Sinykin, Anderson, and Abrahamson. Lucey had learned that Abrahamson had the reputation of having "one of the most gifted legal minds in the state."[12]

Abrahamson did not apply or do anything to advance her candidacy. She did, however, start developing an interest.[13] Others conveyed their support for a woman to be appointed and for Abrahamson to be that woman. The Madison chapter of the National Organization for Women (NOW) included its voice in the chorus. The local chapter published a letter of support in the local newspapers. Still, some resisted the idea of a woman ascending to a powerful judgeship. Elena Cappella, head of the Madison NOW, recalled receiving a troubling phone call in the middle of the night. When Cappella answered the phone, an angry male voice said, "You know, she's a Jew! No Jew is going to judge me!" He may have gotten around to her gender, too, but Cappella hung up and went back to bed.[14]

Abrahamson was pleased when she got a call from the governor's office asking her to see Lucey. It seemed more like a conversation than an interview, and at the conclusion, Abrahamson felt it necessary to clarify whether she had just been interviewed for the Supreme Court vacancy. Lucey confirmed that he had decided to appoint her.[15] Abrahamson was the first woman to join the Wisconsin Supreme Court. Lucey was concerned about whether she could win a statewide election. She won three ten-year terms and served until retiring in 2019.

Lucey opened a number of doors for women. He tapped civil rights activist Vel Phillips for the Milwaukee County Court, making her the state's first African American in that position. She was later elected as secretary of state.

Lucey appointed others who were the first women to serve in their respective positions:

- Norma Briggs, director of the Bureau of Community Service and then executive secretary of the Governor's Commission on the Status of Women

- Virginia Hart, secretary of the Department of Regulation and Licensing and then chair of the Industry, Labor and Human Relations Commission

- Victoria McCormick, Natural Resources Board

- Patricia McIllece, State Medical Examining Board (first woman since 1927)

- Joyce Rhein, Wisconsin Board of Agriculture

- Rebecca Young, Highway Commission

He also improved racial diversity in government positions. In addition to Phillips, he appointed Edward E. Hales, a lawyer from Racine, to the University of Wisconsin Board of Regents and Percy Julian as chair of the State Personnel Board. He reappointed Charles M. Hill Sr. as secretary of the Department of Local Affairs and Development. Governor Knowles had placed Hill in that office in January 1970. And just months after his inauguration, Lucey invited the Great Lakes Inter-Tribal Council to identify someone to join his staff.[16]

### Personnel Management

Another key reform of the early twentieth century Progressive movement was to separate government employment from partisan politics. Public-sector jobs had provided party bosses with the patronage that fueled their machines. Progressives succeeded in passing civil service laws that made it illegal to use partisan loyalty as a requirement or even a preference for hiring public employees.[17] The concern after fifty years of civil service was that public employees enjoyed so much protection that they could no longer be held accountable for their performance. Civil service became synonymous with ossification and an unresponsive bureaucracy.[18]

Lucey agreed with good government advocates active in the 1960s and 1970s who argued that fears of patronage needed to be balanced with concerns about accountability and management. He appointed a task force, the Employment Relations Study Commission, to examine the state's civil service laws.[19] The commission prompted two major changes: first, senior departmental managers serve at the pleasure of the head of their agency, and second, the strict restrictions of initial civil service laws were loosened to allow more managerial discretion in hiring and firing while still prohibiting partisan patronage.[20]

In addition, commission reforms included the creation of a new cabinet-level department to direct personnel management responsibilities such as collective bargaining, training, and diversity. Civil service at the time was under a part-time citizen board with a full-time director. The director had to be selected by the governor from a list of three candidates submitted by the board. In 1976, two years before the establishment of the new department, Lucey was accused of improper interference when the process for naming a director went awry.

Verne Knoll was the deputy director of personnel and sought the top position when it became vacant in 1975. When the personnel board completed its screening of applicants and submitted the top three candidates, two dropped out at the last minute, leaving only Knoll. Lucey insisted he have a choice, and the board again went through a search and screening process. Once again, two of the three top candidates withdrew, leaving only Knoll. Lucey refused to be confined. At this point, Knoll got the support of Senator Dale McKenna, a Democrat, and several Republican legislators who charged Lucey with foul play for refusing to accept the candidate recommended by the board. Knoll also enlisted the support of Howard Koop, who was his partner in a real estate venture and the executive assistant to Attorney General Bronson La Follette. Newspapers ran stories suggesting conspiracy and corruption, and La Follette began an investigation.[21] The AFL-CIO expressed concern and threatened Lucey with a loss of their support.[22]

It turns out that it was Verne Knoll, not Lucey, behind the foul play. Knoll had been an attorney and mayor in Beaver Dam, Wisconsin. On June 18, 1951, he was convicted of thirty-six counts of forgery, larceny, and obtaining money under false pretenses from families in the Beaver Dam area. The judge sentenced him to serve consecutively one to two years for each count. While in the state prison in Waupun, Knoll successfully petitioned Governor Walter J. Kohler to commute his sentence.

On June 1, 1954, Kohler indicated he thought the sentence was too severe and commuted the sentence so that Knoll would be eligible for parole in 1959.[23] Upon his release, Knoll got a job in the state's personnel bureau and started working his way up the ladder.

Since Knoll had been convicted of a felony, he was ineligible for a senior position in state government, such as director of the Personnel Bureau. However, Knoll had been misleading people by saying that Kohler had pardoned him rather than commuted the sentence. A pardon would have had the effect of making him eligible for the director position. A commuted sentence does not eliminate the disqualifying effects of a felony conviction. Not only did he mislead members of the State Personnel Board regarding the nonexistent pardon, but he had contacted other finalists in the selection process to encourage them to withdraw their names, leaving him as the only remaining candidate. While Knoll worked underhandedly to secure his appointment, the position he sought was eliminated with the adoption of the task force recommendation to create a cabinet department of employment relations.

Lucey was cleared of any part in the scandal. Knoll did secure a pardon—from Acting Governor Schreiber in 1978.[24] The scandal demonstrated that part-time citizen boards are no guarantee of clean government. The reform was part of the general effort to provide more discretion and accountability to the governor.

### Court Reorganization

Lucey considered Wisconsin's courts in need of reorganization. The appeals system, in particular, was cumbersome and complex. The Supreme Court had to take all cases brought to it, thus causing a delay of sometimes three or more years before litigants could expect a decision.

When he first took office, Lucey appointed a task force to study the state courts. The task force recommendations required four constitutional amendments. To amend Wisconsin's constitution, two consecutive legislatures must endorse the changes, and voters must then ratify the amendment in a general referendum. The proposed changes simplified the appeals process and allowed the state supreme court to decide which cases it wanted to hear. The reforms also established a one-level trial court and an intermediate court of appeals.

Lucey, Chief Justice Bruce Beilfuss, and Carol Toussaint, former national vice president of the League of Women Voters, went to every Wisconsin city with a television station to urge voters to ratify the constitutional changes. Lucey realized that to reach voters in the western part of the state, he needed to use Minneapolis television stations. He contacted his classmate from Campion, Bob Sheran, who was chief justice of the Minnesota Supreme Court, and persuaded him to hold a press conference with Lucey and Beilfuss and praise the proposed reforms.[25] Wisconsin voters ratified the amendments by a margin of more than 2 to 1.[26]

The study commission on judicial organization also recommended the establishment of a public defender. This proposal was in part a response to instances in which inadequate representation of poor people led to convictions that then were reversed, suggesting the existence of even more cases that might also deserve reversals.[27] County boards supported the proposal, which passed as part of the 1977–79 budget, in part because it provided for full state funding.[28] The public defender initiative easily passed the assembly, but there was concern about its fate in the senate. Fortunately, the senate cochair of the Joint Committee on Finance, Gerald Kleczka, who often opposed new programs with fiscal implications, decided to support the measure because of a television drama about a miscarriage of justice that he had watched the night before the vote.[29]

## Ethics

Lucey considered ethics essential for himself, his appointees, civil servants, and legislators. He was determined that his legacy would include a code of ethics and a board to serve as a watchdog to ensure compliance. He included in his 1973–75 budget a code of ethics that required more than twelve hundred employees who purchased goods and services for the state to disclose their financial interests. While recusal is the most straightforward way to avoid a conflict of interest, it is not always practical or possible, and so the code of ethics required disclosure. A major responsibility of the new State Ethics Board was to receive and review financial interest statements. To show his seriousness, before the appointment of members of the State Ethics Board, Lucey had Keith Clifford, a member of his legal staff, send a memo encouraging everyone in the governor's office to voluntarily submit economic interest statements even if their responsibilities did not include financial matters.[30]

In 1974, the *Milwaukee Sentinel* reported that Harold "Bud" Jordahl, Lucey's choice to head the State Natural Resources Board, had bought land within the boundaries of a proposed $3.5 million public recreation development.[31] In addition, several months before his appointment, Jordahl sold land in Burnett County that was located within the boundaries of a state wildlife project. This transaction netted him a 50 percent profit. Jordahl had disclosed his land holdings to the State Ethics Board and asked for a ruling on whether he was in violation of the code enacted the previous year. Bill Dyke accused Lucey and Jordahl of an indiscretion during the 1974 gubernatorial campaign.[32] The ethics board, however, concluded that Jordahl had disclosed his transactions and had not participated in any Department of Natural Resources decision regarding the land. Jordahl was cleared, and Lucey used the incident as a reminder of the importance of complying with the code.[33]

## ELECTIONS

### *Reapportionment*

Lucey and the legislature had to redraw the boundaries of legislative districts after the US Census Bureau completed its work in 1970. The census led to a reduction in Wisconsin's delegation in the US House of Representatives from ten to nine. Wisconsin had new congressional district boundaries by the time the legislature recessed on March 10, 1972. On that day, however, a suit was filed in federal court because the legislature— with Democrats in the majority in the assembly and Republicans in the senate—had failed to agree on boundaries for state legislative districts. The Wisconsin Supreme Court got involved and set a deadline of April 17, 1972, for the legislature to draw new district lines.

Legislative leaders did not, however, bring their members to the floor to take action. Lucey called a special session on reapportionment on April 19. The legislature responded with a plan that reduced the number of assembly seats from 100 to 99 and then designed the 33 senate districts so that each consisted of three assembly districts. That way, Wisconsin could efficiently comply with the US Supreme Court rulings of *Baker vs. Carr* (1962) and *Reynolds v. Sims* (1964), applying the one-person-one-vote principle to both houses.[34] The plan was adopted, and the court did not need to take further action.

## Voter Registration

One of the first study commissions Lucey established was the Governor's Task Force on Voter Registration and Elections. He directed them to encourage voting. Task force recommendations included allowing registration by mail and at the polls on Election Day, encouraging high school students to register at school, making absentee ballots more available, and providing assistance to voters with disabilities. They also recommended replacing the practice of striking from the registration rolls all individuals who have not voted at least once every two years with a policy of striking only the names of those who have moved out of the municipality or have died.

Some Republicans objected, charging that the changes would lead to fraud, but with full Democratic support, a bill including the task force's proposals passed both the senate and assembly. Lucey signed the bill on October 9, 1975, and considered the emphasis on accessibility as one of his major legacies.[35]

## Campaign Finance

David Adamany was a leading national scholar on campaign finance, and he was pleased that Lucey wanted to curtail the influence of money in politics.[36] Progressives in Wisconsin had outlawed corporate contributions to campaigns when they passed the Corrupt Practices Act of 1911. No changes had been made since then. In 1973, Lucey appointed the Governor's Study Committee on Political Finance, with Adamany as chair. The committee's charge was to design a way to control contributions and expenditures for campaigns for state offices.

Adamany and James Klauser, director of the Republican Senate Caucus, huddled together to work on legislation. Their goal was a bill with bipartisan support. They succeeded in getting nine Republican and nine Democratic senators behind their efforts. After the assembly and senate passed different versions of campaign finance reform, Lucey called a special session. When that session was about to adjourn without agreement on a common bill, Lucey threatened to call another. That pressure had results, and legislation passed with the following major features: disclosure of campaign contributors, limits on amounts that could be contributed, limits on campaign expenditures, and establishment of a bipartisan State Elections Board to monitor and enforce compliance.[37]

Lucey and David Adamany discuss the state budget with the *Wisconsin State Journal* staff on January 28, 1975. J. D. PATRICK, *WISCONSIN STATE JOURNAL*

Missing from the bill was public funding for campaigns. Adamany and Klauser developed a proposal that was to establish a fund of voluntary contributions from income taxpayers. Filers could designate one dollar of their taxes to go to a Clean Election Campaign Fund. Money from the fund would be given to candidates who raised specified amounts in small donations and who agreed to abide by spending and contribution limits. Amounts varied with the office that candidates were seeking.

A critical detail was whether the one-dollar contribution would be added to or included in an individual's income tax bill. Democratic Senator Kleczka of Milwaukee was adamant that legislators, for political reasons, had to support having the contribution increase taxes paid. Others argued that this would discourage participation and the fund would not be sufficient to be effective. The issue was resolved by Schreiber as acting governor after Lucey left office. The legislature worded the bill so it read that the one dollar "shall not be included" in the total tax owed. With the partial veto pen, Schreiber deleted "not."[38]

The US Supreme Court rendered moot the efforts to minimize the influence of money in politics. *Buckley v. Valeo* (1976) considered campaign spending as a form of speech protected by the First Amendment from government regulation. That ruling allowed for limits on contributions, disclosure requirements, and public funding, but these were set aside by subsequent decisions. *Citizens United v. Federal Election Commission* (2010) extended First Amendment rights to corporations and unions and ruled restrictions on contributions as well as expenditures unconstitutional, thereby undercutting meaningful campaign finance limits.

## Crisis Management

### Prison Disturbances

Lucey had to face three disturbances in prisons during his tenure: the reformatory for juveniles in Green Bay in 1971, the maximum security institution at Waupun in 1976, and the medium security prison in Fox Lake in 1977. The 1971 uprising at Attica prison in New York, in which forty-three people died, heightened concern about prison security, and Lucey insisted that the disturbances in Wisconsin be resolved without violence.

The incident at Waupun was especially tense. Upset with overcrowded conditions, inmates took sixteen staff members hostage. They barricaded themselves in the paint shop with lots of flammable material and were armed with knives, chains, spears, and other self-made weapons.

Joe Sensenbrenner had dealt with inmates at Waupun as part of his work on Lucey's legal staff and developed an understanding of the situation that was independent of both the prisoners and the guards. His work earned respect from the prisoners for the governor's office.[39] Sensenbrenner asked Lester Pines to go to the prison to help defuse the 1976 conflict. Pines had worked on the staff of the governor's council on criminal justice and then gone into private practice. After arriving at the prison, Pines got on the phone with the leader of the rebellion to try to calm the situation. He offered, "Why don't I just come in there and we'll talk and work this out." Facing limited options, and knowing that the governor did not want to have to call in the National Guard, the warden let Pines climb up the barricaded staircase into the paint shop, accompanied by the director of prison security. Pines ended up personally negotiating a resolution to the crisis while also staying in phone communication with the warden. He then drafted an agreement, which was signed by the warden and the inmate leader, and the inmates released the hostages. No lives were lost. A July 1976 *Capital Times* editorial, "The Waupun Rebellion," stated:

> It was courageous Madison attorney, Lester Pines, who served as a vital intermediary between prison officials and the inmates and played a key role in the negotiations that led to the end of the rebellion.

After the disturbance ended, Lucey had Bob Dunn spend time in the prison to be sure there were no reprisals by guards or other inmates against those who had been involved in the conflict.[40]

### Novitiate Takeover

Lucey's leadership and negotiating skills were tested when a group calling itself the Menominee Warrior Society seized the Alexian Brothers Novitiate in Gresham, Shawano County, in the early morning hours of New Year's Day 1975. About forty armed young men forced their way into the house where the caretaker, Joe Plonka, his wife, two children, and two guests were celebrating the turn of the calendar.

The Menominee were going through a troubled transition. The federal government had, against the wishes of the Menominee Nation and the state of Wisconsin, terminated official recognition of the tribe in 1954. As critics of the policy had predicted, termination had disastrous results, and the Menominee quickly became impoverished without federal support and struggled to provide basic services. The federal government recognized its mistake and in 1973 agreed to restore the tribe's status. Ada Deer, who had been very active in getting the federal government to reverse the termination action, was elected to lead the Menominee.[41]

Frustrated with the poverty, oppression, and loss of land resulting from the period of termination, and unhappy with the way current tribal leaders had handled it, the Menominee Warrior Society took action. In a plan opposed by Deer, the Warriors sought to obtain the deed to the sixty-four-room novitiate, a twenty-room mansion, the caretaker's cottage, and the surrounding two hundred and sixty acres, a property they believed rightfully belonged to the Menominee under an old treaty. The goal was to convert the novitiate to a hospital or rehabilitation facility.[42] The Alexian Brothers had put the property up for sale in 1969 with an asking price of one million dollars ($6.9 million in 2019), and the building was unoccupied except for the caretaker. The Warriors were led by Mike Sturdevant, who was referred to as "General." Some of the Warriors had been part of the planning process begun seven months earlier; others joined at the last minute and had been drinking. They were accompanied by four children and six women.

Under orders from Sturdevant, the caretaker telephoned the Alexian Brothers headquarters in Chicago. It was, of course, not easy to contact someone in authority in the dark, early hours of the New Year. After some confusion, Plonka described the situation to Brother Maurice Wilson and then put Sturdevant on the line. Sturdevant explained his demand for the deed and then promised that Plonka and the others would be released if the Shawano County Sheriff pledged to stand down. The sheriff, Robert Montour, agreed. The Warriors helped Plonka get his car out of a snow bank, and the family and their guests sped away.

The Alexian Brothers began negotiating with the Warriors over the sale of the property. Meanwhile, deputies and local police established a perimeter around the abbey, and Sheriff Montour demanded that the Menominee leave. He cut off electrical power to the abbey, which quickly caused pipes to freeze and break.

After six days of frustrating, fruitless talks, Montour concluded that he needed help. One of his concerns was that racial tension in the area might escalate. Relations between the Menominee and neighboring whites were fraught with the stereotypes and grievances all too common in these settings. The Menominee Warriors did not trust Shawano law enforcement, and some members of the white community were eager to do what they could to rid the novitiate of the intruders. Vigilante activity began almost immediately, with sporadic gunfire from both sides. The sheriff asked Lucey to call in the National Guard, and Lucey ordered 250 members of the 127th Infantry in Green Bay to the scene.[43]

The National Guard on site was under the command of Colonel Hugh Simonson, the deputy adjutant general of the Wisconsin National Guard. He and Lucey conferred about major policy and strategic issues, but Lucey relied on Simonson to handle detailed matters on the ground. Lucey noted the subzero temperatures and directed that power be restored and that the delivery of subsistence-level food be allowed. The frozen pipes had already done major damage. Colonel Simonson allowed limited traffic in and out of the abbey. Individuals who wanted to cross the security line were searched, and any weapons or drugs were confiscated.[44] Lucey was very upset when he learned that some of the National Guard had allowed beer to go to the Warriors.[45]

The governor asked John Lavine, owner and publisher of the local newspaper, the *Shawano Leader*, and a Lucey appointed member of the University of Wisconsin Board of Regents, to act as a liaison. Lavine agreed and was heavily involved in the almost daily negotiations between the Menominee Warrior Society, the Alexian Brothers, and the National Guard. He accompanied Simonson and frequently kept vigil with him on cold, dark nights.[46]

Tensions were high. Fresh in everyone's mind was the incident two years earlier when two hundred members of the Oglala Lakota and the American Indian Movement took control of Wounded Knee, South Dakota. That occupation ended with a violent confrontation in which two died and thirteen were wounded.

Lucey made it clear to the National Guard, local officials, his staff, and everyone else that he did not want anyone hurt or killed. He faced a challenge that had two major components: one, keeping the peace, and two, facilitating a resolution of ownership of the abbey. Lucey put his most trusted staff members on call. Dunn, one of his closest and longest-serving aides, conferred with Sensenbrenner, whom Lucey had appointed as his executive secretary, and explained that Lucey needed a point person on staff who could serve him in an objective manner. Sensenbrenner responded that he felt confident about playing that role. Dunn continued to be heavily involved, sometimes sleeping in his office as the conflict unfolded and attempts to end it were made.

Lucey appointed Artley Skenandore as his chief negotiator but then had to ask him to withdraw. Skenandore was an Oneida Indian who had served as sheriff of Brown County. Deer rebuked Lucey for what seemed like an assumption that because Skenandore was American Indian he would understand the Menominee concerns. She said he lacked credibility and was not helpful.[47] The takeover garnered national attention and sparked demonstrations sympathetic to the Warriors in Madison and Milwaukee. Dennis Banks of the American Indian Movement went to a rally in Milwaukee on his way to Gresham and the abbey. Father James Groppi, a prominent civil rights activist in Wisconsin, and the actor Marlon Brando added their voices. They both spent a cold and uncomfortable night with the Warriors in the novitiate.[48]

While negotiations seemed at times to be making progress, the movement was slow. The Alexian Brothers offered to sell their property for a reduced price of $750,000 ($5.2 million in 2019). Recognizing the Menominee did not have the money, they said they were willing to give them a year to raise it. Alternatively, they offered to lease the abbey so the Menominee could begin using the novitiate as a hospital, rehabilitation center, or some kind of educational facility.[49] Lucey was not pleased with the Alexian offer, saying it was unrealistic and not very generous. Deer also rejected the offer and made it clear that the Menominee did not want the property for a hospital, rehabilitation center, or any other purpose. The Warrior Society, on the other hand, persisted.

Vigilante activity by white residents of Shawano increased. On January 25, a group calling itself Concerned Citizens of Shawano met with Colonel Simonson to express their impatience and to threaten action. In a situation report, Simonson warned that they might begin "starting fires in area buildings, shooting at the Guardsmen on duty, trying snowmobile runs on the abbey, engaging in fire fights most probably with the Guard, but also with the Indians."[50]

Lucey talked with Simonson and they agreed it was time to set a deadline. On Wednesday, January 29, the Warrior Society was told to leave by Friday, January 31. Simonson had been gradually increasing the number of National Guard troops. When he announced the January 31 deadline, four hundred members of the National Guard plus fifty state troopers were on site. Simonson took steps to bring in more and to move armored personnel carriers and a tank to the novitiate grounds. Sensenbrenner made sure the press covered the preparations, including photos, so that the deadline would be taken seriously by everyone. Simonson readied a unit to use concussion grenades in the event an assault became necessary, and he tightened the perimeter but was lenient about letting individuals leave.

Meanwhile, Lucey got on the phone with the Alexian Brothers in Chicago and explained what might happen on February 1 if the Warriors still occupied the abbey. There might be bloodshed and loss of life. He told the Alexian Brothers he was sure they wanted to avoid that. The Brothers agreed to sell the property to the Menominee tribe for one dollar plus a vague pledge for the Menominee to compensate the order for their expenses to the extent possible.[51]

Lucey then called Sturdevant of the Menominee Warrior Society and told him of the Alexian Brothers' offer. Sturdevant was relieved. He asked Lucey about amnesty or pardons. Lucey wrote in his notes: "I replied that it was improper to discuss this matter and that I was not prepared to make any commitment whatsoever in this regard. Mr. Sturdevant did not seem surprised by my comments."[52]

Sensenbrenner persuaded the Brothers to announce their decision publicly at the abbey rather than from Chicago. Their representatives arrived on February 2. The Warrior Society accepted the Alexian Brothers' offer and peacefully left the next day. Sixteen men and fifteen women, all adults, went from the novitiate to two buses that took them to Shawano—a city near but outside the reservation—for formal charging.[53] Sturdevant and four others were convicted of unlawful assembly, and Sturdevant was found guilty of six counts of false imprisonment, two of armed robbery, and one of armed burglary by an all-white jury of eight women and four men.[54] Everyone served jail time.[55] The plans to transfer the deed to the Menominee and to convert the abbey to a hospital or other health care facility were pursued but never materialized.[56]

Lucey tried to reward Simonson with a promotion but was frustrated by federal rules. He was told by Bo Callaway, secretary of the army, that Simonson could not get the medical clearance required for a promotion and had to be kept at his current rank.[57]

## POLICIES

### Economic Development
Lucey's early initiative to exempt machinery and equipment from property taxes was a powerful signal to the business community that he understood and supported the need for a robust economy. Lucey credited

American Motors President William V. Luneberg with persuading him to foster a business-friendly climate. Edward Wiegner, Lucey's first secretary of the Department of Revenue, translated the general idea into the specifics of the M&E exemption. Lucey argued it was possible to be both progressive and pro-business.[58] The immediate response of American Motors to the M&E exemption was to divert ten million dollars earmarked for another state to the expansion of a plant building compact cars in Kenosha.[59]

Lucey's first budget created a new cabinet-level Department of Business Development. The mission of this agency was to conduct analyses and recommend actions to promote business activity in the state. The department included a unit to advocate for minority enterprises. To recognize more directly the economic impact of tourism, Lucey moved responsibility for this sector from the Department of Natural Resources to the Department of Business Development.

Lucey took action to ensure that the Japanese food processing company Kikkoman had a home in Wisconsin. Milton Neshek, Kikkoman's lawyer, approached Lavine, who he knew to be a close friend of Lucey's, to tell the governor what was happening. Kikkoman feared potential opposition to a Japanese company locating a major soy sauce plant in conservative, Republican Walworth County. This was the first proposed Japanese investment in Wisconsin since World War II. Lavine contacted Lucey, who in turn talked to Senator Walter Hollander, a Republican who represented the area. Lucey and Hollander showed up unannounced and uninvited at the Walworth County Board meeting that was deciding whether to grant Kikkoman the necessary permits. They urged board members to roll out the welcome mat. Lucey concluded by saying he hoped he and Senator Hollander would not have to call a press conference the next day announcing that the board turned down an opportunity for jobs and economic development in the county.[60]

In 1973, the Kikkoman plant in Walworth shipped its first bottles of naturally brewed soy sauce. Shortly thereafter, every bottle of Kikkoman soy sauce in North America came from Walworth. The plant, which has had as many as 160 employees a year, is responsible for thirty-nine Kikkoman products. All but one use soy beans.[61]

## Labor

After four years of impasse, a joint labor and management council in 1976 suggested changes in Wisconsin's workers' compensation and unemployment insurance programs. These programs are among the most frequently touted legacies of the La Follette–McGovern progressive reforms. Lucey had been pushing for the council to agree on measures to be sure the programs remained solvent and to make improvements. He called special sessions to enact council recommendations: in 1975 for workers compensation and in 1976 for unemployment insurance.

Organized labor succeeded in achieving one of its longstanding top priorities: elimination of the requirement that a recipient of unemployment insurance had to wait one week before receiving benefits. Auto workers were especially eager to see this change. When auto companies made changes in assembly lines to begin production of a new model, they typically closed the plants and laid off workers for a week. The layoff saved the companies some money but meant lost wages for workers.

Lucey also brought together representatives of growers and migrant workers in Wisconsin. In 1977, he signed a bill that specified basic rights for the workers and required growers to use contracts. The bill also established a seventeen-member Council on Migrant Labor to oversee administration of the law and provide reports and recommendations.

## Transportation

Lucey was notably unsuccessful in achieving major reforms in Wisconsin's transportation policy. The legislature rejected significant initiatives in 1973 and 1975, and voters refused twice to ratify constitutional amendments that would have enabled more environmentally friendly approaches to transportation. Lucey's failed proposals included a mileage efficiency tax that would vary with the miles-per-gallon rating of a vehicle, placing the highest fee on gas guzzlers; a fee based on the weight class of a vehicle; funding for local mass transit; and funding for bus, rail, water, and air service in rural areas.[62]

Jean Lucey helped to make visible the issue of sixty-five-foot double-bottom trucks. Wisconsin and Iowa were the only Midwestern states that had banned double-bottom (or twin trailer) trucks on state roads. While the trucking industry and most Republicans opposed such restrictions on commerce, Jean felt strongly about retaining the ban. Her concerns were safety and the wear on roads. She also wanted bans on large mobile homes and extra-wide loads.

Republican legislators criticized Wisconsin's first lady when she used gubernatorial stationery and eight-cent stamps from the governor's office to send letters about the truck issue to newspapers and members of the senate and assembly.[63] She, in turn, was critical of the legislature when it passed a joint resolution—which does not need the governor's signature— to allow sixty-five-foot double-bottom trucks on some of the state roads. The joint resolution permitted the Department of Transportation to act administratively to make this change. Lucey had indicated he would have vetoed legislation to accomplish that resolution.[64]

On another issue, the first lady offered a suggestion to Norman Clapp, secretary of the Department of Transportation. She had noted with approval that the department had announced it would plant 102,000 trees in 1974. She had criticized the proliferation of billboards around the state. She wrote, "My suggestion is that the Department of Transportation plant its trees in front of these billboards and save us all from this visual pollution."[65]

### Urban Development

Although Lucey fell short of his goals for transportation policy, he did usher in a new perspective. The national emphasis was on moving people and goods as quickly as possible, which led to the development and expansion of freeways. Lucey balanced that approach and bucked the powerful lobby of companies and unions pushing for road building by considering the effects on urban neighborhoods. He listened to John Norquist, elected to the state assembly in 1974, and others who raised an alarm just as contracts were about to be signed to engineer an expansion of freeways in Milwaukee that would run through communities and further disadvantage low-income families. Lucey directed his chair of the state highway commission to pause the process and allow for more deliberation, which led to abandonment of the plan. He also appointed Rebecca Young, an advocate of mass transit, to the highway commission in an effort to put the brakes on road building.

According to Norquist, who served as mayor of Milwaukee from 1988 to 2004, Lucey valued urban areas. He did not regard them as necessary evils or pity those who lived in cities. He wanted to give people a reason for living in a metropolitan area, not fleeing it. Lucey considered Milwaukee, like other urban areas, as an important part of the state's culture and critical to the state's economy. This vision informed not only his transportation policy but also his approach to health, social services, and education. Lucey also designed his taxation and revenue-sharing reforms in ways to nurture urban areas.

### Health and Social Services

On the morning that Lucey signed the 1973–75 state budget, a group demonstrated outside the executive mansion in hopes he would use his partial veto to void some cuts in welfare payments. The governor avoided confronting the protestors by taking a boat across Lake Mendota to the capitol. Jean Lucey, however, drove to the gate—which the demonstrators had padlocked—and confronted the demonstrators. She argued that they ignored the fact that the budget included a 33 percent increase in state welfare spending and then, in rather colorful language, told them to get off their "duffs" and get a job. She then reached for a nearby hose and doused the demonstrators. When the governor heard of the confrontation, he said he had no comment. The press gave top billing to the incident.[66]

The Milwaukee Tenants Union gave the first lady a dubious "Double Bottom Award" at its 1974 annual party. The tenants group thanked her for taking on the highway lobby on the issue of banning trucks with double trailers or bottoms. The citation went on to say she deserved "something for sitting on your own well-padded bottom while criticizing welfare recipients."[67] Jean did not attend to receive the award but sent a thank-you note, on which she wrote: "Instead of spending your money on meaningless awards, I would humbly suggest you broaden your own horizons. Let's not limit ourselves to only the self-serving issues."[68]

Jean's perspective of people in poverty was very different from that of her husband. She held the general view that poverty resulted from the failure of individuals to take responsibility for their own lives and decried relying on the largesse of government and charities. Pat, by contrast, considered the poor primarily as victims of social injustice and flaws in the economic system. He asserted that government had a responsibility to provide health care assistance and training programs. During Lucey's tenure as governor, health and social services expenditures were second only to education and saw steady increases from $382 million in 1969–71 to $1.4 billion in 1977–79.[69] One reason for the increase in spending was that Lucey had state government assume much of the financing that had been the responsibility of local governments. He felt the state progressive income tax was a more appropriate source of funding than regressive property taxes. Lucey's policy initiatives included revisions in Aid to Families with Dependent Children that allowed fathers to live with their families, protections for those with mental illnesses, services for displaced homemakers, and regulation of nursing homes. Lieutenant Governor Schreiber assumed the role of advocate and ombudsman for those in nursing homes.

Governor Lucey jogs near his Maple Bluff home with *Capital Times* reporters Matt Pommer (left) and Owen Coyle and the Luceys' Yorkshire terrier Beethoven. Lucey followed his doctor's advice to improve his diet and exercise.
DAVID SANDELL, *CAPITAL TIMES*

## Education

Lucey began his tenure as governor with two major education initiatives: merging the state's universities and shifting the funding of K–12 education to a blend of increased state aid and the use of an equalization formula to alter the burdens of property taxes. The issue of racially segregated schools in the state's largest urban area presented an additional challenge. In a landmark case brought by civil rights activist and Wisconsin Representative Lloyd Barbee, Federal Judge John Reynolds ruled that the Milwaukee schools were unconstitutionally segregated and appointed John Gronouski to prepare an integration plan. Outside the courtroom, Barbee, Phillips, and other leaders in the African American community pursued resolutions.

Representative Conta authored a plan to merge the primarily white school districts of Shorewood and Whitefish Bay with a portion of the Milwaukee Public School District that included a substantial number of African American students. The suburbs north of Milwaukee strongly opposed Conta's proposal, and his initiative failed. Also, the court would not order school districts such as Shorewood and Whitefish Bay that were not legally responsible for the segregation problem to be a major part of the solution.[70] However, with the threat of a court-imposed solution in the background, Conta was able to get bipartisan support for another approach.

Lucey readily agreed to have David Riemer, a member of his legal staff, work with Conta. They drafted a plan that provided state aid of up to five million dollars a year to school districts that voluntarily established programs for racial integration. Bussing would happen only with the consent of school boards and the parents of students. The plan spread the costs of implementation to the state as a whole. Lucey supported this proposal and threatened to call a special session if the legislature did not act in a timely manner. He was happy to see the bill, referred to as Chapter 220, on his desk and promptly signed it.[71] In 1993–94, the peak year, 5,900 students participated in Chapter 220. The governor and legislature ended the program in 2015, after forty years of operation.

## Environment and Natural Resources

With the establishment of the federal Environmental Protection Agency in 1970, state agencies such as the Wisconsin Department of Natural Resources spent a significant share of their work on implementing federal

environmental laws. The Badger State prided itself on going further than
the federal government in pursuing a clean and safe environment.

Lucey had been an environmental advocate since his election in 1948
to the state assembly. Initially, he focused on air pollution. As governor,
he worked with legislators and with professionals in the Department of
Natural Resources to address pollution and conservation issues involving water and soil as well as air. The list of concerns included mercury,
polychlorinated biphenyls (PCB), phosphorous, and pesticides. Lucey
emphasized regional approaches and established inland lake districts
to conserve water and preserve its quality.[72] A mining reclamation act
required companies to meet a set of standards. Hazardous waste had to
be disposed of safely, and Lucey's administration established standards
for makers of plumbing, kitchen, and other appliances to minimize the
use of water and natural gas.

The siting of power plants was on the to-do list in Lucey's desk drawer.[73]
Communities where power plants were located benefited from property
taxes paid by these plants. And these communities could keep taxes low if
they did not have to share the revenue with a broad area. Lucey felt a more
equitable arrangement was to have the tax revenue flow to communities
served by the power plant, not just those that provided a home for the
plant. Power plants also raised environmental and economic issues that
argued for permitting to be in the hands of state government rather than
local governments. The 1975 legislature agreed to broaden the perspectives
that went into the approval for siting power plants by requiring approval
from both the state Public Service Commission and the Department of
Natural Resources.

Lucey identified the Kickapoo Dam project as one of his most serious
mistakes.[74] The Kickapoo River in western Wisconsin had been the scene
of devastating floods. Congress passed the Flood Control Act in 1936
authorizing the Army Corps of Engineers to study the problem. In 1938,
the Corps proposed that a dam be built north of La Farge, but nothing
happened for another twenty-three years. After major flooding and ten
deaths, Congress authorized construction of the dam in 1961. The project
began as a 400- to 800-acre reservoir, but the Corps then expanded it
to include a 1,780-acre lake with recreational areas and a hydroelectric
plant. In 1969, the Corps began acquiring more than 9,000 acres of land.

It purchased 140 farms—some from unwilling sellers. Costs ran up to twenty million dollars.

When Lucey took the oath of office in 1971, the federal Environmental Protection Agency raised concerns about endangered plant species and the risk that the recreational lake would become highly eutrophic, meaning it would be choked with decaying plants because of too many nutrients in the water.[75] Lucey was concerned about potential ecological harm and thought the projections for the growth of a thriving tourist industry were exaggerated.[76] He nonetheless told the Corps to proceed, accepting that no other solutions to the flooding had surfaced and hoping that his concerns were unfounded.[77] The Sierra Club sued to stop the project, but Judge Doyle rejected the suit.

By 1974, the project was about half done. Residents had been moved off the land, and shops had been closed. Over half of the dam had been constructed. State Highway 131 and two county highways between La Farge and Rockton were partially relocated. At this point, a study by University of Wisconsin scientists identified severe water quality issues. The estimated cost to complete the project had more than doubled to $51.5 million. People in the area were bitterly divided—some looking forward to a thriving tourist business and others lamenting the environmental and financial costs. Lucey told the Corps to stop any more work on the project, and Senator Nelson blocked further federal funding in 1975.

Three years later, a major flood once again ripped through the valley. The project, however, was not revived. Instead, the Corps pursued other approaches to flood control, and a divided Kickapoo Valley community tried to agree on a future. It took another twenty-five years for the federal and state governments to implement a plan designed by citizen groups. The decades of conflict, damage, and misguided efforts ended with Wisconsin and the Ho-Chunk Nation forming a jointly managed reserve emphasizing conservation, education, and low-impact tourism.[78]

### Energy

The Organization of Petroleum Exporting Countries (OPEC) placed an embargo on shipments of oil to the United States and several other countries in October 1973. The ban was in retaliation for US and European support of Israel in the Yom Kippur War. At the time, the United States was heavily dependent on foreign oil, and OPEC action caused a severe energy shortage just as winter was about to arrive.

Lucey signed an executive order declaring an emergency and establishing the Wisconsin State Energy Office. His first appointment was Stanley York, who had been serving as executive director of the Wisconsin Republican Party.

Lucey and York emphasized the need for conserving energy. Except for hospitals and for research laboratories holding animals, thermostats in state buildings were turned down to sixty-three degrees. Agencies cut back on their use of vehicles, and drivers were encouraged to travel no more than fifty-five miles per hour. In public appearances, Lucey stressed the need for limiting the use of electricity, installing weather stripping, lowering the setting for hot water heaters, and the like. York positioned the state to receive federal assistance to cope with the energy shortage.[79]

The OPEC embargo ended in March 1974, but Lucey continued to pursue energy policies. He hired University of Wisconsin Professor Charles J. Cicchetti to replace York. He also got legislative support to prevent utility companies from disconnecting those who were delinquent in payments during winter months. Lucey reacted with alarm when Cicchetti told him that utilities had nonetheless disconnected about eight thousand homes in Milwaukee in the winter of 1975–1976. In addressing the National Consumer Information Center convention in the nation's capital on January 14, 1976, Lucey suggested serious consideration be given to public ownership of all sources of energy.[80]

Lucey appointed Cicchetti to chair the state's Public Service Commission. The governor then integrated energy with planning generally. He appointed Stephen Born, another University of Wisconsin–Madison professor, to serve as director of the state Office of Planning and Energy.[81]

## CRIMINAL JUSTICE

Lucey pursued a general policy of minimizing the use of prisons. During his 1970 campaign for governor, he had objected to the prison being built in Adams County because of its location. After he became governor, he noted that the state's correctional institutions had a surplus capacity for holding inmates and proposed downsizing. The Governor's Task Force on Offender Rehabilitation went further. In 1972, the members recommended that all state prisons be closed by June 1975 and inmates released to community-based programs. The task force criticized the treatment of inmates in Wisconsin's prisons, labeling some practices as unconstitutional.[82] Lucey agreed with the general recommendation to use community-based institutions and emphasize rehabilitation but rejected the call to close all prisons.[83]

Lucey forwarded the task force report, which included one hundred recommendations, to the Wisconsin Council on Criminal Justice (WCCJ). This council had responsibility for allocating funds the state received under the federal Law Enforcement Assistance Administration. Members were gubernatorial appointees. From 1971 to 1973, the executive director was Walter F. Kelly.

The WCCJ heard a number of perspectives on how best to use the federal funds. Local governments saw an opportunity for budget relief for police equipment and training programs. Universities and nonprofit organizations applied for funds to use for training and research. Lucey's Citizens' Study Committee on Judicial Organization sought support for its work reforming the court system. In Milwaukee, the police chief and the mayor competed for control of the money.

The WCCJ's major goals were to support innovative ways to prevent crime and to develop community-based correctional and rehabilitation programs. Kelly and his staff looked beyond simply providing budget relief for local law enforcement. Besides encouraging innovation, they worked to professionalize criminal justice administration. They had discovered sweetheart, no-bid deals when local governments purchased police communications equipment. The Judiciary Committee in the US House of Representatives asked Kelly to testify and help them expose such arrangements nationally.[84]

Lucey was pleased with the policy direction of the WCCJ. He was concerned, however, because the council became identified with conflict between local governments, police departments, and equipment vendors. Milwaukee was the scene of especially visible struggles involving the mayor and the police force. Focus was shifting from policy issues to WCCJ leadership. Lucey had to do something. He met with Kelly and then, in a January 6, 1973, letter, informed Kelly that he was being dismissed. Lucey wrote:

For the most part I believe that you have achieved during your tenure at the Council even more than I had anticipated in terms of setting in motion the necessary steps to focus additional attention on our courts and our prisons, to utilize funds consistent with the clear mandate of the federal law for experimentation and reform, and to use the influence of the state planning council to genuinely improve the criminal justice system for the state. . . . I have reluctantly concluded that it is in the best interests of the Council and, in fact, in the best interests of many of the reforms you have worked hard to implement, that a new Director be named for the Council. I have reached this conclusion because of the evidence that relations between the Council staff and those with whom it must have intercourse have reached a level of tension which does not bode well for the ability of the staff to carry out its responsibilities.[85]

Despite a January 11 staff petition and numerous letters from judges and local officials supporting Kelly, Lucey held firm.[86] Even after the dismissal, Lucey and Kelly enjoyed a long relationship of friendship and respect.[87]

### Executive Clemency

Governors have authority to check and amend the actions of state courts. After someone has been convicted and sentenced, governors can issue a pardon—which allows the person to be released from prison and state supervision and removes penalties such as ineligibility for certain jobs or programs. Governors can also commute, or reduce, a sentence. Lucey used his legal staff to review requests for clemency and make recommendations. A major question was whether procedural errors led to injustices. Lucey included staff work along with briefing papers, news magazines, and other reading material he brought with him as he left the office every day.[88]

Some staff members weighted heavily evidence that an individual was likely to make good use of a second chance. This consideration was applied most frequently when the conviction was for a nonviolent crime or a minor drug offense. Lucey intervened when Ernesto Chacon was arrested during a demonstration in Milwaukee seeking attention to the needs of the Latino community. During the demonstration, someone broke a window of Chapman Department Store. As a leader of the demonstration, Chacon took responsibility for the act—even though he did not break the window—and pleaded guilty to a misdemeanor. He went to Madison with his attorney, Curry First, and two supporters to seek Lucey's help in clearing his record. Lucey's staff was about to ask them to leave the office area because they were getting too loud. However, Lucey heard the commotion and invited everyone into his office to hear their story. After making some inquiries to confirm Chacon's role, Lucey granted the request.[89]

### No-Fault Insurance

Lucey's Citizens' Study Committee on Judicial Organization recommended that automobile insurance companies compensate victims in accidents regardless of who was at fault. The committee noted that 55 percent of court cases in Wisconsin involved automobile accidents, and these cases were responsible for much of the congestion in the courts.

Another task force looking at the insurance industry generally made a similar recommendation. It added that immediate payment be made to accident victims so they could pay medical bills and have some relief from lost wages. Task force members added that victims should be prevented from suing for pain and suffering, a balancing provision that generated support from the insurance industry.[90]

There was a lot of action but without results. Eight bills, in addition to one coming from task force deliberations, were proposed. Lucey was eager to see no-fault insurance but failed to get the necessary legislative support.[91] It was the lone item he was not able to check on his agenda as "done" when he left the governor's office.[92]

CHAPTER 13

# PROGRESS AND
# FRUSTRATION IN MEXICO

"I will be leaving soon for Washington," Governor Patrick J. Lucey teased in his State of the State address on January 18, 1977. After listening to gasps from the assembled legislators, he smiled and clarified that it would be a visit, not a move, to the nation's capital. He then went on to outline proposals "for the next two years and beyond," indicating an interest in a third term.[1] But plans change. Lucey would not serve a third term, and he did soon leave for Washington, DC, . . . and then for Mexico City.

## THE APPOINTMENT

Lucey's playful references to his future fed into speculation generated by the election of Jimmy Carter to the White House three months earlier. He did not support Carter in Wisconsin's 1976 presidential primary, but when it was clear that the Georgia governor had enough support to win the nomination, Lucey called to congratulate him and casually asked how things were going. Carter responded that he had a big campaign debt and was worried about having resources until public financing became available after the nominating convention. Lucey noted that Carter was visiting Milwaukee to address a national convention of mayors from big cities and offered to sponsor a twenty-five-dollar-a-plate breakfast fundraiser. The future president expressed his gratitude.[2]

Carter was even more grateful when Wisconsin cast its electoral college votes for the Carter–Mondale ticket. Lucey met with the president-elect on

December 9, 1976, fueling speculation about an appointment in the new administration. Lucey had national stature in the Democratic Party and had chaired the Democratic Governors Association when Carter was chief executive in Georgia. Also, the new vice president, Walter Mondale, and Lucey enjoyed a friendship and mutual respect. One rumor emanating from transition team deliberations was that Lucey would be appointed as secretary of the Department of Health, Education, and Welfare or perhaps Commerce or Housing and Urban Development. Another had him as the head of the Department of Energy that Carter planned to create. Lucey diplomatically said that he valued the opportunity to serve as Wisconsin's governor but that he would be inclined to accept a presidential request to serve.[3]

Meanwhile, uncertainty about Lucey's future, combined with Lieutenant Governor Martin J. Schreiber's desire to become governor, sparked other rumors as well as some controversy. Lucey and Schreiber independently positioned themselves to run for governor in 1978. As they each raised money, sought support, and took positions, they gave the appearance that they were competing with one another.[4] Wayne McGown, who had held senior positions in the administrations of Lucey and Republican Governor Warren Knowles, wrote a confidential memo to Schreiber in late summer 1976 suggesting ways for him to distance himself from the governor and prepare to challenge him. Discovery and publication of the memo fueled the speculation and controversy.[5] Would Lucey and Schreiber actually run against each other? Despite gossip, neither seriously envisioned that.[6]

Lucey and Schreiber, with their respective staffs, worked together during November and December on a transition plan in case Lucey was tapped for a senior position in the Carter administration. The hundred-page plan focused primarily on staffing issues. They agreed that if Schreiber stepped in as governor, he would give sixty days' notice for any personnel changes. Other provisions specified how the budget process would be modified and how the governor's office would be restructured.[7]

Lucey began assembling a campaign staff and raising funds on the assumption he would be running for a third term. His main fund-raiser, William Gerrard, had collected more than $150,000 ($634,000 in 2019 dollars) by early 1977—a substantial sum for campaigns at that time. But Lucey's own enthusiasm level was low.[8]

Lucey's daughter, Laurie, was working in the West Wing of the White House as an assistant to Chief of Staff Hamilton Jordan. She was taken aback when Jordan popped his head into her office and said, "Would your dad be interested in being ambassador to Mexico?" She paused before replying, "That's something you should ask him."[9]

A few days later, on March 23, the telephone rang at the governor's residence, and Jean answered. She turned to her husband and said, "President Carter is on the phone." After the governor and the president exchanged greetings, Carter said he wanted Lucey to be the US Ambassador to Mexico. Lucey thanked him and said he would seriously consider the offer and get back to him.[10]

Two days later, Mondale was the keynote speaker at a dinner to raise money for Lucey to seek a third term. Laurie accompanied the vice president. As the event concluded, Mondale and Laurie talked to the governor about the offer of an ambassadorial appointment. Mondale had just helped raise more than one hundred thousand dollars (about $423,000 in 2019) for Lucey's campaign but nonetheless encouraged him to take the assignment south of the border. So did the governor's daughter.[11]

Later that night, Lucey met with Bob Dunn, who was serving as secretary of the Department of Administration at the time. Lucey told Dunn that he was inclined to accept Carter's offer. Lucey was close to achieving almost all the reforms on his wish list and was intrigued with the idea of working on a national level. The speculation that Carter would offer a cabinet appointment encouraged this thinking. Lucey told Dunn that if he accepted the ambassadorial appointment, he wanted Dunn to go with him as a special assistant. Dunn said he would.[12]

Lucey called Carter back and accepted the appointment but indicated that he was in the final stages of getting major court reform and wanted to see that through. Lucey was concerned that he would lose leverage and support if he resigned before the reforms were adopted. He explained to Chief of Staff Jordan that the court reforms depended on four constitutional amendments that needed popular approval in an April 5 referendum. Lucey wanted the appointment kept secret until after the votes were counted, and Jordan agreed.[13] The few others who had been informed kept the secret.

On April 7, Carter announced his first major ambassadorial appointments, which included Lucey and nine others. Lucey announced at a crowded news conference of very surprised people that he would resign as governor, effective after the passage of the 1977–79 state budget, expected by July 1.[14] The day before the announcement, he met with Schreiber to let him know he would become governor.[15]

After Lucey had been in Mexico for a few months and gotten to know Foreign Minister Santiago Roel Garcia, he wondered aloud why he was selected as ambassador. Garcia said, "We picked you." Lucey observed that Mexican authorities did not know him prior to his arrival. Garcia explained that he and President José López Portillo told Carter that they did not want a career diplomat and they did not want a "hyphenated" American. Mexico hosted what was then the largest US embassy, and the country had risen generally in international status, especially with the prospect of becoming a major exporter of oil. It wanted the prestige that goes with having an ambassador who is a major politician, similar to the people who get appointed to London, Paris, and Tokyo.[16]

Hispanic Americans, however, had hoped that Carter would appoint someone who reflected their heritage. Manuel Fierro, president of the National Congress of Hispanic Americans, objected to the selection of Lucey. His organization, which represented 134 Spanish-speaking groups around the country, had lobbied hard for a Latino. Fierro promised to testify before the Senate Foreign Relations Committee in opposition to Carter's choice.[17]

Members of the Texas delegation in Congress also objected to Lucey's nomination. Democratic Representative Robert Krueger telegrammed Carter saying, "It is distressing that a Democratic administration has not found a Hispanic American who it considers deserving of the post." Republican Senator John Tower also publicly criticized the selection of Lucey.[18]

The Foreign Relations Committee unanimously recommended confirmation, and on May 25 the Senate cast a voice vote in agreement. The State Department required that Lucey continue to hold his assets in the blind trust he established when elected as governor. He was also asked to sign an affidavit that the campaign funds raised by Friends of Pat Lucey would not be used for personal expenses but instead returned to donors or given to a political committee that he would not control.[19]

## Departure

While packing his bags, Lucey put the finishing touches on the last of his various initiatives. He had won voter approval of the court reforms. His budget proposal included a number of items on his to-do list and proposals of others that he backed. Among the initiatives were

- Eliminating property taxes on inventories of merchants and manufacturers and on livestock.

- Regulating mining.

- Reforming ethics and lobbying.

- Creating a public defender office.

- Reorganizing the Department of Transportation.

- Making changes to state personnel management.

- Establishing a process for resolving public-sector collective bargaining impasses.

- Enacting safeguards for migrant workers.

- Providing incentives for the preservation of farmland.

- Overseeing nursing homes.

- Overhauling the children's code governing guardianship and custodial arrangements.

- Limiting campaign expenditures.

- Establishing air conditioner efficiency.

- Regulating pesticides.

- Conserving natural gas.[20]

As usual, it was a long list. Predictions varied about how effective Lucey as a lame-duck governor would be.[21] Democrats enjoyed large majorities in both chambers: twenty-three to ten in the senate and sixty-six to thirty-three in the assembly, but the caucuses had divisions within them.

Lucey and legislative leaders could not count on party support for everything they wanted.

Lucey did get the bulk of what he wanted into the budget bill.[22] He
continued to be on the losing side of no-fault automobile insurance but
otherwise felt satisfied with what he had accomplished. On the eve of his
departure, however, he was humbled. Lucey had made partial vetoes in the
budget bill that reached his desk on June 28. The legislature quickly convened to consider overrides. In a sometimes giddy atmosphere, legislators
flexed arms Lucey had twisted for more than six years and raised them to
erase the work of the veto pen. Of the sixty-seven partial vetoes, twenty-one
were overridden. As the last question was put to the assembly, Representative Jonathan Barry shouted, "Stick this in your sombrero!" To cheers and
laughter, representatives voted 99 to 0 to override the partial veto.[23]

Still, Lucey prevailed on major issues. He, for example, vetoed a repeal
of levy limits on local taxing authorities. The senate voted to override,
25 to 8, but the assembly sustained the veto 56 to 43. On another issue,
the governor left standing language to launch a veterinary school at the
University of Wisconsin–Madison but nixed the allocation of money for
the school. This time, it was the senate, by one vote, that upheld his veto.[24]

Dan Wisniewski and Steve Holmgren, Lucey's liaisons to the legislature, left the Capitol for a farewell party at the governor's residence.[25]
They were not looking forward to telling Lucey what had happened to his
other partial vetoes. When Lucey heard their news, however, he laughed.
Years later, he reflected on the episode. He again laughed and said, "You
shouldn't sign a budget the day before you're going to Mexico."[26]

When Lucey was asked, hypothetically, whom he would choose as his
successor, he said, "Tony Earl," referring to a former assembly majority
leader and then cabinet member. Lucey continued, "I would be prepared
to support Tony Earl for president of the United States. And I cannot think
of any other Wisconsin citizen about whom I am prepared to say that."[27]

## AMBASSADOR LUCEY

Lucey was sworn in as ambassador in a ceremony at the White House on
July 6. Vice President Mondale presided, and President Carter made a surprise, unscheduled appearance. Lucey's family was also in attendance.[28]

Lucey with a cartoon depicting the governor's departure for Mexico, drawn by Larry Sanders of the *Milwaukee Journal*.
EDWIN STEIN, *WISCONSIN STATE JOURNAL*

Lucey began his days in Mexico City with Spanish lessons at eight fifteen each morning. His tutor, Marta Wolff, met with him in his marble-walled, parquet-floored office in the large American embassy. Lucey managed eleven hundred employees and an annual budget of thirty-two million dollars ($135 million in 2019).[29] He never did master the Spanish language, but he quickly developed expertise in Mexican politics and economics.

Lucey told Dunn that he wanted as much as possible to get out of Mexico City and see the country. He wanted to have an itinerary as if he were running for sheriff. That meant seeing as much of Mexico as possible, visiting with local officials, hosting a diverse array of prominent Mexicans at the ambassador's residence, and walking around in cities and small towns, even visiting village markets. He asked Dunn to evaluate how US-sponsored projects were doing and assess needs that might be addressed with new or revised programs. As ambassador, it was unrealistic for Lucey to visit everywhere. He had Dunn go places and meet people he could not.

Vice President Walter Mondale swears in Lucey as ambassador with Pat's son David in the background. BOB DAUGHERTY, AP PHOTO

Lucey could not meet with leaders of opposition parties, but Dunn could, and did.[30]

Stan Zuckerman, who served as public affairs officer in the US embassy in Mexico from 1978 to 1983, described some of the bureaucratic challenges Lucey faced. Zuckerman and Lucey had first become acquainted in the early 1960s, when Zuckerman was executive secretary to Governor John Reynolds and Lucey was chair of the Democratic Party of Wisconsin. After Reynolds left office, Zuckerman joined the US Information Agency. He and Lucey maintained contact, and the day after Lucey announced he was accepting the ambassadorial appointment, he asked Zuckerman to join him in Mexico City. Zuckerman told him he would love to, but "things don't work that way." Lucey got a quick lesson in rules regarding federal personnel transfers and assignments.[31] With the exception of the special assistant position filled by Dunn, the ambassador had very limited ability to choose his own team. Lucey was determined and made his way through the State Department bureaucratic maze to get Zuckerman assigned to Mexico.

Lucey was not happy with his public affairs staff. He wanted them to operate like his press secretaries did when he was governor and he expected a proactive approach. Instead, he had employees he considered timid and reactive. Unlike his predecessors, Lucey wanted to go beyond the diplomatic interactions with senior Mexican officials and court understanding and support from local officials and the general population. When Zuckerman arrived, he found that the staff was in the doghouse. He persuaded Lucey to lower his expectations.[32]

Lucey also managed to replace the deputy chief of mission whom he had inherited. This position is second in charge at an embassy and responsible for staff management. Lucey judged the incumbent to be a clock-watcher more than a leader and someone whose contacts with Mexicans were too limited. He engineered a transfer for him, then went to Washington to interview four people who had just finished an assignment and were waiting for another. He chose the youngest, John Ferch—and had another member of the so-called Kiddie Corps.[33]

Lucey was pleased with the work Ferch did. Ferch had agency heads prepare briefing papers for Lucey to let him know what issues they faced and what might be anticipated. Staff meetings became regular and productive. The embassy also began to take clearer positions rather than hedging its recommendations to Washington. In short order, the embassy had a "remarkably good country team."[34] (Ferch would go on to be appointed by President Ronald Reagan as ambassador to Honduras.)

## Panama Canal

Carter was eager to have the US Senate ratify treaties prescribing the fate of the Panama Canal. He asked Lucey to help. That was an extracurricular activity, since it drew more from Lucey's position in national politics than his role as an ambassador. Negotiations leading to the treaties had been going on for decades, but talks between February 15 and August 10, 1977, produced the two treaties. One provided that the United States could take action to maintain the canal as a neutral, international resource, while the other gave Panama control over the canal. As Lucey described the latter, it would end the last vestige of colonialism in the Western Hemisphere.[35]

Lucey attended the meetings of the National Governors Association to secure support from his former colleagues and then went to Washington, DC, to talk with senators. The main opposition came from southern senators. Strom Thurmond led the charge, saying, "The canal is ours, we bought and we paid for it and we should keep it."[36] Lucey was on the winning side. The pact specifying US responsibility for keeping the canal open to ships of all nations was ratified on March 16, 1978, and the treaty giving Panama control over the canal was ratified on April 18. The vote in both instances was 68 to 32.

## CARTER VISIT

Relations with Mexico had grown in importance, especially since the 1976 discovery of a massive oil field in the Gulf of Mexico's Bay of Campeche. The field promised to rival that of Iran and held the promise of prosperity for Mexico and resources for an energy-hungry United States. Partly in response to the issues related to oil, senior administration officials and members of Congress made many high-profile visits.

Carter himself made a visit to Mexico from February 14 to 16, 1979. Mexican officials saw the Carter visit as a chance to leverage their oil into a broad discussion of economic relations between neighbors. Lucey agreed with his hosts that talks should be visionary. The advance team from the White House, however, expressed no interest in the policy briefs and proposals offered by the Mexicans.[37]

Oil had stirred national pride in Mexico. The left in that country's body politic mobilized several thousand protestors in a rally two days before Carter's arrival. Their fear was that the Carter administration "was coming to steal our oil. They will take our oil; they want to take everything away from us."[38] Pressure was on to nationalize the industry.

President Portillo, at some political cost, had made a deal with six US companies to purchase natural gas. It was heralded as the beginning of revenue flows into the country. But US Energy Secretary James R. Schlesinger Jr. blocked the agreement. He complained that the purchase agreed to was above the world price. Portillo was understandably unhappy and said, "The Americans have left me hanging by my paint brush"—invoking the image of a painter working on a ceiling and someone taking away the ladder.[39] Tensions were high as Carter embarked on his visit.

Just before leaving the White House for Mexico, Carter received the news that the US embassy in Tehran had been attacked by demonstrators and that Adolph Dubs, the US ambassador to Afghanistan, had been assassinated. Dubs was kidnapped and shot in the head as Afghan police attempted to rescue him. Carter thought seriously about canceling his visit to Mexico but decided to forge ahead. Lucey met Carter at the airport with a rehearsed group of cheering schoolchildren and a token representation of Mexican officials.[40]

After a visit to Los Pinos, then the official residence and offices of the Mexican president, the delegation attended a formal lunch. Portillo gave a toast that was more fiery than diplomatic. He rebuked Carter and his administration for blocking the natural gas agreement. He said the Americans were guilty of "sudden moves and sudden deceit." Portillo finished with, "We know who our friends really are by the way they treat us." It was an insult that Lucey, other foreign diplomats, and Mexicans understood, but according to Zuckerman, Carter did not.[41] Instead of responding in kind, Carter made matters worse by offering a rambling personal toast and recalling that when he first visited Mexico, he had "Montezuma's revenge." The joke was disrespectful and prompted criticism of Carter.[42]

Zuckerman observed, "The next day, the Mexican press was full of praise for Lopez Portillo because he had stood up to the American President."[43]

Protocol prescribes that a visiting head of state host a formal dinner before departing. Lucey battled with the White House over the menus, the entertainment, and the dinner itself. Initially, Lucey was told that Carter would not host a dinner for President Portillo. Lucey responded that such a move was unacceptable and that if the president would not host a dinner, he would have one himself at the ambassador's residence. The White House relented and then tried to assert control, deciding that the dinner would be a Tex-Mex barbecue. Lucey vetoed that, arguing that a barbecue was below standards and almost anything associated with Texas was not popular in Mexico. He reminded the aides back in Washington that Texas was once part of Mexico and was annexed by force to the United States.

Lucey wanted a more appropriate menu. The White House responded by saying they would send a chef to take charge. Lucey responded, "No, thanks!"[44]

He personally paid for Vicki and Pat Kohlman, two sisters and French-trained chefs from Fond du Lac, Wisconsin, to fly to Mexico City to do the cooking. Their mother, Trudy, a renowned pastry chef, and father, Elmer, volunteered to help. The Kohlman sisters had worked as chefs for Lucey when he occupied the governor's mansion, and they had established a catering business, Chez Vous, in Madison in 1978. The Kohlmans prepared a formal, four-course, French-style dinner. The entrée was beef tenderloin with béarnaise sauce, and dessert was petit fours, one of Trudy Kohlman's specialties[45]

Lucey and Zuckerman proposed that classical pianist Vladimir Horowitz be invited to perform after the dinner. The White House objected because he had played for Carter and then released a record that they felt used the White House for self-promotion. First Lady of Mexico Carmen Romano, an accomplished pianist who founded the Mexico City Philharmonic, also got involved in planning the entertainment. Zuckerman suggested that Lucey ask Leonard Bernstein to conduct the orchestra founded by Romano. Both the Mexican first lady and the White House staff loved the idea. Bernstein agreed and sent ahead a proposed program for the concert that included a mix of American and Mexican music, including the Bernstein Symphonic Dances from *West Side Story*. The first couple of Mexico, who detested *West Side Story* because of its negative portrayal of Hispanics, objected to the selection. Bernstein understood and substituted Beethoven's Fifth Symphony.[46]

The dinner and entertainment were winners, but the visit reinforced doubts Lucey had about Carter's ability to handle presidential responsibilities. Lucey initially had not supported Carter for the White House and had low expectations for him as president. The gaffe at lunch and the approach to the formal dinner seemed to demonstrate a lack of respect for Mexico. The disinterest in policy goals during the visit and the absence of any notable achievement dismayed Lucey.[47] Nonetheless, Lucey continued to be effective as an ambassador.

## PRISONER EXCHANGE

Lucey faced several substantive issues as he began his diplomatic service. One of the first was the fate of US citizens in Mexican prisons. A concern north of the border was that Mexico did not adhere to due

Lucey meets with US prisoners held in Mexico while negotiating an exchange between the two countries. WHI IMAGE ID 143817

process. Also, prison conditions were considered to be lower than those in the United States.

The two countries had signed a prisoner transfer treaty the year before Lucey became ambassador. The treaty excluded some crimes, such as violations of immigration laws and acts of violence. Lucey lobbied the US Senate to ratify the pact, and the response was a positive 90 to 0 vote. He then worked to get implementation language approved. He drafted a statement proposing that the two countries exchange eligible prisoners in accordance with the treaty.[48]

Lucey talked with Portillo and got his agreement to the exchange. To get the cooperation of his own government, Lucey needed to get Carter's signature on the statement and also persuade the US Senate and House of Representatives to pass enabling legislation. After months of waiting to get Carter's attention, Lucey recruited Secretary of State Cyrus Vance, and together they approached Carter while he was making a visit to his peanut farm in Georgia. Carter signed, and Lucey returned to DC to walk the halls of the Capitol. Both houses passed the implementation bill.[49]

The first sixty-one American prisoners were released under the agreement in December 1977. "Ambassador Lucey really went to bat for us," Robin Worthington, one of the prisoners, said when she deplaned in San Francisco. Patricia Bartz from Pewaukee, Wisconsin, added her praise. She had served more than four years of a seven-year term on drug charges.[50] Within a year, almost four hundred Americans and four hundred Mexicans were finishing their sentences in their own countries.

## IMMIGRATION

During his campaign for the presidency, Carter had promised labor unions that he would control illegal immigration from Mexico. He proposed strengthening the border patrol, fining employers of undocumented aliens, and legalizing the status of migrants who had been living in the United States since before 1970. Mexican officials were infuriated not because they disagreed with the measures or with the perennial concerns about illegal immigration but because Carter had not consulted with them. They regarded the issue as a joint problem that should be handled jointly.[51]

Lucey agreed with Carter but also was sympathetic to the Mexican grievance. As Lucey saw it, the major problem was the practice of US employers hiring Mexicans regardless of their documentation. He told Carter that unless American employers observed the law and monitored the status of people working for them, there would be no end to the problem. Without demand, the supply would dwindle.[52]

Lucey scheduled Carter to visit Ixtilco el Grande when he was in Mexico in February 1979. The village was located seventy miles south of Mexico City and was an example of rural development that slowed migration because of improved economic and social conditions at home. It was an alternative to approaching the immigration issue with sanctions. Lucey himself regularly visited rural projects funded in part by loans from the World Bank and the Inter-American Development Bank. Projects ranged from farms to tourist venues to small factories. Carter agreed to increase support for the two banks.[53]

## American Community in Mexico

Lucey did not enjoy broad support from American business representatives in Mexico. At the time, a quarter million US citizens lived in Mexico, forty-four thousand of them in Mexico City. American businesses had an investment of $3.4 billion ($13.4 billion in 2019) in the country. Lucey did not match his predecessor in sponsoring social gatherings and golf parties, but the main grievance of American expatriates was that he did not join them in lobbying Congress for an increase in the deductibility of foreign earnings from US income tax. The expectation of the American Chamber of Commerce in Mexico had been that Lucey would use his political clout and his access to Carter to help get the tax breaks. Lucey thought the business community was adequately protected against double taxation and that it was not appropriate to distort the tax code more than it already was.[54]

Lucey recognized that his job description included throwing parties and enhancing the social life of Americans in Mexico. Visiting dignitaries and Hollywood stars provided occasions for parties. Guests included Walter Mondale, Henry Kissinger, Tom Hayden, Jane Fonda, Helen Hayes, and Jack Anderson.

Lucey arranged to have any American movies that were shown in Mexico City lent to the embassy for a few days. He and Jean then had dinner parties for as many as seventy-two people at the residence followed by a showing of the film. Movie nights occurred at least once a month and were enjoyed by a mix of American business representatives, foreign diplomats, and Mexican officials.[55] A highlight of the evening was to have mint brownies baked from a recipe acquired from Esther Kaplan and made famous by Jean. When Lucey visited Mexico ten years after he had been ambassador, he learned that the American expatriate community held an annual brownie contest and awarded a prize to the one judged to be closest to the "Jean standard."[56]

But movies and brownies were not enough to assuage anger over the tax issue. Prominent members of the American expatriate community complained to the *Wall Street Journal* and the *Los Angeles Times*, saying Lucey was doing a disastrous job. Bob Strauss, who as chair of the Democratic National Committee had had a number of confrontations with Lucey, had a hand in disseminating the critical stories.[57] Strauss had held a grudge against Lucey because he had supported Jean Westwood to be retained as Democratic National Committee chairperson after McGovern's unsuccessful run for president. Lucey prevailed and again successfully opposed Strauss when the DNC tried to end Wisconsin's open primary law in 1975. The charges against Lucey as ambassador were that he did not speak Spanish, had no previous diplomatic experience, failed to listen to American business representatives, and did not work well with embassy staff.[58]

Zuckerman responded to the bad press by inviting the editor of *Excelsior*, the leading paper in Mexico, to have an exclusive, wide-ranging interview with Lucey. The paper had generally been very critical of US policies. The day after the interview, the *Excelsior*'s front page had an eight-column banner headline, a photo of Lucey, and a positive story that took most of two pages. Officials at the State Department called Lucey to congratulate him. The *Excelsior* story was picked up by newspapers throughout the United States, while the critical stories received only limited coverage.[59] However, the rumblings led to discussions about Lucey's future within the Carter administration.

Strauss pressed Carter for an appointment to Mexico for US Representative Krueger, who had been defeated by Tower in 1978 for a seat in the US Senate. Carter responded by creating an ambassador-at-large position back in Washington, DC, and asking Lucey to take it. Carter proposed having the new post coordinate task forces working on Mexican–American relations. It was unusual to have an ambassador-at-large assigned to a single country, and it was not clear what the relationship would be between the ambassador and the ambassador-at-large. When discussions about the possible change leaked, both Carter and Vance issued denials.[60]

According to Zuckerman, in addition to the ambassador-at-large position, Carter told Lucey that he would appoint him secretary of the Department of Energy whenever Schlesinger left. Lucey expressed interest, but when Schlesinger left, Carter named Charles Duncan Jr. without ever saying anything to Lucey. Lucey was miffed.[61]

At the Jefferson–Jackson dinner held by the Democratic Party of Wisconsin in Milwaukee on March 31, 1979, Carter said Lucey would continue as ambassador to Mexico. The president praised Lucey and said that top Mexican officials had called Lucey the most effective American envoy in memory.[62] On June 22, Carter announced he was nominating Krueger to be ambassador-at-large for Mexico. The exact duties of the position and how it would relate to the ambassador were not clear.[63]

Meanwhile, negotiations over natural gas had resumed between the United States and Mexico. Mexicans approached the talks with caution and skepticism because of the Carter administration's blocking the deal that had been reached two years earlier. When that agreement became moot, Mexico decided to use most of its natural gas domestically instead of exporting it. Carter was eager to avoid further inflation of US fuel prices and sought Mexico's agreement to send a guaranteed amount of gas at a fixed price. Lucey worked to smooth relations and was successful in helping the two countries reach agreement before a visit to Washington, DC, by President Portillo in late September 1979.[64]

## RESIGNATION

On October 9, 1979, Lucey announced that he was resigning as ambassador to Mexico, effective November 1. In the weeks prior, Laurie had left her job in the Carter White House to begin her studies at Georgetown Law School, and Dunn had accepted a position as deputy appointments secretary in the White House.

In his letter of resignation, Lucey thanked Carter for the opportunity to serve as ambassador and cited as accomplishments the natural gas agreement, the prisoner exchange treaty, rural development projects, and progress on dealing with immigration issues. He encouraged the development of a respectful approach to our southern neighbor and concluded, "Mexico seeks our friendship as the mature, responsible, independent, and rapidly developing nation that it has become."[65]

Three months after he left Mexico City, a reporter from *Excelsior* interviewed Lucey. The former ambassador shared his concern that despite the progress that had been made, the Carter administration had not adopted a respectful attitude toward Mexico. He said that Carter did not recognize Mexico as mature, responsible, and independent.[66]

The speculation as Lucey left was whether he would help Carter win reelection or would assist Ted Kennedy in his bid to replace Carter.

## CHAPTER 14

# RUNNING FOR VEEP

P atrick J. Lucey knew the odds. The chance of discontents denying a
sitting president of their own party the opportunity to run for reelection was remote at best. Yet Lucey saw firsthand the near success of
Bobby Kennedy in 1968. Could Bobby's brother Ted force Jimmy Carter
to withdraw as Lyndon B. Johnson had done? Were enough people within
the Democratic Party willing to vote against nominating Carter for a second term?

Lucey also knew it was highly unlikely that third-party candidates,
especially when using a new and unfamiliar political label, could successfully compete against Republican and Democratic nominees. In addition
to overcoming issues such as traditional loyalties, name recognition, and
financial resources, new parties must master the labyrinth of state requirements for even getting listed on the ballot.

Lucey knew the odds, but he forged ahead, seeming to welcome the
challenges and motivated by a commitment to progressive values.

## ANOTHER KENNEDY

When Lucey notified Carter that he was resigning as ambassador, the
president suggested he take another assignment. Perhaps in the cabinet?
Perhaps as a special ambassador for human rights? It appeared that Carter
feared Lucey was about to help Senator Ted Kennedy challenge him for
the 1980 Democratic presidential nomination. The fear was well founded.
Lucey declined the offers from Carter and said he was joining the Kennedy
campaign.[1]

Although the tragic car accident at Chappaquiddick continued to haunt Ted Kennedy, the assassinations of his brothers nurtured an almost nostalgic loyalty to the Kennedys and the dream of Camelot. Kennedy was expected to run for president. Moreover, labor union leadership and liberal activists were disappointed with Carter and saw Kennedy as their best hope for the changes they pursued.

The failure to reach an agreement on health care reform played a major role in fueling opposition to Carter. Kennedy and Carter had been negotiating since 1977 on how to achieve universal health care coverage. They both agreed that a plan should be implemented in phases. Kennedy wanted to pass a law that committed the federal government to achieve certain benchmarks by specific dates, whereas Carter wanted flexibility. He wanted to tie phases to economic conditions rather than dates. Neither budged. On December 9, 1978, at the Democratic Party's midterm convention in Memphis, Carter gave an opening speech arguing for budget stringency as the top priority. This was followed by a panel on health care, chaired by then Arkansas Governor Bill Clinton. The panelists were Joseph Califano, Carter's secretary of Health, Education and Welfare; Stuart Eisenstat, Carter's chief White House domestic policy advisor; and Kennedy. Kennedy made a passionate argument for his plan that brought delegates to their feet, cheering enthusiastically. Carter and his staff marked this as the beginning of Kennedy's bid for the nomination.[2]

On November 4, 1979, in an awkward interview with Roger Mudd of CBS News, Kennedy said he was indeed seeking the 1980 nomination.[3] Two days later, Lucey accepted the position of deputy campaign manager. Stephen Smith, Kennedy's brother-in-law, served as campaign manager. At the press conference announcing his appointment, the former ambassador confirmed that Carter had offered him a number of positions. Lucey said he turned them down because of the administration's general failure to accomplish its goals.[4]

Many of Lucey's close associates in the Badger State did not follow him into the Kennedy camp. He met at the home of his former aide, Richard Weening, with about twenty other prominent Democrats to discuss the Kennedy campaign. Lucey's one-time rival David Carley helped raise the five thousand dollars required for Kennedy to qualify for the Wisconsin primary. But leaders such as Anthony Earl, James Wahner, Martin

Schreiber, Daniel Wisniewski, Robert Friebert, Thomas Harnisch, and William Gerrard announced support for the Carter–Mondale ticket.[5]

At the same time that Kennedy was launching his campaign, Iranian student protestors were storming the American embassy in Tehran. They seized fifty-two members of the staff as hostages. As efforts to free the hostages failed, concern grew. The botched April 24, 1980, attempt by Carter's Operation Eagle Claw to rescue American hostages held in Tehran cemented Lucey's negative assessment of the president.[6] The complex and risky effort ended with eight US military crew members dead, five others injured, increased Iranian security placed on the hostages, and international embarrassment. Secretary of State Cyrus Vance, with whom Lucey enjoyed a close relationship, had opposed the rescue plan and resigned when Carter went ahead despite warnings.[7] The hostage crisis plagued Carter throughout his bid for reelection.

Kennedy's campaign foundered initially. Carter notched victories in the Iowa caucuses and primaries in New Hampshire, Vermont, Illinois, and several southern states. Kennedy's only win prior to mid-March 1980 was in his home state of Massachusetts. In a shakeup of Kennedy's campaign staff at the beginning of March, Lucey took over responsibilities as chief spokesperson. Ahead of New York's March 25 primary, polls had Kennedy trailing by twenty points. Kennedy drafted a concession speech.[8] He could pocket this, however. Kennedy beat Carter in New York with 59 percent of the vote and also won neighboring Vermont. Although Lucey was not able to put his home state in the winners' column, he did help win critical contests in Pennsylvania, Michigan, New Jersey, and California.

After completion of the primaries on June 3, Carter had 2,123 delegates—more than the 1,677 votes need to win on the first ballot— and Kennedy had 1,151. Kennedy argued for an open convention in which delegates were free to vote for whomever they wished regardless of pledges or commitments made through the primaries. But some states, including Wisconsin, had laws binding delegates on the first ballot. Lucey acknowledged this but joined in arguing for an open convention. So did Representative Les Aspin, who headed the Wisconsin delegates for Kennedy. David Lasker got support from Dane County Democrats for a resolution asking for an open convention. Senator Gaylord Nelson and

Representatives David Obey, Robert Kastenmeier, and Henry Reuss joined in the call. The Wisconsin delegates pledged to Carter, on the other hand, opposed changing the rules.[9]

The roll call of all national convention delegates was 1,030 in favor of an open convention and 1,936 opposed. Kennedy withdrew his candidacy and gave what many regarded as the best and most moving speech of his life.[10] He had criticisms for Ronald Reagan and for Carter, but he emphasized a vision of justice and fairness.

Lucey walked out of the convention hall before the first vote and sent a letter to Ray Majerus, chair of the Wisconsin delegation, resigning as a delegate. His departure was captured on national television and prompted murmuring throughout the political world. Lucey explained that he could not support Carter and Rule N of the Democratic National Party, which states that delegates "will not publicly support or campaign for any candidate for president or vice president other than the nominees of the convention."[11] A number of Wisconsin delegates, most of whom supported Carter, followed Lucey to his hotel room. They pleaded with Lucey to return, and when some—including a few of his close associates— started yelling at him, Lucey firmly announced, "This conversation is over!" and ushered them out of his room.[12]

Lucey's resignation was not well received by Wisconsin Democrats. He was accused of disloyalty and bad judgment. Some worried his decision would spell victory for Reagan in November. Majerus was particularly vocal. On the other hand, Aspin and Bill Proxmire urged continued respect for Lucey, and Lasker wrote a column defending him.[13] Amidst the controversy, Lucey tried to make it clear that he had resigned as a delegate, not as a Democrat.[14]

## TEAMING UP WITH ANDERSON

The day after Lucey walked out of the convention, John B. Anderson, a Republican member of the House of Representatives representing northern Illinois, invited him to meet. Anderson had competed with Ronald Reagan, Bob Dole, Howard Baker, John Connally, and George H. W. Bush for the Republican presidential nomination.[15] Lucey and Anderson had not worked together and knew one another only by reputation.

Lucey remembered watching Anderson and Reagan debate and was impressed with the performance and the liberal positions of the Illinois representative.[16] Anderson had been a prominent conservative in Congress but supported civil rights and the Equal Rights Amendment and opposed Carter's proposal to reinstate the military draft. Anderson, however, was unable to do better than second place in primaries. After Reagan beat him in Illinois—the home state of both men—Anderson dropped out of the contest for the Republican nomination and announced that he would run for the White House as an independent. He launched the National Unity Party and began the complicated and expensive task of getting on the ballot of each state and the District of Columbia.

Anderson had Lucey on his initial shortlist of preferred running mates. As names dropped off, the choice came down to Lucey and Edward Brooke, a Republican and former US Senator from Massachusetts. A prominent and respected African American, Brooke had endorsed Anderson in the primary contests, but Anderson calculated that Lucey might bring more supporters because of his ties to the Democratic Party and, especially, to the Kennedys. Aspin, who served with Anderson in Congress and worked with Lucey in Wisconsin, urged Anderson to consider Lucey for the vice-presidential slot.[17] Aspin thought that the disaffected Democrats and Republicans concerned about Reagan might be a winning combination, and Lucey had a reputation that made him credible as a potential president if needed.[18]

Before talking with Anderson, Lucey met with Donald Peterson, his erstwhile rival for the Wisconsin Democratic gubernatorial nomination in 1970. Peterson had signed on as the Wisconsin cochair for Anderson and encouraged Lucey to partner with the representative from Illinois.[19] Accompanied by his son David, Lucey met with Anderson for forty-five minutes. They discussed issues and also the possibility of Lucey serving as campaign manager. Lucey said he was not interested in that. Anderson then raised the possibility of Lucey running with him as candidate for vice president.[20] Both men agreed to think about this.

Speculation that Lucey would be Anderson's running mate continued for almost two weeks.[21] Part of the delay in making an announcement was because Anderson wanted to be sure that Jean Lucey was supportive. She had undergone a seven-hour gallbladder operation in early 1980 and seemed to be looking forward to some quiet time. Anderson asked his wife,

Patrick J. Lucey and John Anderson announce their candidacies on the National Unity ticket on August 26, 1980. AP PHOTO

Keke, to meet with Pat and Jean at their vacation home in Door County, Wisconsin. The two women, who proudly shared their Greek heritage and strong wills, immediately established a bond.[22] Three days later, on August 26, Anderson and Lucey held a news conference in Washington, DC, and formally announced they would be running together.[23]

Appearing on the national public television show *The MacNeil/Lehrer Report*, Lucey explained, "I'd rather be working for a candidate about whom it is said he can't win, rather than a candidate about whom it is said he shouldn't win."[24]

Lucey reached out to get people with whom he had worked when he was governor to support the Anderson–Lucey ticket. The reaction was mixed. For example, he was on the phone with longtime supporter and former staff member Keith Clifford for almost an hour trying to get him on board. Clifford respectfully declined, explaining that he learned perhaps too well the lesson Lucey taught about the importance of party loyalty.

Nonetheless, shortly after the phone call, Clifford made sure that Lucey was invited to a gathering organized by Aspin to meet with Walter Mondale. After the two friends who were somewhat awkwardly competing with one another to be vice president talked, someone disparaged Lucey for abandoning the party. Clifford responded, "Pat Lucey has done more for the Democratic Party of Wisconsin than everyone in this room combined. He deserves our respect whether we support him or not." That brought loud applause and quelled further anti-Lucey talk.[25]

Lucey also placed a call to David Lasker, who had remained close to Lucey since 1965, when he helped him in his first campaign for governor. Lucey asked, "Are you willing to jump off a cliff without a parachute with me?" Lasker readily accepted the invitation and staffed the vice-presidential candidate.[26]

## PLATFORM

Anderson's staff was nearing completion of a platform when Lucey agreed to be the vice-presidential candidate. He reviewed the draft before accepting the nomination and then helped complete the 317-page document. Anderson had a reputation of being fiscally conservative and socially liberal, and the National Unity campaign platform reflected those positions. The major policy disagreement between Anderson and Lucey was over health care: Lucey wanted comprehensive federal health insurance, whereas Anderson favored continued reliance on private plans. They agreed to disagree—publicly.[27]

In contrast to the platforms of the Republican and Democratic parties, which are the products of debate and, often, compromise among delegates to the national conventions, the National Unity campaign platform was the work of candidates and their staff. While Republican and Democratic nominees might distance themselves from the positions of their respective parties, the Anderson–Lucey document represented personal pledges by the candidates.

Major positions of the National Unity Party platform were to

- Balance the federal budget before reducing personal income taxes.

- Raise the gasoline tax by fifty cents per gallon to fund a 50 percent reduction in Social Security taxes, while maintaining or increasing benefits.

- Fight inflation with a new system of tax incentives to unions and businesses who agree to wage-price controls.

- Eliminate inheritance and gift taxes on money willed to spouses.

- Emphasize home care for the sick and the elderly.

- Enforce water and air pollution laws more strictly.

- Place a moratorium on new permits for nuclear power plants.

- Create enterprise zones in cities.

- Establish an urban reinvestment trust fund with dedicated revenues from alcohol and tobacco taxes.

- Support adoption of the Equal Rights Amendment.

- Negotiate a nuclear test ban treaty.

- Pursue arms control agreements.

- Uphold principles of the Camp David accords between Israel and Palestine.[28]

## GETTING ON THE BALLOT

States are responsible for election administration, including the placement of candidates for president and vice president on the ballot. A major challenge faced by Anderson and Lucey was to navigate through the rules of the various states and the District of Columbia to get this done. The Democratic Party anticipated the National Unity Party posed more of a threat to Carter–Mondale than to the Republicans and sued in nineteen states to keep the names of Anderson and Lucey off the November 4 ballot.[29]

Five states (Kentucky, Maine, Minnesota, New Mexico, and Ohio) had deadlines for filing candidacy that had passed before Anderson announced his candidacy. Courts set the deadlines aside, ruling that the deadlines had the effect of violating the equal protection rights provided in the Fourteenth Amendment. Texas and four other states had a law prohibiting anyone who had voted in a partisan primary from signing a petition to put an independent or third-party candidate on the ballot.

Lucey's name posed a special problem. In eighteen states, including Wisconsin and Illinois, Anderson was able to meet the deadlines for filing for himself but had to put a placeholder for the vice-presidential slot because he had not yet selected his running mate. In Wisconsin, Anderson included Gerald Larson, a Madison dentist, as a surrogate. When asked to substitute Lucey's name, Kevin Kennedy, legal counsel for the Wisconsin Elections Board, refused because the deadline had passed. Kennedy said a substitution was possible only in the case of a death, and Larson was alive and well. Kennedy, however, agreed with Attorney General Bronson La Follette that the courts would probably rule against the Elections Board if the National Unity Campaign sued to name Lucey in place of Larson. In contrast to the pattern in other states, the Wisconsin Carter–Mondale campaign asked the board to put Lucey's name on the ballot.

At a September 17 meeting, the board met and, with two members absent, voted 3 to 3, effectively rejecting the Anderson–Lucey petition. One of those voting to reject was Esther Kaplan, who had worked hard to get Lucey elected governor in 1970. Carol Skornicka, former staff aid to Governor Lucey, had to miss the meeting because of a hearing in Lancaster, Wisconsin. She had not anticipated the negative outcome and acted to get another meeting scheduled. The board reconsidered and, without going to court, Lucey's name was included.[30]

## Dialing for Dollars

Campaigns cost money, and the Anderson–Lucey quest to get on the ballot added legal and administrative expenses that the Democratic and Republican parties did not have to incur. That effort alone cost over two million dollars ($6 million in 2019).[31] The National Unity campaign also had to build infrastructure, and its candidates had to introduce themselves to voters. Television advertising was essential. And the Anderson–Lucey ticket had less than three months to raise the necessary funds.

The campaign relied heavily on small contributions from individuals excited about the possibility of President Anderson and Vice President

Lucey. The response to general pleas and direct solicitations was gratifying—more than ten million dollars ($31 million in 2019).[32] But even with lots of volunteer help, it was costly in time and money to raise money in such a way.

The Federal Election Commission (FEC) ruled on September 2 that third parties who garnered at least 5 percent of the presidential vote qualified for federal campaign funds. That was key, but the funds would be available only after Election Day in November, and television stations required money up front to run ads. Mitchell Rogovin, the National Unity campaign counsel, approached banks for loans, using the FEC funds as collateral. He had some initial success but then was sabotaged.

On September 9, the White House intentionally leaked to banks a memo written by Tim Smith, Carter campaign committee's legal adviser, warning of the risks of lending money to the Anderson–Lucey campaign. Smith said that if the campaign defaulted on payments, the banks would be subject to court action because the loans would then be considered illegal campaign contributions. At a minimum, he argued, banks would face audits and have legal fees because they were dealing in "unchartered waters." The banks backed off, leaving Anderson and Lucey empty-handed. Rogovin went to the FEC to get clarification. The commissioners ruled on October 2 that Smith's memo was wrong. Loans to the campaign were reasonable business ventures and legally safe. Nonetheless, the damage had been done. Banks feared retribution from the Carter administration despite the FEC ruling, and they worried that the National Unity ticket might not reach the 5 percent threshold. The banks kept the money in their vaults.[33]

Anderson and Lucey were not able to run any television ads in September. They were able to afford some beginning on October 17, less than three weeks before voters went to the polls. The campaign sent out a mailing asking for loans, which would be repaid at 8 percent interest after the election. The appeal generated $1.8 million from 21,800 supporters. It was a help, of course, but well short of the $10 million the campaign had hoped to spend.[34]

The lack of funds affected more than time on television. Anderson and Lucey were not able to commission any polling that could help them target their efforts and guide their scheduling. They were not able to afford a plane for Anderson until the final three weeks. That meant he, as well as Lucey, had to use commercial flights and work around airlines' scheduled routes.[35]

When the campaign was over, the FEC ordered a payment of $4.24 million ($13 million in 2019) to the National Unity campaign. The result was a debt of $620,000 ($1.9 million in 2019), which the two candidates retired in March 1981.[36]

## THE DEBATES

The League of Women Voters announced it was going to sponsor presidential debates in 1980. The League decided that it would invite candidates who had support of around 15 percent in national polls. In late August, Anderson was polling in the 12 to 15 percent range.[37]

The League invited Carter, Reagan, and Anderson to the first debate, held in Baltimore on September 21. Carter refused to participate, arguing that Anderson should not have been included. Because Carter would not be on stage, ABC refused to cover the debate and instead offered viewers the chance to see *Midnight Express*. Reagan and Anderson went ahead, and other networks carried the debate. Polls identified Anderson as having done slightly better than Reagan, although the number who saw the debate was only half of what had been expected.[38]

Anderson and Lucey continued to poll around 15 percent through October. But the League changed its rules and did not invite Anderson to participate in the second debate, held on October 28 in Cleveland. The League also canceled plans for a vice-presidential debate that it had scheduled in Louisville. Reagan, like others, criticized the League, but he decided to attend the second debate. He did considerably better than pundits and voters had expected in his face-off with Carter. What was not widely known at the time was that Reagan had a copy of the briefing books that were written for Carter. Although Carter was clearly the better-informed candidate, Reagan knew what to anticipate and what to attack. He was well prepared, surprisingly confident, and had some memorable lines. Responding to Carter's comments on Medicare, Reagan said, "There you go again." And to viewers, he later asked, "Are you better off now than you were four years ago?"

Who provided the purloined debate briefing books became the subject of a ten-month congressional investigation that was dubbed "Debategate." In 1983, it was revealed that William Casey, Reagan's titular campaign manager and later appointee to direct the Central Intelligence Agency, gave the books to James Baker, the functional campaign manager. The FBI found the fingerprints of Baker and David Gergen, who was working with Baker, on the books. Baker testified before the congressional committee that he indeed had seen the books and that he received them from Casey. Casey, however, denied any knowledge or involvement. The investigation ended without determining who gave the Carter briefing books to Reagan's team.[39]

## ENDORSEMENTS

The Liberal Party in New York broke with a thirty-six-year tradition of backing the Democratic Party candidate and urged its members to support the National Unity pair. Going back to Harry Truman's surprise victory in 1948, the Liberal Party's backing had several times made the difference in who won the state's electoral votes. The hope was that Anderson and Lucey would benefit nationally from what had happened in the Empire State.[40]

There were few other prominent endorsements. Former Interior Secretary Stewart Udall organized a group of prominent environmentalists who issued a declaration of support for Anderson and Lucey. Another environmental group, however, argued that their cause would be better served by voting for Carter and Mondale. The concern was that support for the National Unity campaign would have the effect of electing Reagan.[41] Likewise, auto workers feared supporting Anderson and Lucey would result in a Reagan presidency. They endorsed Carter.[42]

## ON THE STUMP

The National Unity campaign staff scheduled Lucey to deliver a detailed policy speech on energy conservation at Holy Cross College in Massachusetts. Lucey began, "I'm going to do a terrible thing today. I'm going to deliver a serious speech." About midway into his talk, which was received with respectful silence, Lucey paused, cleared his throat, and said, "You know, it's perfectly permissible to clap at any time you want."[43]

Lucey enjoyed campaigning, despite the hectic schedule and the long odds for success. He knew he lacked charisma, but he impressed audiences with his knowledge of the issues and his passion for progressive principles. Lucey and Lasker were constantly on the go, visiting as many as seven cities in six states in a single day, but the energy level never flagged. Lucey napped when he could.[44]

Like his other campaigns, he began most days with greeting workers at a plant gate early in the morning. On Labor Day weekend, the traditional start of the push for votes in the November general election, Lucey and Anderson had rallies in their respective hometowns. Students at the University of Wisconsin–Madison filled the thirteen hundred seats in the Memorial Union Theater, and another thousand waited outside to get a glimpse of the candidates. In Rockford, Illinois, about a thousand supporters stood in a drizzle and listened to Anderson and Lucey.[45] As was generally true in the campaign, the crowds were modest but enthusiastic.

Lucey walked neighborhoods canvassing door to door. His campaigning included going into densely populated areas associated with high crime rates, making the Secret Service personnel assigned to him nervous at times. The agents were especially concerned about providing protection in high-rise apartment buildings. When Lucey went to East St. Louis, Illinois, and Newark, New Jersey, the agents told Lasker that he and Lucey would have to sign a waiver absolving the Secret Service of responsibility for their safety. Lucey signed and proceeded.[46]

Despite the sometimes risky ventures, Secret Service agents confided to Lasker that they enjoyed the assignment of protecting Lucey. According to Lasker, they grew to like him as a person and as a public official. During an extemporaneous, heartfelt speech given at the Kennedy Library, Lucey talked about JFK's vision of people working together and moved one of the hard-nosed agents to tears. The agents felt Lucey, unlike some of the other candidates, listened to people and did not just tell them what he thought they wanted to hear.[47]

Polling suggested that the Anderson–Lucey ticket had a chance to capture Hawaii's electoral votes, so the campaign staff scheduled Lucey to visit the islands. The advance team greeted Lucey with leis, alohas, and a full schedule of photo ops at standard tourist attractions. The leis were gratefully accepted, but the schedule was drastically altered. Lucey wanted

During his campaign for the vice presidency, Lucey greets residents at the Scudder Homes project in Newark, NJ. WHI IMAGE ID 96397

to meet with people, not just photographers. He got both. The highlight of the visit was when Lucey and some of his supporters went to one of the busiest intersections of Honolulu at noon—one of the busiest times—and greeted islanders with smiles and the *shaka*, a Hawaiian gesture of greeting. Drivers reciprocated, and the news coverage was better than any speech or rally could have generated.[48]

On the eve of Election Day, Lasker overheard a discussion of prominent journalists that included representatives from CBS, NBC, the *New York Times*, and the *Wall Street Journal*. The journalists agreed that if one considered the three major presidential candidates and their running mates, the person who stood out as the most qualified was Lucey. He seemed the most able to govern and understood and cared about public policy. Lasker interrupted to be sure he had heard them right, and he had. When he asked in a frustrated voice, "Why didn't that become a story?" the response was that their role was limited to reporting, not opining.[49]

What mattered, of course, was not the judgment of Secret Service agents or reporters but voters. And their decision was to select Ronald Reagan and George H. W. Bush to lead the nation. The results of the 1980

Patrick J. Lucey, accompanied by his wife, Jean, campaigns for the vice presidency in Hawaii in 1980.
WHI IMAGE ID 96395

election (table 14.1) were disappointing to Anderson and Lucey but not unexpected. They qualified for federal funds but came far from winning or even having an impact on who won.

**TABLE 14.1.** 1980 Presidential Election Results

|  | Electoral College | States | Popular Vote | Percent |
|---|---|---|---|---|
| Reagan–Bush | 489 | 44 | 43,903,230 | 50.7 |
| Carter–Mondale | 49 | 6 + DC | 35,480,115 | 41.0 |
| Anderson–Lucey | 0 | 0 | 5,719,850 | 6.6 |

Source: *Statistics of the Presidential and Congressional Election of November 4, 1980* (Washington, DC: Government Printing Office,1981), 73.

The results of what would be Lucey's last campaign were bittersweet. He had known victory was a long shot, but he did not regret the effort.[50]

## CHAPTER 15

# SUNSET YEARS

When Pat Lucey returned to Madison after the 1980 campaign with John Anderson, he pursued a mixture of interests that reflected his first sixty-two years of life. He faithfully practiced his religion, embraced his family, resumed his involvement in real estate, and continued to promote progressive politics. In addition, he shared what he had learned through his unique and rich set of experiences through teaching, mentoring, consulting, and public speaking.

## REAL ESTATE

Lucey's assets had been in a blind trust while he served as governor and ambassador. Madison Attorney Robert Voss administered the trust and sold vacant lots in Wexford Village, Lucey's major real estate development, by lottery. (Wexford is a county and a seaport in Ireland where the Kennedy clan originated.) The last lottery was on November 2, 1979, the day after Lucey resigned as ambassador. The fifteen-year development project launched on Madison's far west side in 1969 had remained on track. When he returned, Lucey announced the start of Wexford Crossing, a thirteen-acre condominium project. Future phases that he envisioned included a shopping center east of the condominiums, park and recreation areas, more residential construction, and possibly an industrial office park.[1]

Lucey did not resume his work in real estate because he wanted to increase his personal wealth. He felt he had all he needed but had his grandchildren in mind.[2]

Because his real estate license had expired, he had to complete a course to get it reissued. While preparing to take the examination, he muttered in annoyance about the governor who was in office when the licensing requirements were strengthened.[3] That governor was the one he saw in the mirror before breakfast each day.

Lucey gradually concluded his active involvement in Wexford Village and in 1989 sold his real estate company to Wauwatosa Realty. He continued as a residential real estate developer, however, focusing primarily on Milwaukee suburbs and a project in Door County, the distinctive peninsula in northeastern Wisconsin. He purchased a 160-acre farm not far from the Lucey vacation home in Jacksonport and designed a plan for a mixture of about eighteen homes. The plan featured land held in common and preserved in its natural state. He reassured an inquiring neighbor of his respect for the rural character of the area.[4]

## CONSULTING AND TEACHING

In addition to continuing his real estate business, Lucey used his knowledge gained from many years as a public servant to provide consulting services. In January 1982, Lucey joined the Madison Consulting Group. He also worked with National Economic Research Associates and Anderson, Benjamin, Read, and Haney. Many of his consulting projects involved Mexico. Others concerned state governments and relations with the federal government.[5]

He served as a trustee of Beloit College and a member of the advisory council of the Robert M. La Follette Institute of Public Affairs at the University of Wisconsin–Madison. The La Follette Institute (later School) of Public Affairs provides graduate training for public sector careers and conducts research on public policy issues.

Lucey also engaged directly with students, teaching both undergraduate and graduate level classes. He shared his experiences and reflected on the history that he helped write. Beginning in 1982, Lucey taught state government courses at Marquette University, a Jesuit college in Milwaukee. In 1983, he was a fellow at the Institute of Politics at the Kennedy School of Government at Harvard University, where he taught state government and conducted a research project on Central America. Lawrence

University in Appleton, Wisconsin, had Lucey conduct a five-day seminar in August 1985.

Noticeable by its absence from his résumé was teaching at his alma mater, the University of Wisconsin–Madison, where I served as director of the La Follette Institute of Public Affairs at the time. This was not for lack of effort. Faculty at the La Follette Institute voted to have me seek a visiting professor position for Lucey to offer a public affairs seminar. Lucey was willing and proposed an outline of topics.[6] E. David Cronon, dean of the College of Letters and Science, however, claimed no funds were available to provide Lucey with even modest compensation and denied permission to proceed. I was able to secure funds from another source within the university, but Cronon continued to deny approval for the appointment. He claimed that it was against university policy to have individuals without advanced degrees and scholarly credentials offer courses.

Chancellor Irving Shain learned of Cronon's action and met with me and the dean. Shain reminded Cronon that the university regularly called upon distinguished individuals with relevant experience to teach. Cronon acknowledged that his motivation was because of Lucey's leadership in merging the University of Wisconsin and Wisconsin State University systems. Shain chastised Cronon and worried about the effects that the denial of an opportunity for students to learn from Lucey would have on relations with legislators. But he did not overrule the decision.

Cronon was not alone on campus in harboring ill feelings toward Lucey. Efforts to award an honorary degree to Lucey met ongoing opposition from the generation of faculty and administrators who had considered merging the state's university systems a mistake. Other universities did bestow honors on the former governor and ambassador.

Classrooms are not the only venues for instruction and reflection. Lucey was generous with his time and agreed to talk to groups of all sizes about his experiences. He spoke at civic groups and Democratic Party functions. He gave commencement addresses. He participated on panels. His topics varied, but he almost always provided a general as well as a personal perspective.

As a former governor with a broad legacy, founding member of the modern Democratic Party of Wisconsin, and a longtime significant player in state politics, Lucey's recollections were of particular interest to historians and history students. The oral history conducted by documentarian

Chip Duncan focused solely on Lucey. He participated in projects on the history of the Democratic Party of Wisconsin and the biography of William Proxmire. Similarly, Lucey made himself available to students completing research for seminars and for theses. Lucey himself contributed to the written record by authoring two short essays about his roots and his early life.[7]

## POLITICS

Not surprisingly, Lucey maintained an avid interest in politics throughout his life. Although he did not run for another office after the 1980 Anderson–Lucey bid for the White House, he continued to follow state and national political dynamics. His friends and former colleagues reported that every phone call and every conversation included a discussion of the latest news and speculation about what and who was around the corner.

Former Democratic governors Martin J. Schreiber, Patrick J. Lucey, Gaylord A. Nelson, John W. Reynolds, and Anthony S. Earl. COURTESY OF LAUREL LUCEY

In 1984, at Walter Mondale's suggestion, Lucey went to the Democratic National Convention as a delegate. He was not active as an advocate and strategist, as he had been in previous meetings to nominate a presidential candidate, but he made the rounds on the floor and cheered Mondale on to victory. While in San Francisco, he stayed at the apartment of longtime aide Bob Dunn.[8]

Lucey occasionally endorsed and contributed to candidates running for state offices. He was happy to see Jim Doyle Jr., son of his friend and mentor, elected governor in 2002 and then reelected four years later. On September 6, 2006, he joined the celebration of Shirley Abrahamson's thirty years of service on the Wisconsin Supreme Court. Three years before she announced her candidacy for another term, Lucey endorsed her 2009 reelection bid.[9]

In 2007, Lucey supported Linda Clifford in her bid to join the state supreme court. He served as chair of her campaign committee and persuaded former governor Republican Lee Dreyfus to join him as cochair. Lucey felt strongly that the judiciary should be independent and nonpartisan.[10] Clifford, however, lost in the first of several costly and highly partisan races for positions on Wisconsin's high court.

In 2011, Lucey agreed to cochair (again with Dreyfus) the committee to reelect David Prosser to the state supreme court. Prosser had been a Republican member of the state assembly and was aligned with conservatives on the court, but he had been widely respected, and Lucey wanted to demonstrate his commitment to an independent, nonpartisan court. After Prosser called Justice Abrahamson a vulgar term and got involved in an altercation with Justice Ann Walsh Bradley,[11] Lucey resigned his position in the campaign and publicly supported Prosser's rival, Joanne Kloppenburg. Prosser narrowly won.

Lucey had some fun endorsing Tommy Thompson when he ran for the US Senate. A group that Lucey regularly had lunch with invited Thompson to meet with them during the 2012 Republican primary. After Thompson gave his pitch, Lucey stood and said that the former governor was competent and experienced and that Lucey was going to vote for him. Thompson thanked Lucey and said, "What about the general election? Are you going to vote for me then, too?" A grinning Lucey emphatically said, "No!"[12] Thompson got the Republican nomination but lost to Democrat Tammy Baldwin.

## LATER YEARS

In 1990, Pat and Jean Lucey moved into a newly built house in Mequon, a suburb north of Milwaukee, where they would be closer to several of their children and grandchildren. Six of the nine grandchildren lived in the Milwaukee area, while the other three (children of Laurie Lucey and Peter Canfield) were in Atlanta.

In 2001, at age eighty-three, Lucey went to Atlanta just days before Christmas to help his daughter, who was recovering from a series of surgeries. He cared for the children, shopped for groceries, cooked, and did last-minute Christmas shopping.[13]

In late 2007, Pat and Jean Lucey moved to the Milwaukee Catholic Home. Jean had developed Alzheimer's disease, and the Lucey children, Paul, Laurie, and David, felt that their dad should no longer try to provide care full time.[14] At the Catholic Home, Jean had a caregiver every day from eight o'clock in the morning until eight o'clock at night.[15]

Pat Lucey, David Lasker, and Jean Lucey at the Luceys' home in Mequon, Wisconsin, on November 21, 2010. COURTESY OF DAVID E. LASKER

Jean had become more conservative in her later years and was an avid viewer of Fox News, but she joined her husband in supporting Barack Obama in 2008. Pat Lucey posted Obama campaign material on their door. When he was informed that it was against the "no politicking" policy of the Catholic Home, he replaced the campaign material with a "family photo"—of himself with Obama.[16]

The Luceys enjoyed their time at the Catholic Home. Pat was happy that Mass was celebrated there every morning.[17] His brother, Father Gregory Lucey, SJ, remembered getting a phone call from Pat on a Sunday afternoon. Pat had forgotten to go to Mass and said, "In my ninety-two years I don't think I ever missed Mass." Father Greg assured him, "With that record or even without that record, the Lord would readily understand."[18]

The Catholic Home also provided Lucey with the opportunity to develop new friendships. He told his son Paul, "I don't think I've ever had so many friends!" adding, "and some of them are Republicans!!"[19] Lucey joined a book group discussing Shakespeare and another that focused

Lucey and his brother Gregory Lucey, SJ, in 2001. COURTESY OF GREGORY LUCEY, SJ

on US presidents.[20] He and Jean had lots of visitors, including former colleagues and staffers they had not seen for years. Naturally, these visits featured a lot of political talk. When Republican governor Scott Walker ran to keep his seat in a recall election, friends teased Lucey and suggested he run for his old office. For at least a flash, Lucey seemed tempted.[21]

Jean, at age 93, died on December 7, 2011. She had led a full life and left even those with whom she at times differed with fond memories. Richard Weening, Lucey's 1970 campaign manager and his first chief of staff, reminisced about how he vied with Jean for Pat's time and attention. He remembered how she fought to protect her husband and preserve family time, even when that meant banning Weening from the governor's residence for a period of time. But when Weening became a regular visitor at the Catholic Home, Jean rewarded him with instant recognition, a smile, and a warm greeting.[22]

Pat asked Father Greg to celebrate Mass and preach the funeral homily for Jean at the Catholic Home. David Lucey shared thoughts about his mother that brought both tears and laughter.[23] He recalled the ups and downs his mother had and how she did all of her swearing in Greek. He and his siblings didn't find out what she was actually saying until they were teenagers and talked with their Greek cousins. By that time, they were old enough to deal with the translations. David stressed how much his mother loved his father, their children, and their grandchildren.

Less than three years after his wife died, at age ninety-six, Lucey became gravely ill. Jane Reynolds, the widow of John Reynolds, former governor and federal judge and Lucey's close friend, went to see him. He opened his eyes when she approached his bed. She said, "Hi Pat. This is Jane Reynolds. You and John were good friends."

Lucey smiled and replied, "Yes. And we soldiered together for good government." Lucey brought his hand up to his forehead and saluted. Just days later, on May 10, 2014, he was gone.[24] But not forgotten.

Lucey's principled but bipartisan style of governing has been celebrated on both sides of the aisle. At a celebration in the Wisconsin State Capitol, former US representative David Obey called Lucey his hero. Obey praised Lucey's principles and his commitment to work things out and maintain civility: "He would outthink you. He would outorganize you. But he would never out-mean you."[25] When he occupied the office, Governor Tommy

Thompson kept the official portrait of Lucey hanging on the wall "because I believed in the man. I wanted to show people the value of bipartisanship."[26] Jim Wood, a former aide and campaign manager, said:

> My constant take on Pat was that he was a man of his times and heritage and a leader ahead of his times. He reflected the traditional values of the first half of the twentieth century—hard work, perseverance, honesty, loyalty to family and friends—and embraced his Irish heritage—humor, a sense of the human tragedy, and the ability of people to overcome adversity. But all of that left him with an intelligence that could not ignore the facts and a sense of responsibility that drove him to do the right thing. When life and events gave him the opportunity to meet that responsibility, he did so with vision and enthusiasm. One of the great ones has moved on. We are richer for his being here and poorer for his passing.[27]

Hal Wilde, one of Lucey's speechwriters, summarized the essence of Patrick J. Lucey and his legacy when speaking at his visitation on May 19, 2014. After quoting Horton from the Dr. Seuss book *Horton Hears a Who*, "I meant what I said and I said what I meant, an elephant's faithful one hundred percent," Wilde shared:

> For ninety-six years Pat Lucey meant what he said and said what he meant—and was faithful one hundred percent:
>
> - Faithful to the vision of do onto others and a merciful God, nurtured in a Catholic home in Crawford County and at Campion—compassionate, generous of spirit, Jesus in the temple speaking truth to power but also the Jesus of the Sermon on the Mount;
>
> - Faithful to the family—Jean, Paul, Laurie, and David, siblings and grandchildren . . . there in his eighties to cook meals and do the laundry in a time of family need, without question;
>
> - Faithful to the nation where his great-grandfather fought for the north in the Civil War after emigrating from Ireland (a picture of

the infant Pat with that great-grandfather and other Lucey men who served the nation in wartime was a prized memento) and where his own World War II service was followed by a lifetime of contributions to America at every level of engagement;

- Faithful to the state of which he was so proud, and Wisconsin's progressive heritage, joyfully shouldering the responsibility that the legacy of Robert La Follette and Francis McGovern place on all who would govern in the name of the people, fairness, justice, and popular democracy.

. . . It is impossible to imagine the twentieth-century history of Wisconsin without the role Pat Lucey played (with Jean's great help) as organizer and manager in the post-war renaissance of the Democratic Party and the rise of Jim (and Ruth) Doyle, Bill Proxmire, Gaylord Nelson, John Reynolds. More than anyone else, he was the catalyst for Wisconsin becoming a two-party state. And when he came out from behind the curtain, he proved to be an equally effective organizer as an elected official—implementing an expansive agenda that balanced progressive steps (that were not always popular) like closing prisons and equalizing aids to local school districts with good government reforms like merger of the University of Wisconsin institutions and cabinet government and pro-business and pro-jobs initiatives such as the elimination of manufacturing equipment taxes.

Often seen as a rabid partisan, he wore the label "politician" with pride. But he was above all a "policy wonk" . . . who cared more about getting things done than getting the credit. A Wisconsin patriot, his objectives were home grown, rooted in deep knowledge of the citizens of the Badger State and the Wisconsin character. He did his homework and wasn't afraid to cross party lines. There are days when the years of Pat's greatest impact—the 1950s, '60s, and '70s—seem as remote from today's hyper-partisan, all-or-nothing politics with imported agendas aimed at national funders and audiences, as Pat was from his great-grandfather who served in the Civil War.[28]

Lucey's impact on Wisconsin has outlasted him. Patrick J. Lucey left a legacy of progressive policies and good government reforms, while demonstrating that one could accomplish much of value through adherence to principles; reliance on analysis; and civil, courteous conduct.

# Appendix A

Wisconsin State Budget Process, 1973–1975

|  | **Governor** | **Legislature** |
|---|---|---|
| **Spring 1972** | Reviews revenue estimates | Reviews revenue estimates |
|  | Sends policy and spending guidelines to agencies |  |
| **Fall 1972** | Updates revenue estimates | Updates revenue estimates |
|  | Holds public hearings |  |
|  | Reviews agency requests |  |
|  | Receives budget from Dept. of Administration |  |
| **Winter 1973** | Submits budget to Joint Finance | Joint Finance receives governor's budget Joint Finance holds hearings |
|  |  | Agencies defend budgets at Joint Finance Committee |

| **Spring 1973** | Receives approved budget from legislature and considers partial vetoes | Joint Finance sends budget to assembly and senate |
| | Signs budget with partial vetoes | Both chambers agree on budget and send to governor |
| **Summer 1973** | Budget implemented | Considers veto override |

# Appendix B

*Policies Adopted by Governor Patrick J. Lucey*
*and Wisconsin State Legislature 1971–1977*

## Governance

Reorganize Courts

Create State Ethics Board and establish ethics standards

Regulate lobbying

Reform and reorganize state civil service

Revise legislative districts to comply with
one-person-one-vote rule

Revise gubernatorial succession: constitutional amendment

Allow bingo (constitutional amendment)

## Taxation

Replace point-of-origin with equalization formula for
revenue sharing

Establish limits on local government property tax levies

Exempt machinery and equipment from property tax

State pay up to 75 percent of county assessment costs if state
standards are met

## EQUAL RIGHTS

Establish rights for women (law passed after constitutional amendment referendum failed)

Allow health professionals to refuse abortions and sterilizations without liability

Provide aid to encourage integration in schools

## ELECTIONS

Simplify voter registration by allowing same day registration and registration by mail; discontinuing removal from rolls of those not voting two elections; and extending the period for requesting absentee ballot

Update campaign finance laws regarding public financing, contribution limits, and spending limits

## BUSINESS DEVELOPMENT AND CONSUMER PROTECTION

Exempt machinery and equipment from property tax

Permit cities and villages to establish tax incremental finance districts

Regulate corporate takeovers, requiring that purchase offers be filed with commissioner of securities and public and permitting the commissioner to go to court to seek injunctions or void sales

Regulate franchises by requiring registration of sales and offers with commissioner of securities and allowing the commissioner to go to court to seek injunctions or void sales

Expand powers of credit unions and savings and loan associations

Provide consumer protection with legislation considered most far-reaching in the country

Regulate siting of power plants

Regulate cable television

## Agriculture

Establish a veterinary school at University of Wisconsin

Create incentive program for preserving farmland

Prohibit corporations from owning or operating farms unless certain standards met regarding kinds and numbers of shareholders

## Labor

Update unemployment compensation law

Update workers compensation law

Allow fair-share agreements with public employee unions

Authorize collective bargaining for state employees

Establish mediation and arbitration procedure for impasse in public sector negotiations

## Transportation

Allow federal and state matching funds to be used for urban mass transit

Reorganize Department of Transportation as a cabinet agency

Restrict use of studded tires

## Health and Social Services

Reorganize Department of Health and Social Services as a cabinet agency

Assume costs of medical assistance and programs for elderly, blind, and disabled not covered by federal government.

Assume costs of local mental health services

Establish rights for mentally ill patients and due process for involuntary commitment

Establish code for services and protections for children

Cover unemployed fathers under AFDC so they can be in home

Regulate nursing homes

Increase state payments for AFDC and Medicaid

Repeal restrictions on sales of contraceptives to unmarried individuals

Extend good Samaritan immunity to anyone rendering emergency assistance

Prohibit use of public funds for abortion

Repeal requirement to wear helmet on motorcycles, except for those under eighteen

Establish services to displaced homemakers

Revise divorce law to include no-fault and adopt Uniform Marriage and Divorce Act

Establish migrant labor regulation

Establish insurance program for medical malpractice

Lower cost of prescription drugs through generic drug pricing

Create housing finance authority to provide assistance to low- and moderate-income families for cost of construction

Expand housing loans and other benefits to Vietnam veterans

## EDUCATION

Merge University of Wisconsin and Wisconsin State University systems

State assume larger share of cost of K-12 education

Use equalization formula for distributing aid

Provide aid to encourage integration in schools

Authorize use of public schools by churches and religious groups (constitutional amendment)

Authorize public schools release students during school hours for religious instruction (constitutional amendment)

## ENVIRONMENT

Direct DNR to monitor industrial waste, hazardous substances and air contaminants

Regulate emission of mercury into air and water

Require state agencies to complete environmental impact statements

Regulate outdoor advertising

Regulate use of snowmobiles and develop trails

Expand powers of metropolitan sewerage commissions

Establish soil and water conservation and require cooperation with regional planning

Give state responsibility for local air pollution control

Preserve lower St. Croix River

Create solid-waste recycling authority

Require permit for air contaminant projects

Create districts and programs for preservation and rehabilitation of inland lakes

Establish waterways commission

Establish natural gas conservation program

Regulate use of pesticides

Limit levels of phosphorus in cleaning agents and
water conditioners

Establish program for management of hazardous waste

Create Wisconsin Fund for nonpoint source pollution

Tighten mining regulation

## CRIMINAL JUSTICE

Establish youthful offenders correctional program

Create public defender program

Close Child Care Center at Sparta and School for Girls at Oregon

Specify degrees of sexual assault

Require reporting of child abuse and neglect

Provide compensation for victims of crime

# NOTES

**Introduction**

1. Tim Wyngaard, "Last Campaign Push, Friends for Dinner Combine in Final Hours of Lucey Election," *Green Bay Press Gazette*, November 8, 1970, A12.
2. Jonathan Kasparek, *Proxmire: Bulldog of the Senate* (Madison: Wisconsin Historical Society Press, 2019).
3. Gordon L. Randolph, "Olson-Lucey Contest May Be Photo Finish," *Milwaukee Journal*, November 1, 1970, 1.
4. James D. Selk, "Election: A Zero-to-Zero Deadlock?" *Wisconsin State Journal*, November 1, 1970, 1.
5. Pat Bauer, remarks at memorial service for David W. Adamany, Madison, WI, December 12, 2016.
6. Wyngaard, "Last Campaign Push."
7. Wyngaard, "Last Campaign Push."
8. Patrick J. Lucey, interview by Bill Broydrick and Tim Cullen, Wisconsin Politics Oral History Project, August 22, 2003, tape transcript 3, 90–91.
9. Wyngaard, "Last Campaign Push."
10. Thomas Bates, *Rads: The 1970 Bombing of the Army Math Research Center at the University of Wisconsin and Its Aftermath* (New York: HarperCollins, 1992).
11. Patrick J. Lucey, handwritten note, November 3, 1970, provided by Patrick Bauer.
12. Vivian Kawatzky, "Jean Lucey's High Hopes Land Safely," *Milwaukee Sentinel*, November 4, 1970, 12.
13. Wyngaard, "Last Campaign Push."
14. Wyngaard, "Last Campaign Push."
15. Joint Committee on Legislative Organization, Wisconsin Legislature, *State of Wisconsin 2015–2016 Blue Book* (Madison: Wisconsin Legislative Reference Bureau, 2015), 699–701.
16. Prior to 1970, Wisconsin had a gubernatorial election every two years. Like the pattern in other states, turnout was generally higher when there was a vote for president.

311

17. The 1971–73 legislature passed a redistricting bill that reduced the number of assembly seats from one hundred to ninety-nine and then configured each of the thirty-three senate seats to comprise three assembly districts. This was done to comply with the one-person-one-vote mandate of the US Supreme Court.

18. Robert Booth Fowler, *Wisconsin Votes: An Electoral History* (Madison: University of Wisconsin Press, 2008), 254, 259.

19. Wyngaard, "Last Campaign Push."

20. Larry Sabato, *Goodbye to Good-Time Charlie: The American Governor Transformed* (Washington, DC: Congressional Quarterly Press, 1976).

21. Dennis L. Dresang and James J. Gosling, *Politics and Policy in American States and Communities*, 6th ed. (New York: Pearson, 2008), 247–49.

22. P. Lucey, interview by Broydrick and Cullen, tape 3 transcript, 73–75.

23. P. Lucey, interview by Broydrick and Cullen, tape 3 transcript, 80.

24. Jeff Smoller, "Detailed Position Papers of Campaign Give Direction to Lucey Administration," *Capital Times*, November 16, 1970, 37.

25. James D. Selk, "Democrat Wins Four-Year Term with Schreiber," *Wisconsin State Journal*, November 4, 1970, 1.

26. Wyngaard, "Last Campaign Push."

### Chapter 1

1. "Ferryville Honors Famous Son Former Gov. Lucey," *La Crosse Tribune*, October 3, 2013.

2. Patrick J. Lucey, interview by Chip Duncan, Duncan Entertainment, December 1, 2009, tape 1 transcript, 12.

3. Ethel Lerum, "History of Ferryville Wisconsin" (no date), www.ferryville.com/History.html.

4. Gregory Lucey, SJ, ed., *"Paddy" Patrick Lucey* (unpublished manuscript, 1993).

5. Patrick J. Lucey, "Paddy (Patrick) Lucey," in G. Lucey, *"Paddy" Patrick Lucey*, 4–7.

6. For a general discussion of Irish immigration to Wisconsin, see David G. Holmes, *Irish in Wisconsin* (Madison: Wisconsin Historical Society Press, 2013).

7. Holmes, *Irish in Wisconsin*, 5.

8. Holmes, 5.

9. Rosella Lucey Nugent, "Margaret Connelly Lucey," in G. Lucey, *"Paddy" Patrick Lucey*, 8, 9.

10. Gregory Lucey, SJ, email to author, August 23, 2017.

11. P. Lucey, "Paddy (Patrick) Lucey," 6; and P. Lucey, interview by Duncan, tape 1 transcript, 2, 3.

12. P. Lucey, interview by Duncan, tape 1 transcript, 3; and Gregory Lucey, SJ, "The Last Lecture: Honor Thy Father and Thy Mother," presented to Alpha Sigma Nu, December 10, 2010.

13. P. Lucey, interview by Duncan, tape 1 transcript, 4.

14. Patrick J. Lucey, interview by John Powell, Temple University Wisconsin Legislative Oral History Project, March 2010, 1.

15. P. Lucey, interview by Duncan, tape 1 transcript , 10.

16. G. Lucey, "The Last Lecture."

17. P. Lucey, interview by Duncan, tape 1 transcript, 14, 15; G. Lucey, email.

18. P. Lucey, interview by Duncan, tape 1 transcript, 15.

19. G. Lucey, "The Last Lecture."

20. P. Lucey, interview by Powell, 10.

21. Gregory Lucey, SJ, interview by author after consulting with his sisters Verona and Kathleen, December 14, 2017.

22. Patrick J. Lucey, interview by Neil Shively, October 17, 2004, tape 1.

23. P. Lucey, interview by Shively.

24. P. Lucey, interview by Powell, 10.

25. In 1958, Lucey's parents retired in Prairie du Chien, where they stayed until they moved into a nursing home in La Crosse in 1972. G. Lucey, email.

26. P. Lucey, interview by Shively.

27. P. Lucey, interview by Shively.

28. S. J. Staber, "A Brief History of Campion Jesuit High School of Prairie du Chien, Wisc." (1972, revised 1975), https://campion-knights.org/History/history72.html.

29. G. Lucey, interview, December 13, 2017.

30. The Wisconsin Evangelical Lutheran Synod purchased the 108-acre campus when Campion closed. The Synod housed a program preparing individuals for their ministry. After reorganizations that downsized that program, the Synod sold the property to the State of Wisconsin, which now uses it for a medium security prison, although the sports complex is separate and operated by the Prairie du Chien recreational department.

31. P. Lucey, interview by Shively.

32. P. Lucey, interview by Duncan, tape 2 transcript, 38.

33. P. Lucey, interview by Duncan, tape 2 transcript, 31.

34. G. Lucey, interview, December 13, 2017.

35. John Ireland, the Archbishop of St. Paul and Minneapolis, founded the college in 1885 as a seminary. He named it in honor of St. Thomas Aquinas, the famed medieval Catholic theologian and philosopher. A liberal arts college program began in 1894, and the student body was all male until 1977. It became the University of St. Thomas in 1990. Throughout its history, the university has been highly respected for its academic standards. It boasts an impressive list of alumni in law, public service, business, and athletics.

36. P. Lucey, interview by Shively, tape 1.

37. P. Lucey, interview by Duncan, tape 3 transcript, 42, 43.

38. P. Lucey, interview by Duncan, tape 3 transcript, 40.

**Chapter 2**

1. Ira Katznelson, *Fear Itself: The New Deal and the Origins of Our Time* (New York: Liveright, 2013).

2. Patrick J. Lucey, interview by Neil Shively, October 12, 2004, tape 2.

3. John E. Miller, *Governor Philip F. La Follette, the Wisconsin Progressives, and the New Deal* (Columbia: University of Missouri Press, 1982), 159–162; Jonathan Kasparek, *Fighting Son: A Biography of Philip F. La Follette* (Madison: Wisconsin Historical Society Press, 2016), 136–51.

4. As pointed out in Chapter 1, the 1971–73 state legislature changed the number of seats in the assembly from one hundred to ninety-nine.

5. E. L. Kirkpatrick and Agnes M. Boynton, *Wisconsin's Human and Physical Resources* (Madison, WI: Research Section, Resettlement Administration, Region II, 1936).

6. Paul W. Glad, *War, a New Era, and Depression, 1914–1940*, The History of Wisconsin, vol. 5 (Madison: State Historical Society of Wisconsin, 1990), 517–39.

7. Patrick J. Lucey, interview by John Powell, Temple University Wisconsin Legislative Oral History Project, March 2010, 2.

8. P. Lucey, interview by Shively, tape 1.

9. Patrick J. Lucey, interview by Chip Duncan, Duncan Entertainment, December 1, 2009, tape 3 transcript, 44.

10. P. Lucey, interview by Duncan, tape 3 transcript, 45.

11. Patrick J. Lucey, interview by Anita Hecht, Proxmire Oral History Project, January 13, 2009, 11.

12. P. Lucey, interview by Duncan, tape 3 transcript, 47.

13. P. Lucey, interview by Powell, 3.

14. P. Lucey, interview by Shively, tape 2.

15. P. Lucey, interview by Shively, tape 2.

16. In 1950, Losey Air Field was renamed Fort Allen.

17. P. Lucey, interview by Shively, tape 2.

18. P. Lucey, interview by Hecht, 12.

19. P. Lucey, interview by Duncan, tape 3 transcript, 52.

20. P. Lucey, interview by Duncan, tape 3 transcript, 53, 54.

21. P. Lucey, interview by Shively.

22. David Lucey, email to author, October 27, 2017.

23. D. Lucey, email.

24. P. Lucey, interview by Duncan, tape 4 transcript, 62, 63.

25. Max Carl Otto, *Science and the Moral Life* (New York: New American Library Mentor Books, 1949).

26. G. C. Sellery, "Max Carl Otto," in *Cleavage in Our Culture Studies*, ed. Frederick Burkhardt (Boston: Beacon Press, 1952); and Frederick Burkhardt, ed., *The Cleavage in Our Culture: Studies in Scientific Humanism in Honor of Max Otto* (New York: Books for Libraries Press, 1969).

27. P. Lucey, interview by Duncan, tape 4 transcript, 64.

28. Patrick J. Maney, *"Young Bob" La Follette: A Biography of Robert M. La Follette, Jr., 1895–1953* (Columbia: University of Missouri Press, 1978), 288.

29. Richard C. Haney, "The Rise of Wisconsin's New Democrats: A Political Realignment in the Mid-Twentieth Century," *Wisconsin Magazine of History* 58, no. 2 (Winter 1974–75), 94.

30. Patrick J. Lucey, interview by Jim Cavanaugh, Wisconsin Historical Society History of the Democratic Party, April 10, 1985, 5.

31. P. Lucey, interview by Duncan, tape 3 transcript, 47.

32. Gregory Lucey, SJ, email to author, August 23, 2017.

33. Edward J. McNamara, "Gregory Lucey," in *"Paddy" Patrick Lucey*, Gregory Lucey, SJ, ed. (unpublished manuscript, 1993), 14.

34. G. Lucey, email.

35. Patrick J. Lucey Papers, 1935–2003, Wisconsin Historical Society, MSS 785, box 1, folder 2.

36. P. Lucey, interview by Duncan, tape 3 transcript, 64, 65.

37. Gregory Lucey, SJ, interview by author, December 14, 2017.

38. Maney, *"Young Bob" La Follette*, 289–91.

39. P. Lucey, interview by Duncan, tape 4 transcript, 69, 70.

40. P. Lucey, interview by Duncan, tape 4 transcript, 68, 69.

41. P. Lucey, interview by Duncan, tape 4 transcript, 70, 71.

42. A 1945 amendment to the state constitution abolished the office of justice of the peace for cities of the first class. In 1966, the state constitution was amended to abolish that office for other municipalities.

43. P. Lucey, interview by Duncan, tape 3 transcript, 65.

## Chapter 3

1. Patrick J. Lucey, interview by John Powell, Temple University Wisconsin Legislative Oral History Project, March 2010, 6.

2. P. Lucey, interview by Powell, 6.

3. Wisconsin Legislature, *The State of Wisconsin Blue Book 1970* (Madison: Wisconsin Legislative Reference Bureau, 1970), 250–58.

4. Wisconsin Constitution, Article IV, section 4, as interpreted in Wisconsin Legislative Council—Legislative Reapportionment Committee, *Report on Reapportionment* (Madison, 1951), Chapter 2; Leon D. Epstein, *Politics in Wisconsin* (Madison: University of Wisconsin Press), 122.

5. Patrick J. Lucey, interview by Jim Cavanaugh, Wisconsin Historical Society Wisconsin Democratic Party Oral History Project, April 10, 1985, tape 60, side 1.

6. Patrick J. Lucey Papers, 1935–2003, Wisconsin Historical Society, MSS 785, box 4, folder 2.

7. Patrick J. Lucey, "With Your Assemblyman," March 9, 1949, in Patrick J. Lucey Papers, 1935–2003, box 4, folder 6.

8. P. Lucey, interview by Powell, 6.

9. Neil Shively, "Running the Farms, Running in '48" (unpublished manuscript), based on taped interview, September 4, 2004.

10. Shively, "Running the Farms."

11. Robert Booth Fowler, *Wisconsin Votes: An Electoral History* (Madison: University of Wisconsin Press, 2008), 130.

12. Michael E. Stevens, "Give 'em Hell, Dan!: How Daniel Webster Hoan Changed Wisconsin Politics," *Wisconsin Magazine of History* 98, no. 7 (Autumn 2014), 17–18; Jonathan Kasparek, "FDR's 'Old Friends' in Wisconsin: Presidential Finesse in the Land of La Follette," *Wisconsin Magazine of History*, 84 (Summer 2001), 16–25.

13. William F. Thompson, *Continuity and Change, 1940–1965*, The History of Wisconsin, vol. 6 (Madison: State Historical Society of Wisconsin, 1988), 436–40, 564–69.

14. Richard C. Haney, "The Rise of Wisconsin's New Democrats: A Political Realignment in the Mid-Twentieth Century," *Wisconsin Magazine of History* 58, no. 2 (Winter 1974–75), 95.

15. P. Lucey, interview by Cavanaugh, tape 60, side 1.

16. Haney, "The Rise of Wisconsin's New Democrats," 96.

17. Patrick J. Lucey Papers, 1935–2003, box 4, folder 2; John Wyngaard, "Government and Politics," *Green Bay Press Gazette*, November 28, 1949, 2.

18. P. Lucey, interview by Cavanaugh, tape 60, side 2.

19. Jonathan Kasparek, *Proxmire: Bulldog of the Senate* (Madison: Wisconsin Historical Society Press, 2019), 31–36.

20. Patrick J. Lucey, interview by Anita Hecht, Proxmire Oral History Project, January 13, 2009, tape 1.

21. John Gurda, *The Making of Milwaukee* (Milwaukee, WI: Milwaukee County Historical Society, 1999).

22. Neil Shively, "Lawmaking and Party Building" (unpublished manuscript), based on taped interview, September 4, 2004.

23. Patrick J. Lucey, interview by Chip Duncan, Duncan Entertainment, December 1, 2009, tape 4 transcript, 83.

24. P. Lucey, interview by Duncan, tape 4 transcript, 85.

25. Neil Shively, "Lawmaking."

26. P. Lucey, "With Your Assemblyman," March 22, 1950.

27. P. Lucey, "With Your Assemblyman." March 16, 1949.

28. P. Lucey, interview by Cavanaugh, tape 60, side 1.

29. P. Lucey, interview by Duncan, tape 4 transcript, 91.

30. Harold G. Vatter, *The U.S. Economy in the 1950s* (Westport, CT: Greenwood Press, 1963).

31. Barton J. Bernstein, *Politics and Policies of the Truman Administration* (Chicago: Quadrangle Books, 1970).

32. P. Lucey, interview by Powell, 6.

33. P. Lucey, interview by Hecht, tape 1.

34. Patrick J. Lucey, "Thomas E. Fairchild" (lecture, University of Wisconsin Law School, Madison, WI, April 19, 2002).

35. David Adamany, *Financing Politics. Recent Wisconsin Elections* (Madison: University of Wisconsin Press, 1966), 62.

**Chapter 4**

1. Note that Jim Doyle's son, Jim Doyle Jr., served as Wisconsin's attorney general (1991–2003) and governor (2003–2011). The references throughout the book are to Jim Doyle Sr. unless his son is explicitly identified.

2. Patrick J. Lucey, interview by Anita Hecht, Proxmire Oral History Project, January 13, 2009, tape 1.

3. In his interview for the Wisconsin Democratic Party Oral History Project for the Wisconsin Historical Society, James Doyle Sr. has a more general recollection than does Patrick J. Lucey. Doyle does not recall a specific agreement with Henry Maier but does recall paying Lucey from funds raised outside Wisconsin (Patrick J. Lucey, interview by Jim Cavanaugh, tape 42, side 1, February 6, 1983).

4. James Doyle Jr., interview by author, January 24, 2019.

5. John Lavine, interview by author, November 15, 2017.

6. David P. Thelen, *Robert M. La Follette and the Insurgent Spirit* (Madison: University of Wisconsin Press, 1985); John D. Buenker, *The Progressive Era (1893–1914)*, The History of Wisconsin, vol. 4 (Madison: State Historical Society of Wisconsin, 1998); Russel B. Nye, *Midwestern Progressive Politics: A Historical Study of Its Origins and Development, 1870–1958* (East Lansing: Michigan State University Press, 1959).

7. Bruce M. Stave, ed., *Urban Bosses, Machines and Progressive Reformers* (Lexington, MA: D.C. Heath, 1972).

8. Nye, *Midwestern Progressive Politics*, 213.

9. Patrick J. Lucey, interview by Jim Cavanaugh, Wisconsin Historical Society Wisconsin Democratic Party Oral History Project, April 10, 1985,

tape 60, side 2; Richard C. Haney, "A History of the Democratic Party of Wisconsin since World War Two" (PhD diss., University of Wisconsin, 1970), 301.

10. Richard C. Haney, "The Rise of Wisconsin's New Democrats: A Political Realignment in the Mid-Twentieth Century," *Wisconsin Magazine of History* 58, no. 2 (1974–75), 91–106.

11. Leon D. Epstein, *Politics in Wisconsin* (Madison: University of Wisconsin Press, 1958), 57–76.

12. Kathy Cramer, *The Politics of Resentment: Rural Consciousness in Wisconsin and the Rise of Scott Walker* (Chicago: University of Chicago Press, 2016), describes the long-lasting nature of urban–rural tensions and notes how after redistricting based on one-person-one-vote principles, perceptions flipped and rural areas felt neglected.

13. Robert Booth Fowler, *Wisconsin Votes: An Electoral History* (Madison: University of Wisconsin Press, 2008), 183–85.

14. David Adamany, *Financing Politics: Recent Wisconsin Elections* (Madison: University of Wisconsin Press, 1969), 62–64.

15. Leon Epstein, "American Parties: A Wisconsin Case Study," *Political Studies* 4, no. 1 (Winter 1956), 35.

16. Adamany, *Financing Politics*, 24.

17. Haney, "The Rise of Wisconsin's New Democrats," 97.

18. P. Lucey, interview by Cavanaugh, tape 60, side 2.

19. Adamany, *Financing Politics*, 98–107.

20. P. Lucey, interview by Cavanaugh, tape 60, side 2.

21. David Halberstam, *The Fifties* (New York: Open Roads Media, 2012).

22. Patrick J. Lucey, "Thomas E. Fairchild" (lecture, University of Wisconsin Law School, Madison, WI, April 19, 2002).

23. P. Lucey, interview by Cavanaugh, tape 60, side 2.

24. Haney, "A History of the Democratic Party of Wisconsin," 160.

25. Haney, 160.

26. P. Lucey, "Thomas E. Fairchild."

27. Michael O'Brien, "The Anti-McCarthy Campaign in Wisconsin, 1951–1952," *Wisconsin Magazine of History* 56, no. 2 (Winter 1972–73), 95.

28. James Doyle Sr., interview by Cavanaugh, tape 41, side 1.

29. P. Lucey, interview by Hecht.

30. P. Lucey, interview by Hecht.

31. P. Lucey, interview by Hecht; John Gronouski, interview by John R. Johannes, Wisconsin Politics Oral History Project, March 29, 1995, tape 1, side 1.
32. Doyle, interview.
33. P. Lucey, "Thomas E. Fairchild."
34. O'Brien, "The Anti-McCarthy Campaign," 107; and P. Lucey, interview by Cavanaugh, tape 60, side 2.
35. O'Brien, "The Anti-McCarthy Campaign," 107.
36. "Vote for State Officers and U.S. Senate, General Election, 1952," in *The Wisconsin Blue Book: 1954*, ed. Wisconsin Legislature (Madison: Wisconsin Legislative Reference Library, 1954), 756, 757.
37. "Vote for State Officers."
38. David P. Thelen and Esther S. Thelen, "Joe Must Go: The Movement to Recall Senator Joseph R. McCarthy," *Wisconsin Magazine of History* 49, no. 3 (Spring 1966), 185–209.
39. P. Lucey, interview by Cavanaugh, tape 60, side 2.
40. Haney, "A History of the Democratic Party of Wisconsin," 345–46.
41. P. Lucey, interview by Hecht, tape 1.
42. Wisconsin Legislature, *The State of Wisconsin Blue Book: 1956* (Madison: Wisconsin Legislative Reference Bureau, 1956), 702.
43. Wisconsin Legislature, 746.
44. Wisconsin Legislature, *The State of Wisconsin Blue Book: 1958* (Madison: Wisconsin Legislative Reference Bureau, 1958), 665.
45. Wisconsin Legislature, 772.
46. Jonathan Kasparek, *Proxmire: Bulldog of the Senate* (Madison: Wisconsin Historical Society Press, 2019), 79.
47. Philleo Nash, interview by Jim Cavanaugh, Wisconsin Democratic Party Oral History Project, Wisconsin Historical Society, September 10, 1986, tape 77, side 1.
48. William F. Thompson, *Continuity and Change, 1940–1965*, The History of Wisconsin, vol. 6 (Madison: State Historical Society of Wisconsin, 1988), 606.
49. William Kraus, email to author, September 4, 2018.
50. Kasparek, 85.
51. Patrick J. Lucey, interview by John Powell, Wisconsin Legislative Oral History Project, March 21, 2010.

52. P. Lucey, interview by Hecht, tape 1.

53. Thompson, *Continuity and Change*, 611.

54. Fowler, *Wisconsin Votes*, 175.

55. Thompson, *Continuity and Change*, 607.

56. Adamany, *Financing Politics*, 44.

57. Nash, interview, tape 77, side 1.

58. Haney, "A History of the Democratic Party of Wisconsin," 301–2; Nash, interview, tape 77, side 2.

59. Gregory Lucey, SJ, interview by author, December 13, 2017.

60. Nash, interview, tape 77, side 2.

61. Haney, "A History of the Democratic Party of Wisconsin," 297–98.

62. John Wyngaard, "Democrats Keep Distance From Labor," *Green Bay Press Gazette*, October 19, 1957.

63. Haney, "A History of the Democratic Party of Wisconsin," 298–99.

64. Haney, 318.

65. Haney, 321–23.

66. Haney, 324, citing an article in the *Milwaukee Sentinel*, May 19, 1958.

67. Haney, 324–25.

68. John Wyngaard, "Lucey Trains Campaign Workers," *Green Bay Press Gazette*, October 7, 1958, cited in Haney, "A History of the Democratic Party of Wisconsin," 349.

69. Esther Kaplan, interview by Jim Cavanaugh, Wisconsin Democratic Party Oral History Project, Wisconsin Historical Society, June 7, 1983, tape 24, side 1.

70. Bill Christofferson, *The Man from Clear Lake: Earth Day Founder Senator Gaylord Nelson* (Madison: University of Wisconsin Press, 2004), 87.

71. Patrick J. Lucey, "Vigorous and Victorious," report to the members of the Democratic Party of Wisconsin, 1959 reelection to state chairman pamphlet (Madison: Amalgamated Lithographers of America).

72. Patrick J. Lucey, interview by Richard Haney, March 17, 1969.

73. Haney, "A History of the Democratic Party of Wisconsin," 330.

74. Haney, 331–37.

75. Haney, 340.

76. Christofferson, *The Man from Clear Lake*, 126.

## Chapter 5

1. Ross Miller, *Here's the Deal: The Making and Breaking of a Great American City* (Evanston, IL: Northwestern University Press, 2003); Jeffrey M. Hornstein, *A Nation of Realtors* (Durham, NC: Duke University Press, 2003); Tamara Venit Shelton, *A Squatter's Republic: Land and the Politics of Monopoly in California, 1850–1900* (Berkeley: University of California Press, 2013); James Howard Kunstler, *The Geography of Nowhere: The Rise and Decline of America's Man-Made Landscape* (New York: Free Press, 1994).

2. David Lucey, email to author, January 16, 2018.

3. Nancy Greenwood Williams, *First Ladies of Wisconsin: The Governors' Wives* (Kalamazoo, MI: Ana Publishing, 1991), 223.i

4. Patrick J. Lucey, interview by Bill Broydrick and Tim Cullen, Wisconsin Politics Oral History Project, August 22, 2003, tape 6 transcript, 144.

5. Jo Eickmann, "Mrs. Lucey: Fighting Spirit," *Milwaukee Journal*, February 12, 1963.

6. Patrick J. Lucey, interview by Chip Duncan, Duncan Entertainment, December 1, 2009, tape 7 transcript, 101.

7. P. Lucey, interview by Duncan, tape 7 transcript, 89.

8. P. Lucey, interview by Duncan, tape 7 transcript, 94.

9. Patrick J. Lucey, interview by Anita Hecht, Proxmire Oral History Project, January 13, 2009, tape 3.

10. Patrick J. Lucey, interview by John Powell for Temple University Wisconsin Legislative Oral History Project, March 21, 2010.

11. Patrick J. Lucey financial statements, in Patrick J. Lucey Papers, Wisconsin Historical Society, MSS 5431, box 1, folder 5.

12. Mark J. Bradley, "Patrick J. Lucey," August 10, 1973, p. 21, in Governor Patrick J. Lucey Papers, Wisconsin Historical Society, MSS 2419, box 2, folder 4.

13. P. Lucey, interview by Duncan, tape 7 transcript, 7.

14. P. Lucey, interview by Duncan, tape 7 transcript, 110; Patrick J. Lucey, memos to GC Lucey, in Patrick J. Lucey Papers, 1935–2003, Wisconsin Historical Society, Series 5431, box 1, folder 6.

15. P. Lucey, interview by Duncan, tape 7 transcript, 112.

16. Bill Malkasian, Senior Vice President, National Association of Realtors, interview by author, September 6, 2017.

17. "'No Seat,' Thompson to Lucey; 'Then Move!' Governor Snaps," *Wisconsin State Journal*, September 14, 1963.

18. "Reynolds Names Counsel in Battle to Seat Lucey," *Capital Times*, September 19, 1963.

19. "Board Seats Lucey on Second Try," *Capital Times*, September 27, 1963.

20. "Senate Confirms 15, Sends 3 Names Back," *Wisconsin State Journal*, November 11, 1963.

21. "Lucey 'Conflict' Possibility Eyed," *Wisconsin State Journal*, November 19, 1963.

22. "Lucey's State Board Position Called Illegal," *Wisconsin State Journal*, November 20, 1963.

23. "Lucey 'Conflict' Possibility Eyed," *Wisconsin State Journal*.

24. "Lucey Heads Real Estate Firm Dealing in Sale of Lake Property," *Wisconsin State Journal*, May 23, 1965; "Lucey Denies Interest Conflict Claim," *Capital Times*, May 24, 1965.

25. Bradley, "Patrick J. Lucey," 11–13.

26. "Lucey to Develop 683-Acre Self-Contained Community," *Capital Times*, April 17, 1969.

27. "Lucey to Develop 683-Acre Self-Contained Community"; "Sprawling Development on Far West Side Eyed," *Wisconsin State Journal*, April 18, 1969.

28. "Lucey Firm Rejects Realty Group's Stand on Rights," *Capital Times*, December 3, 1963.

29. "Anti-Bias Law Backed by Lucey," *Capital Times*, December 6, 1963.

30. Shirley Abrahamson, interview by author, January 3, 2018.

31. Abrahamson, interview.

32. Malkasian, interview.

33. Abrahamson, interview.

34. P. Lucey, interview by Duncan, tape 7 transcript , 117.

### Chapter 6

1. David Adamany, "1960 Elections in Wisconsin" (master's thesis, University of Wisconsin, 1963), 75.

2. Theodore H. White, *The Making of the President 1960* (New York: Harper, 1988).

3. Patrick J. Lucey, interview by Leon Epstein, John F. Kennedy Library Oral History Program, August 1, 1964, 7–8.

4. White, *The Making of the President*, 97.

5. Herman Jessen, mimeographed statement, Wisconsin Democratic Party State Convention Records, 1959 (Wisconsin Democratic Party State Headquarters, Madison).

6. Patrick J. Lucey, "Vigorous and Victorious, A Report to the Members of the Democratic Party of Wisconsin," Wisconsin Democratic Party Convention Records, 1959 (Wisconsin Democratic Party State Headquarters, Madison).

7. Richard C. Haney, "A History of the Democratic Party of Wisconsin since World War Two" (PhD diss., University of Wisconsin, 1970), 395.

8. Adamany, "1960 Election in Wisconsin," 53–53.

9. Haney, "A History of the Democratic Party of Wisconsin," 420–21.

10. Haney, 421–22.

11. P. Lucey, interview by Epstein.

12. P. Lucey, interview by Epstein, 14–15.

13. Haney, "A History of the Democratic Party of Wisconsin," 422.

14. Patrick J. Lucey, interview by Chip Duncan, Duncan Entertainment, December 2, 2009, tape 8 transcript, 134.

15. Jane Hendra, "The 1960 Democratic Campaign in Wisconsin" (master's thesis, University of Wisconsin, 1961), 21.

16. Haney, "A History of the Democratic Party of Wisconsin," 424.

17. White, *The Making of the President*, 134.

18. P. Lucey, interview by Epstein.

19. P. Lucey, interview by Duncan, tape 8 transcript, 141.

20. Gregory Lucey, SJ, email to author, April 3, 2018.

21. P. Lucey, interview by Duncan, tape 8 transcript, 143.

22. G. Lucey, email.

23. Haney, "A History of the Democratic Party of Wisconsin," 430–31.

24. P. Lucey, interview by Duncan, tape 8 transcript, 148.

25. "Humphrey Backers Win Delegate Fight," *Wisconsin State Journal*, January 31, 1960.

26. "Kennedy-Backer Moses Asks Lucey to End Controversy," *Capital Times*, February 11, 1960.

27. "Mayor, Lucey Won't Accept 'Cease Fire'" *Capital Times*, February 9, 1960.

28. Haney, "A History of the Democratic Party of Wisconsin," 432.

29. White, *The Making of the President*, 138.

30. Adamany, "1960 Elections in Wisconsin," 57.

31. Haney, "A History of the Democratic Party of Wisconsin," 440.

32. Larry Tye, *Bobby Kennedy: The Making of a Liberal Icon* (New York: Random House, 2016), 129–43.

33. Andrew Baggaley, "Religious Influence on Wisconsin Voting," *American Political Science Review* (March 1962), 57–69; Harry M. Scoble and Leon D. Epstein, "Religion and Wisconsin Voting in 1960," in *American Ethnic Politics*, ed. Lawrence H. Fuchs (New York: Harper and Row, 1968) 125–48; Adamany, "1960 Elections in Wisconsin."

34. Scoble and Epstein, "Religion and Wisconsin Voting," 136–41.

35. White, *The Making of the President*, 156.

36. Robert Booth Fowler, *Wisconsin Votes. An Electoral History.* (Madison, WI: University of Wisconsin Press, 2008), 444.

37. P. Lucey, interview by Epstein, 45.

38. P. Lucey, interview by Duncan, tape 9 transcript, 154.

39. P. Lucey, interview by Duncan, tape 8 transcript, 146.

40. P. Lucey, interview by Duncan, tape 8 transcript, 146.

41. P. Lucey, interview by Duncan, tape 8 transcript, 146–47.

42. Adamany, "1960 Elections in Wisconsin," 95.

43. Adamany, 73.

44. Hendra, "The 1960 Democratic Campaign," 29.

45. Hendra, 33.

46. "Jasper: Very Fine Kennedy Crowd; Lucey: He's Pleased," *Capital Times*, October 24, 1960.

47. Patrick J. Lucey, interview by Bill Broydrick and Tim Cullen, Wisconsin Politics Oral History Project, August 22, 2003, tape 2 transcript, 41.

48. P. Lucey, interview by Broydrick and Cullen, tape 3 transcript, 77.

49. P. Lucey, interview by Broydrick and Cullen, tape 4 transcript, 93.

50. P. Lucey, interview by Broydrick and Cullen, tape 3 transcript, 73–75.

51. Wisconsin Legislature, *Wisconsin Blue Book: 1962* (Madison: Wisconsin Legislative Reference Bureau), 722.

52. "Lucey to Be at Head of Parade," *Capital Times*, January 18, 1961.

53. P. Lucey, interview by Broydrick and Cullen, tape 3 transcript, 81.

54. Edwin R. Bagley, interview by Larry J. Hackman, John F. Kennedy Library, December 19, 1968.

55. Haney, "A History of the Democratic Party of Wisconsin," 485.

56. John Wyngaard, "Observations about the Nelson-Lucey Quarrel," *Appleton Post-Crescent*, September 26, 1961.

57. Haney, "A History of the Democratic Party of Wisconsin," 486.

58. "Nelson Gives Open Support to Nikolay," *Capital Times*, September 6, 1961.

59. Haney, "A History of the Democratic Party of Wisconsin," 486–88.

60. Gaylord Nelson and Patrick Lucey, joint press release, September 21, 1961, *Capital Times*, September 21, 1961; "The Nelson-Lucey Cease-Fire," *Wisconsin State Journal*, September 25, 1961.

61. "Lucey Favors Nelson for Senate, Reynolds for Governorship Race," *Appleton Post-Crescent*, January 16, 1962.

62. "Gifts Shared, Dems Say," *Capital Times*, May 10, 1962; Mark J. Bradley, "Patrick J. Lucey," August 10, 1973, p. 28, in Governor Patrick J. Lucey Papers, Wisconsin Historical Society Archives, Series 2419, box 2, folder 4.

63. Gaylord Nelson, interview with Jim Cavanaugh, State Historical Society of Wisconsin's Wisconsin Democratic Party Oral History Project, March 28, 1985, tape 53.

64. Patrick J. Lucey, interview by Neil Shively, April 16, 2006.

65. P. Lucey, interview by Shively.

66. Nelson, interview.

67. Haney, "A History of the Democratic Party of Wisconsin," 489–90.

68. 1962 Wisconsin Democratic Party Platform, quoted in *Capital Times*, June 11, 1962.

69. "Nelson Hit on Sales Tax," *Wisconsin State Journal*, June 23, 1962.

70. Haney, "A History of the Democratic Party of Wisconsin," 492–93.

71. William F. Thompson, *Continuity and Change, 1940–1965*, The History of Wisconsin, vol. 6 (Madison: State Historical Society of Wisconsin, 1988), 708–10.

72. Bill Kraus, email to author, September 4, 2018.

73. Haney, "A History of the Democratic Party of Wisconsin," 494.

74. Elie Abel, *The Missile Crisis* (New York: Bantam, 1966), 75.

75. John F. Kennedy to Gaylord Nelson, October 25, 1962, Legislative Reference Library Wisconsin Democratic Party clipping file, cited in Haney, 495–96.

76. Bill Christofferson, *The Man from Clear Lake: Earth Day Founder Senator Gaylord Nelson* (Madison: University of Wisconsin Press, 2004),

77. Leon Epstein, *Politics in Wisconsin* (Madison: University of Wisconsin Press, 1958), 54; John Wyngaard, *Green Bay Press Gazette*, November 14, 1962; Editorial, *New York Times*, November 21, 1962.

78. Lynn Ansfield, interview by author, April 30, 2019.

79. "State Democrats Pick Hanson as Party Chief," *Appleton Post-Crescent*, June 23, 1963.

80. "Party Yearbook Displays Lucey's 'Indelible Print,'" *Wisconsin State Journal*, June 20, 1963.

81. "Turbulent Political Era of Jasper-Lucey Ending," *Capital Times*, June 17, 1963.

82. David Adamany, "Lucey's J-J Dinner, Leadership Lauded by Governor's Aide," *Capital Times*, June 25, 1963.

### Chapter 7

1. "Dems Dinner Didn't Reach Goal, Lucey Says," *Capital Times*, May 7, 1963; Patrick J. Lucey, interview by Chip Duncan, Duncan Entertainment, December 2, 2009, tape 10 transcript, 175.

2. "Lists Sent to Washington for Federal Judge," *Wisconsin State Journal*, March 16, 1963.

3. Richard C. Haney, "A History of the Democratic Party of Wisconsin since World War Two" (PhD dissertation, University of Wisconsin, 1970), 506.

4. Roy S. Wilcox, interview by author, re Francis J. Wilcox, President of State Bar of Wisconsin, 1963–64, April 27, 2018; Haney, "A History of the Democratic Party of Wisconsin," 506.

5. John Wyngaard, "Rabinovitz Bad Choice for Federal Bench," *Green Bay Press Gazette*, September 12, 1963.

6. Patrick J. Lucey, interview by Bill Broydrick and Tim Cullen, Wisconsin Politics Oral History Project, August 22, 2003, tape 3 transcript, 64, 65.

7. James Doyle Jr., interview by author, January 24, 2019.

8. Haney, "A History of the Democratic Party in Wisconsin," 507–10.

9. Haney, 509–11; Miles McMillin, "Dem Committee Job: Lucey-Doyle Fight?," *Capital Times*, June 10, 1963.

10. Haney, "A History of the Democratic Party in Wisconsin," 124.

11. In 1979 the Wisconsin Constitution was amended to remove the role of the lieutenant governor as presiding officer in the state senate.

12. Patrick J. Lucey, interview by Duncan, tape 12 transcript, 206–8.

13. Patrick J. Lucey Papers, "Lucey for Lieutenant Governor Campaign Plan," Wisconsin Historical Society, MSS 785, box 5, folder 1.

14. Patrick J. Lucey Papers, folder 6.

15. Patrick J. Lucey Papers, folder 6.

16. Patrick J. Lucey Papers, folder 5.

17. David Lucey, email correspondence with author, January 16, 2018; Paul Lucey, email correspondence with author, March 5, 2018; Laurie Lucey, email correspondence with author, April 8, 2018.

18. Haney, "A History of the Democratic Party in Wisconsin," 536.

19. Haney, 539; Mark Barbash, *Patrick J. Lucey* (senior honors thesis, University of Wisconsin–Madison, 1971), 37.

20. Patrick J. Lucey, Inauguration Address, January 4, 1965, in Patrick J. Lucey Papers, 1935–2003, Wisconsin Historical Society, MSS 785, box 5, folder 8.

21. Patrick J. Lucey, interview by Anita Hecht, Proxmire Oral History Project, January 13, 2009, tape 2.

22. David Adamany, interview by Patrick McGilligan, Marquette University Wisconsin Politics Oral History Collection, 2011–2012, December 14, 2011.

23. "Lucey Orders Election to Fill Haase Vacancy," *Wisconsin State Journal*, September 18, 1965.

24. "Shouldn't Ethics Code Apply to Lucey, Knowles Bros.?" *Capital Times*, November 10, 1964; "Lucey Leaving CMI Board," *Capital Times*, November 18, 1964.

25. "Lucey Admits Conflict of Interest; What About Knowles," *Capital Times*, November 19, 1964.

26. Adamany, interview.

27. David Adamany, email to Neil Shively, April 12, 2014.

28. Adamany, email.

29. "Peterson Attacks PSC Appointment," *Wisconsin State Journal*, September 22, 1963; "The Adamany Appointment," *Appleton Post-Crescent*, September 24, 1963.

30. Adamany, email.

31. "Adamany's Salary Left up to Lucey," *Wisconsin State Journal*, March 26, 1965.

32. "Knowles Vetoes Adamany Bill," *Wisconsin State Journal*, May 22, 1965.

33. "Senate Fails to Override Veto of Adamany Pay Boost," *Capital Times*, June 10, 1965.

34. Jenann Olsen, interview by author, January 31, 2018.

35. Olsen, interview.

36. Olsen, interview.

37. David Lasker, interview by author, May 3, 2018.

38. Lasker, interview.

39. "UW Aides Can't Work for Lucey," *Wisconsin State Journal*, September 19, 1965.

40. Adamany, interview.

41. "Collection of press releases, speeches and testimony before legislative committees," Patrick J. Lucey, Lieutenant Governor, November 1964–1965, Wisconsin Legislative Reference Library.

42. P. Lucey, interview by Broydrick and Cullen, tape 4 transcript, 101; P. Lucey, interview by Duncan, tape 11 transcript, 204.

43. "Diners Give Lucey Cash, Compliments," *Milwaukee Journal*, August 16, 1966.

44. Patrick J. Lucey, interview by Larry J. Hackman, Robert F. Kennedy Oral History Project of the Kennedy Library, January 6, 1972; P. Lucey, interview by Duncan, tape 11 transcript, 171.

45. "Diners Give Lucey Cash, Compliments."

46. Bill Christofferson, *The Man from Clear Lake: Earth Day Founder Senator Gaylord Nelson* (University of Wisconsin Press: Madison, 2004), 103.

47. Barbash, *Patrick J. Lucey*, 39.

48. Barbash, 41.

49. "Carley Makes His Bid for Governor's Race," *Wisconsin State Journal*, November 5, 1965.

50. John Patrick Hunter, "Carley Calls Lucey Memo 'Shell Game'" *Capital Times*, December 27, 1965.

51. "Lucey Sets State Air Tour to Announce Candidacy," *Capital Times*, May 20, 1966.

52. "All Three Candidates Have Help," *Wisconsin State Journal*, April 17, 1966.

53. Linda Reivitz, interview by author, January 29, 2018.

54. "Carley Raps Lucey for Keynote Refusal," *Milwaukee Journal*, June 4, 1966.

55. "Lucey, Carley to Launch Rival Booms at Dem Convo," *Capital Times*, June 9, 1966.

56. Barbash, *Patrick J. Lucey*, 46.
57. "Lt. Gov. Lucey Announces," *Appleton Post-Crescent*, April 23, 1966; Barbash, 46.
58. Patrick J. Lucey, "Lucey Position on Vietnam" *Capital Times*, June 11, 1966.
59. John Wyngaard, "Lucey-Carley Fight Could Prove Divisive for Democratic Party," *Appleton Post-Crescent*, June 18, 1966.
60. "Lt.-Gov. Lucey States His Position on Vital Viet Nam Issue," *The Capital Times*, June 11, 1966.
61. P. Lucey, interview by Duncan, tape 9, transcript 156.
62. Lasker, interview by author, May 3, 2018.
63. P. Lucey, interview by Duncan, tape 11 transcript, 189.
64. P. Lucey, interview by Duncan, tape 11 transcript, 189; Paul Lucey, email.
65. "Party Hears Lucey Lambaste Knowles," *Wisconsin State Journal*, June 12, 1966.
66. "Adamany Replies to Frinzi Charges," *Capital Times*, August 4, 1966.
67. "Carley Threatens Suit against Lucey," *Capital Times*, August 8, 1966.
68. Barbash, *Patrick J. Lucey*, 57.
69. "Lucey Primary Costs Listed at $85,000," *Appleton Post-Crescent*, September 29, 1966.
70. "Lucey Victory Leaves Party Factions Split," *Wisconsin State Journal*, September 15, 1966.
71. James D. Selk, "Still Smarting, Carley Supports Lucey, Who Makes No Promises," *Wisconsin State Journal*, September 17, 1966.
72. John Patrick Hunter, "Parties Look to Nixon, RFK to Stir Interest in State," *Capital Times*, September 15, 1966.
73. Keith Clifford, interview with author, May 11, 2018.
74. Lasker, interview; Clifford, interview.
75. Clifford, interview.
76. Paul Lucey, email to author, December 15, 2018.
77. P. Lucey, interview by Duncan, tape 11 transcript, 193.
78. P. Lucey, interview by Duncan, tape 11 transcript, 194.
79. James K. Conant, *Wisconsin Politics and Government. America's Laboratory of Democracy* (Lincoln: University of Nebraska Press, 2006), 109.
80. Barbash, *Patrick J. Lucey*, 65.
81. James D. Selk, "Lucey's Final Assault Is on Insurance, Oleo," *Wisconsin State Journal*, November 6, 1966.

82. Selk, "Lucey's Final Assault."

83. Donald Janson, "Knowles Stymies Foe in Wisconsin," *New York Times*, September 29, 1966.

84. Matt Pommer, "Lucey and Knowles Oppose Consolidated College System," *Capital Times*, October 31, 1966.

85. "Milwaukee Rights Leader Stops Talk by Mrs. Lucey," *Appleton Post-Crescent*, November 2, 1966.

86. "Coggs Challenges Mrs. Lucey Over Rights," *Wisconsin State Journal*, November 3, 1966; "Mrs. Lucey Heckled on Rights; Bursts into Tears," *Capital Times*, November 2, 1966.

87. Barbash, *Patrick J. Lucey*, 68.

88. "Knowles, GOP Spent $636,000 in Campaign," *Appleton Post-Crescent*, November 24, 1966; Barbash, *Patrick J. Lucey*, 70.

89. "Aim at State Election," *Appleton Post-Crescent*, November 6, 1966.

90. Edward A. Ziel, "Lucey 'Just Numb' at Defeat, Did Better Than Expected." *Appleton Post-Crescent*, November 9, 1966.

91. John Patrick Hunter, "Lucey Reveals He Almost Quit Campaign Last July," *Capital Times*, November 16, 1966.

92. P. Lucey, interview by Broydrick and Cullen, tape 3 transcript, 73.

## Chapter 8

1. David Maraniss, *They Marched into Sunlight: War and Peace in America, October 1967* (New York: Simon and Schuster, 2003).

2. David Halberstam, *The Unfinished Odyssey of Robert Kennedy: A Biography* (New York: Open Road Media, 2013).

3. Lawrence O'Donnell, *Playing with Fire: The 1968 Election and the Transformation of American Politics* (New York: Penguin Press, 2017), 89–94.

4. Jules Witcover, *85 Days: The Last Campaign of Robert Kennedy* (New York: HarperCollins, 1969), 47–52.

5. Theodore H. White, *The Making of the President 1968*, reissued ed. (New York: Harper Perennial, 2010), 183–85.

6. Patrick J. Lucey, interview by Larry J. Hackman, Robert F. Kennedy Oral History Project of the Kennedy Library, January 6, 1972.

7. Witcover, *85 Days*, 35.

8. White, *The Making of the President 1968*, 130; O'Donnell, *Playing with Fire*, 123–25.

9. Witcover, *85 Days*, 60.

10. P. Lucey, interview by Hackman.

11. O'Donnell, *Playing with Fire*, 180–83; Witcover, *85 Days*, 62–64.

12. David Lasker, email to author, July 3, 2018.

13. O'Donnell, *Playing with Fire*, 184.

14. Witcover, *85 Days*, 73.

15. White, *The Making of the President 1968*, 142–45; O'Donnell, *Playing with Fire*, 250–55.

16. Patrick J. Lucey, interview by Chip Duncan, Duncan Entertainment, December 2, 2009, tape 11 transcript, 157.

17. O'Donnell, *Playing with Fire*, 235–40.

18. P. Lucey, interview by Duncan, tape 11 transcript, 162.

19. O'Donnell, *Playing with Fire*, 254.

20. Witcover, *85 Days*, 55.

21. P. Lucey, interview by Duncan, tape 11 transcript, 166; Patrick J. Lucey, interview by Bill Broydrick and Tim Cullen, Wisconsin Politics Oral History Project, August 22, 2003, tape 3 transcript, 75, 76.

22. P. Lucey, interview by Duncan, tape 11 transcript, 167–69.

23. O'Donnell, *Playing with Fire*, 258.

24. Witcover, *85 Days*, 184.

25. Paul Lucey, note to author, December 11, 2018.

26. P. Lucey, interview by Broydrick and Cullen, tape 3 transcript, 79; P. Lucey, interview by Duncan, tape 12 transcript, 193–96; James D. Selk, "Lucey's View of Shooting Scene: 'Confusion, Hysteria,'" *Wisconsin State Journal*, June 6, 1968.

27. Patrick J. Lucey, speech before the Wisconsin State Democratic Party Convention, Milwaukee, July 19, 1968, cited in Mark Barbash, *Patrick J. Lucey* (senior honors thesis, University of Wisconsin–Madison, 1971), 78.

28. John Wyngaard, "Lucey May 'Sit It Out' but He'll Be Back Again," *Wisconsin State Journal*, June 30, 1968.

29. P. Lucey, interview by Duncan, tape 12 transcript, 196; "Kennedy Aide Lucey Now Backs McCarthy," *Wisconsin State Journal*, August 8, 1968; E. W. Kenworthy, "McCarthy, in Ohio Campaign, Endorsed by Ex-Kennedy Aide," *New York Times*, August 8, 1968.

30. "Lucey Placed on McCarthy 'Cabinet List,'" *Wisconsin State Journal*, August 16, 1968.

31. John Patrick Hunter, "Lucey to Play Major Role in Campaign for McCarthy," *Capital Times*, August 12, 1968.

32. Lasker, email.

33. P. Lucey, interview by Duncan, tape 12 transcript, 198.

34. O'Donnell, *Playing with Fire*, 354–62.

35. John Patrick Hunter, "Lucey Endorses Humphrey-Muskie," *Capital Times*, October 11, 1968.

36. O'Donnell, *Playing with Fire*, 396.

37. Austin Ranney, *Curing the Mischiefs of Factions: Party Reform in America* (Berkeley: University of California Press, 1975); Austin Ranney, "Turnout and Representation in Presidential Primary Elections," *American Political Science Review* 66, no. 1 (March 1972), 21–37.

38. "Lucey Heads Policy Group of New Democratic Coalition," *Capital Times*, December 9, 1968.

39. White, *The Making of the President 1968*, 449–52.

40. "Lucey Asks New Coalition for Liberal 'Continuity,'" *Capital Times*, December 7, 1968.

## Chapter 9

1. Patrick J. Lucey, interview by Chip Duncan, Duncan Entertainment, December 2, 2009, tape 13 transcript, 221.

2. "Lucey Hints He May Be Governor Candidate," *Capital Times*, November 26, 1968.

3. John and Tim Wyngaard, "Lucey Staff Tailors Speech Announcing Bid for Governorship," *Appleton Post-Crescent*, September 21, 1969.

4. James D. Selk, "Lucey Dane County Unit Formed," *Wisconsin State Journal*, May 27, 1969.

5. John Patrick Hunter, "Peterson Tells Democrats He's in Race for Governor," *Capital Times*, October 27, 1969.

6. James D. Selk, "Peterson to Toss Hat into Governor's Derby," *Wisconsin State Journal*, April 22, 1970; John Wyngaard, "Donald Peterson Is Enigmatic Candidate in Primary Election," *Appleton Post-Crescent*, June 18, 1970.

7. "Lucey Calls McCarthy's Planned Visit 'Wonderful,'" *Capitol Times*, July 9, 1970.

8. John Patrick Hunter, "Lucey Soon to Announce Governor Try, Quit NDC Link," *Capital Times*, June 5, 1969.

9. James D. Selk, "Carley Declines Governor's Race," *Wisconsin State Journal*, November 21, 1969.

10. Stephen Holmgren, interview by author, January 8, 2018.

11. Mark Barbash, *Patrick J. Lucey* (senior honors thesis, University of Wisconsin–Madison, 1971), 119.

12. "AFL-CIO Polls Members on Support for Governor," *Milwaukee Journal*, April 3, 1970.

13. Gordon L. Randolph, "26 Legislators Pledge to Support Lucey Bid," *Milwaukee Journal*, March 20, 1970.

14. "Lucey Supported by 26 Legislators," *Milwaukee Sentinel*, March 20, 1970; John Keefe, "Dem Lawmakers Prod Maier to Step Aside," *Wisconsin State Journal*, March 19, 1970.

15. James W. McCulla, "Lucey to Ask Support of Maier in Campaign," *Milwaukee Journal*, May 13, 1970.

16. David Lasker, email to author, July 9, 2018.

17. David Obey, *Raising Hell for Justice: The Washington Battles of a Heartland Progressive* (Madison: University of Wisconsin Press, 2007), 102–46.

18. David Lasker, email to author, July 3, 2018.

19. Dave Wagner, "AFL-CIO Executive Unit Urges Support of Lucey," *Capital Times*, April 13, 1970.

20. Henry Maier, letter to John Schmitt, April 15, 1970, in Barbash, *Patrick J. Lucey*, 122.

21. "Gronouski Supports Lucey for Governor," *Wisconsin State Journal*, December 2, 1969.

22. Patrick J. Lucey, interview by John Powell, Temple University Wisconsin Legislative Oral History Project, March 2010, 29.

23. "Lucey, Zablocki Meeting Friendly," *Milwaukee Sentinel*, August 18, 1970.

24. Holmgren, interview.

25. Dennis Conta, interview by author, December 8, 2017.

26. Richard Weening, interview by Mark Barbash, January 6, 1971.

27. Holmgren interview.

28. David L. Todd, "Lucey Spends $111,747 in His Primary Race," *Appleton Post-Crescent*, September 25, 1970.

29. Patrick J. Lucey Papers, 1935–2003, 1970 Boiler Room Book, MSS 785, box 5B, folder 21, Wisconsin State Historical Society; David Lasker, email to author, July 10, 2018.

30. Jeff Smoller, "Lucey, Peterson Debate; Find Little Disagreement," *Capital Times*, July 30, 1970.

31. Tim Wyngaard, "Lucey Shows Gain in Madison Debates," *Appleton Post-Crescent*, July 31, 1970.

32. "Lucey, Peterson Review Positions," *Capital Times*, September 7, 1970.

33. Arthur L. Srb, "GOP Expected to Influence Democratic Gubernatorial Primary," *Appleton Post-Crescent*, September 1, 1970.

34. Jeff Smoller, "Lucey Wins Right to Oppose Olson," *Capital Times*, September 9, 1970.

35. "Peterson Urges Followers to Join Lucey Campaign," *Capital Times*, September 10, 1970.

36. "It's Lucey Versus Olson," *Appleton Post-Crescent*, September 11, 1970.

37. P. Lucey, interview by Duncan, tape 13 transcript, 226–27.

38. Martin J. Schreiber, interview by author, May 14, 2018.

39. John Wyngaard, "Zimmermann Victory in Democratic Primary Is Disturbing Indeed," *Appleton Post-Crescent*, November 12, 1970.

40. "Lucey, Schreiber Nix Zimmermann," *Wisconsin State Journal*, September 13, 1970.

41. "Lucey Proposes 8 Joint Appearances with Olson," *Capital Times*, September 16, 1970.

42. "Jack Olson Won't Debate Lucey in Governor's Race," *Capital Times*, September 18, 1970.

43. Barbash, *Patrick J. Lucey*, 173–75.

44. "Lucey Underscores Property Tax Inequities," *Appleton Post-Crescent*, September 29, 1970.

45. "Lucey Says Residence Tax Relief Has Top Priority, *Capital Times*, August 11, 1970.

46. "Lucey Says GOP Program Will Tax Property Owners," *Capital Times*, October 12, 1970.

47. Cliff Miller, "Olson-Lucey Clash Sparks Conference of 'Have-Nots,'" *Appleton Post-Crescent*, October 3, 1970.

48. "Lucey Vows Reforms," *Wisconsin State Journal*, September 13, 1970.

49. David Adamany, interview by Patrick McGilligan, Marquette University Wisconsin Politics Oral History Collection, 2011–2012, December 14, 2011.

50. Neil Shively, "Knowles Predicts Tax Increases," *Milwaukee Sentinel*, September 25, 1970.

51. Jeff Smoller, "Knowles, Olson Differ on Tax Hikes," *Capital Times*, September 25, 1970.

52. "Olson Charges Lucey to Hike Income Taxes 60%" *Capital Times*, October 16, 1970.

53. Peter A. Phyrr, *Zero-Base Budgeting* (New York: Wiley, 1973); Dennis L. Dresang, *Public Administration Workbook*, 8th ed. (New York: Pearson, 2017), 329–24.

54. John Wyngaard, "Knowles' Forecast of Higher Taxes Was Unpolitical but True," *Appleton Post-Crescent*, October 5, 1970.

55. "Knowles Hits Lucey's Spending," *Wisconsin State Journal*, October 13, 1970; "Knowles Assails Lucey's Program," *Milwaukee Sentinel*, October 13, 1970.

56. P. Lucey, interview by Duncan, tape 13, transcript 220.

57. "Martin Raps Lucey Shift on War Stand," *Milwaukee Sentinel*, July 27, 1970; "Stung Over Vietnam War Issue, Lucey Hits Back at GOP Critics," *Wisconsin State Journal*, July 21, 1970.

58. "Lucey Outlines Plan for War on State Crime," *Milwaukee Sentinel*, September 18, 1970; "Extremism Blasted by Lucey as 'Menace to Society,'" *Capital Times*, September 23, 1970.

59. "Olson, Lucey Seek 'Position,'" *Appleton Post-Crescent*, September 19, 1970.

60. Tim Wyngaard, "Lucey's Plan Is Thought-Provoking," *Appleton Post-Crescent*, June 29, 1970.

61. Kenneth P. Roesslein, "Lucey Attacks University Critics," *Milwaukee Sentinel*, October 1, 1970; Steven V. Roberts, "Conservatives Press Campus Unrest Issue," *New York Times*, October 11, 1970.

62. "Lucey Picks Froehlich, K-C as Top Issues," *Appleton Post-Crescent*, October 6, 1970.

63. Dave Zweifel, "Secret 'Smear-Lucey' Memos of GOP Bared," *Capital Times*, October 21, 1970.

64. Zweifel, "Secret 'Smear-Lucey' Memos."

65. Dave Zweifel, "Two Disavow Use of Names On 'Smear-Lucey' Flyer," *Capital Times*, October 22, 1970.

66. Jeff Smoller, "TV Ads Intensify as Campaign Nears Close," *Capital Times*, October 31, 1970; Kenneth P. Roesslein, "Lucey Roasted as Hippie Landlord," *Milwaukee Sentinel*, October 23, 1970.

67. Cited in Barbash, *Patrick J. Lucey*, 182–83.

68. Jeff Smoller, "Lucey Says Republicans Erred in 'Smear' Drive," *Capital Times*, November 5, 1970.

69. Barbash, *Patrick J. Lucey*, 208.

70. Barbash, 209, 210.

71. Barbash, 212.

72. Cited in Barbash, 215.

73. John Lavine, interview by author, November 15, 2018.

74. P. Lucey, interview by Duncan, tape 13 transcript, 208

75. Holmgren, interview.

76. Barbash, *Patrick J. Lucey*, 206–8.

77. Dean Showers, " '70 Gift to Lucey Raises Questions," *Milwaukee Sentinel*, August 30, 1974.

78. "Kennedy Home Lucey Fete Site," *Milwaukee Sentinel*, October 8, 1970; Lynn Ansfield, interview by author, April 30, 2019.

79. Jeff Smoller, "Lucey's Campaign Style: Move Fast," *Capital Times*, August 28, 1970; Neil Shively, "Lucey's 'Old School' Campaign Tactics Effective," *Milwaukee Sentinel*, September 3, 1970; James D. Selk, "A Calmer Lucey Is Running Stronger Now," *Wisconsin State Journal*, October 20, 1970.

80. Barbash, *Patrick J. Lucey*, 219–22.

**Chapter 10**

1. Richard Weening, email to author, October 27, 2018.

2. Stephen Holmgren, interview by author, January 8, 2018.

3. Robert H. Dunn, interview by author, November 21, 2017.

4. Patrick J. Lucey, interview by Chip Duncan, Duncan Entertainment, February 11, 2010, tape 13 transcript, 230.

5. P. Lucey, interview by Duncan, tape 14 transcript, 244.

6. Patrick J. Lucey Papers, 1935–2003, Wayne McGown to Dick Weening, November 11, 1971, Wisconsin Historical Society, MSS 785, box 11, folder 4.

7. Patrick J. Lucey Papers, 1935–2003, Joseph E. Nusbaum to Robert Dunn and Jim Fosdick, June 11, 1971, Wisconsin Historical Society, MSS 785, box 11, folder 4.

8. Martin J. Schreiber, interview by author, May 14, 2018.

9. P. Lucey, interview by Duncan, tape 13 transcript, 228.

10. Lon Sprecher, interview by the author, December 19, 2017; Dan Wisniewski, interview by author, November 28, 2017.

11. Tim Cullen, *Ringside Seat: Wisconsin Politics, the 1970s to Scott Walker* (Mineral Point, WI: Little Creek Press, 2016), 84–88, 222–24.

12. Dunn, interview.

13. Thomas Wolanin, *Presidential Advisory Commissions: Truman to Nixon* (Madison: University of Wisconsin Press, 1975).

14. Patrick J. Lucey, interview by John R. Johannes, Wisconsin Politics Oral History Project, May 12, 1995, 38.

15. Dunn, interview.

16. Amy Rabideau Silvers, "Jean Lucey's life wasn't about tea time," *Journal Sentinel*, December 7, 2011, http://archive.jsonline.com/news/obituaries/jean-lucey-wife-of-former-governor-dies-at-93-uf3bra0-135187238.html/.

17. "Governor, Wife Argue at Home; Mrs. Lucey Complains to Police," *Wisconsin State Journal*, March 17, 1972.

18. Amy Rabideau Silvers, "Jean Lucey's life wasn't about tea time."

19. "Lucey Sees '72 Encore for Budget Road Show," *Wisconsin State Journal*, December 26, 1970.

20. John Keefe, "Economic Outlook for State Is 'Bleak,'" *Wisconsin State Journal*, December 6. 1970.

21. "Lucey Austerity Plan Extended til June 30," *Wisconsin State Journal*, January 27, 1971.

22. Charlotte Robinson and Jeff Smoller, "Republicans Heap Scorn on Lucey's Fiscal Plans," *Capital Times*, March 3, 1971; "Froehlich, Conradt Ridicule Budget Bill," *Appleton Post-Crescent*, March 3, 1971.

23. John Wyngaard, "Kellett Adds Prestige to 'Merger' Drive," *Wisconsin State Journal*, September 12, 1971; William Kraus, interview by author, July 5, 2018.

24. Kraus, interview; Neil Shively, *Hitting Every Beehive—Pat Lucey Terrorized the Status Quo in Wisconsin Government, Politics* (unpublished manuscript), 79.

25. Shively, *Hitting Every Beehive*, 82; Weening, email.

26. Stephen Holmgren, email to author, September 17, 2018.

27. James D. Selk, "Governor Will Accept Separate Merger Bill," *Wisconsin State Journal*, May 21, 1971.

28. Shively, *Hitting Every Beehive*, 85.

29. Stephen Holmgren, email to author, November 29, 2018.

30. Stephen Holmgren, interview by author, January 8, 2018; Timothy Cullen, interview by author, January 5, 2018.

31. Shively, *Hitting Every Beehive*, 86.

32. Shively, 87.

33. "Merger Aided as Foe 'Steps Out,'" *Appleton Post-Crescent*, May 21, 1971; Shively, *Hitting Every Beehive*, 87.

34. Anthony Earl, interview by author, October 16, 2017; Weening, email.

35. "Lucey Eyes Session on Merger," *Milwaukee Sentinel*, January 10, 1974.

36. Dan Wisniewski, email to author, December 9, 2018.

37. Earl, interview.

38. James K. Conant, *Executive Decision Making in the State* (PhD dissertation, University of Wisconsin–Madison, 1983.), 150.

39. James D. Selk, "Shared Revenue Backed by Lucey," *Wisconsin State Journal*, March 2, 1971.

40. Charles E. Friederich, "Joint Finance OKs Budget with Merger, Tax Boosts," *Milwaukee Journal*, May 22, 1971.

41. Charles E. Friederich, "Budget Slogged Around in the Trenches for 8 Months," *Milwaukee Journal*, October 27, 1971.

42. Charlotte Robinson, "Lucey Buttonholes Dems to Shore Up Budget Votes," *Capital Times*, July 29, 1971.

43. Tom Foley, "Unify for Lucey, Maier Tells Cities," *Capital Times*, June 18, 1971; "Lucey, Maier, Huber Rip GOP's Tax Stand," *Milwaukee Journal*, August 6, 1971.

44. Cliff Miller, "Lucey Says It's 'Now or Never' for Shared-Tax Reform in State," *Appleton Post-Crescent*, October 22, 1971.

45. James D. Selk, "Budget Finally Clears Senate," *Wisconsin State Journal*, October 27, 1971.

46. James D. Selk, "Governor Hails Fund Measure as 'Landmark,'" *Wisconsin State Journal*, November 4, 1871.

47. Charles E. Friederich, "Lucey Asks Some Shifts in Budget," *Milwaukee Journal*, January 19, 1972.

48. Holmgren, interview.

49. Holmgren, interview; Anthony Earl, interview by author, November 13, 2018; Dennis Conta, interview by author, November 1, 2018; Robert Lang, interview by author, November 14, 2018.

50. Conta, interview.

51. Conta, interview.

52. Conant, *Executive Decision Making*, 274; Eugene C. Harrington, "Tax Relief Gets Top Budget Billing," *Milwaukee Journal*, February 1, 1973.

53. Robert D. Lee Jr., Ronald W. Johnson, and Philip G. Joyce, *Public Budgeting Systems*, 9th ed. (Sudbury, MA: Jones and Bartlett, 2013); Thomas D. Lynch, Jimping Sun, and Robert W. Smith, *Public Budgeting in America*, 6th ed. (Irvine, CA: Melvin & Leigh, 2017); Irene Rubin, *The Politics of Public Budgeting: Getting and Spending*, 7th ed. (Washington, DC: Congressional Quarterly Press, 2013).

54. "Priorities Policy for 1973–1975 Budget," Governor Lucey Records, 1971–1977, Wisconsin State Historical Society, series 2419, box 186, folder 20.

55. "1973–75 Budget and Fiscal Policies," issued by Governor Patrick J. Lucey, May 1, 1972, Governor Lucey Records, 1971–1977, Wisconsin State Historical Society, series 2419, box 186, folder 20.

56. "Productivity Factor in 1973–19756 Budget," Governor Lucey Records, 1971–1977, Wisconsin Historical Society, series 2419, box 186, folder 20.

57. "Governor's Spring Budget Conferences," Governor Lucey Records, 1971–1977, Wisconsin Historical Society, series 2419, box 186, folder 20.

58. Patrick J. Lucey, "Wisconsin's Productivity Policy," *Public Administration Review* 32, no. 6 (November–December 1972), 795–99; Patrick J. Lucey, "Wisconsin's Progress with Productivity Improvements," *Public Administration Review* 38, no. 1 (January–February 1978), 9–12; Patrick J. Lucey, "Productivity: An Essential Strategy for Survival," *Public Productivity Review* 1, no. 1 (September 1975), 30–35; Harold Wilde, email to author, August 24, 2018.

59. Thomas P. Lauth, "Budgeting and Productivity in State Government: Not Integrated but Friendly," *Public Productivity Review* 10, no. 3 (Spring, 1987), 21–32; Gary W. Florkowski and Donald E. Lifton, "Assessing Public-Sector Productivity Incentives: A Review," *Public Productivity Review* 11, no. 1 (Autumn 1987) 53–70.

60. William S. Becker, "State Budget Battle—The Inside Story," *Capital Times*, January 25, 1973.

61. "Tax Relief Plan Centers on Lucey Idea vs. Direct Cut," *Milwaukee Journal*, February 2, 1973.

62. Conant, *Executive Decision Making*, 275.

63. Neil H. Shively and Dean Showers, "Legislative Panel OKs $3 Billion State Budget," *Milwaukee Sentinel*, June 30, 1973.

64. "Budget Attacks Renew," *Wisconsin State Journal*, April 24, 1975.

65. Tommy G. Thompson and Doug Moe, *Tommy: My Journey of a Lifetime* (Madison: University of Wisconsin Press, 2018), 46–47.

66. "Lucey's Comprehensive Budget," *Milwaukee Journal*, February 3, 1973.

67. Neil Shively, "Maier, Lucey Strike Note of Shared Tax Harmony," *Milwaukee Sentinel*, April 11, 1974.

**Chapter 11**

1. Gary D. Wekkin, *Democrat versus Democrat: The National Party's Campaign to Close the Wisconsin Primary* (Columbia: University of Missouri Press, 1984), 137.

2. Commission on Party Structure and Delegate Selection, *Mandate for Reform*, (Washington, DC: Democratic National Committee, 1970), 34–48.

3. Theodor H. White, *The Making of the President, 1972: A Narrative History of American Politics in Action* (New York: Atheneum, 1973), 105–8.

4. "Governor Patrick J. Lucey for Vice President: Right on the Issues, Right for the Ticket," in Patrick J. Lucey Papers, 1935–2003, Wisconsin Historical Society, MSS 785, box 11, folder 9.

5. Charles E. Friederich, "Just a Dark Horse, Lucey Says," *Milwaukee Journal*, July 6, 1972; Eugene C. Harrington, "Lucey Still Wants Kennedy on Ticket," *Milwaukee Journal*, July 9, 1972.

6. Stephen Holmgren, interview by author, September 26, 2018.

7. White, *The Making of the President, 1972*, 196, 197.

8. White, 198.

9. Keith Clifford, email to author, September 20, 2018.

10. Patrick J. Lucey, interview by Chip Duncan, Duncan Entertainment, February 11, 2010, tape 13 transcript, 215.

11. Holmgren, interview.

12. David Adamany, "Crossover Voting and the Democratic Party's Reform Rules," *American Political Science Review* 70, no. 3 (June 1976), 536–41; Frank A. Sorauf, *Party Politics in America*, 3rd ed. (Boston: Little, Brown, 1976), 216; and Wekkin, *Democrat versus Democrat*, 33.

13. Wekkin, *Democrat versus Democrat*, 68.

14. Linda Reivitz, interview by author, October 8, 2018.

15. Wekkin, *Democrat versus Democrat*, 90, 91, 96.

16. Wekkin, 107.

17. Wekkin, 71–76.

18. Tim Cullen, interview by author, September 10, 2018.

19. Wekkin, *Democrat versus Democrat*, 121, 122.

20. Wekkin, 125–30; Brady Williamson, email to author, September 5, 2018.

21. Wisconsin Legislature, *The State of Wisconsin Blue Book: 1977* (Madison: Wisconsin Legislative Reference Bureau, 1977), 872–77.

22. James T. Sykes, memo, n.d., Wisconsin Historical Society, Wisconsin Governor Lucey (1971–1977), series 2419, box 203, folder 39.

23. *State Ex. Rel. La Follette v. Democratic Party* (1980).

24. *Democratic Party of U.S. v. La Follette* (1981).

25. Patrick J. Lucey, interview by Jim Cavanaugh, Wisconsin Historical Society, History of the Democratic Party, April 10, 1985, tape 65; P. Lucey, interview by Duncan, tape 14 transcript, 239; Stephen Holmgren, interview by author, January 8, 2018.

26. Bob Woodward and Carl Bernstein, *All the President's Men* (New York: Simon and Schuster, 1974); *Richard Nixon and Watergate: The Life of the President and the Scandal That Brought Him Down* (Charles River Editors, 2014).

27. Patrick J. Lucey, interview by John Powell, Temple University Wisconsin Legislative Oral History Project, March 2010.

28. James B. Wood, interview by author, July 16, 2018.

29. Wood, interview.

30. Wood, interview.

31. P. Lucey, interview by Duncan, tape 8 transcript, 130.

32. William Kraus, interview by author, September 10, 2018.

33. Dale Van Atta, *With Honor: Melvin Laird in War, Peace, and Politics* (Madison: University of Wisconsin Press, 2008).

34. Van Atta, *With Honor*; Kraus, interview.

35. Dean Showers, "Dyke Sees Lucey 'Way Out in Front,'" *Milwaukee Sentinel*, May 25, 1974.

36. Charles E. Friederich, "Lucey Joins Race, Talks of Debates," *Milwaukee Journal*, June 12, 1974; Neil H. Shively, "Lucey Unwinds after Vote Trip," *Milwaukee Sentinel*, June 22, 1974.

37. Neil H. Shively, "Dyke Tries New Tack in Campaigning," *Milwaukee Sentinel*, July 24, 1974.

38. W. L. Christofferson, "Lucey Outspends Dyke by 4 to 1," *Wisconsin State Journal*, November 1, 1974.

39. Neil H. Shively, "Capitol Control A Rarity," *Milwaukee Sentinel*, November 6, 1974.

40. Tim Cullen, interview by author, January 5, 2018; Dan Wisniewski, interview by author, November 28, 2017.

41. Tim Cullen, interview by author, May 15, 2019.

42. Tim Cullen, interview by author, January 5, 2018.

43. Tim Cullen, *Ringside Seat: Wisconsin Politics, the 1970s to Scott Walker*, (Mineral Point, WI: Little Creek Press, 2016).

44. Neal R. Peirce and John Keefe, *The Great Lakes States of America* (New York: W.W, Norton, 1980), 256.

### Chapter 12

1. Joe Sensenbrenner, interview by author, July 2, 2018; Patrick J. Lucey, interview by Bill Broydrick and Tim Cullen, Wisconsin Politics Oral History Project, August 22, 2003, tape 6 transcript, 150.

2. Michael E. Stevens, "'A Fair Chance for All': McGovern's Progressivism," *Wisconsin Magazine of History* 100, no. 4 (Summer 2017), 46–51.

3. David Riemer, interview by author, June 5, 2018.

4. George E. Mowry, *The Progressive Era* (Washington, DC: American Historical Association, 1972); Russell Blaine Nye, *Midwestern Progressive Politics: A Historical Study of Its Origins and Development, 1870–1950* (Lansing: Michigan State College Press, 1959); John D. Buenker, *The Progressive Era, 1893–1914*, The History of Wisconsin, vol. 4 (Madison: State Historical Society of Wisconsin, 1998), 405–420.

5. Robert C. Bjorklund, "Lucey Appointment Bid Called a 'Power Grab,'" *Wisconsin State Journal*, June 19, 1973.

6. Robert Dunn, interview by author, November 21, 2017.

7. James D. Selk, "Lucey Slaps State Vets' Dept." *Wisconsin State Journal*, December 2, 1972.

8. Reid Beveridge, "Veterans Board Completes Cycle," *Wisconsin State Journal*, April 24, 1978.

9. "Appointments by Governor Patrick J. Lucey, 1971–1977," Madison, Wisconsin, Legislative Reference Library.

10. Jeff Smoller, "Times Do Change: 'Dove' on Vet Board," *Capital Times*, April 16, 1971.

11. Shirley Abrahamson, interview by author, January 3, 2018.

12. Patrick J. Lucey, interview by Chip Duncan, Duncan Entertainment, February 12, 2010, tape 13 transcript, 211; Matt Pommer and Diane Sherman, "Picks Abrahamson for High Court," *Capital Times*, August 5, 1976.

13. Abrahamson, interview.

14. Elena Cappella, email to author, January 12, 2018.

15. Abrahamson, interview.

16. "Lucey Opens Staff to Indian Representation," *Appleton Post-Crescent*, September 13, 1971.

17. Ari Hoogenboom, *Outlawing the Spoils: A History of the Civil Service Reform Movement, 1865–1883* (Urbana: University of Illinois Press, 1961); Carl R. Fish, *The Civil Service and the Patronage* (New York: Longman, Green, 1935); Paul P. Van Riper, *History of the United States Civil Service* (Evanston, IL: Row, Peterson, 1958).

18. Patricia W. Ingraham and David H. Rosenbloom, eds., *The Promise and Paradox of Civil Service Reform* (Pittsburgh, PA: University of Pittsburgh Press, 1992); Dennis L. Dresang, *Personnel Management in Government Agencies and Nonprofit Organizations*, 6th ed. (New York: Routledge, 2017).

19. The author served as research and staff director. Task force cochairs were business executive John Stevens and State Senator Paul Offner.

20. *Wisconsin Civil Service: Report of the Employment Relations Study Commission, 1975–1977*, Papers of Wisconsin Governor Lucey (1971–1977), Wisconsin Historical Society, series 2419, box 145, folder 9.

21. Matt Pommer, "GOP: Lucey Tampered with Civil Service," *Capital Times*, January 13, 1977; Neil H. Shively, "La Follette Blasts Lucey on Probe," *Milwaukee Sentinel*, January 14, 1977; Patricia Simms, "Personnel Board Hearing Is Ordered," *Wisconsin State Journal*, March 5, 1977.

22. Patricia Simms, "Labor Lessens Lucey Support," *Wisconsin State Journal*, March 30, 1977.

23. *Journal of the Proceedings of the Wisconsin State Assembly*, 1955, 180.

24. *Journal of the Proceedings of the Wisconsin State Senate*, December 31, 1978, 88; Patricia Simms, "Personnel Official Withdraws Pardon Request," *Wisconsin State Journal*, May 11, 1978.

25. P. Lucey, interview by Duncan, tape 8 transcript, 165.

26. Official records of the Election Board, *The State of Wisconsin Blue Book: 1977* (Madison: Wisconsin Legislative Reference Bureau, 1977), 868, 869.

27. Summary of Executive Budget Proposal Creating the Office of the Wisconsin Public Defender (1977 Senate Bill 77); Robb Kurz, memorandum to Hal Bergen, Charles M. Hill Sr., Greg Hyer, Jim Gosling, David Riemer, Rep. Peter Tropman, Dan Wisniewski, and Ed Parsons, February 15, 1971, Patrick J. Lucey Papers, 1935–2003, Wisconsin Historical Society, MSS 2419, box 158, folder 27.

28. Position paper from Wisconsin Counties Association, Patrick J. Lucey Papers, 1935–2003, Wisconsin Historical Society, MSS 2419, box 158, folder 27.

29. Riemer, interview.

30. Keith Clifford, interview by author, September 18, 2018; Keith Clifford, memorandum to Executive Office Staff, August 10, 1973.

31. Neil Shively, "Lucey Calls for Land Data," *Milwaukee Sentinel*, September 18, 1974.

32. "Dyke Uses Jordahl Case as Issue," *Milwaukee Sentinel*, September 18, 1974.

33. "Jordahl Report Satisfies Lucey," *Milwaukee Sentinel*, November 22, 1974.

34. Peter J. Dykman, "Summary of Significant Legislative Action 1971 Wisconsin Legislature," in *State of Wisconsin Blue Book: 1973* (Madison: Wisconsin Legislative Reference Bureau, 1973).

35. P. Lucey, interview by Duncan, tape 17 transcript, 249.

36. David Adamany, interview by Patrick McGilligan, Marquette University Wisconsin Politics Oral History Collection, 2011–2012, December 14, 2011; David Adamany, *Financing Politics* (Madison: University of Wisconsin Press, 1969), *Campaign Finance in America* (Boston: Brooks Cole, 1972), and *Political Money: A Strategy for Campaign Financing in America* (Baltimore: Johns Hopkins Press, 1975).

37. Paul C. Pokorney, "Summary of Significant Legislative Action 1973 Wisconsin Legislature," in *State of Wisconsin Blue Book: 1975* (Madison: Legislative Reference Bureau, 1975), 279.

38. Dan Wisniewski, interview by author, November 28, 2017.

39. Sensenbrenner, interview.

40. Dunn, interview.

41. Nicholas C. Peroff, *Menominee Drums: Tribal Termination and Restoration, 1954–1974* (Norman: University of Oklahoma Press, 1982).

42. J. Patrick Rick and Curt Knocke, *The Abbey and Me: Renegades, Rednecks, Real Estate and Religion* (Berkeley, CA: Counterpoint, 2012).

43. Governor Patrick J. Lucey to Major General James Lison, Adjutant General, Wisconsin National Guard, January 6, 1975, Wisconsin Governor Patrick J. Lucey records, 1971–1977, Wisconsin Historical Society, series 2419, box 201, folder 30; "Guard Called Up in Siege," *Milwaukee Sentinel*, January 7, 1975.

44. Rick and Knocke, 96–144.

45. Stephen Holmgren, interview by author, September 26, 2018.

46. Handwritten notes and daily log kept by National Guard, Wisconsin Governor Patrick J. Lucey records, 1971–1977, Wisconsin Historical Society, series 2419, box 201, folder 30; Rick and Knocke, 159.

47. "Skenandore Not Serving Menominee Interest," Ada Deer press release, January 19, 1975, Wisconsin Governor Patrick J. Lucey records, 1971–1977, Wisconsin Historical Society, Series 2419, Box 201, Folder 29.

48. Rick and Knocke, *The Abbey and Me*, 228–32.

49. Rick and Knocke, 256–60.

50. Confidential situation report, January 26, 2018, Wisconsin Governor Patrick J. Lucey records, 1971–1977, Wisconsin Historical Society, series 2419, box 201, folder 22.

51. Statement of Intent and Contract, Alexian Brothers, January 29, 1975, Wisconsin Governor Patrick J. Lucey records, 1971–1977, Wisconsin Historical Society, series 2419, box 201, folder 21; Richard P. Jones, "Lucey Says Guard Was Set for Assault," *Milwaukee Journal*, February 13, 1975.

52. Handwritten notes from Lucey to file, February 3, Wisconsin Governor Patrick J. Lucey records, 1971–1977, Wisconsin Historical Society, series 2419, box 201, folder 30.

53. Rick and Knocke, *The Abbey and Me*, 266; Sensenbrenner, interview.

54. "Indian Convicted in '76 Takeover," *New York Times*, April 22, 1976, www.nytimes.com/1976/04/22/archives/indian-convicted-in-75-takeover-menominee-found-guilty-in-wisconsin.html.

55. Richard W. Jaeger, "Leader of Menominee Indian Takeover of Abandoned Monastery Dies," *Wisconsin State Journal*, January 15, 2005.

56. The property was eventually sold to a Texas savings and loan association for $1.4 million.

57. Howard H. Callaway, Secretary of the Army, letter to Governor Patrick J. Lucey, February 27, 1975, Wisconsin Governor Patrick J. Lucey records, 1971–1977, Wisconsin Historical Society, series 2419, box 201, folder 22.

58. "Lucey Welcomed by Industrialists," *Milwaukee Sentinel*, January 15, 1974.

59. Neil Shively, "State Invests in New Jobs," *Milwaukee Sentinel*, January 15, 1973.

60. John Lavine, interview by author, November 15, 2017.

61. Nick Hines, "Why Your Soy Sauce Actually Comes from Wisconsin," April 10, 2017, https://vinepair.com/cocktail-chatter/soy-sauce-actually-comes-wisconsin/.

62. Neil H. Shively, "Transit Measure Defeat Would Be First for Lucey," *Milwaukee Sentinel*, December 11, 1975; John Wyngaard, "Rejection of Transportation Referendum Was Significant," *Appleton Post-Crescent*, November 10, 1976.

63. "Mrs. Lucey's Use of Stamps in Truck Fight Criticized," *Appleton Post-Crescent*, February 10, 1974.

64. Diane Sherman, "Mrs. Lucey Slaps 65-Ft. Truck Ploy," *Capital Times*, June 20, 1973.

65. "Jean Says Cover Ugly Billboards," *Capital Times*, April 29, 1974.

66. Mike Miller, "Mrs. Lucey Battles Welfare Protestors," *Capital Times*, August 3, 1973.

67. "Mrs. Lucey Citation Has a Double Edge," *Milwaukee Sentinel*, March 22, 1974.

68. "Jean Doubles Up over Tenant Union Award," *Capital Times*, March 23, 1974.

69. *State of Wisconsin Blue Books* for 1973, 1975, 1977, and 1979–80.

70. Riemer, interview.

71. Dennis Conta, interview by author, December 8, 2017; Riemer, interview; Charles E. Friederich, "Integration Bill to Get Prompt OK by Lucey," *Milwaukee Journal*, March 27, 1976.

72. Steve Born, interview by author, January 11, 2018.

73. Wisniewski, interview.

74. Patrick J. Lucey, memorandum to author, April 15, 1981.

75. Briefing La Farge Dam and Lake Project at Madison Wisconsin, April 15, 1971, Wisconsin Governor Patrick J. Lucey records, 1971–1977, Wisconsin Historical Society, series 2419, box 209, folder 10.

76. Governor Patrick J. Lucey, letter to the People of Kickapoo Valley, May 20, 1971, Wisconsin Governor Patrick J. Lucey records, 1971–1977, Wisconsin Historical Society, series 2419, box 209, folder 10.

77. Governor Patrick J. Lucey, letter to General B. G. Ernest Graves Jr., District Engineer, US Army Corps of Engineers, May 20, 1971, Wisconsin Governor Patrick J. Lucey records, 1971–1977, Wisconsin Historical Society, series 2419, box 209, folder 10.

78. Al Anderson, "La Farge Dam Project" (no date), http://kvr.state.wi.us/About-Us/History/La-Farge-Dam-Project/.

79. "York Quits as Energy Director," *Milwaukee Sentinel*, January 15, 1974.

80. Richard Bradee, "Government Utility Stirs Lucey Interest," *Milwaukee Sentinel*, January 14, 1976.

81. Born, interview.

82. Report of the Governor's Task Force on Offender Rehabilitation, Patrick J. Lucey Papers, 1935–2003, Wisconsin Historical Society, MSS 2419, box 158, folder 27.

83. Owen Coyle, "Lucey Disagrees, But Backs Offender Unit," *Capital Times*, August 3, 1972.

84. Memoranda of January 18, 1971, and October 7, 1971, from Burch H. Falkner, Area Manager for General Electric, Patrick J. Lucey Papers, 1935–2003, Wisconsin Historical Society, MSS 2419, box 142, folders 18 and 21; Walter F. Kelly, interview by author, September 19, 2018.

85. Patrick J. Lucey, letter to Walter Kelly, January 6, 1973, Patrick J. Lucey Papers, 1935–2003, Wisconsin Historical Society, MSS 2419, box 143, folder 4.

86. Patrick J. Lucey Papers, 1935–2003, Wisconsin Historical Society, MSS 2419, box 143, folder 4.

87. Kelly, interview.

88. Keith Clifford, interview by author May 11, 2018; Riemer, interview; Sensenbrenner, interview.

89. Curry First, email to author, October 28, 2017, and interview by author, November 24, 2017; Sandy Allen, interview by David Adamany, July 10, 2016.

90. Mike Miller, "Lucey Says He's Behind Task Force No-Fault Version," *Capital Times*, May 2, 1973.

91. Governor Patrick J. Lucey, letter to Richard B. Antaramian, March 8, 1977.

92. P. Lucey, interview by Duncan, tape 16 transcript, 257; Wisniewski, interview.

## Chapter 13

1. Eugene Harrington, "Lucey's State of the State: More Austerity, Reforms," *Milwaukee Journal*, January 18, 1977.

2. Patrick J. Lucey, interview by Chip Duncan, Duncan Entertainment, February 12, 2010, tape 18 transcript, 310; Patrick J. Lucey, interview by Bill Broydrick and Tim Cullen, Wisconsin Politics Oral History Project, August 22, 2003, tape 6 transcript, 139.

3. Stuart Levitan, "Lucey Would Answer Carter Call," *Capital Times*, December 9, 1976; Matt Pommer, "Lucey May Get Top Energy Post," *Capital Times*, December 16, 1976.

4. Kenneth R. Lamke, "Schreiber May Challenge Lucey," *Milwaukee Sentinel*, January 24, 1977; Patricia Simms, "Halt-Schreiber Memo Written," *Wisconsin State Journal*, February 25, 1977.

5. Dean Showers, "Strategy Memo to Schreiber Bared," *Milwaukee Sentinel*, May 8, 1977.

6. Martin J. Schreiber, interview by author, May 14, 2018; P. Lucey, interview by Duncan, tape 15 transcript, 226; Robert Dunn, interview by author, November 21, 2017.

7. Patricia Simms, "Transition Plan Was Set Last Fall," *Wisconsin State Journal*, April 8, 1977.

8. Patrick J. Lucey, interview by Jim Cavanaugh, Wisconsin Historical Society, History of the Democratic Party, April 10, 1985, tape 65; P. Lucey, interview by Duncan, tape 15 transcript, 249.

9. Laurie Lucey, telephone conversation with author, December 20, 2018.

10. P. Lucey, interview by Cavanaugh, tape 65.

11. P. Lucey, interview by Broydrick and Cullen, tape 6 transcript, 139.

12. Dunn, interview.

13. P. Lucey, interview by Duncan, tape 15 transcript, 269.

14. "Lucey's Acceptance of Mexico Post Surprises Both Wisconsin Parties," *New York Times*, April 9, 1977.

15. Martin J. Schreiber, interview by author, May 14, 2018.

16. P. Lucey, interview by Duncan, tape 15 transcript, 269; Patrick J. Lucey, interview by John Powell, March 2010.

17. "Hispanic Spokesman Hits Choice of Lucey," *Wisconsin State Journal*, May 9, 1977.

18. "Lucey to Meet Critics," *Milwaukee Sentinel*, May 20, 1977.

19. Richard Bradee, "Lucey Backed for Envoy Post, *Milwaukee Sentinel*, May 25, 1977.

20. Legal Section, Legislative Reference Bureau, "Summary of Significant Legislation, 1977 Wisconsin Legislature," *Wisconsin Blue Book 1979–1980* (Madison: Wisconsin Legislative Reference Bureau, 1979), 377–93.

21. "Surprised Legislators Mull Lucey Decision," *Milwaukee Sentinel*, May 18, 1977.

22. Reid Beveridge, "Lucey's Priority Bills Enacted," *Wisconsin State Journal*, July 10, 1977.

23. "Kill Key Lucey Vetoes, Keep Local Tax Limits," *Milwaukee Sentinel*, July 1, 1977.

24. Reid Beveridge, "21 of Lucey Vetoes Fall," *Wisconsin State Journal*, July 1, 1977.

25. Dan Wisniewski, interview by author, November 28, 2017; Stephen Holmgren, interview by author, January 8, 2017.

26. P. Lucey, interview by Duncan, tape 15 transcript, 262.

27. Neil H. Shively, "Lucey Says Earl Would Make Good Successor," *Milwaukee Sentinel*, June 18, 1977; P. Lucey, interview by Duncan, tape 15 transcript, 263.

28. "Appearance by President Surprises New Ambassador," *Wisconsin State Journal*, July 7, 1977.

29. Neil H. Shively, "Lucey Finding Politics Useful," *Milwaukee Sentinel*, January 24, 1978.

30. Dunn, interview.

31. Stanley Zuckerman, interview by Charles Stuart Kennedy, Association for Diplomatic Studies and Training Foreign Affairs Oral History Project, July 26, 2004.

32. Zuckerman, interview; P. Lucey, interview by Duncan, tape 18 transcript, 334.

33. P. Lucey, interview by Duncan, tape 18 transcript, 336.

34. Zuckerman, interview.

35. Donald Pfarrer, "Lucey Lobbies for Canal Pacts," *Milwaukee Sentinel*, September 9, 1977.

36. J. Michael Hogan, *The Panama Canal in American Politics: Domestic Advocacy and the Evolution of Policy* (Carbondale: Southern Illinois University Press, 1986).

37. Zuckerman; Alan Riding, "Mexico Angry at U.S. as Carter Visit Nears," *New York Times*, February 11, 1979.

38. Zuckerman, interview.

39. Zuckerman, interview.

40. Zuckerman, interview.

41. Zuckerman, interview.

42. Edward Walsh, "Carter Gets Stiff Mexican Warning," *Washington Post*, February 15, 1979; P. Lucey, interview by Duncan, tape 18 transcript, 324.

43. Zuckerman, interview.

44. P. Lucey, interview by Duncan, tape 18 transcript, 335.

45. Vicki Kohlman, interview by author, December 28, 2018.

46. Zuckerman, interview.

47. P. Lucey, interview by Duncan, tape 18 transcript, 332.

48. "US Jail Shifts to Aid Many," *Milwaukee Sentinel*, August 13, 1977.

49. P. Lucey, interview by Duncan, tape 18 transcript, 337.

50. "Lucey Cited in Prisoner Swap," *Wisconsin State Journal*, December 11, 1977.

51. Walsh, "Carter Gets Stiff Mexican Warning"; Patrick J. Lucey, "The United States and Mexico," *Vital Speeches of the Day* (February 1, 1979), 45, 8.

52. P. Lucey, interview by Duncan, tape 18 transcript, 333; Zuckerman, interview.

53. Alan Riding, "Mexican Plan Slows Emigrant Flow to U.S.," *New York Times*, February 15, 1979.

54. Zuckerman, interview.

55. P. Lucey, interview by Duncan, tape 19 transcript, 338.

56. P. Lucey, interview by Duncan, tape 17 transcript, 269.

57. Zuckerman, interview.

58. "Carter to Recall Lucey As Envoy to Mexico," *Los Angeles Times*, September 5, 1978.

59. Zuckerman, interview.

60. Dunn, interview; Zuckerman, interview; Matt Pommer, "Carter May Shift Lucey's Job. Lucey May Leave Mexico," *Capital Times*, March 23, 1979.

61. Zuckerman, interview.

62. "Carter Pledges to Retain Lucey as U.S. Ambassador to Mexico," *New York Times*, April 1, 1979.

63. Dunn, interview.

64. Alan Riding, "Mexico and U.S. Still Split on Natural Gas," *New York Times*, August 21, 1979.

65. Ambassador Patrick J. Lucey to President Jimmy Carter, October 9, 1979, Patrick J. Lucey Papers, 1935–2003, Wisconsin Historical Society, MSS 785, box 11, folder 13.

66. "Paranoia toward Mexico in the Carter Administration. Lucey" *Excelsior*, January 4, 1980, Patrick J. Lucey Papers, 1935–2003, Wisconsin Historical Society, MSS 785, box 11, folder 13.

**Chapter 14**

1. Patrick J. Lucey, interview by Chip Duncan, Duncan Entertainment, February 12, 2010, tape 19 transcript, 339.

2. Stuart E. Eizenstat, *President Carter: The White House Years* (New York: St. Martin's Press, 2018), 823–31.

3. Roger Mudd interview by Karen Herman, Television Academy Foundation, Nov. 18, 2011, http://interviews.televisionacademy.com/interviews/roger-mudd.

4. "Lucey Named Ted's Deputy Manager," *Wisconsin State Journal*, November 6, 1979.

5. "State Steering Unit Readied for Kennedy," *Capital Times*, November 12, 1979; Matt Pommer, "Several State Leaders Reveal Carte Support," *Capital Times*, December 4, 1979.

6. P. Lucey, interview by Duncan, tape 19 transcript, 338.

7. Eizenstat, *President Carter*, 794–802.

8. Eizenstat, 858.

9. "Obey Favors 'Open' Convention," *Wisconsin State Journal*, August 5, 1980; Patricia Simms, "Wisconsin's Carter Delegates Endorse Binding-Ballot Rule," *Wisconsin State Journal*, August 5, 1980.

10. Eizenstat, *President Carter*, 861; P. Lucey, interview by Duncan, tape 19 transcript, 339; Patricia Simms, "State's Delegates Cheer for Kennedy," *Wisconsin State Journal*, August 13, 1980.

11. Robert H. Spiegel, "Lucey Doesn't Know Whom He'll Support," *Wisconsin State Journal*, August 13, 1980.

12. David Lasker, interview by author, May 3, 2018.

13. David Lasker, "Lucey Deserves Praise, Not Abuse, Delegate Says," *Capital Times*, August 18, 1980.

14. P. Lucey, interview by Duncan, tape 19 transcript, 341.

15. Jim Mason, *No Holding Back: The 1980 John B. Anderson Presidential Campaign* (Lanham, MD: University Press of America, 2011).

16. P. Lucey, interview by Duncan, tape 19 transcript, 344.

17. Mason, *No Holding Back*, 347–49.

18. Mason, 350.

19. John Patrick Hunter, "Lucey to Meet with Anderson Today," *Capital Times*, August 13, 1980.

20. P. Lucey, interview by Duncan, tape 19 transcript, 353.

21. Warren Weaver Jr., "Lucey, Ex-Governor of Wisconsin, Seen Likely to Run with Anderson," *New York Times*, August 22, 1980.

22. Mason, *No Holding Back*, 352; "Lucey Sees Mrs. Anderson, Criticizes Carter," *Wisconsin State Journal*, August 23, 1980.

23. Warren Weaver Jr., "Anderson Chooses Lucey for His Ticket, *New York Times*, August 26, 1980.

24. Mason, *No Holding Back*, 352.

25. Keith Clifford, email to author, November 14, 2018.

26. Lasker, interview.

27. Bill Peterson and Kathy Sawyer, "Anderson Unveils National Unity Platform," *Washington Post*, August 31, 1980.

28. Clifford W. Brown and Robert J. Walker, *A Campaign of Ideas: The 1980 Anderson/Lucey Platform* (Westport, CT: Greenwood Press, 1984).

29. Mason, *No Holding Back*, 369.

30. Patricia Simms, "Lucey Placed on Ballot," *Wisconsin State Journal*, September 23, 1980.

31. Mason, *No Holding Back*, 369.

32. Mason, 377.

33. Mason, 377; Lasker, interview; Bill Peterson, "Anderson Campaign, Alleging Sabotage, Gives Up Effort to Borrow from Banks," *Washington Post*, October 16, 1980; Jerry Landauer, "Obscure Section of Federal Election Law Could Shatter Anderson's Hopes for Loan," *Wall Street Journal*, October 2, 1980; "Anderson Aides Blast Memo on Loan Risk," *Los Angeles Times*, September 19, 1980.

34. Mason, *No Holding Back*, 397–400.

35. Mason, 417.

36. Mason, 409.

37. "With Kennedy Aid, Carter Cuts Reagan Lead in Poll," *New York Times*, August 19, 1980.

38. Mason, *No Holding Back*, 379.

39. House Committee on Post Office and Civil Service, Subcommittee on Human Resources, *Unauthorized Transfers of Nonpublic Information During the 1980 Presidential Election*, 98th Cong., 2d sess., 1984.

40. Frank Lynn, "Liberal Party Unit, Rebuffing Carter, Endorses Anderson," *New York Times*, September 7, 1980.

41. "Environmentalists Back Anderson," *Capital Times*, November 3, 1980.

42. Bill Peterson, "Auto Worker Chiefs Voice 'Enthusiastic' Support for Carter," *Washington Post*, August 27, 1980.

43. Jackson Diehl, "Lucey Invokes Kennedy Liberalism in Anderson Campaign," *Washington Post*, September 20, 1980; remarks prepared for Governor Patrick J. Lucey to be delivered at the College of the Holy Cross, Worcester, Massachusetts, September 17, 1980, Wisconsin Historical Society, M2003–138, box 1, folder 15.

44. Lasker, interview.

45. Paul A. Rix, "Anderson, Lucey Woo Students," *Wisconsin State Journal*, August 31, 1980; Bill Peterson, "Anderson Given Tepid Reception by Ill. Hometown," *Washington Post*, September 1, 1980.

46. Lasker, interview.

47. Lasker, interview.

48. David Lasker, interview by author, June 6, 2018.

49. Lasker, interview, June 6, 2018.

50. P. Lucey, interview by Duncan, tape 19 transcript, 358.

### Chapter 15

1. Thomas W. Still, "Lucey Back at Home in Real Estate Game," *Wisconsin State Journal*, June 30, 1981.

2. Robert Dunn, email to author, December 8, 2018.

3. William Malkasian, Wisconsin Realtors Association, interview by author, September 6, 2017.

4. Patrick J. Lucey, letter to Gretchen Werts Hanson, November 2, 1993. Courtesy Paul Lucey.

5. Communication from Broydrick & Associates, September 9, 2003. Courtesy Paul Lucey.

6. Patrick J. Lucey, letter to author, April 15, 1981.

7. Patrick J. Lucey, "My Irish Roots," Wisconsin Governor Patrick J. Lucey Records, 1971–1977, Wisconsin Historical Society, M2003–138, box 1, folder 1.

8. John Patrick Hunter, "Now Lucey Finds Time for Relaxing," *Capital Times*, July 1, 1981.

9. Patrick J. Lucey, "Introduction of Chief Justice Shirley Abrahamson," September 6, 2006.

10. Paul Lucey, email to author, December 8, 2018.

11. Crocker Stephenson, Cary Spivak and Patrick Marley, "Justices' Feud Gets Physical: Prosser, Bradley Clash on Eve of Union Ruling," *Milwaukee Journal Sentinel*, June 25, 2011.

12. Tommy G. Thompson, interview by author, September 25, 2018.

13. Laurie Lucey, email to author, December 5, 2018.

14. Paul J. Lucey, email to author, December 4, 2018.

15. Patrick J. Lucey, email to Neil Shively, February 6, 2008.

16. Paul Lucey, note to author, December 11, 2018.

17. Patrick J. Lucey, commencement address, Edgewood College, May 17, 2009.

18. Gregory Lucey, SJ, interview by author, December 14, 2017.

19. Paul Lucey, email.

20. Gregory Lucey, SJ, interview by author, December 13, 2017.

21. Tim Cullen, interview by author, December 4, 2018.

22. Richard Weening, email to Paul Lucey, December 19, 2011.

23. G. Lucey, interview, December 14, 2017, and email, December 11, 2018.

24. Jane Reynolds, interview by author, May 7, 2018.

25. "Dem Icon Lucey Remembered as Big-Hearted, Bipartisan Tactician," *Wispolitics.com*, September 14, 2014.

26. "Dem Icon Lucey Remembered."

27. "Patrick Lucey's 'Hobby' Helped Transform Wisconsin Politics," *Milwaukee Journal Sentinel*, May 12, 2014.

28. Hal Wilde, "An Extraordinary Life," Mass of Christian Burial, Patrick Joseph Lucey, May 19, 2014.

# Acknowledgments

This project was possible because of the extraordinary admiration and affection of the many people whose lives were affected by Patrick J. Lucey. This includes people who worked with him and many who were political opponents. Given his place in the history of Wisconsin, it was obvious that there was a need for a biography of Lucey. But the research and writing got off to an inauspicious start.

Neil Shively and David Adamany, separately, began working on a Lucey biography. Neil had retired as a reporter for the then *Milwaukee Sentinel*. He and Lucey had a high level of respect for each other and enjoyed a warm friendship. Pat spent several days being interviewed by Shively, recounting highlights of his life on a reel-to-reel tape recorder. Pat also shared boxes of mementos with Neil. Shively began drafting chapters of a Lucey biography but then became too ill from cancer to continue. Neil passed away on September 30, 2014, just four months after Pat died.

Meanwhile, in Philadelphia, David Adamany, a longtime aide and friend of Pat, had been collecting materials about Lucey and his administration since 2008. David's long, distinguished academic career as a political science scholar and education administrator had been capped off as president of Temple University. With the help of graduate students and his personal assistant, Bridget Huggins, he gathered years of newspaper articles, academic works, and oral histories that could be used in writing a Lucey biography. Neil's family graciously gave Neil's work to David to supplement his own research. Tragically, David died unexpectedly on November 10, 2016, before he was able to begin writing.

David's siblings, Tom and Doreen Adamany and Sandra Brusewitz, were eager to identify someone to complete the project. Doreen assembled a small group together in Madison. Among those attending were David's longtime personal friend and former Madison mayor Joel Skornicka; former Lucey staff members Stephen Holmgren, David Riemer, Jeff Smoller, and Jim Wood; Professor David Canon (chair of the University of Wisconsin–Madison Department of Political Science); and Terry Shelton (outreach director of the University of Wisconsin–Madison Robert M. La Follette School of Public Affairs). I was pleased and honored to be their choice.

Pat Lucey had cooperated with a number of people completing oral histories. The most extensive of these resources was the twenty-two hours of interviewing done by Chip Duncan, a noted photographer, author, and documentarian. Bill Broydrick, Tim Cullen, Leon Epstein, Larry Hackman, Anita Hecht, John Powell, Jim Cavanaugh, and John R. Johannes did more focused but equally valuable oral histories. My research included very useful—and enjoyable—interviews of the following: Shirley Abrahamson, Lynn Ansfield, Pat Bauer, Hal Bergan, Steve Born, Keith Clifford, Dennis Conta, Tim Cullen, Governor Jim Doyle, Robert Dunn, Governor Anthony Earl, Curry First, Stephen Holmgren, Walter Kelly, Vicki Kohlman, William Kraus, Robert Lang, David Lasker, John Lavine, Father Gregory Lucey, SJ, Bill Malkasian, Samuel Martino, George Mitchell, Jenann Olsen, Harry Peterson, Linda Reivitz, Jane Reynolds, David Riemer, Governor Martin Schreiber, Joe Sensenbrenner, Carol Skornicka, Joel Skornicka, Jeff Smoller, Lon Sprecher, Governor Tommy Thompson, Jim Wahner, Tony Walter, Roy Wilcox, Harold Wilde, Brady Williamson, Daniel Wisniewski, and Jim Wood.

My wife, Maxine Austin, and my brother, Joel Dresang, lovingly and expertly reviewed early drafts of the entire manuscript. Likewise, Michael Stevens, State Historian of Wisconsin emeritus, read a draft of the manuscript and offered insightful comments and suggestions. In addition, a number of people who knew and worked with Lucey responded to early drafts and did important fact checking. These included Doreen Adamany, Keith Clifford, Dennis Conta, Tim Cullen, Robert Dunn, Stephen Holmgren, William Kraus, Robert Lang, David Lasker, John Lavine, David Lucey, Gregory Lucey, SJ, Laurie Lucey, Paul Lucey, Jenann Olsen, Linda Reivitz, David Riemer, Joe Sensenbrenner, Terry Shelton, Jeff Smoller, Richard Weening, Harold Wilde, Daniel Wisniewski, and Jim Wood. My grandson, Denico Chapman, helped organize documents and other material.

Joel Skornicka and Michael Youngman provided helpful guidance in seeing this project through to publication. Many thanks to the Patrick J. Lucey friends and family members who contributed to a fund that defrayed some of the publication costs of this book and supported the digitization of the Society's extensive Wisconsin Democratic Party Oral History Collections, and accessible via the Society's website.

Special gratitude is extended to the staff of the Wisconsin Historical Society Press, especially Erika Wittekind, the developmental editor for this book. Throughout the process, Erika posed questions and made suggestions that invariably were insightful and helpful.

Working with so many talented and knowledgeable people has been enjoyable and a real honor. I, of course, take responsibility for any errors.

# Index

Page numbers in *italic type* indicate illustrations.

Lucey, Patrick J.: 1950 Congressional
election, 51–55; 1966
gubernatorial election, 5, 120,
126, 134, 136–50, 170; 1970
gubernatorial election, 1–6, 164–
88; 1974 gubernatorial election,
223–27; 1978 gubernatorial
election, 260–61; as ambassador,
261–75; birth of, 16; and
campaign strategy, 1–4, 40, 42–
44, 54–79, 124, 133, 139, 141, 149,
170–71, 184–85, 224, 288; and
capitalism, 25; cartoons of, 193,
196; as chair of Democratic Party
of Wisconsin, 72–79, 94–100,
108, 111–18, 266; children of, 83,
125, 126, 141, 145, 154, 165, 186,
261, 296–98; and civil rights, 32,
51, 90–91, 117, 135, 147, 162; and
civility of, 9, 13, 44, 95, 136, 140,
191, 203, 298; early life, 8, 11–12,
16–28; early political career, 38–
55; family background, 13–24,
33, 44; and fiscal responsibility,
10, 76, 177–79, 195–97, 204,
208; and journalism, 23–24;
and law school, 29, 31, 33, 35; as
lieutenant governor, 4, 88, 120–
39; and lumber business, 83–84;
and Madison development,
89–91, 291–92; Madison
residence, 5, 29, 33, 51, 83, 92,
251; military service, 29–33;
Milwaukee residence, 291–301;
and oration/speeches, 7–8,
23–24, 287–88; and philosophy

major, 34; and poetry/literature,
23; and presidential campaigns,
4–5, 13, 95–114, 118, 130, 153–65,
215–21, 260, 276–90, 294; and
progressive principles, 7–10,
13, 37, 45, 56–47, 75, 96, 117,
126, 135, 137, 163, 188–213, 217,
225, 229, 300; and real estate
business, 2, 68, 80–93, 118,
124, 128, 136, 150, 291–92; and
reinventing Democratic Party
of Wisconsin, 9–10, 45–47,
56–73, 108, 117–18, 214–18,
282, 293, 300; and religion, 4,
19–23, 34, 90, 96, 104, 132, 291,
299; retirement of, 291–301;
romantic life, 23, 28, 32, 37,
81–83; and scandal, 235–36,
238; and teaching, 292–93; and
trusteeship at Beloit College, 292;
and Vietnam War protests, 4–5,
92, 120, 140, 143–45, 152–55,
173, 179–83; and workers, 1–3, 9,
135, 148–50, 248
Lucey, Paul, 83, 125–26, 125
Lucey, Peter, 13
Lucey, Verona, 21, 33, 101
Luneberg, William V., 247
Lutheranism, 15–16, 19, 61
Lynch, John, 97

machine politics, 57–59, 163, 214,
217, 229, 234
MacIver, John, 7, 181
Madigan, Robert SJ, 23
Madison Board of Realtors, 90–91

National Unity Party, 280–88

Nebraska, 99, 157–58

Nelson, Gaylord, 35, 47, 57, 64,
    70–72, 75–79, 98, 94–121, 113,
    136–43, 165–66, 186, 191, 216,
    226, 231, 254, 278, 294, 300

Nelson, William L., 89–90

Neshek, Milton, 247

Nestingen, Ivan, 97, 98, 100, 102,
    111, 114

Nestingen, John, 64

New Deal, 9, 27, 35, 37, 45, 49, 53,
    60, 117, 163

Nikolay, Frank, 97, 106, 111–12, 120,
    175

Nixon, Richard, 106–7, 123, 162–64,
    176, 179, 184, 204, 216, 222–25

no-fault insurance, 258, 264

Nonpartisan League, 59

Norquist, John, 249

Northland Hotel (Green Bay, WI), 47,
    81, 154

Northwestern University (Evanston,
    IL), 117

nuclear weapons, 152

Nusbaum, Joseph E., 191–92, 208

Nye, Russel B., 59

O'Brien, Don, 157

O'Brien, Lawrence, 143

O'Donnell, Kenneth, 100, 106, 116

O'Malley, John F., 175

Obama, Barack, 297

Obey, David, 139, 168, 279, 298

Oglala Lakota, 244

Olsen, Jenann, 132–33

Olson, Jack, 3–6, 107–8, 123–26,
    138, 150, 173–90, 176

one-person-one-vote rule, 7, 219,
    238

Oregon primary (1968), 158–59

Organization of Petroleum Exporting
    Countries (OPEC), 254–55

Oscar Mayer Corporation, 1, 2

Otto, Max Carl, 34, 97

Padden, Philip, 87

Panama Canal, 30, 267–68

Park Hotel (Madison, WI), 64

Pasch, Maurice, 89

patronage, 58–60, 75

Patterson, Rita, 28, 32, 37

Payne, Henry, 58

Pearl Harbor attack, 30

Peirce, Neal R., 228

Pennsylvania, 11, 278

People's Park, 91–93

Peterson, Donald O., 161–62, 165–
    66, 169–76, 172, 280

Petri, Thomas, 226

Pfankuchen, Gretchen, 97

Pfankuchen, Llewellyn, 97

Pfister Hotel (Milwaukee, WI), 6–7,
    9, 136–37, 223

Philippines, 30

Phillips, Vel, 97, 111, 117, 146, 233,
    252

Pierce County, 62

Pines, Lester, 241–42

Plonka, Joe, 242–43

political advertising, 4, 67, 184–85,
    237, 284–85